American Statesmen
On Slavery and the Negro

American Statesmen

On Slavery

and the Negro

NATHANIEL WEYL

and

WILLIAM MARINA

ARLINGTON HOUSE   *New Rochelle, N.Y.*

FOR OUR CHILDREN

Anita Marie Marina, Craig Allen Marina,

Virginia Grace Marina,

Jonathan Vanderpoel Weyl and Walter Castleton Weyl.

Library of Congress Catalog Card Number 79-143275

ISBN 0-87000-117-5

MANUFACTURED IN THE UNITED STATES OF AMERICA

Introduction

In these pages, we have attempted a full and, we hope, unbiased presentation of the views of American statesmen on slavery and the Negro from Colonial times to the assassination of President John F. Kennedy.

We decided for a variety of reasons to cut off the narrative in 1963. The record of the Johnson Administration is too fresh in the minds of readers to require any recapitulation. At present, we have little more than the bare record of official events. We lack those memoirs of participants and observers which illumine the pages of history and provide an understanding of the motivation and dynamics of social processes. These considerations apply with even greater force to the record of the Nixon Administration, which at the time of this writing (November 1970) is still incomplete.

Were we dealing with Chief Executives of the learning and intellectual depth of Thomas Jefferson, John Quincy Adams or, for that matter, Theodore Roosevelt and Woodrow Wilson, the absence of memoirs and analogous accounts would not be a fatal obstacle. These men were, to use David Riesman's phrase, inner-directed. They had evolved their own personal philosophies of life and of society. They were capable of solitude and concentrated thought. The views they expressed were powerfully stamped with their own individuality of thought and purpose. They were not afraid to stand against the currents of public opinion. They spoke to voice their beliefs, not merely to win the approval of electoral majorities.

In the present era of television politics, which reached full florescence circa 1960, things are not so simple. Presidential utterances are more calculated. They are often the composite work of many hands and minds. They have an anonymous and homogenized aspect. They are more likely to express lofty aspirations than opinions that come from the heart. They seldom form good raw material for biography and they sometimes remind one of Marcel Proust's remark that the purpose of speech is to conceal one's thoughts.

Another area we have avoided is the philosophy of Chief Justices of the United States and Associate Justices of the Supreme Court insofar as they are expressed in their judicial opinions. Supreme Court decisions cannot intelligently be discussed without analyzing their relationship to the Common Law and the Constitution. Fascinating as that terrain is, it seemed extraneous to the present volume. Moreover, competent studies of American case law on slavery and the Negro exist and are available.

We have gone beyond the frontiers suggested by the title. The Appendix deals with Hebraic, Greek, Roman, Medieval Christian and Enlightenment thinkers whose views influenced the Founding Fathers and other American political leaders. We have included in our cast of characters, politicians who did little or nothing to deserve the title of statesman, but who nonetheless influenced events. We have included Abolitionists, Populists, racist agitators, Socialists, Klansmen, political economists and philosophers of government, men whose views helped shape the course of history, but who never held high political office and never stood at or near the helm of power.

The amassing of this material and sometimes its interpretation have been facilitated by an immense amount of recent research on the American Negro and his role in our history, much of it thoughtful, perceptive, comprehensive in its scope and exacting in its scholarship. Among liberal historians of slavery, we acknowledge a special debt to David Brion Davis, Winthrop D. Jordan and Leon F. Litwack, who have added to our knowledge and at times provided us with valuable insights. Among Marxists, Eugene D. Genovese has contributed important and original analyses of some of the most fundamental problems of slavery as an institution and is distinguished from many of his contemporaries by his positive appreciation of the ethos and way of life of the patrician slaveholding South.

Other contemporary studies of slavery and the Negro suffer from an intense moralistic bias and from the fact that their authors seem more interested in scolding their subjects than in understanding their reasons for their action. The proper business of the historian is not to inflict his prejudices on his readers, but, in the vernacular of modern American youth, "to tell it like it was." As the German historian of civilization, Leopold Ranke, put it, perhaps a bit more eloquently: *"Ich will bloss sagen wie es eigentlich gewesen ist."*[1] The Greek Sophist, Lucian, once observed: "Historical characters are not prisoners on trial." It may be tempting for the historian to arraign great men, prosecute them and convict them. It panders to his prejudices, inflates his ego and is invariably successful, since they are not present to defend themselves. Nevertheless, it is none of his business.

We believe that the record of the judgments made by American political leaders on slavery and the Negro, their analyses of the underlying problems and their proposed remedies cast light on the difficulty and durability of the problem and its imperviousness to easy solutions. This record now stretches over two centuries which are almost bisected by a civil war that many thought might reduce racial strife in America to inconsequential dimensions. In presenting this record, our purpose is not to place American statesmen in pigeonholes and still less to moralize concerning their doubts and conclusions. It is simply to write down, to the best of our ability, the record of the past in the hope that it may shed light on this vexing topic for the present and the future.

We are indebted to our wives, Sylvia Castleton Weyl and Dorita Roca Marina, for more help than we can here acknowledge. The cooperation of William Axford, Director of Library Services, Florida Atlantic University, and that of his staff was invaluable. We also found the resources of the University of Miami useful. We thank Thelma Spangler and Donna Smith for

[1]"I shall merely state how it actually was."

their successful and devoted labor in deciphering and typing this manuscript. We are equally grateful to Andy and Candy Mead for careful reconciliation of typescript and proofs.

—Nathaniel Weyl
—William Marina

Boca Raton, Florida
November 14, 1970

American Statesmen
On Slavery and the Negro

CHAPTER ONE

|ꞁꞁ|ꞁꞁ|ꞁꞁ|ꞁꞁ|ꞁꞁ|ꞁꞁ|ꞁꞁ|ꞁꞁ|ꞁꞁ|ꞁꞁ|ꞁꞁ|ꞁꞁ|

Benjamin Franklin and
the Colonial Age

|ꞁꞁ|ꞁꞁ|ꞁꞁ|ꞁꞁ|ꞁꞁ|ꞁꞁ|ꞁꞁ|ꞁꞁ|ꞁꞁ|ꞁꞁ|ꞁꞁ|ꞁꞁ|ꞁꞁ|ꞁꞁ|ꞁꞁ|ꞁꞁ|ꞁꞁ|ꞁꞁ|ꞁꞁ|ꞁꞁ|ꞁꞁ|ꞁꞁ|ꞁꞁ|ꞁꞁ|ꞁꞁ|ꞁꞁ|

> And while we are, as I may call it, *Scouring* our Planet, by
> clearing America of Woods, and so making this Side of our
> Globe reflect a brighter Light to the Eyes of Inhabitants in
> Mars or Venus, why should we in the Sight of Superior Beings
> darken its People? why increase the Sons of Africa, by Plant-
> ing them in America, where we have so fair an Opportunity,
> by excluding all Blacks and Tawneys, of increasing the
> lovely White and Red?
>   —BENJAMIN FRANKLIN, *Observations concerning the*
>   *Increase of Mankind, Peopling of Countries, &c.*
>   (1751)[1]

During the century before the American Revolution, the morality of Negro slavery was considered chiefly a religious issue.
The immensely influential Massachusetts Congregationalist
divine, Cotton Mather (1663–1728), had read and absorbed Aristotle on natural slavery and believed the Negro natives of
Africa to be possibly descendants of Ham and certainly "the
most Brutish of Creatures upon Earth." Nevertheless, they had
immortal souls and should therefore be brought to Christianity:
    "Let us make a Trial, Whether they that have being Scorched
and Blacken'd by the Sun of *Africa,* may not come to have
Minds Healed by the more Benign *Beams* of the *Sun of Righteousness.*"[2]

[1]Leonard W. Labaree (ed.), *The Papers of Benjamin Franklin* (New Haven,
1961), IV, 229–30.
[2]David Brion Davis, *The Problem of Slavery in Western Culture* (Ithaca,
1966), p. 217, quoting Mather's *Diary.* Cotton Mather's zeal for the religious

Opposition to slavery as an immoral institution was strong-est among the nonconformist Protestant denominations. John Wesley, the founder of Methodism, who had visited Georgia in 1735, wrote a tract against slavery on the eve of the American Revolution. He denounced the African slave trade as "that ex-ecrable sum of all villainies" and proclaimed that it would be better to have the West Indies inundated by the Atlantic Ocean than that its soil should continue to be tilled by slave labor.[3]

William Penn traded in slaves and leading Quaker families in Philadelphia and Newport were engaged in the interna-tional slave trade until the middle of the 18th Century. As late as 1756, Negroes were not accepted for Quaker burial.[4] The Society of Friends moved from acquiescence in slavery to mili-tant opposition to the institution only in the decades immedi-ately preceding the Revolution.

The nature and intensity of Colonial opposition to slavery and the slave trade has often been exaggerated by Abolitionist writers. Henry Wilson, the zealous Abolitionist historian and politician who became Vice President of the United States un-der Grant, exemplifies this naïveté.

"Georgia, however, was settled by colonists under the lead of James Oglethorpe," Wilson wrote, "who held slavery to be a horrid crime against the gospel, as well as against the laws of England, and slavery was there forbidden."[5] Actually, Ogle-thorpe was Deputy Governor of the Royal African Company, the British chartered company engaged in the slave trade. While he once expressed the hope that the opening up of Georgia should not cause the enslavement of African natives, he was himself a slaveowner. Davis points out that slaves were excluded from the colony, not by its 1732 charter, but by a spe-cial defense measure (1735). The most weighty reason ad-vanced for the banning of Africans was that the Spaniards in Florida might use them to start a servile insurrection in which

---

instruction of slaves did not mean that he considered the institution of slavery unjust. He told Massachusetts Negroes that they were better off as slaves than as free men and should give up their "fondness for freedom."

[3]John Wesley, *Thoughts upon Slavery* (Philadelphia, 1774), p. 58ff.
[4]Davis, *Slavery,* p. 305.
[5]Henry Wilson, *History of the Rise and Fall of the Slave Power in America* (Boston, 1872), I, 4.

the English colonists would be expelled or slaughtered.[6]

As Christianity became more liberal and less preoccupied with the doctrine of Original Sin, religious opposition to slavery tended to fuse with that of the philosophers of the Enlightenment. The contradiction between the resounding claim that all men are created equal and the prevalence of chattel slavery was not lost on either side. With some justice, Ambrose Serle, secretary to Admiral Lord Howe, who commanded the British fleet that stood off superior French forces during the Revolutionary War, observed that the Americans treat their Negroes "as a better kind of Cattle. . . . while they are bawling about the Rights of *human Nature.*"[7]

This contradiction was noted by James Otis (1725–1783), the Massachusetts lawyer, orator and publicist. While mental illness prevented Otis from playing any politically significant role in the Revolution,[8] his influence on the course of events during the decade before hostilities broke out was enormous. No New Englander played a larger part in controlling the course of events in those critical years and no American was more frequently quoted, approved or assailed in Parliament and the British press during the 1760s.

In the 1764 pamphlet in defense of the right of the Colonies to self-government upon which his fame rests, Otis made a revolutionary assertion concerning slavery:

> The Colonists are by the law of nature free born, as indeed all men are, white or black. No better reasons can be given, for enslaving those of any color than such as baron Montesquieu has humorously given. . . . Does it follow that tis right to enslave a man because he is black? Will short curl'd hair like wool, instead of christian hair, as tis called by those, whose hearts are as hard as the nether millstone, help the argument? Can any logical inference in favour of slavery be drawn from a flat nose, a long or a short face?[9]

[6]Davis, *Slavery,* pp. 145–46.
[7]Edward H. Tatum, Jr. (ed.), *The American Journal of Ambrose Serle, Secretary to Lord Howe, 1776–1778* (San Marino, Cal., 1940), p. 249. Quoted in Winthrop D. Jordan, *White Over Black: American Attitudes Toward the Negro, 1550–1812* (Chapel Hill, 1968), p. 291.
[8]Although insane from 1769 on, Otis had lucid moments and served as a volunteer at Bunker Hill in 1775.
[9]James Otis, *The Rights of the British Colonies Asserted and Proved* (Boston, 1764), p. 29. Quoted in Jordan, *Black,* p. 278.

A man of greater cultivation than most of his contemporaries, Otis followed Rousseau in rejecting the views of Grotius and Pufendorf that, because slavery had existed since ancient times, it was consonant with the laws of nations. Negro slavery, he warned, "threatens one day to reduce both Europe and America to the ignorance and barbarity of the darkest ages."[10]

Benjamin Franklin

Chronologically, Benjamin Franklin belongs more to the Colonial era than to that of the American Revolution and the Constitution. Born in Boston in 1706, the fifteenth child of a highly respected Presbyterian tallow chandler, Franklin was seventy when he worked with Thomas Jefferson and John Adams on the Declaration of Independence and eighty-three when the Constitution was adopted.

While he was an opponent of slavery, there were times in his life when Franklin himself owned slaves. He had little direct contact with slavery or with Negroes and his voluminous writings deal only occasionally or peripherally with either topic.

Franklin's most revealing comments concerning slavery, the Negro and immigration in general were made in his *Observations concerning the Increase of Mankind, Peopling of Countries, &c.*, written in 1751 and published, after considerable hesitation on the part of its author, three years later. The central argument of this essay, which was later to be praised by Thomas Malthus, is that immigration to new countries is unnecessary because natural increase always cures underpopulation. The political purpose of the essay was to convince the Colonies that they should discourage both free immigration from the European Continent and Catholic Ireland and the forced immigration of Negroes by the slave trade. Franklin believed that America should remain a preponderantly Anglo-Saxon and Protestant country.

He thought it was "an ill-grounded Opinion that by the Labour of Slaves, America may possibly vie in Cheapness of Manufactures with Britain." Slave labor involved hidden ex-

[10]Otis, *Rights*, p. 38. Quoted in Davis, *Slavery*, p. 441.

penses. They neglected their work for "Neglect is natural to the Man who is not to be benefited by his own Care or Diligence." A driver had to be employed to keep them at work. One had to consider their "Pilfering from Time to Time, almost every Slave being *by Nature?* a Thief. . . ." All in all, industrial labor in England was much cheaper "than it ever can be by Negroes here." Franklin then asked:

"Why then will America purchase Slaves? Because Slaves may be kept as long as a Man pleases, or has Occasion for their Labour; while hired Men are continually leaving their Master (often in the midst of his Business,) and setting up for themselves."[11]

If slavery was, in Franklin's opinion, uneconomic, it was also one of the things which "must diminish a Nation" by encouraging the emigration and discouraging the immigration of white settlers. In the same essay, Franklin wrote:

The Negroes brought into the English Sugar Islands, have greatly diminish'd the Whites there; the Poor are by this Means depriv'd of Employment, while a few Families acquire vast Estates; which they spend on Foreign Luxuries, and educating their Children in the Habit of those Luxuries; the same income is needed for the Support of one that might have maintain'd 100. The Whites who have Slaves, not laboring, are enfeebled, and therefore not so generally prolific; the Slaves being work'd too hard and ill fed, their Constitutions are broken, and the Deaths among them are more than the Births; so that a continual Supply is needed from Africa. The northern Colonies having few Slaves increase in Whites. Slaves also pejorate the Families that use them; the white Children become proud, disgusted with Labour, and being educated in Idleness, are rendered unfit to get a Living by Industry.[12]

Predicting that the natural increase of the American population would create a state of affairs in which there would be more English people in North America than in the British Isles in a century, Franklin concluded his essay with a plea for preservation of the Colonies as an area of Anglo-Saxon, Protestant settlement:

[11]Labaree, *Franklin, IV*, 229–30.
[12]*Ibid.*, p. 231.

And since Detachments of English from Britain sent to America, will have their Places at Home so soon supply'd and increase so largely here; why should the Palatine Boors be suffered to swarm into our Settlements, and by herding together establish their Language and Manners to the Exclusion of ours? Why should Pennsylvania, founded by the English, become a Colony of *Aliens,* who will shortly be so numerous as to Germanize us instead of our Anglifying them, and will never adopt our Language or Customs, any more than they can acquire our Complexion.

24. Which leads me to add one Remark: That the Number of purely white Peoples in the World is proportionately very small. All Africa is black or tawny. Asia chiefly tawny. America (exclusive of the new Comers) wholly so. And in Europe, the Spaniards, Italians, French, Russians and Swedes, are generally of what we call a swarthy Complexion; as are the Germans also, the Saxons only excepted, who with the English, make the principal Body of White People on the Face of the Earth. I could wish their Numbers were increased. And while we are, as I may call it, *Scouring* our Planet, by clearing America of Woods, and so making this Side of our Globe reflect a brighter Light to the Eyes of Inhabitants in Mars or Venus, why should we in the Sight of Superior Beings, darken its People? why increase the Sons of Africa, by Planting them in America, where we have so fair an Opportunity, by excluding all Blacks and Tawneys, of increasing the lovely White and Red? But perhaps I am partial to the Complexion of my Country, for such Kind of Partiality is natural to Mankind.[13]

As the quoted passage shows, Franklin was not primarily concerned with excluding Negroes. He was concerned about the quality of the future population of North America. As such, he objected as strenuously to the immigration of penniless German settlers and the forceful deportation to the Colonies of Anglo-Saxon convicts as he did to the slave trade which "has blacken'd half America."

In 1751, he published a letter in the *Pennsylvania Gazette* under the signature of "AMERICANUS," in which he proposed that, if Britain continued to export "felons-convict" to North America, the Colonies should send England rattlesnakes in return. Complaining that "all the Newgates and Dungeons in Britain are emptied into the Colonies," Franklin asked ironically: "What is a little *Housebreaking, Shoplifting,* or *High-*

[13] *Ibid.,* p. 234.

way Robbing; what is a *Son* now and then *corrupted* and
hang'd, a Daughter *debauch'd* and *pox'd,*[14] a Wife *stabb'd,* a
Husband's *Throat cut,* or a Child's *Brains beat out* with an
Axe, compar'd with this 'IMPROVEMENT and WELL PEO-
PLING of the Colonies.'

"And *Rattle-Snakes,"* Franklin continued, "seem the most
suitable Returns for the *Human Serpents* sent us by our
Mother Country. In this, however, as in every other Branch of
Trade, she will have the Advantage of us. She will reap *equal*
Benefits without equal Risque of the Inconveniencies and Dangers. For the *Rattle-Snake* gives Warning before he attempts
his Mischief; which the Convict does not."[15]

Probably in 1753, Franklin wrote Peter Collinson to endorse
the latter's proposal that further immigration of Germans be
discouraged. He thought that Collinson's suggestion that German settlers be assimilated through subsidizing their marriage
to people of English stock was impractical. "The German
Women are generally so disagreeable to an English Eye,"
Franklin thought, "that it wou'd require great Portions to induce Englishmen to marry them. Nor would the German Ideas
of Beauty generally agree with our Women; *dick und starke,*
that is, *thick and strong,* always enters into their Description
of a pretty Girl: for the value of a Wife with them consists much
in the Work she is able to do."[16]

Franklin conceded that these critical observations did not
apply to all Germans indiscriminately. "They say," he admitted, "the Germans that came formerly were a good sober industrious honest People; but now Germany is swept, scour'd and
scumm'd by the Merchants, who, for the gain by the Freight,
bring all the Refuse Wretches poor and helpless who are bur-
thensome to the old Settlers, or Knaves and Rascals that live by
Sharking and Cheating them."[17] He recommended that, instead
of Germans, "English, Welsh and Protestant Irish" be encouraged to settle in Pennsylvania.

Franklin's strange view that Germans, French and Swedes
should be classed as "swarthy" people and his refusal to include
south Europeans and Russians in the ranks of the White race

[14]i.e., infected with syphilis.
[15]Labaree, *Franklin,* IV, 133.
[16]*Ibid.,* V, 159.
[17]*Ibid.,* p. 160.

scarcely merits critical comment. As for the Germans, about 100,000 had settled in Pennsylvania by the outbreak of the Revolution and they comprised a third of the population of the Colony. They came, for the most part, from the Palatinate and other areas of southwest Germany and had been impelled to emigrate by economic and religious pressures.[18] Franklin was not alone in holding a low opinion of them. When George Washington first encountered them on crossing the Blue Ridges in 1748 as a 16-year-old surveyor, he described them as "ignorante" in his diary and noted that they "would never speak English . . ."[19]

From the 1750s on, Benjamin Franklin was interested in Negro education. He supported a school for Black children run by the Reverend William Sturgeon, which taught them reading and the Catechism. Franklin visited this school in 1763 and examined the pupils. "I was on the whole much pleas'd," he wrote, "and from what I then saw, have conceiv'd a higher Opinion of the natural Capacities of the black Race, than I had ever before entertained. Their apprehension seems as quick, their Memory as strong, and their Docility in every Respect equal to that of white Children. You will wonder perhaps that I should ever doubt it, and I will not undertake to justify all my Prejudices, nor to account for them."[20]

This is one of the first expressions of the view that Negro intelligence is innately equal to that of Whites and it puts Franklin in opposition to the prevailing viewpoint of his age. The last sentence quoted may seem to contradict this conclusion, but Franklin's letter was written to a minister who played a prominent role in Negro education and who held strong views about Negro potential abilities. On March 20, 1774, Franklin wrote the Marquis de Condorcet, the French mathematician and philosopher, that the Negroes were "not deficient in natural Understanding, but they have not the Advantage of Education."[21]

[18]Dieter Cunz, "German Americans," in Francis J. Brown and Joseph S. Roucek, *One America* (Englewood Cliffs, 1960), pp. 104–07.

[19]Richard O'Connor, *The German-Americans* (Boston, 1968), p. 41.

[20]Letter to John Waring, Philadelphia, December 17, 1763. Labaree, *Franklin*, X, 396.

[21]*Ibid.*, ftn. 1.

Franklin opposed the immigration of Negroes into the American Colonies on the grounds that they were difficult to assimilate and would prevent the creation of a homogeneous Anglo-Saxon nation. He was hostile to slavery and the slave trade primarily because he believed chattel slavery was economically inefficient and because slavery discouraged the white population from working. Until he reached the age of 57, he considered, as did most of his contemporaries, that Negroes were innately inferior to Caucasians in mental ability. His visit to the Negro school in 1763 convinced him that the Negro intellectual potential was equal to the white and he persisted in this viewpoint until his death.

In August 1772, Franklin wrote his Quaker Abolitionist friend, Anthony Benezet, concerning slavery and the slave trade. He called the latter "a detestable commerce" and added:

"I am glad to hear that the disposition against keeping Negroes grows more general in North America. Several pieces have been lately printed here against the practise, and I hope in time it will be taken into consideration and suppressed by the legislature."[22]

The following year, Franklin wrote Dean Woodward in London to state that he had learned "that a disposition to abolish slavery prevails in North America; that many of the Pennsylvanians have set their slaves at liberty; and that even the Virginia Assembly have petitioned the king for permission to make a law for preventing the importation of more into that Colony."[23] He predicted correctly that Virginia's request to ban further slave imports into the Commonwealth from Africa would be denied by the British king.

During the stormy years of the American Revolution, Benjamin Franklin took part in editing the Declaration of Independence, brought France into the war on the American side and performed many other valuable services. He wrote and did little of any importance during this period concerning slavery and the slave trade.

At the Federal Convention of 1787 which drafted the Consti-

[22]Jared Sparks (ed.), *The Works of Benjamin Franklin* (Boston, 1836–42), VIII, 16–17.

[23]*Ibid.*, p. 42.

tution, Franklin, who had by now entered his ninth decade, supported a strong Federal Government and urged unsuccessfully that the sessions begin with prayer,[24] but took little part in the controversies over slavery and the slave trade.

Although he was too old and sick to take an active part in running its affairs, Franklin was elected President of an organization called the Pennsylvania Society for Promoting the Abolition of Slavery and Relief of Free Negroes Unlawfully Held in Bondage and for Improving the Condition of the African Race. In the autumn of 1789, Franklin submitted his Plan for Improving the Condition of the Free Blacks to the Society. This proposed that four committees be established to educate, employ and govern the free Negro community. The Committee of Inspection "shall superintend the morals, general conduct, and ordinary situation of the free Negroes, and afford them advice and instruction, protection from wrongs, and other friendly offices." The Committee of Guardians was to "place our children and young people with suitable persons, that they may (during a moderate time of apprenticeship or servitude) learn some trade or other business or subsistence." The Committee on Education was to see that the children and youth of the free Negroes "receive such learning as is necessary for their future situation in life" and be inculcated with "moral and religious principles." Finally, the Committee of Employ was to find work for the free Negroes so they might avoid "poverty, idleness, and many vicious habits."[25]

Franklin's plan thus involved running the lives of the free Negroes for the benevolent purpose of rescuing them from "vicious habits"; superintending their morals and conduct, and seeing to it that their children were educated in sound religious principles and were put to work in "apprenticeship or servitude."

The reasons for advocating this plan were set forth in an "Address to the Public," dated November 9, 1789, which appeared under Benjamin Franklin's signature. The excessively

---

[24]"How has it happened, Sir," Franklin asked, "that we have not hitherto once thought of humbly applying to the Father of lights to illuminate our understandings?" Max Farrand, *Records of the Federal Convention* (New Haven, 1911), I, 451–52.
[25]Sparks, *Franklin*, X, 320–21.

ornate and flowery style of this document creates the suspicion that it was not written by Franklin. It presumably had his approval since, although 84 at the time, he was in possession of most of his mental powers.

Slavery was "such an atrocious debasement of human nature," the Address declared, that its abolition was sometimes "a source of serious evils." Slavery impaired "the intellectual faculties and . . . social affections" of the slave. "Reason and conscience" had "little influence over his conduct, because he is chiefly governed by the passion of fear." Consequently, "freedom may often prove a misfortune to himself, and prejudicial to society."

In short, turning the manumitted Negroes loose would create serious problems of pauperism, delinquency and crime. The Address recommended that the Federal Government eventually assume responsibility for these people. Meanwhile, the Society appealed to the public for funds so that the freed slaves might be instructed "for the exercise and enjoyment of civil liberty," taught "habits of industry" and given suitable employment. Their children should receive "an education calculated for their future situation in life."[26]

In February 1790, the Society sent a memorial on slavery to Congress under Franklin's signature. Asserting that "equal liberty . . . is still the birth-right of all men," the memorial asked Congress to "loosen the bands [sic] of slavery" and "countenance the restoration of liberty to those unhappy men, who alone, in this land of freedom, are degraded to perpetual bondage" and "are groaning in servile subjection . . ." It hoped that Congress would "step to the very verge of the power vested in you" to discourage "traffic in the persons of our fellow men."[27]

This eloquent memorial was presented to Congress on February 12, 1790. The previous autumn, Benjamin Franklin had lost a good deal of weight and had become weak. After a partial rally, he was bedridden and in such acute pain that he had to be drugged with opium. On the 17th of April 1790, in his 84th year, Franklin died.

---

[26]Quoted in Matthew T. Mellon, *Early American Views on Negro Slavery* (New York, 1934), pp. 20–22.

[27]*Annals of the Congress of the United States,* I, 119f.

Given these conditions, it is doubtful that Franklin actually wrote the memorial to Congress and it is even possible that he never saw it. Henry Wilson, the Abolitionist historian of slavery, and former Vice President of the United States, refers to the memorial as "from the 'Pennsylvania Society for Promoting the Abolition of Slavery' signed and *said to have been written by Franklin.*"[28] Nor does McMaster, in his classic American history, mention Franklin's name in connection with the document.[29]

The Quaker memorial was treated by Congress with contempt. Tucker of South Carolina said that he was "surprised to see another memorial upon the same subject, and that signed by a man who ought to have known the Constitution better." Smith of the same State observed that the Southern States would "never have entered the Confederation unless their property had been guaranteed to them."

Congress debated the memorial and decided that it had no power to interfere with the slave trade until 1808 and no power to interfere with slavery at any time. On March 27, 1790, President George Washington wrote David Stuart:

"The memorial of the Quakers (and a very malapropos one it was) has at length been put to sleep, and will scarcely awake before the year 1808."[30] Stuart replied with an account of the alarm the petition had caused among Virginia slaveholders, inducing some to sell their slaves for ridiculously low prices from fear that Congress might emancipate them. On June 15, 1790, Washington wrote Stuart again:

"The introduction of the Quaker memorial respecting slavery was, to be sure, not only *ill-timed,* but occasioned a great waste of time. The final decision, thereon, however, was as favorable as the proprietors of this species of property could well have expected, considering the light in which slavery is viewed by a large part of the Union."[31]

---

[28]Wilson, *Slave,* I, 62. Emphasis supplied.
[29]John Bach McMaster, *A History of the People of the United States from the Revolution to the Civil War* (New York, 1911).
[30]Jared Sparks (ed.), *The Writings of George Washington* (Boston, 1834–1837), X, 82.
[31]*Ibid.,* 94.

Thomas Paine

Foremost among the propagandists for the American Revolutionary cause was Thomas Paine, a new arrival in the Colonies, who had left England in 1774, only a few months before the events which precipitated the final rupture with the Mother Country.

One of the most eloquent and effective pamphleteers of the age, Paine was envious and quick to make enemies, but fortunate in enjoying the protection of Thomas Jefferson. "The ferocious sneer with which Thomas Paine regarded what he called the 'No-ability,'" wrote William Gaunt, "seemed to be imprinted on his face rather than kindliness toward humanity in general."[32]

Paine's pamphlet *Common Sense,* published early in 1776, was a clear and brilliantly effective tocsin call to resistance that convinced thousands of Americans that conciliation was no longer possible and that independence was the only solution. Shortly after his arrival in America, Paine also attacked slavery. In his article "African Slavery in America," which appeared in the *Pennsylvania Journal and the Weekly Advertiser* on March 8, 1775, Paine painted an idyllic picture of tropical West Africa as a fertile land, inhabited by "industrious farmers" who "lived quietly averse to war, before the Europeans debauched them with liquors." Then the slave traders appeared on the scene "willing to steal and enslave men by violence and murder" for financial gain.[33] The British, above all, were responsible for enslaving a hundred thousand Negroes annually, "of which thirty thousand are supposed to die by barbarous treatment in the first year."

Negro slavery could not be justified, Paine asserted, as the merciful sparing of lives that already were forfeited, since the Negroes had committed no crime. Nor did the buyers' ignorance of how these men were enslaved validate their purchase. The true owner always "has a right to reclaim his goods that

---

[32]William Gaunt, *Arrows of Desire: a Study of William Blake and his Romantic World* (London, 1956), pp. 76–77.

[33]This and the quotations that follow, unless otherwise stated, are from Thomas Paine, "African Slavery in America," reprinted in Philip S. Foner (ed.), *The Complete Writings of Thomas Paine* (New York, 1945), pp. 15–18.

were stolen, and sold; so the slave, who is proper owner of his freedom, has a right to reclaim it however often sold."

It was argued that slavery was justified by the practices of the ancient Jews as recorded in the Bible. Paine retorted that the Jews practiced many customs which "may not be imitated by us," such as the extermination of peoples they conquered, "polygamy and divorces." Nor did ancient history justify slavery. There, it had resulted from sparing the lives of prisoners of war. "But to go to nations with whom there is no war. . . . purely to catch inoffensive people, like wild beasts, for slaves, is the height of outrage. . . ."

The "chief design" of Paine's essay was "to entreat Americans to consider" with what "consistency, or decency they complain so loudly of attempts to enslave them, while they hold so many thousands in slavery."

The great remaining question was: "What should be done with those who are enslaved already? To turn the old and infirm free, would be injustice and cruelty; they who enjoyed the labours of their better days should keep, and treat them humanely."

The others might be given land at reasonable rentals, where they could live and work with their families. Other manumitted Negroes "might sometime form barrier settlement on the frontiers." As the Cossacks defended Russian borders, so emancipated Negroes might guard America's western wilderness. This was far better, Paine thought, than their "being dangerous, as now they are, should any enemy promise them a better condition." The point was prescient since, within a few years, the British would be promising American slaves their freedom if they would take up arms against the Continental Army.

An emancipation policy of this sort, Paine asserted, would persuade the Negroes to adopt Christianity sincerely and thus help spread the gospels. This argument may well have been effective with his readers, but it came with strange grace from a man who would soon be publishing tracts excoriating religion.

An early member of the first anti-slavery society in America (established in Philadelphia in 1775 under the leadership of Benjamin Franklin), Paine wrote the preamble to the first legislative act for the emancipation of American slaves. This measure was passed by the Pennsylvania Assembly on March 1, 1780, at a time when Paine was its Clerk. It provided for gradual liberation instead of the total and immediate emancipation Paine had hoped to see.[34]

A few years later, Paine left America to observe and applaud the French Revolution. Imprisoned and almost executed, he there discovered that revolutions devour their children.

[34]Thomas Paine, "A Serious Thought," *Pennsylvania Journal,* October 18, 1775, reprinted in Foner, *Paine,* pp. 19–20.

CHAPTER TWO

George Washington

The benevolence of your heart, my dear Marquis, is so conspicuous upon all occasions, that I never wonder at any fresh
proofs of it; but your late purchase of an estate in the colony
of Cayenne, with a view to emancipating the slaves on it, is
a generous and noble proof of your humanity. Would to God
a like spirit might diffuse itself generally into the minds of
the people of this country. But I despair of seeing it.... To
set the slaves afloat at once would, I really believe, be productive of much inconvenience and mischief; but by degrees it
certainly might, and assuredly ought to be effected; and that
too by legislative authority.

—George Washington to the Marquis de Lafayette,
May 10, 1786.[1]

When he was not engaged in public life either as a military or
a civilian leader, George Washington lived by preference in his
beloved Mount Vernon, associated with fellow members of the
Virginia planter aristocracy and devoted most of his attention
and energy to the management of his farms and his slave work-
force. He was not only a planter, but one of the largest estate
owners in the Commonwealth. During his entire life he owned
slaves and, at his death, possessed 124 Negroes in his own right,
another 153 dower Negroes (belonging to Martha Custis Washington), and in addition leased forty from a Mrs. French.

Washington's formal education was rudimentary and by the
age of fifteen he was working as a surveyor. His evolving views
on slavery and the Negro, as on other topics, were shaped less
by reading and theorizing than by practical experience. Conse-

[1]Sparks, *Washington,* IX, 163.

quently Washington's grasp of the slavery issue in relation to history, ethics and anthropology was far less comprehensive than that of Thomas Jefferson. However, his insights were generally keen and his practical judgment was perhaps unsurpassed by any of his contemporaries. Disapproving of the institution of chattel slavery both on moral grounds and on those of expediency, George Washington saw no practical way out of the impasse. Like Jefferson, but less urgently, he was oppressed by the fear that the issues of slavery and the Negro might destroy the nation or at least dismember it.

In the management of his slaves, Washington was a kindly master who demanded work and obedience but behaved according to a strict sense of justice. He generally referred to his Negroes as "my people." On one occasion, he urged his manager to be "particularly attentive to my negroes in their sickness" and complained that overseers as a general rule "view the poor creatures in scarcely any other light than they do a draught horse or ox, neglecting them as much when they are unable to work instead of comforting and nursing them when they lie on a sick bed."[2]

He imported slaves from the West Indies, but not from Africa. Thus in 1772, Washington ordered "musty" flour from wheat raised on his estates sold in Jamaica and the proceeds laid out in Negroes, provided the "choice ones" could be had for 40 pounds sterling or less. As he was overburdened with aged and feeble slaves, he ordered: "Let there be two-thirds of them males, the other third females. The former not exceeding (at any rate) 20 years of age, the latter 16. All of them to be straight-limbed and in every respect strong and likely, with good teeth and good countenances, to be sufficiently provided with clothes."[3]

Like other Virginia slaveholders, Washington made no provision for the education of his Negroes and accepted their promiscuity as a matter of course.[4] He expected a full day's work

[2]Worthington Chauncy Ford (ed.), *The Writings of George Washington* (New York, 1892–1899), XII, 240.

[3]Douglas Southall Freeman, *George Washington, a Biography* (New York, 1948–1957), III, 296.

[4]Paul Leland Haworth, *George Washington, Country Gentleman* (Indianapolis, 1925), p. 193.

from them and, being a methodical and experienced administrator, sometimes calculated exactly how many hours each agricultural task should require. When his slaves became unruly Washington sometimes sent them to the West Indies. On July 2, 1766 we find him ordering "Negro Tom" sold "in any of the islands you may go to, for whatever he will fetch . . . That this fellow is both a rogue and a runaway (tho' he was by no means remarkable for the former, and never practiced the latter till of late) I shall not pretend to deny—But he is exceedingly healthy, strong and good at the hoe . . . which gives me reason to hope he may, with your good management, sell well, if kept clean and trim'd up a little when offered for sale."[5] Washington added that Tom should be kept "handcuffd till you get to sea." Twenty-five years after this incident, the squire of Mount Vernon sold a Negro named "Waggoner Jack" for "one pipe and one quarter cask of wine" as punishment for misbehavior.[6]

As early as 1774 Washington expressed strong opposition to the African slave trade, but not to the institution of slavery. As chairman of the meeting which drafted the Fairfax Resolutions of July 18 of that year, Washington presumably agreed with the resolve that "during our present difficulties and distress, no slaves ought to be imported into any of the British colonies on this continent; and we take the opportunity of declaring our most earnest wishes to see an entire stop for ever put to such a wicked, cruel and unnatural trade."

Opposition to the slave trade, however, was not at all tantamount to hostility toward slavery. Since Virginia bred slaves for sale to other colonies, she often viewed the African "blackbirders" as undesirable competitors. The unrestricted admission of freshly caught slaves was viewed by many Southerners as a dangerous practice, conducive to servile insurrection. It was also argued that the abolition of the slave trade would result in substantial improvement in the conditions under which slaves lived. As long as deaths from overwork and disease could be made up for by African imports, there was little economic motivation for betterment of living conditions. Once the African trade was outlawed, the slaveowners would have a

[5]Ford, *Writings*, II, 211–12.
[6]Haworth, *Washington*, p. 204.

powerful financial incentive to treat their Negroes well enough so that births would be substantially in excess of deaths. On June 21, 1775, Washington proceeded to Cambridge to assume his duties as Commander-in-Chief of the American Continental Army, comprising at the moment the militias of Massachusetts, Connecticut, Rhode Island and New Hampshire. En route he learned that these troops had behaved well under fire at Bunker Hill. Among them were such Negroes as Peter Salem, who shot and killed a British major, and Salem Poor, who was commended by twelve officers for having "behaved like an experienced officer as well as an excellent soldier."[7]

In May 1775, the Committee of Safety of Massachusetts had resolved "that the admission of any persons as Soldiers into the Army now raising, but only such as are Freemen, will be inconsistent with the principles that are to be supported, and reflect dishonor on this Colony: and that no Slaves be admitted into this Army upon any consideration whatever."[8] While slaves were denied the right to bear arms, the free Negroes of Massachusetts and the other New England colonies were admitted into the Army without dispute. "They took their place not in a separate corps, but in the ranks with the white man."[9] According to Livermore, "Hundreds of blacks—slaves and freemen— were enlisted, from time to time, in the regiments of state troops and of the Connecticut line."[10] Since the muster rolls did not identify soldiers by race, the number of Negroes in the Continental Army is unknown.

In his first report to Congress, written in July 1775, Washington wrote pessimistically: "From the number of Boys, Deserters and Negroes which have been inlisted in the troops of this Province, I entertain some doubts whether the number required can be raised here."[11] His fellow Virginian, General Horatio Gates, simultaneously instructed recruiting officers: "You are not to enlist any deserter from the ministerial (Brit-

---

[7]Walter H. Mazyck, *George Washington and the Negro* (Washington, D. C., 1932), p. 31.

[8]*American Archives, Fourth Series,* II, 762.

[9]George Bancroft, *A History of the United States* (Boston, 1834–1874), VII, 421.

[10]George Livermore, *An Historical Research respecting the Opinions of the Founding Fathers of the Republic on Negroes as Slaves, as Citizens and as Soldiers* (Boston, 1863), p. 148.

[11]Ford, *Writings,* III, 16.

ish) army, nor any stroller, negro, or vagabond, or person suspected of being an enemy to the liberty of America nor any under eighteen years of age."[12] Their classing of Negroes with boys, deserters, strollers, suspects and vagabonds indicates the Virginia commanders' evaluation of the former as troops.

Washington's policy of eliminating all free Negroes and slaves from the armed forces was supported by Edward Rutledge of South Carolina in the Continental Congress. Despite strong Southern support, Rutledge's motion was defeated. Nevertheless, on October 8, 1775, Washington held a Council of War at which the officers present unanimously agreed to exclude all slaves from the armed forces and by a large majority agreed to exclude free Negroes as well. On the following day, orders were issued to guards to "seize and confine until sunrise any Negro found straggling about any of the roads and villages near the encampments at Roxbury or Cambridge."[13]

Between October 18th and 24th, a Committee of the Continental Congress, consisting of Benjamin Franklin, Thomas Lynch of South Carolina and Benjamin Harrison of Virginia, conferred with Washington on matters of military policy. One of the questions proposed by the Commander-in-Chief was: "Ought not Negroes to be excluded from the new enlistment, especially such as are slaves? All were thought improper by the Council of Officers."[14] The civilian committee endorsed the decision of the Council of War. Washington had temporarily succeeded in eliminating all Negroes from the Continental Army.

Before the year came to an end, however, the issue of Negro troops again arose. On November 7, 1775, Lord Dunmore, the British Governor of Virginia, announced by proclamation: "I do hereby further declare all indented servants, Negroes or others (appertaining to Rebels,) free, that are able and willing to bear arms, they joining His Majesty's Troops, as soon as may be, for the more speedily reducing this Colony to a proper sense of their duty to His Majesty's Crown and dignity."[15]

This British policy of arming slaves threatened, in Washington's opinion, to transform the American revolutionary strug-

[12]*American Archives, Fourth Series*, II, 1630.
[13]Mazyck, *Washington*, pp. 38–39.
[14]*American Archives, Fourth Series*, III, 1049.
[15]Mazyck, *Washington*, p. 42.

gle into a race war. On December 15, 1775, he wrote Joseph Reed: "If the Virginians are wise, that arch-traitor to the rights of humanity, Lord Dunmore, should be instantly crushed, if it takes the force of the whole Colony to do it—otherwise, like a snow-ball, in rolling, his army will get size, some through promises, and some through inclination, joining his standard; but that which renders the measure indispensably necessary, is the negroes,—for if he gets formidable, numbers of them will be tempted to join who will be afraid to do it without."[16]

His sensitivity to the possible consequences of British recruitment of a slave army made Washington swiftly reverse his prior policy. On December 30th, the Orderly Book contains this entry:

"As the General is informed that numbers of free negroes are desirous of enlisting, he gives leave to the recruiting officers to entertain them, and promises to lay the matter before the congress, who, he doubts not, will approve it."[17]

On the 31st, Washington wrote the President of Congress that "the free negroes, who have served in this army, are very much dissatisfied at being discarded. As it is to be apprehended, that they may seek employ in the ministerial army, I have presumed to depart from the resolution respecting them, and have given license for their being enlisted. If this is disapproved of by Congress, I will put a stop to it."[18]

In response to this request, the Congressional Committee led by Benjamin Franklin decided on January 16, 1776, that "the free negroes who have served faithfully in the army at Cambridge may be re-enlisted therein, but no others." The Continental Army, however, ignored this restriction. All recruits, regardless of color, were accepted if fit for service. In 1777, Connecticut passed a law that "slaves of good life and conversation" were to be enlisted if approved of by the selectman.[19]

Meanwhile, Washington had received on adulatory poem from Phillis Wheatley, a slave who had been brought from Africa when seven years old. She had been educated by her

---

[16]William Reed, *Life and Correspondence of President Reed* (Philadelphia, 1797), I, 135.
[17]Mazyck, *Washington*, p. 43.
[18]Sparks, *Washington*, III, 218.
[19]Mazyck, *Washington*, p. 46.

Boston master and, after writing *Poems on Various Subjects,*
was sent to London and received by British aristocratic circles.
Her tribute to Washington began with the lines:

> "Celestial choir! enthron'd in realms of light,
> "Columbia's scenes of glorious toils I write."

and ended with the thought:

> "Proceed great chief with virtue on thy side,
> "Thy every action let the goddess guide.
> "A crown, a mansion, and a throne that shine,
> "With gold unfading, Washington be thine."

Several months after receiving these flowery verses, Washington sent them to his secretary, Joseph Reed, for his amusement. Learning that the author of the poem was a slave,
Washington wrote a gracious letter to "Miss Phillis" in which
he thanked her for her "elegant lines," called them "striking
proof of your poetical talents" and invited her to visit him at his
headquarters in Cambridge.[20] The slave poetess thus became
the first (and last) member of her race to pay a social visit to
Washington. She received "the most polite attention of the
Commander-in-Chief."[21] Whether Washington was really impressed by her qualities as a poet or was merely acting in accordance with *noblesse oblige* is an open question.

Thomas Jefferson was less gracious. "Religion, indeed, has
produced a Phyllis Whately;" he wrote in *Notes on Virginia,*
"but it could not produce a poet. The compositions published
under her name are below the dignity of criticism."[22]

By the beginning of the year 1778, the plight of the Continental Army was sufficiently serious for Washington to stifle some
of his misgivings concerning the policy of arming Negroes. On
January 2, General Varnum requested that a battalion of
Negroes be raised in Rhode Island and Washington forwarded
the recommendation to the state governor without adverse
comment. To facilitate this recruitment, the Rhode Island

[20]Ford, *Writings,* III, 417, 440.
[21]Benson John Lossing, *The Pictorial Field Book of the Revolution* (New
York, 1851–1860), I, 556.
[22]Quoted in Philip S. Foner (ed.), *Basic Writings of Thomas Jefferson* (Garden
City, N.Y., 1950), p. 146.

Legislature passed a law providing that, upon enlistment, every slave "is absolutely made free, and entitled to all the wages, bounties, and encouragements given by congress to any soldier enlisting into their service."[23] Masters were paid up to 120 pounds for each Rhode Island slave thus emancipated.

Washington was not in agreement with this policy. A month after Varnum's request, the Commander-in-Chief proposed to Congress that Negroes in Carolina, Virginia, and Maryland be hired as wagon drivers for the Army, since they were cheaper than white men. "They ought however to be freemen," he added, "for slaves could not be sufficiently depended on. It is to be apprehended that they would too frequently desert to the enemy to obtain their liberty, and for the profit of it, or to conciliate a more favorable reception would carry off their waggon horses with them."[24]

In 1779, Washington expressed his views on the military expedient of arming slaves in a letter to Henry Laurens. Laurens was an atypical South Carolinian for he loathed slavery and had no qualms about the mass arming of Negroes. He had unsuccessfully attempted to persuade the South Carolina legislature to allow him to raise a force of three thousand Negroes with which he proposed to drive the British out of Georgia and conquer eastern Florida. He was on good terms with Washington largely because his son, Colonel John Laurens, was an intimate friend of Alexander Hamilton.

Washington wrote him on March 20, 1779:

> The policy of our arming slaves is in my opinion a moot point, unless the enemy set the example. For, should we begin to form battalions of them, I have not the smallest doubt, if the war is to be prosecuted, of their (the British) following us in it, and justifying the measure upon our own ground. The contest must then be who can arm (Negroes) fastest. And where are our arms? Besides, I am not clear that a discrimination will not render slavery more irksome to those who remain in it. Most of the good and evil things in this life are judged of by comparison; and I fear a comparison in this case will be productive of much discontent in

[23]Mazyck, *Washington*, p. 61.
[24]Ford, *Writings*, VI., 349.

those,who are held in servitude. But, as this is a subject that has never employed much of my thoughts, these are no more than the first crude ideas that have struck me upon the occasion.

This remarkable letter concluded with some comments about the way in which the enemy was waging war. "Sir Guy Carleton is using every art to soothe and lull our people into a state of security," Washington wrote. "Admiral Digby is capturing all our vessels, and suffocating as fast as possible in prisonships all our Seamen, who will not enlist into the service of his Britannic Majesty; and Haldimand, with his savage allies, is scalping and burning on the frontiers. Such is the line of conduct pursued by the different commanders, and such their politics."[25]

Thus, Washington believed that any initiative taken by the Continental Army in recruiting slaves would be matched by the British. He thought the enemy was in a better position to win the allegiance of the Negroes because it had more and better arms and because men prefer freedom to bondage. He was keenly aware of the possibility that a competition between the two sides to see which could arm more black men could end in servile insurrection and racial war. He did not, however, close the door on Laurens's plan because he believed that the British were resorting to such atrocious methods of combat that expedients might be justified which he would not normally consider. His statement that these views were merely "crude ideas" on "a subject that has never employed much of my thoughts" was indicative of his courtesy and diplomatic style. It was designed to soften the blow of his negative verdict. Washington had thought about this matter. He had thought hard and for a fairly long time.

Despite his distaste for the institution of slavery, Washington resisted all efforts of outsiders to free his slaves or those of his fellow planters. As Commander-in-Chief of the Continental Army and later as President of the United States, he used his enormous influence to have slaves emancipated by the British returned to their former masters and to assure France of American support in crushing the slave uprising in Haiti.

[25]Sparks, *Washington,* VI, 204.

In April 1778, Washington learned from Lafayette that a British sloop had come up the Potomac and several of his Mount Vernon Negroes had absconded and joined the enemy. Lund, Washington's manager, knew that planters who refused to supply the British with provisions sometimes had their houses burned down. To avoid this result and to get the Mount Vernon slaves back, Lund had resorted to appeasement. "You ought to have considered yourself as my representative," Washington wrote him in a stinging reprimand, adding,

... To go on board their vessels; carry them refreshments; commune with a parcel of plundering scoundrels and request a favor by asking the surrender of my Negroes, was exceedingly ill-judged, and 'tis to be feared, will be unhappy in its consequences, as it will be a precedent for others, and may become a subject of animadversion.

He predicted that the enemy would "prosecute the plundering plan they have begun" and

unless a stop can be put to it by the arrival of a superior naval force, I have as little doubt of its ending in the loss of all my Negroes and in the destruction of my houses."[26]

On May 6, 1783, Washington wrote Lieutenant General Sir Guy Carleton, who had succeeded Sir Henry Clinton and represented British interests in the United States, to protest the fact that "a large number of negroes" had been taken out of the country on English ships. "Whether this conduct is consonant to, or how far it may be deemed an infraction of the treaty," he observed, "is not for me to decide. I cannot, however, conceal from you, that my private opinion is, that the measure is totally different from the letter and spirit of the treaty."[27] Sir Guy replied on May 12 with understandable sharpness that the Negroes he had taken out of the country he had "found free when I arrived at New York. I had therefore no right, as I thought, to prevent their going away to any part of the world they thought proper." He stated that commissioners would be

[26]Freeman, *Washington,* V, 283.
[27]Sparks, *Washington,* VIII, 431.

appointed to see that slave property was not removed in British vessels and rebuked Washington for "the mere suspicion" that the King's minister could be guilty of "a notorious breach of the public faith."[28]

Five years later, Washington was in Pennsylvania. He found himself in the unpleasant situation of facing possible loss of his slaves because of a state law declaring that all adult bondsmen must be declared free six months after their master moved into Pennsylvania and became a citizen of the state. Washington had not, of course, taken out Pennsylvania citizenship, but he feared somebody might try to "entice" his Negroes and that they would then become "insolent." He wrote Tobias Lear:

"As all (the slaves of the Presidential establishment) except Hercules and Paris are dower negroes, it behooves me to prevent the emancipation of them, otherwise I shall not only lose the use of them but may have them to pay for.[29] If upon taking good advice, it is found expedient to send them back to Virginia, I wish to have it accomplished under pretext that may deceive both them and the public, and none, I think, would so effectually do this as Mrs. Washington coming to Virginia next month . . ."[30] His wife, he proposed, would then return to Mount Vernon, taking the slaves with her as a matter of course.

Washington had gradually come to believe that slavery was a pernicious institution and that it should be abolished by law. This did not make him tolerant either of Negro insurrectionaries, who sought freedom with arms, or those he considered outside agitators, who sought emancipation through propaganda. In a letter to Robert Morris, which is worth quoting extensively, he expressed his views clearly and succinctly:

Mount Vernon, 12 April 1786.

DEAR SIR,

I give you the trouble of this letter at the instance of Mr. Dalby of Alexandria, who is called to Philadelphia to attend what he considers a vexatious lawsuit respecting a slave of his whom a society of Quakers in the city, formed for such purposes, have

---

[28] *Ibid.,* p. 545.
[29] Because Washington was responsible under law for the conservation of dower property.
[30] Freeman, *Washington,* VI, 308–09.

attempted to liberate. The merits of this case will no doubt appear upon trial. From Mr. Dalby's state of the matter, it should seem, that this society is not only acting repugnantly to justice, so far as its conduct concerns strangers, but in my opinion impoliticly with respect to the State, the city in particular, without being able, except by acts of tyranny and oppression, to accomplish its own ends. He says that the conduct of this society is not sanctioned by law. Had the case been otherwise, whatever my opinion of the law might have been, my respect for the policy of the State would on this occasion have appeared in my silence; because against the penalties of promulgated laws one may guard, but there is no avoiding the snares of individuals, or of private societies. If the practice of this society, of which Mr. Dalby speaks, is not discountenanced, none of those whose *misfortune*[31] it is to have slaves as attendants, will visit the city if they can possibly avoid it; because by so doing they hazard their property, or they must be at the expense (and this will not always succeed) of providing servants of another description.

I hope it will not be conceived from these observations, that it is my wish to hold the unhappy people, who are the subject of this letter, in slavery. I can only say that there is not a man living who wishes more sincerely than I do to see a plan adopted for the abolition of it; but there is only one proper and effectual mode by which it can be accomplished, and that is by legislative authority; and this, as far as my suffrage will go, shall never be wanting. But when slaves, who are happy and contented with their present masters, are tampered with and seduced to leave them; when masters are taken unawares by these practices; when a conduct of this kind begets discontent on one side and resentment on the other; and when it happens to fall on a man whose purse will not measure with that of the society, and he loses his property for want of means to defend it; it is oppression in such a case, and not humanity in any, because it introduces more evils than it can cure. [32]

As President, Washington was concerned with the fact that fugitive slaves from Georgia were not being returned to their masters by the Spanish authorities governing Florida. On May 20, 1791 he instructed James Seagrove, the Indian agent in Georgia:

Your first care will be to arrest the farther reception of fugitive slaves; your next to obtain restitution of those slaves, who have fled to Florida, since the date of Governor Quesada's letter to Mr.

[31]Emphasis in the original.
[32]Sparks, *Washington,* IX, 158–59.

Jefferson, notifying the orders of his Catholic Majesty; and your last object, which may demand the greatest address, will be to give a retrospective force to the orders of the court of Spain . . .[33]

On September 24, 1791, President Washington informed the French Minister that he was supplying France with money, arms and ammunition to put down the Negro uprising which had broken out in Haiti a month previously. "Sincerely regretting as I do the cause, which has given rise to this application," he wrote, "I am happy in the opportunity of testifying how well disposed the United States are to render every aid in their power to our good friends and allies, the French, to quell 'the alarming insurrection of the negroes in Hispaniola,' and of the ready disposition of the executive authority to effect it."[34] The sum of $40,000 was made available by Secretary of the Treasury Alexander Hamilton. In October, he wrote a private letter to the French Minister, in which he characterized the servile uprising as "unfortunate," "daring and alarming," adding that it was difficult to predict its outcome.[35]

Two years after the end of the War of American Independence Lafayette wrote Washington: "Now, my dear General, that you are going to enjoy some ease and quiet, permit me to propose a plan to you, which might become greatly beneficial to the black part of mankind. Let us unite in purchasing a small estate, where we may try the experiment to free the Negroes, and use them only as tenants. Such an example as yours might render it a general practice; and if we succeed in America I will cheerfully devote a part of my time to render the method fashionable in the West Indies. If it be a wild scheme, I had rather be mad in this way, than to be thought wise in the other task."[36]

Lafayette's letter was dated February 5, 1783. There is no evidence that Washington ever answered it. However, on August 19, 1784, the Marquis visited Mount Vernon and spent twelve days with his former Commander-in-Chief. There is some reason to conjecture that Washington discussed the pro-

[33] *Ibid.*, X, 163.
[34] *Ibid.*, p. 194.
[35] *Ibid.*, p. 195.
[36] Quoted in Mazyck, *Washington*, p. 81.

ject with Lafayette on that occasion.[37] At least, Lafayette bought an estate in Cayenne (French Guiana) and contributed 100,000 francs to launch the project. In this venture he had the backing of Marshal de Cartries, the French Minister of the Navy. When Washington learned of this he wrote Lafayette from Mount Vernon on May 10, 1786:

> The benevolence of your heart, my dear Marquis, is so conspicuous upon all occasions, that I never wonder at any fresh proofs of it; but your late purchase of an estate in the colony of Cayenne, with a view to emancipating the slaves on it, is a generous and noble proof of your humanity. Would to God a like spirit might diffuse itself generally into the minds of the people of this country. But I despair of seeing it. Some petitions were presented to the (Virginia) Assembly, at its last session, for the abolition of slavery, but they could scarcely obtain a reading. To set the slaves afloat at once would, I really believe, be productive of much inconvenience and mischief; but by degrees it certainly might, and assuredly ought to be effected; and that too by legislative authority.[38]

Whatever Washington's intentions may have been in regard to this matter, the imminence of the Federal Convention of 1787 made affirmative action impossible. The great need of the hour was to arrest the centrifugal forces destroying the new nation and to unite the states in a Federal Republic. Washington's great task would be to serve as the symbol and orchestrating brain of this new political entity. For him to succeed in making a Constitution possible, acceptable and efficacious, it was indispensable that he avoid participating in controversies over matters which he deemed of secondary importance.

Lafayette had been a consistent champion of the Negro from the moment of his arrival in America. He doubted that the Negro was equal to the white man in intelligence, but held that inequality of ability could never justify slavery. "It is unquestionable," he wrote, "that differences of intelligence exist among different races of men, and that in this respect some appear far superior to others, but none are on that account the less entitled to the enjoyment of civil and political liberty. In

[37] *Ibid.*, p. 90.
[38] Sparks, *Washington*, IX, 163–64.

each of these races, the same differences exist among the individuals comprising them; and for that reason men gifted by nature with superior intelligence do not, or at least ought not to sell their inferiors like beasts of burden."[39]

During the more moderate, initial phases of the French Revolution, Lafayette put through a decree in the National Assembly, entitling free Negroes in the French colonies to full civil rights. When the Jacobin faction took power, Lafayette was proscribed as a traitor and held in prison for five years. Despite the protests of Madame de Lafayette, the revolutionary government confiscated his Cayenne estate and sold the Negroes he had liberated back into slavery.

In 1785, Washington told the Reverend Francis Asbury, who was to become the first Methodist Bishop in America, that he was opposed to slavery.[40] The following year he wrote John F. Mercer: "I never mean (unless some particular circumstance should compel me to it) to possess another slave by purchase; it being among my first wishes to see some plan adopted, by which slavery in this country may be abolished by slow, sure and imperceptible degrees."[41] This and similar statements did not prevent Washington from asking Henry Lee to buy a slave bricklayer for him provided the price was not over 100 pounds. Nor did it prevent his accepting five Negro slaves from Mercer in settlement of a debt, provided they were all males and good workers. This was not evidence of logical inconsistency on Washington's part and certainly not of hypocrisy; it merely meant that he did not regard slavery as the overshadowing moral issue that later generations considered it. The "particular circumstances" which would induce Washington to buy more slaves were matters of convenience and good farm management.

Knowing much more about farming than Benjamin Franklin, Washington did not agree that chattel slavery was uneconomic. On June 18, 1792 he wrote:

[39]Mazyck, *Washington*, p. 92, citing Cloquet, *Recollections of the Private Life of General Lafayette*, I, 144–45.
[40]John Fitzpatrick (ed.), *The Diaries of George Washington, 1748–1799* (Boston, 1925), II, 379.
[41]Ford, *Writings*, XI, 62.

High wages is not the worst evil attending the hire of white men in this country; for being accustomed to better far than, I believe, the labourers of almost any other country, add considerably to the expense of employing them, whilst blacks, on the contrary, are cheaper, the common food of them (even when well treated) being bread made of Indian corn, butter-milk, fish (pickled herrings) frequently, and meat now and then; with a blanket for bedding. [42]

At the same time, he was aware that Negro slavery was a burden on the South, that it discouraged white immigration, perpetuated agricultural backwardness and was part of the reason for the fact that Virginia and Maryland land, though in his opinion as good as that of Pennsylvania, was cheaper. In a letter to John Sinclair, dated Philadelphia, 11 December 1796, Washington wrote that there was more agricultural prosperity in Pennsylvania "because there are laws here for the gradual abolition of slavery, which neither of the two States above mentioned (Maryland and Virginia) have at present, but which nothing is more certain than that they must have, and at a period not remote."[43]

As he became older, his disapproval of slavery became stronger and more articulate. In 1794, he wrote Tobias Lear concerning his desire to sell some of his western land: "I have another motive which makes me earnestly wish for these things—it is indeed more powerful than all the rest—namely to liberate a certain species of property—which I possess very repugnantly to my own feelings . . ."[44] He could not liberate his slaves, however, unless he found other means of defraying his expenses and other financial obligations.

Around the same time he wrote Alexander Spotswood:

With respect to the other species of property concerning which you ask my opinion, I shall frankly declare to you that I do not like even to think, much less talk of it. However, as you have put the question, I shall, in a few words, give *my ideas* about it. Were it not then, that I am principled against selling negroes, as you would cattle at a market, I would not in twelve months from this

[42]Mazyck, *Washington,* p. 124.
[43]Sparks, *Washington,* XII, 326.
[44]Haworth, *Washington,* p. 214.

date, be possessed of one as a slave. I shall be happily mistaken
if they are not found to be a very troublesome species of property
ere many years pass over our heads.[45]

In 1797, Washington expressed the hope that the legislature
of Virginia "could see the policy of gradual abolition of slavery.
It might prevent much future mischief."[46] Two years later, he
wrote his nephew, Robert Lewis, that he had "more working
negroes by a full moiety, than can be employed to any advantage in the farming system" at Mount Vernon. He could not sell
them because of his principles. He would not hire them out to
others because he had "an aversion" to breaking up families.
Unless he could solve this problem, he believed he would be
ruined. Although Washington had sold lands for $50,000 over
the past four years, this had barely sufficed "to keep [him]
afloat."[47]

In his will, Washington directed that all slaves he held in his
own right be freed upon Martha Washington's death. He did not
order them emancipated on his own death "though earnestly
wished for by me," because they were intermarried with the
dower Negroes whom he had no legal power to free. Immediate
emancipation would break up marriages and families, occa-
sioning "the most painful sensations" among those freed and
among the dower Negroes kept in slavery.

Washington willed that the old infirm Negroes "be comfortably fed and clothed by my heirs while they live" and that infants and children without parents able to provide for them be
bound by the court as apprentices until the age of 25, taught
some useful trade and how to read and write. He categorically
forbade his executors to sell any of his Negroes or send them
out of the Commonwealth of Virginia.[48]

To his mulatto man, William, Washington gave immediate
freedom and an annuity of $30 a year for life. But if he should
prefer it on grounds of age and infirmity, he could remain in
"the situation he now is," receiving food, clothes and $30 annu-
ally. "And this I give him," Washington concluded, "as a testi-

---

[45] *Ibid.*
[46] Sparks, *Washington,* XII, 323.
[47] Ford, *Writings,* XIV, 196.
[48] Sparks, *Washington,* I, 569–74.

mony of my sense of his attachment to me, and for his faithful services during the revolutionary war."[49]

Above all else, Washington believed in order, justice and the rule of law. He considered the slave trade iniquitous at all times. His views on slavery gradually changed during his lifetime from conventional acceptance of the institution to tacit misgivings and, finally, to outright hostility. He believed that slavery was a moral evil. He also considered that it was ruinous to the agriculture and the economy of the South because it discouraged white immigration, perpetuated agricultural backwardness and routinized farming methods, and because it saddled the planters with huge fixed costs which prevented them from trying technological innovations.

This forthright opposition to the institution of slavery did not make Washington either an abolitionist or a friend of abolitionism. He thought the Quakers were pernicious meddlers in affairs which did not concern them and that, under the cover of righteousness, they were ruining honest men and sowing distrust and hatred where cooperation and harmony had previously prevailed. He was implacably hostile to slave uprisings, such as that of Haiti, and he resisted to the best of his ability the efforts of the British to take American slaves they had emancipated out of the country with them at the end of the Revolutionary War. Like Thomas Jefferson, he was vigorous in seeing that the machinery of government was employed to pursue fugitive slaves and have them returned to their masters.[50]

He wanted to see slavery abolished, but gradually and by law, with the acquiescence of the slave owners, by means of persuasion rather than civil strife and cataclysm. Thus, he could express his sympathy with Lafayette's scheme of voluntary colonization of emancipated slaves outside of the United States.

There are very few places in which Washington expressed his opinion of the abilities of Negroes. His praise of the slave poetess, Phillis Wheatley, has been interpreted by some as recognition on Washington's part of the potential capacity of individual Negores. It is at least equally probable that this was an expression of his natural kindness and attitude of *noblesse*

---

[49] *Ibid.*
[50] His instructions to James Seagrove illustrate this point.

oblige. Washington's extreme reluctance to admit Negroes of any sort into the Continental Army until British recruitment of blacks made it necessary for him to reverse his policy suggests that his appraisal of their ability was unfavorable. The fact that he classified free Negro soldiers with boys and deserters reinforces this conclusion.

If Washington's views on this matter are not entirely clear, the probable reason is his prodigious self-discipline, reticence and diplomacy. He knew the value of not wearing one's heart on one's sleeve. His views were generally cautiously expressed with appropriate reservations and disclaimers of infallibility. These character traits enabled Washington to unify a divided nation behind his leadership and to preside over and dominate a Cabinet containing such incompatible elements as Alexander Hamilton and Thomas Jefferson. Both men were probably Washington's intellectual superiors, but they were not his superiors in fortitude, self-discipline, perseverance and character.

CHAPTER THREE

Slavery and the Framers of the Constitution

It appears by the Journal of the Convention that formed the Constitution of the United States, that I was the only member of that body that ever submitted the plan of a constitution completely drawn in articles and sections; and this having been done at a very early state of their proceedings, the article on which now so much stress is laid, . . . and which is in these words: 'the citizens of each State shall be entitled to all privileges and immunities in every State,' having been made by me, it is supposed that I must know, or perfectly recollect, what I meant by it. In answer, I say, that, at the time I drew that constitution, I perfectly knew that there did not then exist such a thing in the Union as a black or colored citizen, nor could I then have conceived it possible that such a thing could have ever existed in it; nor, notwithstanding all that has been said on the subject, do I now believe one does exist in it.

— Charles Pinckney, Speech in the House of Representatives, February 13, 1821.[1]

When the Federal Convention met in May 1787 to form a Constitution for the United States, a significant minority of its delegates were staunch opponents of slavery. This opposition was concentrated in those who adhered to the Federalist philosophy—the conservative element in the nascent Republic, consisting of men who believed in sound money, the protection of property rights, national development, and government by men of education and substance.

[1]Farrand, *Records,* III, 444.

Benjamin Franklin and Alexander Hamilton were ardent abolitionists. John Jay, who would become the first Chief Justice of the United States, was president of the New York anti-slavery society. Such Northern Federalist leaders as Rufus King and Gouverneur Morris were in the forefront of the opposition to slavery and the slave trade.

Southern and Border State Federalists also openly opposed the institution. Introducing a bill in the state legislature to permit Negro manumission, William Pinckney asked how Maryland could be both "the school for patriots and the mother of petty despots." Luther Martin, "the bulldog of Federalism," and Samuel Chase, later Associate Justice of the Supreme Court, played leading roles in the anti-slavery society established in Maryland in 1789. It is not accidental that Luther Martin was Jefferson's lifelong enemy or that Chase was impeached by the Jeffersonian political machine. In Delaware, Bayard and Rodney were prominent opponents of slavery and, in North Carolina, the versatile and scholarly Federalist political leader, Hugh Williamson, worked against any extension of slavery.

In contrast to the Declaration of Independence, which was essentially an eloquent instrument of persuasion, filled with resounding phrases that committed no government or nation to anything, the Constitution was an enduring compact made by sovereign states, each phrase of which carried implications for the sort of society Americans would constitute in the long, indefinite future that stretched ahead. Representatives of the several states came to Philadelphia keenly aware of the interests they were to defend and the sort of Republic they wished to build, but prepared to make the sacrifices necessary if sometimes discordant particular interests were to be served in a single body politic. Slavery was never mentioned by name, but the Constitution nonetheless dealt with the problems and conflicts it created in realistic and comprehensive fashion.

A minority among the delegates saw that the issue of slavery was the most important source of schism in the newborn nation. With characteristic prescience James Madison observed on June 30, 1787 that the divisions of interest between the states were based not primarily on "difference of size," but from "their having or not having slaves."[2] Not even Madison, however, could foresee that the slavery question would cause the only conflict in the history of the nation so grave that it could not be resolved without civil war or that the tensions occasioned by the co-existence of Negroes and Whites in the same nation would continue throughout an indefinite future.

The most hotly debated issue concerned the representation of slaves in Congress. Should they or should they not be counted in determining the number of Representatives to which each State was entitled and in measuring the extent to which Congress could levy taxes on the several states? The underlying legal issue was whether the slave was a *person,* and thus entitled to political representation, or mere *property,* and as such entitled to be counted solely for purposes of tax assessment.

The compromise finally adopted was that slaves should be counted as three-fifths of a person for both purposes. There were indignant objections. William Paterson of New Jersey said he could regard Negro slaves "in no light but as property. . . . and if Negroes are not represented in the States to which they belong, why should they be represented in the Gen'l. Govt.?"[3] The compromise plan was objectionable because it would stimulate the African slave trade by increasing the political power of those Southern States which continued to import Negroes.

Gouverneur Morris was opposed both to slavery and to the creation of a democracy in which political power was based on mere numbers. As Madison reported his remarks, Morris

could not persuade himself that numbers would be a just rule at any time. The remarks of (Mr. Mason) relative to the Western Country had not changed his opinion on that head. Among other objections it must be apparent they would not be able to furnish men equally enlightened, to share in the administration of our common interests. The Busy haunts of men not the remote wilderness, was the proper School of political Talents. If the Western people get the power into their hands they will ruin the Atlantic interests. The Back members are always most averse to the best measures.... Another objection with him against admit-

[2] *Ibid.,* I, 486.
[3] *Ibid.,* p. 560.

ting the blacks into the census, was that the people of Pena. would revolt at the idea of being put on a footing with slaves. They would reject any plan that was to have such an effect.[4]

Morris said bluntly that if the two southernmost States, South Carolina and Georgia, refused to ratify the Constitution unless it contained full protection of the slave interest, then the other States should form a Union without them. On August 8th, he delivered his views concerning slavery eloquently and at length:

"He never would concur in upholding domestic slavery," Madison's notes read.

It was a nefarious institution—It was the curse of heaven on the States where it prevailed. Compare the free regions of the Middle States, where a rich & noble cultivation marks the prosperity & happiness of the people, with the misery & poverty which overspread the barren wastes of Va. Maryd. & the other States having slaves. (Travel thro' ye whole Continent & you behold the prospect continually varying with the appearance & disappearance of slavery. The moment you leave ye E. Sts. & enter N. York, the effects of the institution become visible; Passing thro' the Jerseys and entering Pa- every criterion of superior improvement witnesses the change. Proceed Southwdly, & every step you take thro' ye great regions of slaves, presents a desert increasing with ye increasing proportion of these wretched beings.)[5]

The three-fifths compromise was adopted. As it turned out, this was a major triumph for the South since the States were never assessed to finance the Federal Government. Hence, the slave-holding States obtained extra representation and political power without any corresponding loss of revenue.

The compromise gave the South, in every election between 1790 and the Civil War, from a quarter to a third more Representatives in Congress than her free population entitled her to have. The inclusion of slaves as three-fifths of free men enabled Thomas Jefferson to defeat John Adams for the Presi-

[4]Remarks on July 11, 1787. *Ibid.,* p. 583.
[5]*Ibid.,* II, 221–22. Slavery had been abolished in New England and gradual emancipation had been legislated in Pennsylvania. In New York State, however, Negroes had comprised a sixth of the population on the eve of the Revolution and were still numerous.

dency in 1800 and thus destroy the Federalist Party and bring
about the "second American Revolution." In this momentous
contest, the Electoral College cast 73 votes for Jefferson and 65
for Adams. The Jeffersonian victory was due to the support of
the slave states and the fact that Southern political power in
the Lower House and hence in the Electoral College was in-
flated.

It is amusing to speculate on what might have happened if
the three-fifths compromise had been rejected and the South
had accepted the Constitution on the basis of representation in
proportion to the free population. Adams would have served a
second term; the split in the Federalist Party would almost
certainly have been healed because of Alexander Hamilton's
death in 1804; the nation would probably have been dominated
by a strongly nationalistic, industry-oriented North, hostile to
slavery and allied with the West. This might have forced peaceful emancipation earlier or else led to secession a generation
before it occurred. What would probably have been obviated is
a state of affairs in which political power was frozen in such
a manner that it ceased to represent either population or economic strength.

The African Slave Trade

Opposition to the African slave trade was more deep-seated
than to slavery itself. Delegates who were willing to compromise on toleration of domestic slavery regarded the international slave trade as a moral enormity and an abomination. It
was deemed an incitement to tribal warfare over half of Africa,
which had turned "man-stealing" and murder into a vast industry. The horrors of the Mid-Atlantic Passage on slave ships had
been widely publicized and were well known to many of the
delegates.

Continuation of the African trade, delegates believed, would
not only perpetuate slavery, but force a continuous infusion of
African savages into American society. This meant increasing
the dangers of slave insurrection and making solution of the
race problem, whether by segregation or total deportation, increasingly difficult. An unlimited supply of cheap slave manpower from Africa would also act as a brake on improvement

in the living and working conditions of the black population. With abundant new supplies available, the Negro labor force might be worked to death, as in Surinam and parts of the West Indies. Finally, the African slave trade was a perpetual source for the aggrandizement of Southern political power.

The geographical division of economic interest was complex. Georgia and South Carolina had seen their plantations ravaged and their slave labor force seized by the British during the Revolutionary War. These states faced an acute labor shortage for their lucrative rice and indigo plantations. The Negro gangs worked in swamp land, exposed to malaria and other fevers; mortality was high, and the demand for replacements continuous and heavy.

These two southernmost states waged a stubborn struggle against restrictions on the slave trade and were supported, to some extent, by Massachusetts and Rhode Island, which were anti-slavery in their moral outlook but economically involved in the African trade as financiers, merchants, shipbuilders, captains and seamen.

The slave trade was opposed by the Middle Atlantic States. With their depleted tobacco lands and surpluses of Negroes, Maryland and Virginia tended to join in this opposition. These states were interested in high prices for Negroes and would increasingly serve as breeding areas which would export their surplus Blacks to the newer and more fertile slave-operated agricultural areas south and west of their frontiers.

A more basic cleavage concerned the nature of American society, the sort of commonwealth which the delegates envisioned. The nation was united in its opposition to integration of the Negro in American society on any basis of citizenship, equality or even freedom. The yeomen of the South wanted a white democracy, as did virtually the entire North. This meant that the Negro population must be kept enslaved, freed on a segregated and pariah basis, or emancipated only to be deported. The problem could be kept within manageable limits only by restricting the sources of supply, and this meant outlawing the African slave trade. As against this prevalent viewpoint, the aristocratic element in South Carolina and Georgia envisaged a society comparable to that of ancient Greece, in which all manual labor was performed by slave gangs whose owners formed a cultural, economic and political elite.

In the great debate on the African slave trade, George Mason of Virginia made an eloquent plea for its illegalization.

> This infernal trafic originated in the avarice of British Merchants. The British Govt. constantly checked the attempts of Virginia to put a stop to it. The present question concerns not the importing States alone but the whole Union. The evil of having slaves was experienced during the late war. Had slaves been treated as they might have been by the Enemy, they would have proved dangerous instruments in their hands. . . . Slavery discourages arts & manufactures. The poor despise labor when performed by slaves. They prevent the immigration of Whites, who really enrich & strengthen a Country. They produce the most pernicious effect on manners. Every master of slaves is born a petty tyrant. They bring the judgment of heaven on a Country.[6]

Oliver Ellsworth, the Connecticut Federalist leader, viewed the matter more dispassionately:

> As he (Ellsworth) had never owned a slave could not judge of the effects of slavery on character. He said however that if it was to be considered in a moral light we ought to go farther and free those already in the Country.—As slaves also multiply so fast in Virginia & Maryland that it is cheaper to raise than import them, whilst in the sickly rice swamps foreign supplies are necessary, if we go no farther than is urged, we shall be unjust towards S. Carolina & Georgia—Let us not intermeddle. As population increases; poor laborers will be so plenty as to render slaves useless. Slavery in time will not be a speck in our Country. . . . As to the danger of insurrections from foreign influence, that will become a motive to kind treatment of the slaves.[7]

General Charles C. Pinckney warned that outlawing the slave trade would mean "an exclusion of S. Carola from the Union." He pointed out that his state and Georgia could not do without African supplies. "As for Virginia she will gain by stopping the importations. Her slaves will rise in value, & she has more than she wants."[8]

[6] *Ibid.*, p. 370.
[7] *Ibid.*, pp. 370–71.
[8] *Ibid.*, p. 371.

The provision finally adopted read: "The Migration or Importation of such Persons as any of the States now existing shall think proper to admit, shall not be prohibited by the Congress prior to the Year one thousand eight hundred and eight, but a Tax or duty may be imposed on such Importation, not exceeding ten dollars for each Person."[9]

This was designed to give South Carolina and Georgia twenty years of unrestricted importation of Africans to repair the manpower losses caused by British depredations during the Revolutionary War. There was no assurance that Congress would pass legislation outlawing the trade in 1808 or thereafter. If it did so, the gap could presumably be filled by the reproduction of the existing servile population.

The South also gained from the "full faith and credit clause" designed to compel all the states to extend comity to each other, to recognize each other's laws, and to extradite criminals on demand. The South demanded assurance that the Federal Government would "require fugitive slaves and servants to be delivered up like criminals." Roger Sherman of Connecticut "saw no more propriety in the public seizing and surrendering a slave or servant, than a horse" and thought the Constitution should not be burdened with petty details concerning the return of stolen goods. James Wilson added that there was no reason why the Federal Government should be saddled with the cost of catching fugitives for the Southern States. The clause demanded by Butler and Pinckney of South Carolina was nonetheless incorporated in the Constitution, where it became the basis for two fugitive slave laws, and thus inflamed passions that brought the nation eventually to the Civil War.

James Madison justified the constitutional compromise on the African slave trade in a speech to the Virginia Convention on June 17, 1788. He observed that the representatives from South Carolina and Georgia had pointed out that they already had the right to bring in slaves from Africa and hence nothing new was being given them. Moreover, they had acquired land on the assumption that they could import African Negroes to cultivate it. "Great as the evil is," Madison observed, "a dismemberment of the union would be worse. If those states should disunite from the other states, for not indulging them,

[9] *Constitution of the United States,* Article I, Section 9.

in the temporary continuance of this traffic, they might solicit and obtain aid from foreign powers. . . ."[10]

In defending the Constitution in *The Federalist,* Madison called the right to abolish the slave trade, which had "so long and so loudly upbraided the barbarism of modern policy," a "great point gained in favor of humanity." He added: "Happy would it be for the unfortunate Africans if an equal prospect lay before them of being redeemed from the oppression of their European brethren!"[11]

Moralists objected to the constitutional provision which considered the slave worth three-fifths of a free man, as implying that the former was infra-human. The task of justifying this again fell to the brilliant pen of Madison. Pretending to state the Southern pro-slavery position, Madison observed that slaves are considered by the law

> in some respects, as persons, and in other respects as property. In being compelled to labor, not for himself, but for a master; in being vendible by one master to another master; and in being subject at all times to be restrained in his liberty and chastised in his body, by the capricious will of another—the slave may appear to be degraded from the human rank, and classed with those irrational animals which fall under the legal denomination of property. In being protected, on the other hand, in his life and in his limbs, against the violence of all others, even the master of his labor and his liberty; and in being punishable himself for all violence committed against others—the slave is no less evidently regarded by the law as a member of the society, not as a part of the irrational creation; as a moral person, not as a mere article of property.[12]

Abraham Baldwin of Georgia declared in 1790 that the provisions of the Constitution concerning slavery were "more cautiously expressed, and more punctiliously guarded than any other part." The Constitution had gone to great pains to ensure that the imprint it had made would not "easily be eradicated," for "the moment we go to jostle on that ground (slavery), I fear we shall feel it tremble under our feet."[13]

[10]Farrand, *Records,* III, 325.
[11]James Madison, Alexander Hamilton and John Jay, *The Federalist Papers* (New Rochelle, 1965), No. 42, p. 266.
[12]*Ibid.,* No. 54, p. 337.
[13]Farrand, *Records,* III, 360.

In the opinion of General Charles Cotesworth Pinckney, the provisions on slavery were a resounding victory for the South. He told the South Carolina House of Representatives in January 1788 in a speech urging ratification:

> By this settlement we have secured an unlimited importation of negroes for twenty years. Nor is it declared that the importation shall be then stopped; it may be continued. We have a security that the general government can never emancipate them, for no such authority is granted; and it is admitted, on all hands, that the general government has no powers but what are expressly granted by the Constitution, and that all rights not expressed were reserved by the several states.[14] We have obtained a right to recover our slaves in whatever part of America they may take refuge, which is a right we had not before. In short, considering all the circumstances, we have made the best terms for the security of this species of property it was in our power to make. We would have made better if we could; but, on the whole, I do not think them bad.[15]

The Constitution had been unambiguous on the issue of slave representation, on the regulation of the African slave trade, on the duty to catch and return fugitive slaves, and on the obligation of all the States to extend comity to one another.

It had left other areas ambiguous. Did the Federal Government exercise plenary powers in the District of Columbia and the territories or was it merely a trustee for sovereign States in these areas? Did the United States have the right to legislate freedom in the nation's capital or the territories? Could it declare men free when they entered these regions and, if so, was that freedom indelible and permanent or limited to their sojourn there? These and other questions remained unanswered and would rise to haunt American statesmen and jeopardize the nascent Republic. Yet, all in all, the authors of the Constitution had proceeded, by means of masterly compromises, to forge a viable nation from a matrix of states divided against one another by many issues, but by that of slavery more than any other.

[14]Although this constitutional doctrine would be made explicit by the Tenth Amendment, it would be systematically violated and destroyed through subsequent legislative aggrandizement and judicial construction.

[15]Farrand, *Records*, III, 254–55.

CHAPTER FOUR

Alexander Hamilton and John Adams

Suppose Congress should at one vote, or by one act, declare all the negroes in the United States free, in imitation of that great authority, the French sovereign legislature, what would follow? Would the democracy, nine in ten, among the negroes, be gainers? Would not the most shiftless among them be in danger of perishing for want? Would not nine in ten, perhaps ninety-nine in a hundred of the rest, petition their old aristocratical master to receive them again, to protect them, to feed them, to clothe them, and to lodge and shelter them as usual?

Would not some of the most thinking and philosophical among the aristocratical negroes ramble into distant states, seeking a poor and precarious subsistence by daily labor? Would not some of the most enterprising aristocrats allure a few followers into the wilderness, and become squatters? or, perhaps, incorporate with indians?

—John Adams to John Taylor of Carolina, 1814.[1]

Upon the retirement of George Washington, the Federalist Party was torn by a factional dispute centered around its two dominant leaders, Alexander Hamilton and John Adams. The slavery issue was not a major factor in this split, which was a harbinger of the eventual extinction of the Federalist Party as a force in American politics. Nevertheless, Adams' views concerning slavery were more cautious and moderate than those of his rival and significant numbers of Southern, slaveholding

[1]Quoted in Charles Francis Adams (ed.), *The Works of John Adams* (Boston, 1856), VI, 511.

Federalists swung their support behind the Massachusetts statesman.[2]

Neither Adams nor Hamilton ever considered Negro slavery to be the most important issue dividing the American people. On at least one occasion, Adams suggested the exact contrary. Despite the negative aspects of slavery, the presence of a large slave population in the South, in his opinion, acted as a deterrent to secession.[3]

Whatever differences divided Hamilton and Adams on the slavery issue, both were Federalists. The common philosophy they shared concerning the nature of man and society outweighed their differences of opinion.

It has become fashionable for liberal historiography to characterize the Federalists as men who placed the protection of property and wealth as primary and the assertion of basic human values as secondary.[4] The Federalists have thus been caricatured as, not merely conservatives, but archetypes of reaction.[5]

If this view were true, we would expect to find that Hamilton and Adams, as leaders of the two factions of the Federalist Party, were staunch champions of slavery, since slaves were property. The contrary was the case. Both men disliked the institution of slavery and regarded it as morally repugnant. Their fundamental philosophy was that of statesmen who championed both property rights and the other fundamental rights and liberties of free men.[6]

Alexander Hamilton

Hamilton's early life stands out in contrast to the New England upbringing of John Adams. Born on the island of Nevis in the West Indies, Hamilton grew up in an atmosphere in

---

[2]Manning J. Dauer, *The Adams Federalists* (Baltimore, 1953), p. 18.

[3]John R. Howe, Jr., *The Changing Political Thought of John Adams* (Princeton, 1966), p. 223.

[4]The contrast drawn between property rights and human rights is more rhetorical than real. Property rights are the rights of human beings to security in what they own and what they have earned.

[5]This theme is woven through such a liberal classic as Vernon Louis Parrington, *Main Currents in American Thought* (New York, 1927).

[6]Adams' philosophy concerning rights is brought out in a competent and readable new biography, Anne Husted Burleigh, *John Adams* (New Rochelle, 1969).

which Negro slaves were an integral part of the plantation economy that dominated the islands.

Little is known of Hamilton's early years. As an illegitimate child whose father had deserted his mother, Rachel Levine, his first years were apparently difficult. His mother died when he was only eleven, and the next year, 1769, found him apprenticed as a clerk in the trading house of Nicholas Cruger, one of the wealthiest merchants on the island of St. Croix. Hamilton's rise within the firm was rapid and by the age of fifteen he was, in the absence of the owner, successfully managing the business.[7]

In late August of his fifteenth year a violent hurricane struck the island. Hamilton wrote a vivid account of the event for the local newspaper. His literary ability was immediately recognized and with the help of some of the leaders on the island he was sent off to college.

Hamilton landed in the Colonies on the eve of their break with England. He tried to enter Princeton but, refused permission to move into an advanced class, enrolled in Kings College in New York, now Columbia University. The turmoil over the Boston Tea Party challenged his ability both as a writer and an orator. As the conflict widened he found himself drawn into it. Early in 1776 he joined the army as a Captain of Artillery, and, within a little over a year, was made a lieutenant-colonel and aide-de-camp to the Commander-in-Chief of the Continental Army, George Washington.

It was in this position, as aide to Washington, that Hamilton, then only twenty-three, faced the Negro problem and slavery in the American Colonies for the first time. Even before hostilities, Thomas Paine had predicted that an unfriendly power might seek to foment slave insurrections and thus weaken the Colonies. As the war dragged on the British recruited Negro troops, promising those who were slaves their freedom. Defeats suffered by the Continental Army aggravated the shortage of manpower.

Hamilton thought that the utilization of Negro troops on a

[7]The data on Hamilton's early life are found in Nathan Schachner, *Alexander Hamilton* (New York, 1946), pp. 1–34. Schachner does not agree with those historians who emphasize Hamilton's illegitimacy as a psychological explanation of his ambition and drive.

large scale would fill the gaps in the ranks of the Army and counteract British efforts to muster slaves. In a letter to his friend, John Jay, Hamilton stated that Colonel John Laurens of South Carolina hoped "to raise two, three or four battalions of negroes; with the assistance of the government of that state, by contributions from the owners in proportion to the number they possess." If Jay approved the plan, Hamilton hoped "to have it recommended by Congress to the state; and, as an inducement, that they would engage to take those battalions into Continental pay." He added that adoption of this plan was urgent as British operations in the South were growing every day more "serious and formidable."

Hamilton had "not the least doubt, that the negroes will make very excellent soldiers, with proper management." "It is a maxim," he noted, "with some great military judges, that with sensible officers soldiers can hardly be too stupid; and on this principle it is thought that the Russians would make the best troops in the world, if they were under other officers than their own."

"I mention this," Hamilton wrote, "because I frequently hear it objected to the scheme of embodying negroes that they are too stupid to make soldiers. This is so far from appearing to me a valid objection that I think their want of cultivation[8] (for their natural faculties are probably[9] as good as ours) joined to that habit of subordination which they acquire from a life of servitude, will make them sooner became [sic] soldiers than our White inhabitants. Let officers be men of sense and sentiment, and the nearer the soldiers approach to machines perhaps the better."

He foresaw "that this project will have to combat much opposition from prejudice and self-interest. The contempt we have been taught to entertain for the blacks, makes us fancy many things that are founded neither in reason nor experience; and an unwillingness to part with property of so valuable a kind will furnish a thousand arguments to show the impracticability

[8]Here Hamilton made two changes. For "want of cultivation," he first wrote "spontaneity" and then crossed it out. He next wrote "want of knowledge," but then crossed out "knowledge" and substituted "cultivation."
[9]He first wrote "perhaps," then crossed it out and inserted "probably."

or pernicious tendency of a scheme which requires such a sacrifice."

Nonetheless, Hamilton warned, if the Americans did not recruit the Negroes, the British would, and "the best way to counteract the temptations they will hold out will be to offer them ourselves. . . . An essential part of the plan is to give them their freedom with their muskets. This will secure their fidelity, animate their courage, and I believe will have a good influence upon those who remain, by opening a door to their emancipation."

In closing his letter to Jay, Hamilton confessed that this last consideration, that of emancipation, "has no little weight in inducing me to wish the success of the project; for the dictates of humanity and true policy equally interest me in favor of this unfortunate class of men."[10]

In the months that followed, Hamilton kept in close touch with Laurens, but the project failed. The South Carolina legislature vetoed it. "I was outvoted, having only reason on my side," Laurens wrote Hamilton, "and being opposed by a triple-headed monster that shed the baneful influence of avarice, prejudice, and pusillanimity, in all our assemblies."[11]

As the nations of Europe armed against England, the emergency subsided and opposition to Laurens's plan grew. "I think your black scheme would be the best resource the situation in your country will admit," Hamilton wrote. "I wish it success, but my hopes are very feeble. Prejudice and private interest will be antagonists too powerful for public spirit and public good."[12] Nevertheless, as one historian has remarked, "Hamilton continued to insist that the victory would go to the side with the strongest battalions regardless of whether they were black or white."[13]

With the war over, Hamilton protested officially against the British failure to return the two thousand or so Negroes they

---

[10]Hamilton to Jay, March 14, 1779, in Harold C. Syrett (ed.), *The Papers of Alexander Hamilton* (New York, 1961), II, 17–18.
[11]*Ibid.*, III, 121 (July, 1782).
[12]*Ibid.*, II, 166 (September 11, 1779).
[13]John C. Miller, *Alexander Hamilton: Portrait in Paradox* (New York, 1959), p. 42.

had carried off, despite provisions in the peace treaty that all seized property was to be restored to its owners.[14] Disliking slavery, he was obligated to take this position as an American official and in the light of bitter complaints from Southern planters. As late as Jay's treaty (1794), Hamilton was undecided on the matter, but essentially sympathetic to the British course of action.[15]

Though it has sometimes been argued to the contrary, Hamilton owned slaves throughout his life.[16] Nevertheless, on February 4, 1785 Hamilton was one of thirty-two prominent New Yorkers who met to establish the Society for Promoting the Manumission of Slaves. John Jay was elected president. Hamilton, along with two others, was selected as "a Committee to Report a Line of Conduct to be recommended to the Members of the Society in relation to any Slaves possessed by them; and also to prepare a Recommendation to all such Persons as have manumitted or shall Manumit Slaves to transmit their names and the names and Ages of the Slaves manumitted; in Order that the same may be Registered and the Society be the better Enabled to detect Attempts to deprive such Manumitted Persons of their Liberty."[17]

Hamilton prepared a resolution "that the members of the society begin by freeing their own slaves." This direct action found no favor with the humanitarian members and the resolution was quashed.[18] The Society was never popular with the mass of New Yorkers, and it was rumored in 1792, during Jay's campaign against DeWitt Clinton for the governorship, that his presidency of the Society would work against him.[19]

Not long after the founding of the Manumission Society,

[14]Syrett, *Hamilton,* III, 365, 369, 540.
[15]Broadus Mitchell, *Alexander Hamilton, the National Adventure, 1788–1804* (New York, 1962), p. 339. Syrett, *Hamilton,* X, 494, reproduces a letter from George Hammond, the British representative in America, to George Grenville, the Foreign Secretary, reporting that "Hamilton seemed partly to acquiesce in my reasoning up to this point (that the seized Negroes be treated as booty of war) and added that this matter did not strike him as an object of such importance as it had appeared to other members of his government." (January 9, 1792.)
[16]Schachner, *Hamilton,* p. 183.
[17]"Minutes of the Society," in Syrett, *Hamilton,* III, 597.
[18]Schachner, *Hamilton,* p. 183.
[19]Syrett, *Hamilton,* XI, 344.

Henry Laurens, the father of John, who had been killed in the war in August 1782, wrote Hamilton: "Could I but prevail, upon my fellow Citizens to prohibit further importations (of Negroes from Africa), I should deem it progress equal to carrying all the outworks; my attempts hitherto have been fruitless; . . . speaking generally a whole Country is opposed to me . . ."[20] Laurens added:

> Some of my Negroes to whom I have offered freedom have declined the Bounty, they will live with me, to some of them I already allow Wages. . . . I will venture to say the whole are in more comfortable circumstances than any equal number of Peasantry in Europe, . . . the Lash is forbidden." He concluded on a note of optimism: "I think I see the rising gradations of unlimited freedom and view the prospect with pleasure. When we shall be wise enough to stop importation, such happy Families will become more general and time will work manumission or a state equal to it.[21]

Hamilton in the meantime kept up his own attack on slavery. On March 13, 1786, he, along with other members of the Society, sent a petition to the New York Legislature urging the end of the slave trade "as a commerce so repugnant to humanity, and so inconsistent with the liberality and justice which distinguish a free and enlightened people."[22] Shortly before leaving for the Constitutional Convention in Philadelphia Hamilton again made known his opposition to slavery.[23]

In *The Federalist* and later before the New York Ratification Convention, Hamilton defended the constitutional compromise which counted slaves as three-fifths of free citizens for purposes of Federal taxation and representation. He spoke sympathetically of "the unfortunate situation of the Southern States, to have a great part of their population, as well as property in blacks" and supported the decision to outlaw the African slave trade after 1808.[24]

---

[20] *Ibid.*, III, 606.
[21] *Ibid.*, 606–7.
[22] *Ibid.*, 614, quoting *The New-York Packet,* March 13, 1786.
[23] Bower Aly, *The Rhetoric of Alexander Hamilton* (New York, 1965), p. 48, citing the *New York Journal and Weekly Register,* May 24, 1787.
[24] Syrett, *Hamilton,* V, 23–24, 153.

In the years that followed Hamilton's energies were devoted to consolidating the new national government and vying for leadership of the Federalist Party. His premature death in a duel with Aaron Burr in 1804 prevented him from contributing to the debates over slavery that would culminate in the Missouri Compromise.

John Adams

As a New Englander, John Adams never had the intimate and extensive involvement with Negro slavery of such Virginia revolutionary leaders as Washington, Jefferson and Madison. He probably had more contact with Negroes in the years prior to the Revolution than is suggested in a recent volume on the color problem in early America.[25] In an imaginative attempt to recreate the milieu in which Adams grew up, Page Smith, Adams' most definitive biographer, noted that the church which the family attended seated the men to the right of the pulpit, the women to the left, "with the gallery reserved for the boys of the town, Negroes and Indians. . . . (and that) the Negroes languished during the sermon and only revived for the psalm-singing."[26]

The first powerful expression of opinion by Adams on the subject of slavery and the Negro was occasioned by the failure of Britain's West Indian colonies to join the American Colonies in protesting the imposition of the Stamp Tax.

> But can no Punishment be devised for Barbadoes and Port Royal in Jamaica? For their base Desertion of the Cause of Liberty? . . . Their mean, timid Resignation to slavery? . . . They deserve to be made Slaves to their own Negroes. But they live under the scortching Sun, which melts them, dissipates their Spirits and relaxes their Nerves. Yet their Negroes seem to have more of the Spirit of Liberty, than they. . . . I could wish that some of the Blacks had been appointed Distributors and Inspectors &c. over their Masters.[27]

[25]Frederick M. Binder, *The Color Problem in Early National America as Viewed by John Adams, Jefferson and Jackson* (The Hague, 1968), p. 11.
[26]Page Smith, *John Adams* (New York, 1962), I, 5–6.
[27]L. H. Butterfield (ed.), *Diary and Autobiography of John Adams* (Cambridge, 1961), I, 285.

In the early 1770s, Adams became interested in the condition of Negro slaves. He observed that his friend, Dr. Cooper, had quoted a "proverb from his Negro, Glasgow, . . . and then told us another instance of Glasgow's intellect, of which I had before thought him entirely destitute."[28] Shortly thereafter, Adams recorded another encounter with a Negro, in which the slave "soon began to open his heart," complaining about his master and expressing a desire to be sold to someone else. From this experience Adams drew the conclusion: "Thus I find discontents in all men—the black thinks his merit rewarded with ingratitude, and so does the white; the black estimates his own worth and the merit of his services higher than anybody else, so does the white. This flattery, fond opinion of himself, is found in every man."[29]

As the crisis between England and the Colonies deepened, the New Englander had his first opportunity to strike a blow against the slave trade which British policy had so vigorously promoted. Only three months before the signing of the Declaration of Independence, he joined with other delegates to the Continental Congress from Massachusetts, Maryland and Virginia in urging the passage of a resolution abolishing the importation of slaves into any of the thirteen colonies.[30]

Once the Congress had declared America independent, such issues relating to Negro slaves as taxation and representation had to be debated. The South wanted to count the Negro slaves for purposes of representation, but not for taxation. In his *Diary,* Adams recorded something of the debate. "Slaves prevented freemen cultivating a country," James Wilson of Pennsylvania charged.[31] When Delegate Lynch argued that slaves ought not to be taxed any greater amount than "Land, Sheep, (or) Cattle," Benjamin Franklin retorted: "Slaves rather weaken than strengthen the State, and there is therefore some difference between them and sheep. Sheep will never make any Insurrection."[32]

It was Jefferson who noted for posterity Adams's own views

[28] *Ibid.,* II, 140.
[29] *Ibid.,* 36.
[30] *Ibid.,* III, 377.
[31] *Ibid.,* II, 245–8.
[32] *Ibid.*

on the subject. Adams held that "in some countries the labouring poor were called freemen, in other they were called slaves; but that the difference as to the state was imaginary only." It is of interest that Adams compared the condition of laborers in the North with those of the slaves in the South in a way that anticipated the arguments of Southern apologists for slavery over half a century later. He pointed out that the working conditions and hours of the Northern fishermen were as "painful" and "abject" as that "of slaves." He concluded that "a slave may indeed from custom of speech be more properly called the wealth of his master, than the free labourer might be called the wealth of his employer; but, as to the state, both were equally its wealth, and should therefore equally add to the quota of its tax."[33]

While Adams was no friend of slavery, he was concerned, like most American statesmen of the time, that the issue might disrupt the young American union. In 1777, writing to his friend James Warren about an emancipation bill then pending in Massachusetts, he observed: "The Bill for freeing the Negroes, I hope, will sleep for a time. We have cause enough of Jealousy, Discord and Division and this Bill will certainly add to the Number."[34] No doubt Adams was relieved when the legislature tabled it.

Some months later, Adams had occasion to visit Maryland and recorded his assessment of the effect of slavery upon Southern attitudes toward work. Farming and other trades were performed by slaves, enabling the poor whites as well as the planters to strut about like gentlemen. "They hold their Negroes and convicts, that is, all laboring people and tradesmen, in such contempt, that they think themselves a distinct order of beings." They did not allow their sons to work or to learn a trade, "but they bring them up in idleness, or, what is worse, in horse racing, cockfighting, and card playing."[35]

During the war and the years that followed, Adams was frequently abroad representing his country. While in England in 1785, Adams read Jefferson's *Notes on the State of Virginia,*

[33] Julian P. Boyd (ed.), *The Papers of Thomas Jefferson* (Princeton, N.J., 1952–), I, 321.
[34] *Warren-Adams Letters* (Boston, 1917), I, 339.
[35] Quoted in Smith, *Adams,* I, 314.

and was impressed with the attack upon slavery. In a letter to his Virginia friend, he noted: "The passages upon slavery are worth Diamonds. They will have more effect than Volumes written by mere Philosophers."[36]

Several years before, Adams had received an essay on slavery from the Comte de Sarsefield, an acquaintance. In his *Diary* he noted with approval that the Count had "assembled every Appearance of Argument in favour of the Slavery of the Glebe (villeinage) or domestic Slavery, and has refuted them all."[37] Adams often expressed a desire to get away from the concerns of state and study nobility and aristocracy, a project which Jefferson urged him to undertake.[38]

In 1786, Adams discussed the slavery problem with Grenville Sharp:

> The idea that captives in war are slaves, is the foundation of the misfortunes of the negroes. This principle is honored and admitted by all the powers of Europe who pay tribute to the states of Barbary. I expect that one part of Africa will avenge upon my fellow citizens the injury they do to another by purchasing their captives. Yet I presume we shall be compelled to follow the base example of submission, and pay tribute or make presents, like the rest of Christians to the mussulmen. . . . I wish you would take up the whole of this African system and expose it altogether. Never, never will the slave trade be abolished, while Christian princes abase themselves before the piratical ensigns of Mahomet.[39]

Adams was in England during the debates over the Constitution in which the issue of slavery played such a significant role. When he returned to assume the Vice Presidency, he was much upset by the abolitionist petitions being presented to Congress by the Quakers under the signature of Benjamin Franklin. These petitions aroused violent anger and Adams was concerned that they would embitter the South and make the Union insecure.[40]

[36]Lester J. Cappon (ed.), *The Adams-Jefferson Letters* (Chapel Hill, 1959), I, 21.
[37]Butterfield, *Diary*, III, 15–16.
[38]Adams, *Works*, VIII, 371.
[39]*Ibid.*, 387–88.
[40]Smith, *Adams*, II, 759.

Adams said and did practically nothing about Negro slavery during his years as Vice President and later as President. This was probably due to his concern lest the issue erupt into the political arena and threaten the existence of the Union. Negro slavery did, however, cause certain problems in his household. Abigail Adams, though ill, would not have a slave as a house servant, although "most of the whites were recently arrived immigrants, without experience as domestics, usually stupid and lazy and invariably addicted to the bottle."[41]

It was not until after his defeat by Jefferson in 1800 that Adams expressed himself clearly on the issue of slavery. Writing to George Churchman and Jacob Lindley he stated: "Although I have never sought popularity by any animated speeches or inflammatory publications against the slavery of the black, my opinion against it has always been known, and my practise has been so conformable to my sentiments that I have always employed free men; both as domestics and laborers and never did I own a slave."

As to ending the institution, "The abolition of slavery must be gradual and accomplished with much caution and circumspection." Surely even those who favored immediate emancipation would fear "to venture an exertion which would probably excite insurrections among the blacks to rise against their masters, and imbrue their hands in innocent blood." There were other, more important evils in the country, Adams argued, and slavery was in the process of being extinguished anyhow.[42]

As the crisis over the expansion of slavery that resulted in the Missouri Compromise approached, Adams began to show increasing concern for the Union. While again expressing a hatred of slavery, and reiterating a desire for eventual emancipation, he displayed growing concern for the slaveholders, "who are so unfortunate as to be surrounded with these fellow creatures. . . ." He repeated that he had never owned slaves, even "when the practise was not disgraceful, when the best men in my vicinity thought it was not inconsistent with their character, and when it has cost me thousands of dollars for the labor and subsistence of free men, which I might have saved by the

[41] *Ibid.,* p. 794.
[42] Adams, *Works,* IX, 92–93.

purchase of negroes at times when they were very cheap."[43]

On the Missouri question, Adams opposed the extension of slavery, especially the huge plantations with their "great hordes of black serfs." They would discourage immigration by "the middle class of people: who were the backbone of the country." To Louisa Adams he wrote: "The Missouri question. . . . hangs like a cloud over my imagination."[44] Again, "I shudder when I think of the calamities which slavery is likely to produce in this country. You would think me mad if I were to describe my anticipations. If the gangrene is not stopped, I can see nothing but insurrection of the blacks against the whites. . . . till at last the whites will be exasperated to madness—shall be wicked enough to exterminate the Negroes as the English did the Rohillas."[45]

Adams feared that England might attempt to arouse the slaves to revolt, as she had attempted, he believed, several times before. In Nova Scotia, he thought, she was planning to train Negroes already stolen from the United States to infiltrate the South and incite the slaves to rebellion.[46]

In the end, Adams simply had no answer to the problem of the Negro and slavery. If slavery were done away with, the South would still face the problem of dealing with the Negro. "All possible humanity" should be shown the Negro as long as this was "consistent with the public safety."[47] As John R. Howe, Jr., has concluded of Adams' dilemma: "What should be done with the free Negroes, he did not know. He considered the feasibility of colonization, but concluded reluctantly that it would not work."[48]

Perhaps it was to his friend, Thomas Jefferson, that Adams best expressed his feelings about slavery:

[43]To Robert J. Evans, June 8, 1819, in *Ibid.*, X, 380.
[44]December 23, 1819, quoted in Smith, *Adams,* II, 1125–26.
[45]*Ibid.,* (January 13, 1820). The Rohillas were a tribe of Afghan descent which occupied territories in Uttar Pradesh, India, who were subjugated and broken by the British in alliance with the Nawab of Oudh in 1774.
[46]Adams to Rev. Henry Colman, January 13, 1817, cited in Howe, *Adams,* pp. 244–45.
[47]Adams to Peter Ludlow, Jr., February 20, 1819, in Howe, *Adams,* p. 245.
[48]*Ibid.,* based on Adams to Rev. Henry Colman, January 13, 1817. See also Howe, "John Adams's Views of Slavery," *Journal of Negro History,* XLIX (July 1964), 201–206.

Slavery in this Country I have seen hanging over it like a black cloud for half a Century. If I were drunk with enthusiasm as Swedenborg or Westley [sic], I might probably say I had seen Armies of Negroes marching in the air, shining in Armour. I have been so terrified with this Phenomenon that I constantly said in former times to the Southern Gentlemen, I cannot comprehend this object; I must leave it to you. I will vote for forcing no measure against your judgments. What we are to see, GOD knows, and I leave it to him, and to his agents in posterity. I have none of the genius of Franklin, to invent a rod to draw from the cloud its Thunder and lightning.[49]

[49]Cappon, *Letters,* II, 571, February 3, 1821.

CHAPTER FIVE

Thomas Jefferson: The Natural Aristocracy and Deportation of the Negro

> Nothing is more certainly written in the book of fate than that these people are to be free; nor is it less certain that the two races, equally free, cannot live in the same government. Nature, habit, opinion have drawn indelible lines of distinction between them. It is still in our power to direct the process of emancipation and deportation, peaceably, and in such slow degree that the evil will wear off insensibly, and their place be, *pari passu*, filled up by free white laborers. If, on the contrary, it is left to force itself on, human nature must shudder at the prospect held up.
>
> —Thomas Jefferson, *Autobiography*.[1]

Of the men who served as architects of the American constitutional system and of the American nation, none played a larger role in articulating a body of significant doctrine concerning slavery and the American Negro than Thomas Jefferson. As author of the Declaration of Independence, codifier of the laws of Virginia, father of the Bill of Rights, exponent of the doctrine of legitimate secession, and leader of what his partisans called the Second American Revolution, Jefferson exercised an influence on the *ante-bellum* American mind that can scarcely be exaggerated. It was he who organized and dominated the political party which governed the United States with few interrup-

---

[1]Quoted in Foner, *Jefferson*, pp. 439–40.

tions from the beginning of the Nineteenth Century to the outbreak of the Civil War. Twice President of the United States,
Jefferson was succeeded by his friends and proteges James
Madison and James Monroe, each of whom also served two
terms. As the most significant political spokesman and philosopher of the governing party during those 36 years, Jefferson
established a record of unbroken national leadership which not
even Franklin Delano Roosevelt would be able to match. As the
sectional and slave conflicts became increasingly menacing to
the life of the new republic, spokesmen for the insurgent South
embraced Jefferson's views on the right to revolution and
secession, the moral superiority of yeomanry over urban proletariat, the importance of states' rights and individualism to the
survival of free institutions and the inferiority and unassimilable nature of the Negro.

Upon the death of David Rittenhouse in 1796, Jefferson succeeded to the presidency of the American Philosophical Society, the one significant national organization of philosophers,
scientists and other members of the creative elite of the nascent republic. Despite perennial protests on his part that advancing age and residence in Washington and Virginia made
him unable to discharge his responsibilities toward the Society,
Jefferson was re-elected President regularly until 1815 when
finally, at the age of 72, he was allowed to resign. This office, as
Daniel J. Boorstin has pointed out in his significant critical
analysis *The Lost World of Thomas Jefferson,*[2] involved recognized leadership of the American intellectual community. As
distinct from his contemporaries and rivals in the world of
public affairs, Jefferson was the dominant intellectual force
within a coterie of versatile and creative minds affiliated with
the Society. This circle included David Rittenhouse, the astronomer and inventor; Dr. Benjamin Rush, physician, abolitionist
and penal reformer; Benjamin Smith Barton, botanist and
natural historian; Joseph Priestley, the Unitarian minister who
discovered oxygen and pioneered in the study of electricity;
Charles Wilson Peale, the self-taught painter and natural historian, and Thomas Paine. Jefferson not only cast a long
shadow on his time and that following his death, but did so over

[2](Boston, 1948).

an unusually extended time-span. Born in 1743, he lived until the age of 83, dying finally on the same day as his old comrade-in-arms John Adams—July 4th, 1826, the fiftieth anniversary to the day of the adoption of the Declaration of Independence.

Jefferson and the Natural Aristocracy

Perhaps the central intellectual conflict in Jefferson's political thinking was the contradiction between his belief in the equality of mankind—a corollary of his uncritical acceptance of natural rights doctrine and of his religious beliefs—and his empirical observation that the inequality of men in terms of innate and acquired mentality and morals was one of the most fundamental facts of social organization. The a priori philosophizing which led Jefferson to his dogma of equality is discussed succinctly and competently by Boorstin[3] and need not be recapitulated here. His more fervent expressions in favor of the equality of mankind were sometimes lettered for practical political purposes, in the course of conflict with such opponents as the British Crown and the Federalist Party or else under the euphoric influence of the French Revolution. The extent to which this benign and rather gentle philosopher could be stirred to political fanaticism by the latter event is illustrated by his justification of the Reign of Terror:

> The liberty of the whole earth was depending on the issue of the contest, and was ever such a prize won with so little innocent blood? My own affections have been deeply wounded by some of the martyrs to this cause, *but rather than it should have failed I would have seen half the earth desolated.*[4]

The most famous Jeffersonian aphorism concerning the equality of man is, of course, the second sentence of the Declaration of Independence: "We hold these truths to be self-evident, that all men are created equal . . ." But the primary purpose of the Declaration was to rally the widest possible support to the Revolutionary cause. It was designed to win men's hearts, rather than to expound a valid political philoso-

[3]Boorstin, *Jefferson,* pp. 41–98.
[4]Paul Leicester Ford (ed.), *The Writings of Thomas Jefferson* (New York, 1892–1899), VI, 154. Emphasis supplied.

phy. As Jefferson himself put it, "Neither aiming at originality of principle or sentiment, nor yet copied from any particular and previous writing, it was intended to be an expression of the American mind, and to give to that expression the proper tone and spirit called for by the occasion. *All its authority rests then on the harmonizing sentiments of the day.*"[5]

Throughout his long life, Thomas Jefferson believed in the existence and supreme importance of a natural aristocracy of talent and virtue, which had been placed on earth by Providence to give mankind the possibility of just government. He made a sharp distinction between this natural aristocracy, the members of which could come from any social class and almost any race, and the artificial aristocracy of birth and privilege, the rule of which he equated with injustice and usurpation.

In Jefferson's *Literary Bible,* a compilation of quotations which he copied as a young man from such writers as Homer, Cicero, Shakespeare, Milton and Bolingbroke, there is a significant passage from Euripides which he evidently thought worth committing to memory: "To be of the noble born gives a peculiar distinction clearly marked among men, and the noble name increases in lustre in those who are worthy." Perhaps in a half jocular mood, Jefferson had expressed interest in acquiring a coat of arms. Summing up his attitude as a young man, Dumas Malone, Jefferson's most authoritative biographer, concluded:

> It would have been surprising if he had wanted to substitute for leadership of this sort [that of the Virginia gentry of which he was a member—authors] the rule of the uneducated crowd about whom so many grave doubts had been expressed by the ancient writers. The fact is that never in his life did he believe it necessary to choose between such alternatives. By the time of the Declaration of Independence, he was convinced that aristocracies of birth and wealth were artificial and unjust, but that what he sought to liberate and promote was a 'natural' aristocracy of talent and virtue. He himself first appeared in the forum as one who had inherited a noble tradition of responsibility along with great privileges.[6]

[5]Andrew A. Lipscomb and Albert Ellery Bergh (eds.), *The Writings of Thomas Jefferson* (Washington, D.C., 1904–1905), XVI, 118. Jefferson to Henry Lee, May 8, 1825. Emphasis supplied.
[6]Quoted in Dumas Malone, *Jefferson the Virginian* (Boston, 1948), p. 178.

Discussing his bill to allow tenants to hold their entailed lands in fee simple, introduced in 1781, Jefferson pointed out in his *Autobiography* that perpetual tenant status created great landed, patrician families, representing inherited wealth and dominating the Colonial governments. "To annul this privilege, and instead of an aristocracy of wealth, of more harm and danger, than benefit to society, to make an opening for the aristocracy of virtue and talent, which nature has wisely provided for the direction of the interests of society, and scattered with equal hand through all its conditions, was deemed essential to a well-ordered republic."

In 1779, Jefferson drew up a statute for public education in Virginia, which has been hailed as an audacious and prophetic effort to establish free education for the gifted. In addition to an entire network of "hundred" or primary schools to teach all white children to read, there were to be grammar schools to give a handful of children of superior intellectual gifts, "raked from the rubbish annually," a much more comprehensive higher education. This system, Jefferson pointed out, would teach all white children in the Commonwealth, male and female, the elements of reading, writing and arithmetic. In addition, it would turn out "ten annually of superior genius, well taught in Greek, Latin, geography, and the higher branches of arithmetic; turning out ten others annually, of still superior parts, who, to those branches of learning shall have added such of the sciences as their genius shall have led them to . . ."[7]

The preamble to the bill avoided referring to the people as "rubbish," but pointed out candidly that the purpose was to educate "those persons, whom Nature hath endowed with genius and virtue" with a "liberal education, worthy to receive and able to guard, the sacred deposit of the rights and liberties of their fellow citizens, and that they should be called to that charge without regard to wealth, birth, or other accidental condition or circumstance." This was entirely consonant with Jefferson's definition of the American goal as "an aristocracy of ability arising out of a democracy of opportunity."

Long after he had completed his Presidential terms and retired to his beloved Monticello, Jefferson made a full and

[7] *Notes on Virginia*, in Ford, *Jefferson*, III, 252.

frank statement of his beliefs about innate human differences, natural aristocracy and eugenics in his correspondence with his old friend, comrade-in-arms and rival, John Adams. This thoughtful exchange of letters is in refreshing contrast to the eloquence of such public documents as the Declaration of Independence. The two old statesmen wrote each other, not to sway the passions of multitudes, but in the belief that "we ought not to die before we have explained ourselves to each other." At the time the letters concerning natural aristocracy were written, Jefferson was in his seventieth year, but with his intellect vigorous and unimpaired and no longer responsive to any need to distort or prettify his true beliefs in the service of political expedience.

The topic was introduced by Adams, who wrote Jefferson on August 14, 1813:

> "Behold my translation
> " 'My friend Curnis, When We want to purchace, Horses, Asses, or Rams, We inquire for the Wellborn. And every one wishes to procure, from the good Breeds. A good Man does not care to marry a Shrew, the Daughter of a Shrew; unless They give him, a great deal of Money with her.'
> "What think you of my translation? Compare it with that of Grotius, and tell me, which, is nearest to the Original in letter and in Spirit."

The quotation was from Theognis, the Sixth Century Greek poet from the city of Megara on the Isthmus of Corinth. An eyewitness of the revolutions of his time, Theognis had been expropriated by the democratic faction, which he hated. His verse consists primarily of moralizing on the sins of the democrats and on the fact that, in his day, men chose wives on the basis of wealth, rather than beauty, lineage, character or intelligence.

Living 544 years before Jesus Christ, Adams observed, Theognis was as enlightened on this subject as your Nineteenth-Century American. Nobody had proved to mankind that "the Idea of the 'Well born' is a prejudice, a Phantasm, a Point of no point, a Gape Fly away, a dream? I say it is the Ordonance of God Almighty, in the Constitution of human nature, and wrought into the Fabrick of the Universe."[8]

On September 1st, Adams returned to the same subject in another letter to Jefferson. He submitted an additional translation of Theognis:

"Nor does a Woman disdain to be the Wife of a bad rich Man. But She prefers a Man of Property before a good Man. For Riches are honoured; and a good Man marries from a bad Family, and a bad Man from a good one. Wealth mingles all Races."

Adams then observed that the five pillars of aristocracy were "Beauty, Wealth, Birth, Genius and Virtues. Any one of the three first, can at any time over bear any one or both of the two last."[9]

On October 28, 1813 Jefferson replied from Monticello in what is the classic statement of his views on natural aristocracy and the control of human reproduction. He began by pointing out that the passage Adams had quoted from Theognis was "a moral *exhortation*, . . . a reproof to man, who, while with his domestic animals he is curious to improve the race by employing always the finest male, pays no attention to the improvement of his own race, but intermarries with the vicious, the ugly, or the old, for considerations of wealth or ambition."

After quoting the Pythagorean philosopher Ocellus to the effect that "the powers, the organs and desires for coition have not been given by god to man for the sake of pleasure, but for the procreation of the race," Jefferson continued with a strong, and quite unexpected, plea for a policy of controlled human breeding:

> The selecting of the best male for a Harem of well chosen females also, which Theognis seems to recommend from the example of our sheep and asses, would doubtless improve the human, as it does the brute animal, and produce a race of veritable *aristoi*. For experience proves that the moral and physical qualities of man, whether good or evil, are transmissible in a certain degree, from father to son. But I suspect that the equal rights of men will rise up against this privileged

[8] Adams to Jefferson, August (14?), 1813, in Cappon, *Letters*, II, 365.
[9] Adams to Jefferson, September 1, 1813, in *Ibid.*, p. 371.

Solomon, and oblige us to continue acquiescence under the Αμαυρωσα γενεοα ἄδτων('the degeneration of the race of men') which Theognis complains of, and to content ourselves with the accidental aristoi produced by the fortuitous concourse of breeders. For I agree with you that there is a natural aristocracy among men. The grounds of this are virtue and talents. Formerly bodily powers gave place among the aristoi. But since the invention of gunpowder has armed the weak as well as the strong with missile death, bodily strength, like beauty, good humor, politeness and other accomplishments, has become but an auxiliary ground of distinction. There is also an artificial aristocracy founded on wealth and birth, without either virtue or talents; for with these it would belong to the first class. *The natural aristocracy I consider as the most precious gift of nature for the instruction, the trusts, and government of society.* And indeed it would have been inconsistent in creation to have formed man for the social state, and not to have provided virtue and wisdom enough to manage the concerns of the society. *May we not even say that that form of government is the best which provides the most effectually for a pure selection of these natural aristoi into the offices of government?* The artificial aristocracy is a mischievous ingredient in government, and provision should be made to prevent its ascendancy. On the question, What is the best provision, you and I differ; but we differ as rational friends, using the free exercise of our own reason, and mutually indulging its errors. *You* think it best to put the Pseudoaristoi into a separate chamber of legislation where they may be hindered from doing mischief by their coordinate branches, and where also they may be a protection to wealth against the Agrarian and plundering enterprises of the Majority of the people. I think that to give them power in order to prevent them from doing mischief, is arming them for it, and increasing instead of remedying the evil . . .

I think the best remedy is exactly that provided by all our constitutions, to leave to the citizens the free election and separation of the aristoi from the pseudoaristoi, of the wheat from the chaff. In general they will elect the really good and wise. In some instances, wealth may corrupt, and birth blind them; but not in sufficient degree to endanger their society.[10]

The revolutionary view of American society propounded in this letter was never elaborated in any of Jefferson's public documents, probably because of the predictably hostile reaction it would have aroused in the public mind. Even after a

[10]Jefferson to Adams, October 28, 1813, in *Ibid.,* pp. 386–87. Emphasis on *You* and *I* by T.J.; all other emphases by the authors.

century and a half, no American President would risk public support by suggesting a controlled breeding plan under which declines in the mental potential of the population might be arrested by encouraging the creative minority to acquire plural spouses.

Jefferson's exposition, admirable as it is, contains logical weaknesses. His dismissal of "beauty, good humor and politeness" as merely ancillary grounds of distinction due to the invention of gunpowder is a somewhat bizarre view. As Adams was quick to point out, women of unusual beauty have always been able to attain power by influencing their men.

Jefferson used his doctrine of the natural aristocracy as a bludgeon with which to pummel the "artificial aristocracy" of birth and wealth. He accentuated the contrast by the sophistry of asserting that those who belonged to both groups should automatically be excluded from the second. Neither he nor Adams came to grips with the really pertinent issue, the extent to which the two aristocracies coincided. Yet a strong case could be made for rule by the "artificial" aristocracy if it in fact monopolized much of the ability and virtue of the nation.

Typical of Jefferson's theological approach to scientific issues was his assumption that God created the universe with an economy of means and, therefore, would never have made man a social animal without simultaneously bringing into existence a class of people capable of providing good government—the natural aristocracy. On similar grounds, Jefferson also argued that no animal species had ever become extinct. For it to have done so, he believed, would have argued inefficiency on the part of the Deity in creating it.[11] Finally, the optimistic faith that majorities will generally choose governments composed of the creative minority of virtue and talents will sound extraordinary to anyone who has ever seriously reflected about the calibre of political leadership in the Twentieth Century.

After allowing a month to elapse, John Adams replied in a somewhat garrulous and disjointed communication. He refused to accept the distinction between artificial and natural aristocracies on the grounds that wealth and lineage were conferred on some individuals by nature in just as arbitrary a manner as she distributed virtue and intelligence. He believed

---

[11]Boorstin, *Jefferson*, pp. 38–40.

that aristocracies of wealth and power were allowed to become hereditary only after "Corruption in Elections becomes dominant and uncontroulable." Rapacious and bickering aristocracies were then followed by periods of Caesarism, an idea that seemed to anticipate Oswald Spengler.[12] Adams concluded with the assertion that "both artificial Aristocracy and Monarchy, and civil, military, political and hierarchichal Despotism, have all grown out of the Natural Aristocracy of 'Virtue and Talents.' " As for the United States:

"We, to be sure, are far remote from this. Many hundred years must roll away before We shall be corrupted. Our pure, virtuous, public spirited federative Republick will last for ever, govern the Globe and introduce the perfection of Man, his perfectability being already proved by Price Priestly, Condorcet, Rousseau Diderot and Godwin."[13]

Whether Jefferson found Adams' irony unpalatable or concluded that he was not able to communicate meaningfully on this subject with his old associate, he made no further reference to the theory of natural aristocracy in his correspondence.

Faith in the natural aristocracy and in its unique fitness to govern was a constant navigational star in Jefferson's long and varied public career. He believed that the American people would consistently choose these natural aristoi to govern them. This should ensure that the new republic would escape from that oscillation between amoral anarchy and immoral despotism which had characterized much of European history and that it would become, as Jefferson termed it, "the world's best hope."[14] He believed that enormous differences existed in the intellectual and moral capacities of men. He considered that a good society could only be established and preserved if its foundation was a people capable of appreciating justice, law, representative institutions and human freedom. Holding these beliefs, Jefferson was deeply concerned throughout his life with the danger that American society would be fatally poisoned by the intrusion of people whom he considered incapable of civilization. It was in these terms that he appraised the abilities and

---

[12] *The Decline of the West* (New York, 1926).

[13] Adams to Jefferson, November 15, 1813. Cappon, *Letters,* II, 400.

[14] *First Inaugural Address,* March 4, 1801. Reprinted in Foner, *Jefferson,* pp. 332–35.

prospects of the two non-white ethnic groups inhabiting the United States: the Indians and the Negroes. His judgment was that the shortcomings of the former were wholly the result of an adverse environment and that those of the latter were probably largely innate.

Notes on the State of Virginia

Jefferson's *Notes on the State of Virginia* were written in 1781–82 in response to inquiries from François Barbé-Marbois, the secretary of the French legation in Philadelphia. One of Jefferson's motives was to have his French friends as fully informed as possible concerning the American scene and clearly aware of the extent to which Americans enjoyed greater political and intellectual freedom than Europeans.[15] Another concern was to refute a theory of American degeneracy, first proposed by Buffon and later elaborated by the Abbé Raynal, to the effect that excessive heat and moisture made the Americas unfavorable to the development of animals and that hence American species were more stunted than those of the Old World.[16]

Jefferson's masterful exposition of the resources, natural history, institutions and customs of Virginia was published anonymously in Paris in 1785. While he sent copies to friends, Jefferson wished to keep his authorship secret as, "I fear the terms in which I speak of slavery and of our Constitution may produce an irritation which will revolt the minds of our countrymen against reformation . . ."[17]

In discussing the American Indian, whom he had known well since childhood, he made short shrift of such claims on Buffon's part as that he was cowardly, without strong emotional family ties, inert, antisocial and without a powerful emotional life. The root of these defects, Buffon had asserted, was sexual inadequacy and indifference. The Indians, having practically no body hair or beards, were allegedly "weak and small" in their "reproductive organs."

Jefferson retorted that he could state from personal observa-

[15]Dumas Malone, *Jefferson and the Rights of Man* (Boston, 1951), p. 93.
[16]Boorstin, *Jefferson,* pp. 98–108.
[17]Jefferson to Monroe, June 17, 1785, in Ford, *Jefferson,* IV, 418–19.

tion that the Indian "is neither more defective in ardor, nor more impotent with his female, than the white reduced to the same diet and exercise; that he is brave, when an enterprise depends on bravery; . . . also he meets death with more deliberation and endures tortures with a firmness unknown . . . with us; that he is affectionate to his children, careful of them, and indulgent in the extreme; . . . that his vivacity and activity of mind is equal to ours in the same situation; hence his eagerness for hunting and for games of chance."[18] Jefferson added that the reason Indians had practically no beards or body hair was not sexual inadequacy, but that they considered this hair disfiguring and carefully plucked it out.

If virility was associated with abundance of body hair, Jefferson asked, how did Buffon and Raynal explain the fact that "Negroes have notoriously less hair than the whites; yet they are more ardent." Factual evidence for the assertion that the excessive heat and moisture of the Americas stunted either "the races of animals" or man was lacking. When an allowance was made for "those circumstances of their situation which call for a display of particular talents only," it would probably be found that the Indians "are formed in mind as well as in body, on the same module with the *Homo sapiens Europaeus.*"[19]

Jefferson concluded his discussion of the Indians with the assertion:

"The principles of their society forbidding all compulsion, they are to be led to duty and to enterprise by personal influence and persuasion. Hence eloquence in council, bravery and address in war, become the foundations of all consequence with them. To these acquirements all their faculties are directed. Of their bravery and address in war we have multiplied proofs, because we have been the subjects on which they were exercised. Of their eminence in oratory we have fewer examples,

[18] *Notes on the State of Virginia,* Query VI.
[19] Linnaeus in his *Systema Natura* divided the *Genus Homo* into two species: *homo (sapiens) diurnus,* or mankind, and *homo (troglodytes) nocturnus,* or the anthropoid apes. *Homo (sapiens) diurnus* was divided into the varieties: *Europaeus, Americanus, Asiaticus, Afer, Ferus* and *Monstrosis.* The first four were the aboriginal inhabitants of their respective continents. *Ferus* was man who had become savage by living in a state of nature; *Monstrosis* was a class of monsters or mutants.

because it is displayed chiefly in their own councils. Some, however, we have, of very superior lustre."[20]

Jefferson's Negro Expatriation Plan

While he denied that the American Indian had shortcomings *vis-à-vis* the white man or else attributed any that existed to purely environmental causes, Jefferson took a radically different approach to the Negro. Query XIV, concerning "the administration of justice and the description of the laws," deals primarily with slavery and the Negro. Since it is Jefferson's most carefully considered exposition on both topics, it is worth quoting extensively. Among the "most remarkable alterations" of the laws of Virginia Jefferson proposed was:

> To emancipate all slaves born after passing of the act.[21] The bill reported by the revisors does not itself contain this proposition; but an amendment containing it was prepared, to be offered to the legislature whenever the bill should be taken up, and further directing that they should continue with their parents to a certain age, then be brought up, at the public expence, to tillage, arts or sciences, according to their geniusses, till the females should be eighteen, and the males twenty-one years of age, when they should be colonized to such place as the circumstances of the time should render most proper, sending them out with arms, implements of household and of the handicraft arts, seeds, pairs of the useful domestic animals, &c. to declare them a free and independent people, and extend to them our alliance and protection, till they shall have acquired strength; and to send vessels at the same time to other parts of the world for an equal number of white inhabitants; to induce whom to migrate hither, proper encouragements were to be proposed.

At the time Jefferson wrote, proposals for the voluntary colonization of free Negroes in Latin America or Africa were beginning to come into vogue. Jefferson went far beyond this. He proposed nothing less than the total and mandatory deporta-

---

[20] *Notes on the State of Virginia,* Query VI. Jefferson added that the speech of Logan, a Mingo chief, to Lord Dunmore, Governor of Virginia, was oratorically equal to the best of Demosthenes and Cicero.

[21] Bill No. 51 "concerning Slaves," proposed by Jefferson. Nothing came of it and, as Jefferson explained decades later in his *Autobiography,* "The public mind would not yet bear the proposition."

tion of all persons of African origin. For a small nation, jealous of the powers of government and regarding taxation as an infringement on personal liberty,[22] Jefferson's plan was drastic and sweeping. In 1790, at the time the *Notes* were published, there were 750,000 Negroes in the United States, of whom about 300,000 were in Virginia. The plan, therefore, entailed the movement of a million and a half people across the Atlantic, the Negro half of whom were to be trained, fed, equipped and supplied at government expense until they became self-supporting, and the white half of whom were to be attracted to the United States presumably with financial concessions.

Although this proposal involved a revolutionary expansion of the functions of the Federal Government, Jefferson never swerved from it during the remaining third of a century of his public life. Thus, in 1801, Governor James Monroe of Virginia forwarded to President Jefferson a resolution that land be bought abroad to which Negroes implicated in conspiracy or insurrection might be deported. Jefferson endorsed the plan with the significant proviso that no Negroes be sent "within our limits" or to any place which might in future "become part of our Union." After the rebellion led by Toussaint l'Ouverture in Santo Domingo, Jefferson had "become daily more and more convinced that all the West India Islands will remain in the hands of the people of colour, and a total expulsion of the whites sooner or later take place."[23]

Thus, settlement of Negroes in either Africa or the West Indies seemed to him satisfactory. Their deportation to the mainland of Central or South America should be ruled out, he wrote Monroe, because of the future time "when our rapid multiplication will . . . cover the whole northern, if not the southern continent . . . nor can we contemplate with satisfaction either blot or mixture on that surface." The ideal place to send them would be Haiti, whose Negro ruler, Dessalines, might consider as meritorious actions "deemed criminal by us." If Haiti rejected these turbulent elements, they should be shipped back to

---

[22]In 1794, for example, the "Watermelon Army" of west Pennsylvania farmers took up arms against the United States because of an excise tax of 9¢ to 25¢ a gallon on domestically produced whiskey.

[23]Thomas Jefferson to James Monroe, July 14, 1793.

Africa.[24] Deportation was, in his opinion, absolutely imperative, because justice demanded that these people be free, while
self-preservation required that they be removed from the
United States.
Computing the value of an average adult slave at $200 and
that of a newborn Negro baby at $12.50, Jefferson estimated
that to buy up all the slaves, send them to Africa and support
them for a year would cost $900 million. This, in his opinion,
could be done by having the inhabitants of the lands in the
Northwest Territory, ceded by Virginia, foot the bill. At the
time, the national income of the United States was about $855
million annually, of which some $300 million came from
agriculture.[25] Given the ingrained hatred of governmental authority and taxes of white Americans of the period, Jefferson's
deportation scheme seemed chimerical.

On Negro-White Race Differences

Immediately after proposing emancipation and deportation
in the *Notes,* Jefferson considered in great detail the reasons
which, in his opinion, made the second step necessary.

> It will probably be asked, Why not retain and incorporate the
> blacks in the state, and thus save the expence of supplying, by
> importation of white settlers, the vacancies they will leave?
> Deep rooted prejudices entertained by the whites; ten thousand
> recollections by the blacks, of the injuries they have sustained;
> new provocations; the real distinctions which nature has made;
> and many other circumstances, will divide us into parties, and
> produce convulsions which will probably never end but in the
> extermination of one or the other race.—To these objections,
> which are political, may be added others, which are physical and
> moral.

Of these physical and moral differences, the first and most
striking one, Jefferson asserted, was that of color. Believing
that beauty was not a matter of subjective taste, but objective

[24]Thomas Jefferson to James Monroe, November 24, 1801.
[25]Estimates of the National Industrial Conference Board for 1819. Bureau of
the Census, *Historical Statistics of the United States* (Washington, D.C., 1942),
p. 14.

and absolute, Jefferson associated blackness with esthetic inferiority.

> And is this difference of no importance? Is it not the foundation
> of a greater or less share of beauty in the two races? Are not the
> fine mixtures of red and white, the expressions of every passion
> by greater or less suffusions of colour in the one, preferable to
> that eternal monotony, which reigns in the countenances, that
> immoveable veil of black which covers all the emotions of the
> other race? Add to these, flowing hair, a more elegant symmetry
> of form, their own judgment in favour of the whites, declared by
> their preference of them, as uniformly as is the preference of the
> Oran-ootan for the black women over those of his own species.
> The circumstance of superior beauty, is thought worthy atten-
> tion in the propagation of our horses, dogs, and other domestic
> animals, why not in that of man?[26]

Jefferson proceeded with the observation that Negroes
sweated more, "which gives them a very strong and disagreeable odour" and that this greater transpiration "renders them
more tolerant of heat, and less so of cold, than the whites." He
also noted the Negro's "disposition to sleep when abstracted
from their diversions, and unemployed in labour. An animal
whose body is at rest, and who does not reflect, must be disposed
to sleep, of course."

In discussing temperamental differences between Negroes
and Whites, Jefferson noted that the former seemed to require
less sleep. They were "at least as brave," but their courage
might be due to "a want of forethought." He then added:

[26]This passage has stirred generations of liberal and negrophile writers to
wrath. Among the latest is Winthrop D. Jordan, who concludes on fragmentary
evidence that Jefferson's "picture of Negroes as crudely sensual beings" was
"a functional displacement of his own drives" (*Black,* p. 459.) While Jefferson's
belief that orangutans preferred Negroes to their own species as sexual partners was part of the folklore of his day, his references to the "eternal
monotony" of the Negro countenance and to the "immoveable veil of black
which covers all emotions of the other race" has some scientific support. Carleton S. Coon points out that "communication through facial expression. . . . has
reached its peak among two racial groups, the European and Western Asian
Caucasoids and the Mongoloids of China and Japan." Anatomically, this depends upon "the specialization of certain bundles of thin muscles derived from
the platysma—the subcutaneous muscle sheath of mammals which permits
them to shake their coats" and these platysmal fiber patterns "are completely
different from race to race." [*The Living Races of Man* (New York, 1965), p.
257.]

They are more ardent after their female; but love seems with them to be more an eager desire, than a tender mixture of sentiment and sensation. Their griefs are transient. Those numberless afflictions, which render it doubtful whether heaven has given life to us in mercy or in wrath are less felt, and sooner forgotten with them. In general, their existence appears to participate more of sensation than reflection.

The Quality of African Negro Mind

"Comparing them by their faculties of memory, reason, and imagination," Jefferson wrote, "it appears to me that in memory they are equal to the whites; in reason much inferior, as I think one could scarcely be found capable of tracing and comprehending the investigations of Euclid; and that in imagination they are dull, tasteless, and anomalous. It would be unfair to follow them to Africa for this investigation. We will consider them here, on the same stage with the whites."

After making every allowance for differences in condition and education, Jefferson continued, millions of them had been born in America. Many of these had been trained in handicrafts and given a liberal education, enabling them to benefit from conversations with their masters and from living in a country "where the arts and sciences are cultivated to a considerable degree." With none of these advantages, the Indians showed creative ability in the plastic arts and a gift for "the most sublime oratory", which proved to Jefferson "the existence of a germ in their minds which only wants cultivation." By contrast, in the case of the Negroes:

> But never yet[27] could I find that a black had uttered a thought above the level of plain narration; never see even an elementary trait of painting or sculpture. In music they are more generally gifted than the whites with accurate ears for tune and time, and they have been found capable of imagining a small catch. Whether they will be equal to the composition of a more extensive run of melody, or of complicated harmony, is yet to be proved. Misery is often the parent of the most affecting touches

[27]Jefferson's manuscript contains these words, later deleted: "but never yet . . . as far as I have heard, has a black excelled in any art, in any science." Thomas Jefferson, *Notes on the State of Virginia,* William Peden (ed.), (Chapel Hill, 1955), p. 288.

in poetry.—Among the blacks is misery enough, God knows, but no poetry. Love is the peculiar oestrum of the poet. Their love is ardent, but it kindles the senses only, not the imagination. Religion indeed has produced a Phyllis Whately; but it could not produce a poet.[28] The compositions published under her name are below the dignity of criticism. The heroes of the Dunciad are to her, as Hercules to the author of that poem.

Jefferson turned next to Ignatius Sancho, born on a slave ship, and author of *Letters,* published in London in 1782. He gave Sancho "first place among those of his own colour who have presented themselves to the public judgment," but found his thought "as incoherent and eccentric, as is the course of a meteor through the sky." In comparison with the white epistolary writers among whom he lived, Sancho would have to be enrolled "at the bottom of the column."

All this left the question open of whether the mentally degraded condition of the Negro was due to his race or to the fact that he was enslaved. Jefferson approached this issue from two different angles. "The improvement of the blacks in body and mind, in the first instance of their mixture with the whites," he observed, "has been observed by every one, and proves that their inferiority is not the effect merely of their condition of life." In short, the mental superiority of mulattoes over full-blooded Negroes proved to Jefferson that slavery alone could not explain the African's failure to reach mental parity with his masters.

Jefferson's second argument was a comparison of the condition and accomplishments of Roman slaves, who were white, with Virginia slaves, who were black. The status of the former, particularly during the Augustan Age, "was much more deplorable than that of the blacks on the continent of America." The Romans kept male and female slaves in separate apartments, because it was cheaper to buy a slave than to rear one. Cato advised a fellow farmer "to sell his old oxen, old waggons, old tools, old and diseased servants, and everything else become useless." Slaves who were seriously ill were habitually exposed

[28]The same Phyllis Whately (or Wheatley) whose verse Washington had either admired or politely pretended to admire. The modern reader will tend to agree with Jefferson's appraisal.

on the island of Aesculapius on the Tiber to die of hunger and neglect. Jefferson cited the case of Vedius Pollio who proposed feeding one of his slaves to his fish because he had broken a glass. He observed that the evidence of slaves in Rome was regularly taken under torture and that, when a master was murdered, all slaves in the same house or within earshot were condemned to death, whether guilty or innocent.

Jefferson concluded:

"Yet notwithstanding these and other discouraging circumstances among the Romans, their slaves were often their rarest artists. They excelled too in science, inasmuch as to be usually employed as tutors to their master's children. Epictetus, (Diogenes, Phaedon), Terence, and Phaedrus, were slaves. But they were of the race of whites. It is not their condition then, but nature, which has produced the distinction."

Jefferson proceeded to a discussion of the morals of Virginia slaves. "That disposition to theft with which they have been branded, must be ascribed to their situation, and not to any depravity of the moral sense." He believed that men could not be expected to respect the property rights of others if they were denied the opportunity to acquire property themselves. Despite all this, many Negro slaves were "of the most rigid integrity." If the mental difference between the two races could in all probability be ascribed to heredity, whatever moral differences existed were the result of the institution of slavery and its evil effects.

The belief that the Negroes were mentally inferior as a race was based on Jefferson's observations at close range over many years, but it went against his grain as a political philosopher of equal rights. He voiced his final conclusion with hesitation:

The opinion, that they are inferior in the faculties of reason and imagination, must be hazarded with great diffidence. To justify a general conclusion, requires many observations, even where the subject may be submitted to the Anatomical knife, to Optical glasses, to analysis by fire, or by solvents. How much more then where it is a faculty, not a substance, we are examining; where it eludes the research of all the senses; where the conditions of its existence are various and variously combined; where the effects of those which are present or absent bid defiance to calculation; let me add too, as a circumstance of great tenderness, where our conclusion would degrade a whole race of men from the rank in the scale of beings which their Creator may perhaps have given them. To our reproach it must be said, that though for a century and a half we have had under our eyes the race of black and of red men, they have never yet been viewed by us as subjects of natural history. I advance it therefore as a suspicion only, that the blacks, whether originally a distinct race, or made distinct by time and circumstances, are inferior to the whites in the endowments both of body and mind. It is not against experience to suppose, that different species of the same genus, or varieties of the same species, may possess different qualifications. Will not a lover of natural history then, one who views the gradations in all the races of animals with the eye of philosophy, excuse an effort to keep those in the department of man as distinct as nature has formed them? This unfortunate difference of colour, and perhaps of faculty, is a powerful obstacle to the emancipation of these people. Many of their advocates, while they wish to vindicate the liberty of human nature, are anxious also to preserve its dignity and beauty. Some of these embarrassed by the question, 'What further is to be done with them?' join themselves in opposition with those who are actuated by sordid avarice only. Among the Romans emancipation required but one effort. The slave, when made free, might mix with, without staining the blood of his master. But with us a second is necessary, unknown to history. When freed, he is to be removed beyond the reach of mixture.

The Case of Benjamin Banneker

In an effort to refute the verdict of Jefferson's *Notes on the State of Virginia,* enemies of chattel slavery trotted out a procession of exceptional Africans. One of these was Thomas Fuller, or "Negro Tom," a "self-taught Arithmetician," born in Africa and brought to the United States as a slave at the age of fourteen. He was able to perform such feats as to calculate in his head in a few minutes the number of seconds a man had lived at the age of seventy years, seventeen days and twelve hours.[29] The *Columbian Centinel* hailed him as a prodigy who, had his opportunities been equal to those of the whites, would have been acknowledged by Newton himself as "a Brother in

[29]Jordan, *Black,* p. 449.

Science." It seems probable that Fuller belonged to the bizarre and imperfectly understood category of *idiots savants.*

A more serious contender was a Negro named Benjamin Banneker, born free in Maryland, who had developed an early interest in mathematical puzzles, had allegedly constructed a clock and, upon being given books by a Quaker neighbor named Andrew Ellicott, had studied astronomy. In 1791, Banneker was appointed to Major l'Enfant's commission to survey the new capital city of Washington, enabling the *Georgetown Weekly Ledger* to editorialize that his abilities "already prove that Mr. Jefferson's concluding that that race of men were void of mental endowment was without foundation." Ironically, Banneker owed his appointment to Thomas Jefferson, who had a lifelong interest in discovering Negroes of talent or genius whose existence might disprove his hypothesis.[30]

Between 1791 and 1796, Banneker published a series of almanacs which were sold as "an extraordinary Effort of Genius" by a Negro and as refutation of Hume's and Jefferson's theories of African racial inferiority.

On receiving a manuscript copy of the almanac, Secretary of State Jefferson wrote Banneker a generous letter in which he declared:

> No body wishes more than I do to see such proofs as you exhibit, that nature has given to our black brethren, talents equal to those of the other colors of men, and that the appearance of a want of them is owing merely to the degraded condition of their existence, both in Africa and in America.[31]

Enthusiastic about Banneker's achievement, Jefferson wrote the Marquis de Condorcet on the same day:

> I am happy to be able to inform you that we now have in the United States a negro, the son of a black man born in Africa, and of a black woman born in the United States, who is a very respectable mathematician.[32] I procured him to be employed under one of our chief directors in laying out the new federal city on

[30] *Ibid.,* p. 450.
[31] Thomas Jefferson to Benjamin Banneker, August 30, 1791.
[32] Banneker had a white grandmother.

the Potowmac, and in the intervals of his leisure, while on that work, he made an Almanac for the next year, which he sent me in his own hand writing, and which I inclose to you. I have seen very elegant solutions of Geometrical problems by him. Add to this that he is a very worthy and respectable member of society. He is a free man. I shall be delighted to see these instances of moral eminence so multiplied as to prove that the want of talents observed in them is merely the effect of their degraded condition, and not proceeding from any difference in the structure of the parts on which intellect depends.

Based on this letter and an earlier one to Chastellux on June 7, 1785, in which Jefferson merely reiterated his unwillingness to make an unqualified, dogmatic judgment of Negro mental inferiority on the basis of the evidence available to him, such writers as J. R. Wiggins, then executive editor of the *Washington Post,* have advanced the untenable view that Jefferson's views on the Negro became more mellow with age.[33]

The one instance of Banneker could not have changed Jefferson's verdict that Negroes, as a whole, were less endowed with mental ability. Moreover, further acquaintance with Banneker led to disillusionment. On October 8, 1809 Jefferson wrote to his friend Joel Barlow from Monticello: "We know he had spherical trigonometry enough to make almanacs, but not without the suspicion of aid from Ellicot, who was his neighbor and friend, and never missed an opportunity of puffing him. I have a long letter from Banneker, which shows him to have had a mind of very common stature indeed."

Eight months previously Jefferson had received a book entitled *Literature of Negroes* from the Abbé Henri Gregoire. He informed Barlow that the book was a preposterous collection of unverified, puffed-up accounts of black achievement, but wrote Gregoire diplomatically, assuring the Frenchman of his hope that the Negro would prove to be mentally "on a par with ourselves" and adding that "whatever be their degree of talent it is no measure of their rights. Because Sir Isaac Newton was superior to others in understanding, he was not therefore lord of the person or property of others."[34]

[33]J. R. Wiggins, Address at Monticello, April 13, 1959.
[34]Thomas Jefferson to Henri Gregoire, February 25, 1809.

The Evils of Slavery

The fact that Jefferson held a low opinion of Negro ability did not reconcile him in any way to the moral evil of chattel slavery. As a young lawyer he had vainly defended Samuel Howell, an octoroon, who was bound to involuntary servitude until the age of thirty-one, as his grandmother and mother had been before him, under a Virginia law which punished sexual intercourse between whites and Negroes by the enslavement of their progeny. After informing the court that by the law of nature "we are all born free," Jefferson added that "it remained for some future legislature, if any should be found wicked enough, to extend it (slavery) to grandchildren and other issue more remote."[35]

In his draft instructions for the Virginia delegation to the Congress of 1774, published as *A Summary View of the Rights of British America,* Jefferson charged the British crown with having prevented the colonies from abolishing slavery in the interests of avarice and greed:

> The abolition of domestic slavery is the great object of desire in those colonies, where, it was, unhappily introduced in their infant state. But previous to the enfranchisement of the slaves we have, it is necessary to exclude all further importations from Africa. Yet our repeated efforts to effect this by prohibitions, and by imposing duties which might amount to a prohibition, have been hitherto defeated by his Majesty's negative. . .

This draft was rejected because of its strong anti-slavery stance.

He resumed this attack on King George III in his draft of the Declaration of Independence. "He has waged cruel war against human nature itself," Jefferson charged, "violating its most sacred rights of life and liberty in the persons of a distant people who never offended him, captivating and carrying them into slavery in another hemisphere, to incur miserable death in their transportation hither." This arraignment was rejected at the instigation of Georgia and South Carolina.

[35]Lipscomb and Bergh, *Writings of Jefferson,* I, 135.

In 1784, when an effort was unsuccessfully made to exclude slavery from the Northwest Territory, Thomas Jefferson and Hugh Williamson of North Carolina were the only Southern delegates to support it. In 1787, the ban was approved.

If Jefferson opposed slavery as a denial of natural rights to the slaves, he opposed it equally as a corrupting influence on their masters. Since his fundamental concern was with the achievement of a republic of white citizens, destined to serve as "the world's best hope," this perception of a tendency to corrupt the masters was crucial to his thinking.

"The whole commerce between master and slave," he wrote in the *Notes on the State of Virginia,*

> is a perpetual exercise of the most boisterous passions, the most unremitting despotism on the one part, and degrading submissions on the other. Our children see this, and learn to imitate it; for man is an imitative animal . . . The parent storms, the child looks on, catches the lineaments of wrath, puts on the same airs in the circle of smaller slaves, gives a loose to his worst of passions, and thus nursed, educated, and daily exercised in tyranny, cannot but be stamped by it with odious peculiarities. The man must be a prodigy who can retain his manners and morals undepraved by such circumstances . . . With the morals of the people, their industry also is destroyed. For in a warm climate, no man will labour for himself who can make another labour for him. This is so true, that of the proprietors of slaves a very small proportion indeed are ever seen to labour. And can the liberties of a nation be thought secure when we have removed their only firm basis, a conviction in the minds of the people that these liberties are the gift of God? That they are not to be violated but with his wrath?[36]

Jefferson and Sally Hemings

In 1802, James T. Callender attacked Jefferson in the columns of the *Richmond Recorder* for keeping a slave concubine named Sally Hemings and fathering children by her. Callender was a Scottish scribbler and character assassin whom Jefferson had subsidized to libel his political enemies. When Jefferson failed to appoint Callender postmaster at Richmond, the two had a falling-out and, in the dispute, it was the Virginia philoso-

[36]Jefferson, *Notes* (Peden, ed.), pp. 162–63.

pher and not the pen prostitute who was guilty of outright mendacity.[37]

Sally Hemings; her brothers, James and John; and her mother, Betty, came to Monticello in 1774 as part of the estate of Jefferson's father, John Wayles. Betty was the daughter of a British sea captain and a slave girl. Her children were believed to have been fathered by John Wayles and were, therefore, only one quarter Negro at most.

Sally was described as unusually pretty and "mighty near white." As a teen-ager, she was sent to France, when Jefferson was United States Minister there, ostensibly to serve as maid to his daughter, Polly. She had five children. The eldest had features which were "said to bear a striking resemblance to those of the president himself."[38] Another son, Madison Hemings, was named for Jefferson's closest colleague and "learned to be a great fiddler."[39]

The Hemings family received favored treatment at Jefferson's hands and three of them were given their freedom by his will. Most serious Jefferson scholars have rejected the charge that their subject kept a slave mistress and fathered five children by her. Dumas Malone does so primarily on moralistic grounds in the, to our mind mistaken, belief that conduct of this sort was incompatible with Jefferson's character. Thomas Fleming repeats the assertion, made by Edmund Bacon, Jefferson's overseer at the time, that the father of Sally's children was one of Jefferson's Carr nephews. "The fundamental pattern of Jefferson's whole life is the best answer," Fleming writes. "That such an idealistic man could, at the age of fifty-five, have openly maintained this illicit relationship and retained the respect and affection of his daughters and the numerous other relatives who visited Monticello is simply incredible."[40]

Fleming's somewhat fatuous comment is quoted as typical of

[37]William W. Crosskey, *Politics and the Constitution* (Chicago, 1953), pp. 780–81. For Jefferson's side of the story, see Henry Adams, *History of the United States* (New York, 1931), I, 322–27.

[38]James T. Callender in the *Richmond Recorder,* September 1, 1802. Quoted in Jordan, *Black,* p. 465.

[39]Isaac Jefferson, *Memoirs of a Monticello Slave,* (Charlottesville, 1951), p. 13.

[40]Thomas Fleming, *The Man from Monticello,* (New York, 1969), p. 282.

the school of biography which believes that great men must be paragons of middle-class morality. If the story of the liaison is true, Jefferson began it when in his early forties and fathered Sally's last child when sixty-five, by no means an advanced age for paternity. Fleming's assumption that Jefferson's daughters and friends were apprised of the relationship is gratuitous. The Bacon version of the matter could well be a cover story for public consumption. Finally, there is no obvious reason why a widower, who evidently had strong private reasons to avoid remarriage, should not have satisfied some of his sexual and emotional needs by maintaining a young and attractive mistress, one incidentally who was preponderantly white.

On March 13, 1873, the *Pike County Republican* of Pee Pee, Ohio, published the recollections of Madison Hemings, who was then in his seventies. He stated that his mother, Sally Hemings, had become Jefferson's mistress in France when she was a girl of about fifteen. She was reluctant to return to the United States with him, but consented to do so when he promised her exceptional privileges and freedom for their children when they reached the age of twenty-one. Of the four children who survived to maturity and were emancipated, two passed for white, married white men and lived in Washington. Eston married a Negro woman and moved to Wisconsin. Madison lived in Ohio as a carpenter, where he married and raised a large family. Concerning his mother, he said: "It was her duty, all her life which I can remember, up to the time of father's death, to take care of his chamber and wardrobe, look after us children and do such light work as sewing, etc."[41]

The Callender story is rendered overwhelmingly probable by a fact which has been established only by recent research. During the years in question, Thomas Jefferson spent approximately only a third of his time in Monticello. Yet he was present there nine months before the birth of each of Sally's children.[42] The odds against this being due to random chance are $(\frac{1}{3})^5$ or 243 to one!

Jordan analyzes the affair with Sally in terms of an elaborate

---

[41]Merrill D. Peterson, *The Jefferson Image in the American Mind* (New York, 1960), pp. 185–86.
[42]Jordan, *Black* p. 466.

long-distance psychoanalysis of Jefferson. "Evidently women loomed as threats to masculinity, as dangerously powerful sexual aggressors," he writes.[43] The slender evidence on which he bases this charge is that Jefferson opposed punishing rape by castration on the grounds that women might be tempted to charge rape in order to punish unfaithful lovers and the further fact that he admonished his daughter: "Nothing is so disgusting to our sex as a want of cleanliness and delicacy in yours." In an age when clothing was excessive and neither detergents nor deodorants had been invented, the advice was doubtless sound. The fact that Jefferson fathered six children by his wife and probably five more by Sally and had at least one extra-marital affair constitutes some sort of *prima facie* evidence against a lifelong fear of female sexual aggression.

Jefferson's alleged relationship with Sally Hemings has seemed to some historians incompatible with his disapproval of the racial mixture of whites and Negroes. Actually, his views concerning miscegenation[44] were considerably more temperate than those of many of his contemporaries. As a young lawyer, he wrote of "that confusion of species, which the legislature *seems to have considered* as an evil."[45] Later, he persuaded the Virginia legislature to reduce the definition of mulatto from one-eighth to one-quarter Negro, a standard by which Sally Heming's children should have been adjudged white.[46]

As against this, there is his forceful statement in the *Notes on the State of Virginia* that, once emancipated, all Negro slaves must be "removed beyond the reach of mixture" to prevent them from "staining the blood" of their masters.

Jefferson opposed a blending of the two races because he believed it would produce a stock mentally inferior to the white population of the United States. He did not, however, accept the condemnatory folklore concerning mulattoes which falsely asserted that they inherited the vices, but not the virtues, of their

---

[43] *Ibid.,* p. 464.
[44] Negroes and negrophiles sometimes object to the word *miscegenation* as implying a stigma and moral judgment. It does not mean that the *breeding* is *amiss* or a *mistake,* but derives from the Latin verb, *miscere,* meaning to mix. The term is, therefore, descriptive, not invidious.
[45] Emphasis supplied.
[46] v. Jordan, *Black,* p. 468.

parents and that they were inferior to both the white and the
Negro race. In the *Notes,* in fact, he asserted the direct contrary, that interbreeding with the whites produced "the improvement of the blacks in body and mind."[47] Since the presence of the Negro population in the United States was a *fait
accompli,* Jefferson may well have considered that in siring
Sally's children he was improving the colored population. This
view would certainly have been in accord with his approval of
eugenics and a policy of supplying superior men with harems
for breeding purposes. In general, one can probably assert that
the blanket objection to miscegenation is a lower-class and
lower-middle-class attitude. The upper class in slaveholding
societies has tended to tolerate, and on occasion to approve, the
miscegenation of male masters and female slaves, provided
that the progeny of these unions are not accepted as full-
fledged members of the dominant race.

Callender's charges plagued Jefferson's later years and occasioned extravagant denunciations from white supremacy advocates and abolitionists alike. Callender and other scandalmon-
gers of the same stripe wrote of Jefferson's "African brothel"
and of the "sooty charms" of "Black Sal."

Mrs. Trollope led the forces of slander on the other side and
in her *The Domestic Manners of the Americans* (1832) said it
was common knowledge that the author of the Declaration of
Independence had fathered "unnumbered generations of
slaves." She asserted that "the hospitable orgies for which his
Montecielo (sic) was so celebrated were incomplete unless the
goblet he quaffed was tendered by the trembling hand of his
own slavish offspring." Writing six years after Jefferson's
death and having no understanding whatsoever of his character, she made the silly assertion that, when his slave children
tried to run away, Jefferson said laughingly: "Let the rogues get
off if they can; I will not hinder them."[48]

In 1838, a certain Dr. Levi Gaylord of New York claimed that
an unidentified Southern gentleman told him that he had personally seen the daughter of Thomas Jefferson sold in New
Orleans for a thousand dollars. This was accepted as sober fact

---

[47]Jefferson, *Notes* (Peden, ed.), p. 141.
[48]Quoted by J. C. Furnas, *Goodbye to Uncle Tom* (New York, 1956), p. 141.

in abolitionist circles and trumpeted across the land. William Lloyd Garrison published an anonymous poem, entitled "Jefferson's Daughter," in the *Liberator,* which ended with these lines:

> "The daughter of Jefferson sold for a slave!
> "The child of a freeman for dollars and francs!
> "The roar of applause, when your orators rave,
> "Is lost in the sound of her chain, as it clanks."[49]

William Wells Brown, the Negro writer, contributed verse in which the unfortunate woman was sold on the auction block; Frederick Douglass embroidered the story by selling a granddaughter as well; in still another version, a child of Jefferson committed suicide rather than work as a slave in a brothel.

Thus, the abolitionists sought to reduce Thomas Jefferson's life to a shabby hypocrisy and the Declaration of Independence to a conjuror's trick. Federalist opponents of Jefferson's vision caricatured his attractive and charming mistress as a misshapen savage imported from the jungle, conveniently forgetting that she was American-born and three-quarters white. A spate of British travelers to the United States during the first half of the Nineteenth Century used this alleged instance of hypocrisy and sexual depravity on the part of one of America's most revered statesmen as further proof of the coarseness and inferiority of the new republic.

Fire Bell in the Night

When in his late seventies, Jefferson saw sectional conflict over slavery seizing the stage of public affairs and threatening the existence of the Union. He saw the Missouri Compromise, which banned slavery from territories north of 36 degrees 30 minutes latitude acquired under the Louisiana Purchase, as condemning the nation to incessant and intensifying sectional strife. This, he believed, would delineate North and South as two separate and incompatible social systems, whereas a *laissez-faire* policy toward the territories would spread the slave population more evenly, mitigate the territorial concentration of blacks, and improve the condition of the bondsmen.

[49]Peterson, *Jeffersonian Image,* pp. 182–83.

He wrote in anguish and alarm to John Holmes, a Massachusetts Senator who had broken with the Federalist Party:

> I had for a long time ceased to read newspapers, or pay any attention to public affairs, confident they were in good hands, and content to be a passenger in our bark to the shore from which I am not distant. But this momentous question, like a fire bell in the night, awakened and filled me with terror. I considered it at once as the knell of the Union. It is hushed, indeed, for the moment. But this is a reprieve only, not a final sentence. A geographical line, coinciding with a marked principle, moral and political, once conceived and held up to the angry passions of men, will never be obliterated; and every new irritation will mark it deeper and deeper. I can say, with conscious truth, that there is not a man on earth who would sacrifice more than I would to relieve us from this heavy reproach, in any *practicable* way. The cession of that kind of property, for so it is misnamed, is a bagatelle which would not cost me a second thought, if, in that way, a general emancipation and *expatriation* could be effected; and gradually, and with due sacrifices, I think it might be. But as it is, we have the wolf by the ears, and we can neither hold him, nor safely let him go. Justice is in one scale, and self-preservation in the other. Of one thing I am certain, that as the passage of slaves from one State to another, would not make a slave of a single human being who would not be so without it, so their diffusion over a greater surface would make them individually happier, and proportionally facilitate the accomplishment of their emancipation by dividing the burthen on a greater number of coadjutors . . .
>
> I regret that I am now to die in the belief, that the useless sacrifice of themselves by the generation of 1776, to acquire self-government and happiness to their country, is to be thrown away by the unwise and unworthy passions of their sons, and that my only consolation is to be, that I live not to weep over it.[50]

On this note of bleak and sombre despair, Thomas Jefferson ended his long struggle to extirpate the moral evil of slavery, to remove the former slaves from the present and future territorial confines of the United States and to create on the foundation of an essentially homogeneous white population a strong, viable, free and unified republic.

[50]Thomas Jefferson to John Holmes, April 22, 1820.

CHAPTER SIX

The Jeffersonians: Madison, Monroe and John Quincy Adams

> Stratford Canning: Can you conceive any greater and more atrocious evil than this slave trade?
>
> John Quincy Adams:Yes: Admitting the right of search by foreign officers of our vessels in time of peace; for that would be making slaves of ourselves.[1]

Between 1801 and 1825, the White House was occupied by Thomas Jefferson and two of his friends, collaborators and protégés, James Madison and James Monroe. Each of these members of the Virginia dynasty served two terms. James Monroe had the good fortune to serve as President during eight years which came to be known as "the era of good feeling" because of the absence of party strife and the undisturbed pre-eminence of the Republican party, or Democratic-Republican party as it then called itself.

This period of one-party rule culminated in the presidency of John Quincy Adams, the son of Jefferson's old Federalist foe, John Adams. After the inauguration of John Quincy Adams in 1825, it became apparent that the opposing political views of such powerful personalities as Andrew Jackson, John C. Cal-

---

[1]John Quincy Adams, *Memoirs,* IV, 310. Quoted in Samuel Flagg Bemis, *John Quincy Adams and the Foundations of American Foreign Policy* (New York, 1955), p. 409. Stratford Canning was the British Minister Plenipotentiary to the United States during 1820–23 when Adams was Secretary of State under President Monroe.

houn and Henry Clay could not be reconciled within a single political party.

The election of Andrew Jackson in 1828 thus symbolized the end of an era in which Jeffersonian ideas had been dominant. It brought to power men who, in the name of the "common man," opposed that expanding role of the Federal Government in the economic and social life of the nation which had characterized some of the presidential policies of the Jeffersonians.

James Madison

Born in 1751, James Madison grew up at the family plantation of Montpelier in Virginia. As his biographer Irving Brant has noted, "The institution of slavery as he grew up with it at Montpelier combined the personal ease of the master with lifelong consideration for the servant, the two factors uniting to quiet the conscientious antagonism Madison felt to it in principle."[2]

Indian attack was a constant danger during these early years of the Virginia frontier. "The contrast in Madison's childhood between his reliance on Negroes and his dread of Indians greatly affected his attitude toward these two 'tributary races.' " Inclined by nature to sympathize with the downtrodden and ready to recognize the rights which were commonly ignored by Americans, he had seen the tomahawk and torch too vividly . . . to permit him to view the Indian as anything but a savage."[3]

Orange County, in which Madison grew up, had formerly been notorious for its harsh treatment of slaves. When a Negro slave named Eve was convicted of poisoning her master, Sheriff Thomas Chew, Madison's great-uncle had her burned at the stake. The Madison family was one of the larger slaveowners in the area and boasted possession of 118 Negroes in 1782. James Madison played with slave children as a boy; and, when the family sold slaves, it took care to avoid separating families.[4]

Madison treated his slaves "with a consideration bordering

[2]Irving Brant, *James Madison* (Indianapolis, 1946), I, 44.
[3]*Ibid.*, p. 48.
[4]*Ibid.*, pp. 49–50.

upon indulgence. He never sold any of them until two years before his death, when straightened circumstances compelled him to dispose of several, with their own consent, to certain of his kinsmen."[5]

Graduating from Princeton in 1771, Madison, like many of his contemporaries, was caught up in the American Revolution. Elected to the Continental Congress in 1779, he proposed that slaves be counted as three-fifths of free citizens in apportioning the burden of import duties.[6] This formula would later be adopted by the Federal Convention of 1787 and incorporated in the Constitution as the basis for determining State representation in the lower House. During the Revolution, Madison urged that Negro slaves be offered their freedom if they would enlist in the Continental Army and fight the British. Such a policy would be "consonant to the principles of liberty which ought never to be lost sight of in a contest for liberty."[7]

As early as 1785, he voiced his opposition to slavery in a letter to Edmond Randolph: "My wish is, if possible, to provide a decent and independent subsistence . . . Another of my wishes is to depend as little as possible upon the labor of slaves."[8] The following year, he reported to Jefferson that several petitions "in favor of a gradual abolition of slavery" had been submitted to the Virginia legislature, mainly by Methodists, and these "were not thrown under the table but were treated with all the indignity short of it." By contrast, a bill to outlaw manumission of slaves was narrowly defeated.[9]

Slavery was a major source of contention at the Constitutional Convention of 1787. To avoid dissension, delegates attempted to avoid open discussion of the issue, but without success. The "institution of slavery and its consequences," Madison wrote, "furnished the line of discrimination" that divided the delegates.[10] Great as the evil was, he considered dismemberment of the Union worse. "As to the present property in

[5]Edward McNall Burns, *James Madison, Philosopher of the Constitution* (New Brunswick, 1938), quoted in Brant, *Madison,* I, 51.
[6]Matthew T. Mellon, *Negro,* p. 125.
[7]*Letters and Other Writings of James Madison* (New York, 1884), II, 161; and Gaillard Hunt, *The Life of James Madison* (New York, 1902), pp. 70–71.
[8]*Ibid.*
[9]*Writings of Madison,* I, 217–18.
[10]Wilson, *Slave,* I, 41.

slaves," Madison observed, "the new Constitution linked taxation with representation in such a way that no tax could force
the freeing of them."[11]

The Constitution provided that Congress could pass no law to
restrict or outlaw the African slave trade until 1808. Madison
opposed the compromise. "Twenty years will produce all the
mischief that can be apprehended from the liberty to import
slaves," he predicted. "So long a term will be more dishonorable
to the National character than to say nothing about it in the
Constitution." He maintained that it was "wrong to admit in
the Constitution that there could be property in men."[12]

At one point in the debates, Madison argued that representation "in the House should be based on the whole number of free
inhabitants, and the Senate, which represented property, on
the whole number, including slaves."[13] He observed in his notes
on the Convention that a decision had been taken not to use the
word "slave" in the Constitution. Years afterward, writing to
Lafayette, Madison recollected: "I scarcely express myself too
strongly in saying that any illusion[14] in the Convention to the
subject . . . would have been a spark to a mass of gunpowder."[15]
He thought: "Where slavery exists, the republican theory
becomes still more fallacious."[16]

In his brilliant defense of the Constitution in *The Federalist
Papers,* which he co-authored with Alexander Hamilton and
John Jay, Madison deplored the fact that the right to outlaw the
slave trade had been postponed until 1808. Nevertheless, "It
ought to be considered as a great point gained in favor of
humanity, that a period of twenty years may terminate forever,
within these states, a traffic which has so long and so loudly
upbraided the barbarism of modern policy . . ."[17]

Shortly after the new Federal Government was inaugurated,
the Quakers submitted petitions to Congress demanding the
abolition of slavery. Madison wrote one of the petitioners de-

[11]Brant, *Madison,* III, 216.
[12]Charles C. Tansill (ed.), *Documents Illustrative of the Formation of the
Union of the American States* (Washington, D. C., 1927), pp. 616, 618.
[13]Wilson, *Slave,* I, 43.
[14]Allusion.
[15]*Madison,* III, 150.
[16]*Ibid.,* I, 322.
[17]No. XLII.

clining to support the request, as he would not "become a volunteer in giving a public wound" to the nascent republic. At the same time, he decried the "shamefully indecent" argument of those pro-slavery Southerners who described Negroes "as inherently inferior beings who would be harmed by freedom."[18] Madison was attracted by legalistic arguments; Jefferson delighted in broad intellectual speculation. Henry Clay thought "that Jefferson had more genius, Madison more judgment and common sense; that Jefferson was a visionary and a theorist; that Madison was cool, dispassionate, practical and safe."[19] The violently hostile reception that Congress gave these early Quaker petitions may have deterred Madison from "agitation of the subject."[20] There were few debates on slavery in the twenty years that followed. During his two terms as President, Madison mentioned the subject formally only twice. On both occasions, he expressed pleasure at the nation's progress toward eradication of the institution.

In 1802, Napoleon's forces were engaged in suppressing the Negro government of Haiti under Toussaint l'Ouverture. As Secretary of State, Madison attempted to avoid American involvement. In 1812, Pichon, the French representative, "recalled to Mr. Madison that the President (Jefferson) . . . made me hope for more in saying positively that the United States would join in starving Toussaint."[21]

At the end of his public career, after eight years as Secretary of State and an equal period in the Presidency, Madison turned his attention to the growing movement to colonize Negroes in Africa. Societies dedicated to this purpose were sprouting up in Virginia and enlisting the support of such eminent Americans as Chief Justice John Marshall, James Monroe and John Tyler. In 1819 Madison wrote Robert J. Evans, a Philadelphia aboli-

[18]Brant, *Madison*, III, pp. 308–09; *Madison*, IV, 188.
[19]Mellon, *Negro*, p. 133.
[20]Brant, *Madison*, III, 309.
[21]Quoted in *Ibid.*, IV, 74. Those writers who are in the habit of comparing American treatment of slaves unfavorably with that of the Spanish, French and Portuguese may find the orders of General Leclerc, the commander-in-chief in Haiti, sent to Napoleon on October 7, 1802, of interest: "It is necessary to destroy all Negroes in the mountains, men and women, sparing only children under twelve years, to destroy half of those in the plains and not leave in the colony a single colored man (mulatto) who has worn the epaulette." Quoted in *Ibid.*, IV, 494.

tionist, that three points were essential to the "eventual extinguishment of slavery in the United States. . . . A general emancipation of slaves ought to be 1. Gradual. 2. Equitable, and satisfactory to the individuals immediately concerned. 3. Consistent with the existing and durable prejudices of the nation."[22]

In elaborating on these principles, Madison pointed out that emancipation, "like remedies for other deep-rooted and widespread evils" must be gradual. The masters should be compensated for the loss of property "guarantied by the laws, and recognized by the Constitution." As for the slave, it was essential "that his condition in a state of freedom be preferable, in his own estimation, to his actual one in a state of bondage."

He dwelt at some length on the third point. Because of "probably unalterable prejudices in the United States," the freed Negroes "ought to be permanently removed beyond the region occupied by, or allotted to, the white population."

If the free Negroes had to remain in the United States, he suggested, their condition would be so debased that many might prefer slavery. Under "the degrading privation of equal rights, political and social, they must be always dissatisfied with their condition, as a change from one to another species of oppression; always secretly confederated against the ruling and privileged class; and always uncontrolled by some of the most cogent motives to moral and respectable conduct." He urged "the removal of the blacks" to preclude "jealousies and hostilities . . . the contempt known to be entertained for their peculiar features. . . . their vindictive recollections" and "predatory propensities."[23]

The removal and colonization of the Negroes could not, in the long run, be left to private initiative, philanthropy and patriotism. "It is the nation which is to reap the benefit. The nation,

[22]Madison to Evans, June 15, 1819, in *Madison*, III, 133–38. Adrienne Koch points out the importance of this message in *Madison's "Advice to My Country"* (Princeton, 1966), p. 187. She challenges Robert McColley's conclusion that George Wythe was the only Virginia leader who was willing "to reason from the fundamental principle of the Negro's right as a human being." See his *Slavery and Jeffersonian Virginia* (Urbana, 1964). Koch concludes a two-page analytical note with the comment: "These statements would not be worth this perfunctory analysis if it were not for the fact that they are similar to others on almost every page of a study that purports to be an 'objective' work of modern 'scholarship.' " (pp. 184–85.)

[23]*Madison*, III, 134.

therefore, ought to bear the burden." This could be done without new taxes or any increase in the public debt. He estimated that the purchase, transportation and colonization of one and one-half million Negroes at an average cost of $400 would amount to $600 million. This would require the sale of about 200 million acres of public land at $3 an acre or 300 million acres at $2 an acre. This would dispose of about one-third of the national domain but, in Madison's opinion, it was not too high a price to pay for the abolition of slavery and the elimination of the Negro from American society.[24] If necessary, Madison thought, the Constitution could be amended to authorize establishment of a Colonizing Society under the Chief Executive.[25]

As the crisis over Missouri gathered in intensity, Madison expressed "no slight anxiety" in a letter to Robert Walsh dated November 27, 1819. "Should a state of parties arise," he speculated, "founded on geographical boundaries, and other physical and permanent distinctions which happen to coincide with them, what is to control those great repulsive masses from awful shocks against each other?"[26] He wrote President Monroe that the zealots who were unwilling to compromise on the extension of slavery might have this as their secret aim. This was "an additional reason for a conciliatory" attitude.[27] When the Missouri Compromise was accepted, he welcomed it.

In 1821 he wrote Lafayette to express doubts about any settlement of the problem of Negro slavery: "No satisfactory plan has yet been devised for taking out the stain. If an asylum could be found in Africa, that would be the appropriate destination for the unhappy race among us." He was not "sanguine" that the American Colonization Society "will accomplish such a provision, but a very partial success seems the most that can be expected."[28] Regions other than Liberia should be found to which free Negroes might emigrate.

[24] *Ibid.*, p. 136.
[25] *Ibid.*, p. 138.
[26] *Ibid.*, p. 157.
[27] *Ibid.*, pp. 164–65. (February 10, 1820).
[28] *Ibid.*, pp. 239–40. This would seem to refute Binder, *Color Problem*, p. 78, who states that Madison was more optimistic about colonization than Jefferson. As a pillar of the Society, he found it necessary to express optimism to its supporters.

"Even in States, Massachusetts, for example, which displayed most sympathy with the people of colour on the Missouri question, prohibitions are taking place against their becoming residents," Madison observed. The Negroes "are every where regarded as a nuisance, and must really be such as long as they are under the degradation which public sentiment inflicts upon them." He also noted that the free Blacks were "rapidly increasing from manumissions and from offsprings," thus reducing the proportion of slaves to white people. He hoped that this tendency might prove "favorable to the cause of a universal emancipation."[29] Yet, in his answers to questions about the Negro submitted to him on March 13, 1823 by a Dr. Morse, Madison had taken the opposite view. "Is it considered that the increase in the proportion of free blacks to slaves increases or diminishes the danger of insurrection?" Morse had asked. "Rather increases" was Madison's reply.[30]

Writing to Lafayette five years later, Madison noted that "manumissions now more than keep pace with the outlets provided," that is, with opportunities for emigration. More Negroes would be freed if it were certain they would leave the country. With a grant of power to Congress, "what would be more simple, . . . than to purchase all female slaves at their birth, leaving them in the service of the holder to a reasonable age, on condition of their receiving an elementary education?"[31] Yet "no such effort would be listened to" as long as the "indelible" impression remained "that the two races cannot coexist, both being free and equal. The great *sine qua non,* therefore, is some external asylum for the coloured race."[32]

Madison had hoped that the Virginia Constitutional Convention of 1830 would deal with the question of slavery. Though it was "composed of the *elite* of the community, and exhibited great talents in the discussions," the gathering manifested "violent" opposition to anti-slavery action and a discussion of emancipation "would have been a spark to a mass of gunpowder."[33] Several years later, Madison wrote Thomas R. Dew, a

[29] *Madison,* III, 240.
[30] *Ibid.,* pp. 310–15.
[31] *Ibid.,* p. 541.
[32] *Ibid.,* p. 542.
[33] *Ibid.,* IV, 60.

Southern intellectual who was one of the first Americans to defend slavery as a positive good, to express disagreement with Dew's writings and urge "deportation with emancipation" as the only solution to the Negro problem.[34] As he approached the end of his long life, Madison accepted the Presidency of the American Colonization Society and devoted much of his time and energy to its work.

James Madison's views on the need to couple emancipation with colonization of the Negro were essentially the same as those of Thomas Jefferson and Henry Clay. He differed from them and from most of his contemporaries in his refusal to brand the Negroes as a mentally inferior race or to attribute the visibly degraded condition of the free Negroes to any other cause than the monumental prejudice and discrimination which they ubiquitously encountered.

James Monroe

Despite the fact that Monroe was President during the struggle over slavery that led to the Missouri Compromise, he was less intimately involved in the issue than his friends, Jefferson and Madison. Since he was primarily a lawyer rather than a planter, he spent much of his life after his two Presidential terms in New York, and died there in 1831. Yet some of his attitudes and responses to the slavery issue are of interest in that they reflect American opinion of his era.

When Monroe was Governor of Virginia, slaves in the Commonwealth planned an uprising and a march on Richmond. The Gabriel Conspiracy, as it was called, involved at least a thousand Negroes and was probably inspired by events in Haiti.[35] In contrast to French genocide of the Negroes and mulattoes in Haiti, Monroe believed the death penalty was too harsh a punishment and considered "banishing insurgent slaves and other criminals."[36]

The Virginia Assembly requested Governor Monroe to com-

---

[34]*Ibid.*, pp. 274–79.

[35]Kenneth M. Stampp, *The Peculiar Institution* (New York, 1956), p. 135.

[36]W. P. Cresson, *James Monroe* (Chapel Hill, 1946), pp. 174–75. Of the Gabriel conspiracy Negroes, 25 were executed after trial and 40 were pardoned. See Arthur Styron, *The Last of the Cocked Hats: James Monroe and the Virginia Dynasty* (Norman, 1945), p. 223.

municate with President Jefferson concerning the feasibility of purchasing Western land for the colonization of such Negroes. Although the two Virginians exchanged letters on the subject, nothing came of the plan, partly because Jefferson objected to having free Negroes settle in any area which was likely to become part of the United States in the future.

Like Madison, Monroe was active in the American Colonization Society for resettlement of free Negroes in Africa. He approved legislation, enacted by Congress in 1819, for the return to Africa of illegally captured Negroes and was zealous in enforcing it. Refusing to involve the Federal Government in the purchase of territory in Africa for colonization because he regarded such action as unconstitutional, Monroe nonetheless appointed two agents and sent an American ship to the land acquired by the Colonization Society in Liberia. In recognition of this support, the American Negro emigrés to that settlement named their capital Monrovia in 1824.[37]

Monroe said little about slavery or the Negro. "Like most Virginians of his class," Styron writes, "while he would have scorned any pious justification of slavery to obscure its commercial aspects, he took slavery for granted as a sort of metaphysical evil like war and the prison system."[38] When he sold his own slaves, Monroe did so "by families and to good masters, since the God who made us made the black people and they ought not to be treated with barbarity."[39]

During the crisis over the admission of Missouri, President Monroe agreed to accept any solution arrived at by Congress.[40] Later, he expressed doubts of the constitutionality of congressional exclusion of slavery from a territory, but, after discussion with his Cabinet, decided not to press the issue.[41] Unlike the pessimistic Jefferson and the doubting Madison, Monroe believed that the Compromise of 1820 had settled the issue of extension of slavery and prevented any disruption of the Union.[42]

[37]Cresson, *Monroe,* p. 340.
[38]Styron, *Cocked Hats,* p. 360.
[39]*Ibid.*
[40]Daniel C. Gilman, *James Monroe* (Boston, 1899), p. 246.
[41]Styron, *Cocked Hats,* p. 362.
[42]Binder, *Color Problem,* p. 79.

John Quincy Adams

The last of the Jeffersonian Presidents, John Quincy Adams, evinced little interest in the issue of slavery during the early phases of his career.[43] As a diplomat, he acted impartially, presenting Southern claims for indemnities for slaves seized by the British during the Revolution and attempting to extradite fugitive slaves who had escaped to Canada.[44]

He had little sympathy for the American Colonization Society. In 1819, he told President Monroe that its program "meant imperialism . . . the grafting of an overseas colonial establishment upon the Constitution of the United States." At one point, he termed the Society an "abortion," adding:

> There are men of all sorts and descriptions concerned in this Colonization Society: some exceedingly humane, weak-minded men, who have really no other than the professed objects in view, and who honestly believe them both useful and attainable; some, speculators in official profits and honors, which a colonial establishment would of course produce; some, speculators in political popularity, who think to please the abolitionists by their zeal for emancipation, and the slave-holders by the flattering hope of ridding them of the free colored people at the public expense; lastly, some cunning slave-holders, who see that the plan may be carried far enough to produce the effect of raising the market price of their slaves.[45]

Adams' views on slavery began to crystallize during the debates over the admission of Missouri. He believed that Congress had the right to regulate slavery in the territories, but not to abolish it in any state where it already existed. With the prophetic gloom that was to characterize the Adams family by the end of the century, he confided to his *Diary:* "I take it for granted that the present question is a mere preamble—a title page to a great tragic volume."[46]

Late one afternoon in February 1820, while the debate over Missouri raged in Congress, Adams had a long discussion of the

---

[43]Samuel Flagg Bemis, *Foundations*, p. 122.

[44]*Ibid.*, p. 416.

[45]*Ibid,*. Quoting Charles Francis Adams (ed.), *The Memoirs of John Quincy Adams* (Philadelphia; 1874–77), IV, 292. Also see Allan Nevins, *The Diary of John Quincy Adams* (New York, 1928), pp. 228–29.

[46]Adams, *Memoirs*, IV, 502, quoted in Bemis, *Foundations*, p. 416.

question with John C. Calhoun. "I do not think . . . [slavery] will produce a dissolution of the Union," Calhoun said, "but if it should, the South would be from necessity compelled to form an alliance, offensive and defensive, with Great Britain."

Adams replied, "That would be returning to the colonial state."

"Yes, pretty much, but it would be forced upon us," answered Calhoun.

"If by the effect of this alliance . . . the population of the North should be cut off from its natural outlet upon the ocean," questioned Adams, "do you think it would fall back upon its rocks bound hand and foot, to starve, or would it not retain its powers of locomotion to move southward by land?"

"Then," countered Calhoun, "we shall find it necessary to make our communities all military."

It was late in the evening when Calhoun finally left the State Department and afterwards Adams reflected upon what had been said: "Slavery is the great and foul stain upon the North American Union, and it is a contemplation worthy of the most exalted soul whether its total abolition is or is not practicable: . . . A dissolution, at least temporary, of the Union, as now constituted, would be certainly necessary, and the dissolution must be upon a point involving the question of slavery and no other. The Union then might be reorganized upon the fundamental principle of emancipation. This object is vast in its compass, awful in its prospects, sublime and beautiful in its issue. A life devoted to it would be nobly spent or sacrificed."[47]

Later on, walking home from a cabinet meeting, Adams and Calhoun returned to the subject. "The principles which you have avowed," Calhoun said, "are just and noble; but in the Southern country, whenever they are mentioned they are understood as applying only to white men." Adams' reaction was that slavery "taints the very sources of moral principle . . . If the Union is to be dissolved, this is precisely the question upon which it ought to break."[48]

Unlike almost all of his contemporaries, John Quincy Adams believed that the ultimate solution for the Negro would be his

[47]Adams, *Memoirs*, IV, 531, quoted in Bemis, *Foundations*, pp. 417–18.
[48]Nevins, *Diary*, pp. 231–32.

disappearance as a race through widespread miscegenation. Another agency would be race war. He seems to have regarded both with equanimity. "A more remote but perhaps not less certain consequence," he confided to his *Diary,* "would be the extirpation of the African race upon this Continent, by the gradual bleaching process of intermixture, where the white portion is already so predominant, and by the destructive progress of emancipation, which, like all great religious and political reformations, is terrible in its means, though happy and glorious in its ends."[49]

Since he was part of the Monroe Administration, Adams took no part in the debates on the Missouri issue. After retiring from the Presidency, Adams returned to Washington as a Representative from Massachusetts and remained in the House until his death in 1845. For these last fifteen years, he conducted a long fight to make the House receive the petitions of abolitionists.

Yet, he was not an abolitionist himself. He favored abolishing the slave trade, but not slavery, in the District of Columbia, arguing that the latter demand would stir up "ill blood" in the South. While he believed that emancipation would come, he considered himself bound by the Constitution. Accordingly, one State should not meddle in the affairs of another.[50]

His virtually single-handed defeat of the "gag rule" was a personal triumph which brought Adams death threats from the South. He opposed the annexation of Texas because it would enlarge slave territory. His defense of the slave mutineers of the *Amistad* and his successful fight to have them returned to Africa brought him the plaudits of his abolitionist friends.[51]

Yet, when all the rhetoric is stripped away, John Quincy Adams had very little of consequence to say about either the Negro or slavery. His acceptance of Negro-white interbreeding to transform Americans into a mulatto race did not indicate tolerance of other ethnic and national groups. He often spoke of Jews in such a way as to suggest a strong antisemitic prejudice. His *Memoirs* contains such phrases as "the alien Jew

[49]*Ibid.,* p. 228.
[50]Samuel Flagg Bemis, *John Quincy Adams and the Union* (New York, 1956), p. 331.
[51]*Ibid.*

delegate" or "the Jew delegate from Florida."[52] He believed the American Indians to be "an inferior race, declining in virility and perhaps not worth preserving."[53]

Elected to the Presidency by less than a plurality of either the popular or the electoral vote, Adams was soundly defeated for re-election by Andrew Jackson. His reputation rests less on his political power or originality of thought than on his achievements as a diplomat, his prominence in the political life of the nation for three decades, his longevity, the sheer mass of his writings, and his identification with the anti-slavery cause.

[52]George A. Lipsky, *John Quincy Adams: His Theory and Ideas* (New York, 1950), pp. 121–22. The "Jew delegate from Florida" was David Levy Yulee, who served in the House from 1841 to 1845 and in the Senate from 1845 to 1851 and from 1855 to 1861.

[53]*Ibid.*

CHAPTER SEVEN

The Jacksonians

To the Free Colored Inhabitants of Louisiana
Through a mistaken policy, my brave fellow Citizens, you
have heretofore been deprived of a participation in the Glorious struggle for national rights, in which our Country is engaged. This shall no longer exist. As sons of freedom, you are
now called upon to defend our most estimable blessings. . . .
Your intelligent minds are not to be led away by false repre-
sentations. . . . I shall not attempt it. In the sincerity of a
Soldier, and the language of truth I address you.
—Andrew Jackson, September 21, 1814.[1]

As early as Madison's first term in the Presidency, strict inter-
preters of the Jeffersonian tradition such as John Randolph of
Roanoke and John Taylor of Caroline had begun to warn
against a dangerous drift toward Federalist policies. They objected to a national bank, to the granting of monopoly charters
in other areas, to increased governmental support of internal
improvements and to other forms of governmental interven-
tion in the life of the average citizen. As agrarians, they opposed legislation along these lines because it seemed to favor
the manufacturing and commercial interests.

Jeffersonians such as William H. Crawford, an unsuccessful
Presidential candidate in 1824, called John Quincy Adams "a
Federalist in sheep's clothing."[2] In 1828, dissatisfaction with
the policies of Jefferson's successors culminated in the election
of Andrew Jackson. Chosen by the voters primarily because of

---

[1]Quoted in John Spencer Bassett (Ed.), *Correspondence of Andrew Jackson*
(Washington, D. C., 1926–1935), II, 58–59.
[2]Arthur M. Schlesinger, Jr., *The Age of Jackson* (Boston, 1945), p. 19.

his personal popularity as a military leader and because he
represented the American dream of rising from humble origins
to high office, Jackson gave no evidence during his first years
in office of having any broad program which would correct the
policies of the last two decades.

Before the end of his first term, however, Old Hickory's political program began to crystallize. Those elements who opposed
governmental involvement in economic affairs in the interests
of the favored few rallied under the banner of Jacksonian
Democracy. Firm believers in *laissez-faire,* they backed Jackson's crusade to destroy the Bank of the United States, a hated
monopoly that vividly symbolized the mercantilist policies of
Madison, Monroe and Adams.

The Democratic Party that emerged from Jackson's battle
with the "monster" bank was truly national in its appeal.
Equality of opportunity for all white men, coupled with a cur-
tailed role for government, won the support of all classes. New
York financial circles benefited from the destruction of the
Bank of the United States, supported Jackson, and soon made
Wall Street the financial capital of the nation.

A major element in the Jacksonian program was strong advocacy of westward expansion, offering cheap land to farmers
and expanded markets to industry. Most Americans found
little merit in James Madison's suggestion that the proceeds
from sale of the public lands be used to free the Negro from
slavery and colonize him outside the United States. Land hunger was general and intense. What the agrarians wanted was
free land.

The Jacksonian commitment to expansion was a two-edged
sword. As new land was added to the nation, an insistent question was raised: Would slavery be allowed in these territories,
or would they be preserved for the white man exclusively? This
issue was first debated under Monroe and resolved temporarily
by the Missouri Compromise of 1820. It continued to crop up in
the years that followed. Despite intermittent crisis and conflict
over the extension of slavery, the Democratic Party, under the
leadership of men such as Andrew Jackson, Martin Van Buren,
James K. Polk, Thomas Hart Benton, James Buchanan and Stephen A. Douglas, dominated American politics during the three
decades prior to the Civil War.

Andrew Jackson

Andrew Jackson was born on the Carolina frontier in 1767.
Orphaned at an early age, he spent his boyhood in poverty. In
his ambitious efforts to get ahead, he tried a variety of businesses, including storekeeping, land speculation, the practice
of law and trading in slaves. During most of his adult life, he
was engaged in three major careers, those of plantation owner,
soldier and politician. In each field, Jackson was in intimate
contact with the Negro and the institution of slavery.

In his young manhood, Jackson was involved, according to a
lifelong friend, "in many schemes for the accumulation of fortune, not usually resorted to by professional men."[3] In 1790 he
operated a small trading post in the Mississippi territory and
sold slaves to Abner Green, father-in-law of his friend W. H.
Sparks. An item in Jackson's papers entitled "List of Negroes
for A. Jackson" under date of November 8, 1790 indicates the
extent of his slave-trading activities. The list of purchases in-
cludes: "One Fellow Daniel, One Wench Kate" and "three
young ones." Since Jackson was not engaged in farming at the
time, it is a fair inference that he bought these slaves for re-
sale at a profit.[4]

Five years later, John Overton, a Nashville attorney who was
engaged in land speculation with Jackson, suggested that some
of their profits be used to "purchase somewhere in the lower
part of the eastern states such Negroes (as) we might want
for Joel Rice." In 1804, Jackson wrote a customer that "a fellow answering the description you wanted was bought, but I
was fearful he would not suit you as he had once left his master."[5]

Beginning in 1806, Jackson changed his role from that of
slave trader to that of master and soon acquired plantations in
Tennessee, Alabama and Mississippi. At the outbreak of the
War of 1812, he owned twenty slaves in Davidson County,
Tennessee. By 1825, he owned 83 slaves and in 1842, near the
end of his life, he reported possession of "about one hundred
and fifty negroes, old, middle aged and young."[6]

[3]W. H. Sparks, *The Memories of Fifty Years* (Philadelphia, 1870), p. 149.
Quoted in Binder, *Color*, p. 120.
[4]*Ibid.*, p. 121.
[5]Bassett, *Correspondence*, I, 8, 13.
[6]*Ibid.*, pp. 212, 272; VI, 138.

Except for the Adamses, all of the Presidents from Washington through Jackson were slave owners and believed the Negro to be inferior to the white man. Those who belonged to the Virginia dynasty also considered that slavery was a moral evil which should be done away with as soon as possible. Andrew Jackson did not share this view. As Frederick Binder observes: "Jackson does not appear to have been troubled by slavery or, for that matter, to have ever given serious consideration to the question of the morality of the institution."[7]

Jackson used similar methods in his roles as plantation owner and as soldier. He imposed discipline without cruelty or undue harshness. As a slave owner, Jackson kept a close eye on the operation of his plantations and inquired about the health of his Negroes by name.

"I am happy to hear that Adam is mending," he wrote his adopted son, Andrew, Jr., in 1833. "with regard to him and Dick Hanny, I have wrote Sarah. let the advice I have given be attended to, and both will get well. little hanah has been too long neglected, let the bandage be put on her as directed at once, get saml, and Dr. Hogg to prepare and place it, and prescribe the liniment and treatment, the leg must be bandaged so that the hip *cannot move,* and her position must be on her back—*attend* to this."[8]

In periods of prosperity, Jackson bought slaves; in times of financial difficulty, he would sell as many as fifty in one batch to pay debts.[9] Even when burdened with the duties of the Presidency, Jackson showed paternalistic concern over the death of his Negroes. "I learn old Ned and Jack are both dead," he wrote. "Jack was a fine boy, but if he was well attended, I lament not, he has gone the way of all the earth." When he learned that foul play may have been involved, Jackson blamed the "exposure and bad treatment" of an overseer who had "ruled with a rod of iron." He blamed this man, Graves W. Steele, for "the inhumanity that he has exercised toward my poor Negroes" and added that "unless he changes his conduct" he was to be dismissed. When Jackson found that one of his slaves had commit-

[7]Binder, *Color,* p. 122.
[8]Bassett, *Correspondence,* V , 228.
[9]*Ibid.,* VI, 87, 148, 244.

ted suicide, he considered the episode "a mortifying experience to me."[10]

At times, he was forced to deal with the problem of insubordination and with runaways. The former were particularly a problem for his wife when Jackson was away on military expeditions. "I hate chains," he once observed, but this did not prevent him from using them on recalcitrant Negroes or from selling others down the river. "As far as lenience can be extended to these unfortunate creatures," he explained to one of his men, "I wish you to do so; subordination must be obtained first, and then good treatment."[11]

Having no moral scruples about the institution, Jackson took no steps to free his slaves when death approached. But since his financial situation was straitened, he began to sell them off in large numbers. The most he could promise them was that they would have a better life in heaven than they had enjoyed on earth. As one of his slaves recalled his last words:

"He then turned to us all and said, 'I want you to prepare to meet me in Heaven: I have a right to the Tree of Life. My conversation is for you all. Christ has no respect to color. He dwelleth in me and I dwell in him.' "[12]

On the eve of the Battle of New Orleans in 1815, Jackson promised "every noble hearted generous brave freeman of colour volunteering to serve during the contest with Great Britain" the same salary, clothing, allotment, cash, and land bounties that were promised white soldiers. He assured them that "as a distinct, independent Battalion or Regiment, pursuing the path of glory, you will undivided receive the applause, reward, and gratitude of your countrymen."[13]

Enough free Negroes to form a battalion accepted Jackson's offer. Marquis James notes that the crowds cheered enthusiastically as the white soldiers paraded by shortly before the battle. "They cheered again, though with less abandon, for the 'Battalion of Free Men of Color,' Santo Dominican negroes under white officers. Their mobilization had been Jackson's own idea, carried out in the face of a considerable body of local

[10]*Ibid.,* IV, 42, 49.
[11]*Ibid.,* III, 158.
[12]*Ibid.,* VI, 415.
[13]*Ibid.,* II, 58–59.

opinion as to the propriety of placing arms in the hands of former slaves."[14]

Jackson's decision had been motivated less by the "sincerity of a soldier" than by considerations of security. He explained to Governor Claiborne of Louisiana that "an activating motive for the address" to the free Blacks was to get the Negroes into the army so that they "may when danger appears be moved to the rear where they will be kept from doing us injury." They might be used against the British if "their pride and merit entitle them to confidence. . . . If not they can be kept from uniting" with the enemy. After the victory at New Orleans, Jackson reported to James Monroe that there had been "great fears" that the Negroes might "unite themselves to the enemy on his approach, and become the means of stirring up insurrection among the slaves." In the General's opinion, it was simply a question of having "their part of the population in our ranks . . . or in the ranks of the enemy; and my first efforts were therefore exerted to inspire them with attachments to their feelings and prejudices."[15]

If Jackson recruited the Negroes for ulterior motives, he nevertheless treated them fairly. Although some whites protested, the Negroes were allowed to retain their arms after each battle. When a paymaster balked at the equal pay rule, Jackson ordered him to use the same scale "whether the troops are white, Black or Tea." He did not hesitate to commend those Negro soldiers who fought well and "manifested great bravery."[16]

At the time of the Missouri Compromise, Jackson complained that the "Eastern interests" were using the slavery issue to acquire "political ascendency and power." He feared this might excite the slaves "to insurrection and massacre." Yet he, too, could play politics with the slavery issue. Thus, in 1821, he wrote Calhoun and John Quincy Adams, urging a quick occupation of Florida to stop that "dreaded evil" and "barbarous

[14]Marquis James, *The Life of Andrew Jackson: The Border Captain* (Indianapolis, 1938), p. 230.

[15]Bassett, *Correspondence*, II, 88. Binder, *Color*, p. 127, notes, that while two standard histories of the American Negro refer to Jackson's appeal for colored volunteers, they omit any reference to his doubts about their loyalty. See Carter G. Woodson, *The Negro in Our History* (Washington, D. C., 1941), pp. 200–201; John Hope Franklin, *From Slavery to Freedom* (New York, 1956), p. 169.

[16]*Ibid.*, II, 165.

traffic," the slave trade. His desire for the annexation of Florida was sincere, but there is no other evidence in his writings that he opposed the slave trade or even regretted his own previous involvement in it.[17]

Andrew Jackson and almost all of his followers, from Martin Van Buren to such radical reformers as Fanny Wright and Albert Brisbane, disliked the abolitionists.[18] As a recent historian of Nineteenth-Century Liberalism put it:

> Jacksonians were generally opposed to abolitionism on the ground that it distracted attention from social issues within the Northern states. . . . As a last consideration, the whole idea of abolitionism violated *laissez faire*. . . . An activist government was exactly what Jacksonians did not want. The new puritans in politics, calling for abolitionism and temperance and blue laws, gave the impression that there were many things to be done. The voice of the people must be felt. The government must be used.[19]

Jackson also rejected the Southern tendency to raise the slavery issue for sectional purposes. He criticized Calhoun for his "weakness and folly" in thus arousing Eastern opposition to the "annexation of Texas."[20] Jackson wanted Texas acquired, not to expand slavery, but to increase the power and extent of the United States.

Thomas Hart Benton

Old Bullion Benton, as he was called, emerged as a leader of the pro-slavery forces during the debates concerning the admission of Missouri. A friend of Jackson, he had fought in the Senate for hard money and the agrarian interests. Writing under the *nom de plume* of La Salle in 1829, Benton combined all three positions in an assault on the tyranny of the Northeast against the farming interests of the South and West. He charged the Northern "federal" party with having "discouraged the settlement of the West by refusing . . . to vote for equitable prices for the public lands." The East, moreover, "in

[17]Bassett, *Correspondence,* III, 57–58.
[18]Schlesinger, *Jackson,* p. 425.
[19]Robert Kelley, *The Transatlantic Persuasion: The Liberal Democratic Mind in the Age of Gladstone* (New York, 1969), pp. 267, 269.
[20]Jackson to Francis P. Blair, May 11, 1844. Bassett, *Correspondence,* VI, 287.

every question in the South West between the white people and the negroes or Indians, regularly, officially, impertinently, and wickedly, takes part with the Indians and negroes against their white fellow citizens and fellow Christians." All Northern activity was "tending to one point, . . . *the abolition of slavery, under the clause of the Declaration of Independence, which asserts the natural equality of all men.*"[21]

Despite his dislike for the abolitionists, one that his distinguished biographer, Theodore Roosevelt, enthusiastically shared,[22] Benton was unwilling to follow Calhoun's proposal that it be made a Federal crime to distribute abolitionist literature among slaves. He regarded the proposal as an invasion of freedom which was not even justified by "suppression of so great an evil."[23] He disagreed with Clay's efforts to compromise the slavery issue in 1850, reiterating his loyalty to the Missouri Compromise. One of Benton's last political acts was to oppose the Kansas-Nebraska Bill of Stephen A. Douglas. Originally pro-slavery, Benton wanted the West to remain "free soil" for the white man. He could not accept "popular sovereignty," which took the power to legislate for the territories away from Congress and vested it in the people who lived there. Benton ended his days convinced that a bitter conflict was impending.[24]

Martin Van Buren

The heir apparent and successor to President Jackson was Martin Van Buren, a man who, like the Dutch farmers whom he represented and from whom he was descended, was "prejudiced against free Negroes."[25]

As early as 1827, Van Buren urged using "Genl Jacksons personal popularity with the portion of the old party feeling yet remaining. . . ." to bring about *"substantial reorganization* of the old Republican Party."[26] Van Buren's plan was to substitute *"party principle* for *personal preference."* Instead of a re-

[21]William Nisbet Chambers, *Old Bullion Benton, Senator from the New West* (Boston, 1956), p. 159.
[22]Theodore Roosevelt, *Thomas Hart Benton* (Boston, 1887).
[23]Chambers, *Benton,* pp. 332–334.
[24]*Ibid.,* p. 400.
[25]Kelley, *Transatlantic Persuasion,* p. 267.
[26]Robert V. Remini, *Martin Van Buren and the Making of the Democratic Party* (New York, 1959), p. 130, quoting a letter to Thomas Ritchie.

gional division, there must be a political division based on policy.

Van Buren believed that the party system was probably the only way of preventing the conflict between the free and slave states from reaching the point of explosion. If the old party feelings were suppressed, "prejudices between free and slave-holding states will inevitably take their place." Only if traditional party allegiances evaporated, could "the clamour against the Southern Influence and African Slavery" gain decisive influence in the North.[27]

"It would be a mistake," writes Robert V. Remini, "to interpret Van Buren's words as a defense of the slave system of the South." He merely understood the power of the plantation owners of the South and wished to ally it with that of Jacksonian Democracy. As for slavery, Van Buren was "neither its foe nor its friend. His papers are remarkably free of any discussion of the question, and while he had great affection for Southerners as a group, he had no strong feeling about their 'peculiar institution.' His later opposition had not developed."[28]

Basically, Van Buren shared a position not unlike that of many statesmen of the era and similar to that which Abraham Lincoln would later expound. He believed the Negro to be inferior to the white man. He liked the South and Southerners and would do nothing to interfere with slavery where it already existed. But he would not tolerate the expansion of slavery into new areas, which he wished reserved for free labor and free farmers.

Given these beliefs, Van Buren's attitude toward Texas was predictable. The issue of annexation arose when he assumed the Presidency and he postponed action on the matter. As another Jacksonian Democrat, Preston King, put it, his opposition to annexing Texas hung "upon the single point of slavery." Without that problem, "I would take Texas to night."[29]

It was probably his stand on Texas that lost Van Buren renomination for the Presidency. The prize went to James K. Polk, who had more accurately gauged the temper of the public,

---

[27]*Ibid.*, p. 132.
[28]*Ibid.*
[29]Quoted in Schlesinger, *Jackson*, p. 430.

and who swept to victory on the pledge of expansion. The resulting war with Mexico and acquisition of additional territory again raised the troubling issue of slavery.

In the spring of 1848, Van Buren crystallized his final position on slavery and expansion during his successful bid for nomination as Presidential candidate of the Free Soil Party. He viewed American history in terms of a struggle between labor and capital for their fair share of income. "Shall we," he asked, "whose government was instituted to elevate. . . . the laboring man" open our territories to slavery and thus force down wages?[30]

The problem of the relationship of slavery to democracy now faced the nation "in a practical form." Van Buren urged that "it can no longer be evaded or postponed. It is upon us. We must decide it. Shall these vast communities (acquired from Mexico) be the creations of free or slave labor?" The two systems, Van Buren argued, could not indefinitely coexist. Which people should be excluded: the planter and his slaves or the free laboring man?

"It is against the hundreds of thousands of our own descendants, who must earn their bread by the sweat of their brows, and hundreds of thousands of children of toil from other countries, who would annually seek a new home and a refuge from want and oppression in the vacant territories, that this unjust exclusion is sought to be enforced."[31] Van Buren closed by urging that it was the duty of government to protect "the laboring masses" in their rights "to political and social equality, and in the secure enjoyment of the fruits of their industry."[32]

Van Buren's defeat virtually eliminated him from the political scene. In the meantime, the Compromise of 1850 caused a tremendous realignment of political forces. Some Northern conservatives, like William H. Seward and Abraham Lincoln, began to move toward the philosophy of Thomas Jefferson, while others, such as Daniel Webster and Rufus Choate, moved toward the views of the Southern slaveowners. "Whatever

[30] *Ibid.*
[31] *Ibid.*
[32] *Ibid.*, p. 463.

remained of the Jacksonian tradition had in the main, by 1858, entered the Republican Party," Schlesinger says.[33]

Lincoln in 1859 commented on the changed positions of the parties. The party that had supposedly originated with Jefferson had ceased to mention his name, while the party that had developed from his opponents now quoted him constantly. It reminded him of two drunken men in greatcoats, brawling in the street, who, after a long and tiring scuffle, found they had somehow exchanged garments.

Toward the end of his life, in 1858, Martin Van Buren told a former associate that he still held the same views as ten years earlier. He added with great emotion: "The end of slavery will come—amid terrible convulsions, I fear, but it will come."[34]

James K. Polk

Polk assumed the Presidency in 1845 committed to a program of national expansion. At the end of the War with Mexico, the Wilmot Proviso, excluding slavery from the territories thus acquired, became a subject of acrimonious national controversy. In December 1846, Polk told David Wilmot, the author of the proviso, that he "did not desire to extend slavery" but that, in the territories acquired from Mexico "the great probability was that the question would never arise in the future organization of territorial or State Governments in these territories."[35]

Polk's position in the ensuing debate was basically that the issue was an artificial one, since the land acquired was not suitable for slave labor. Texas, which was natural slave territory, had been acquired earlier. There is no substance to the view once held that Polk's expansionism was part of a slaveholders' conspiracy. Like Jackson, he was first and foremost a nationalist.

Polk also resembled Jackson in his hatred of political opponents and in his propensity to impute to them the lowest possible motives, motives bordering on treason. Both men saw Calhoun in this light because the South Carolinian constantly

[33] *Ibid.*, pp. 471, 489.
[34] *Ibid.*, p. 487.
[35] Quoted in Charles G. Sellers, *James K. Polk; Continentalist, 1843–46* (Princeton, 1966), II, 618.

pressed for the inclusion of the slavery issue in every debate concerning the territories.[36] While Polk had supported the right of abolitionists to present petitions to the House, he was truthful when he said, "I put my face alike against Southern agitators and Northern fanatics."[37]

In a debate in the House over slavery in 1826, Polk observed that, when the United States became free, "this species of population was found amongst us. It had been entailed upon us by our ancestors, and was viewed as a common evil; . . . affecting the whole nation. Some of the States which then possessed it have since gotten rid of it: they were a species of property that differed from all other: they were rational; they were human beings."[38]

At the end of his Presidential term, Polk predicted, with a gloom equal to Van Buren's, that the quarrel over slavery "will be attended with terrible consequences to the country, and cannot fail to destroy the Democratic Party, if it does not ultimately threaten the Union itself."[39]

Stephen A. Douglas

A bitter struggle in the long crisis over slavery that would eventually split the party of Andrew Jackson began in 1854 when Stephen A. Douglas of Illinois introduced the Kansas-Nebraska Bill in the Senate. The key to an understanding of Douglas' policy is the importance he placed on expansion as a necessity for the United States.[40] "Popular sovereignty" was merely a means by which the territories could be opened to settlement and lines of communication and transportation to the Pacific completed, thus linking American farm and industrial products with the markets of Asia. Douglas hoped that his proposed solution would remove the problem of organizing the territories from the immediate jurisdiction of Congress. With the polarization of political forces, each debate over the status of the territories found diehard abolitionists arrayed against

[36]*Ibid*., p. 612.
[37]Polk, *Diary,* IV, 299; quoted in Schlesinger, *Jackson,* p. 453.
[38]Charles Allan McCoy, *Polk and the Presidency* (Austin, 1960), pp. 162–163.
[39]*Ibid*., p. 156.
[40]Harry V. Jaffa, *Crisis of the House Divided: An Interpretation of the Issues of the Lincoln-Douglas Debates* (Garden City, 1959), p. 48.

equally recalcitrant Southern champions of slavery. The clash of these bands of implacable zealots threatened, in Douglas' opinion and in that of other political analysts, to escalate into disunion and civil war.

The passage of Douglas' Kansas-Nebraska bill led to bloody struggles in which armed bands of pro-slavery and pro-freedom settlers terrorized entire regions in the hope of thus winning an electoral majority in the contests over "popular sovereignty." The events in "bloody Kansas" inaugurated a period in which violence over slavery became more endemic, culminating in John Brown's raid on Harper's Ferry in 1856.

Douglas next came to grips with the slavery issue in his famous debates with Lincoln for the Illinois Senate seat in 1858. "The civilized world," he observed, "have always held that when any race of men have shown themselves so degraded, by ignorance, superstition, cruelty, and barbarism, as to be utterly incapable of governing themselves, they must, in the nature of things, be governed by others, by such laws as are deemed applicable to their condition."[41]

At another point in the debates, Douglas stated: "Now, I do not believe that the Almighty ever intended the negro to be the equal of the white man. If he did, he has been a long time demonstrating that fact. For thousands of years the negro has been a race upon the earth, and during all that time, in all latitudes and climates, wherever he has wandered or been taken, he has been inferior to the race which he has there met. He belongs to an inferior race, and must always occupy an inferior position."[42]

He agreed that the Negroes and "all other dependent races" should have those privileges which they could safely exercise. "Humanity" and "Christianity" required that. The extent and nature of these privileges must be decided by the individual States. Illinois "tried slavery . . . for twelve years, and finding it not profitable, . . . abolished it . . ."[43]

To suggestions that he favored slavery, Douglas replied: "I am not pro slavery. I think it is a curse beyond computation to

[41] *Ibid.*, p. 32.
[42] *Ibid.*, p. 339.
[43] *Ibid.*, p. 35.

both white and black. But we exist as a nation by virtue only of the Constitution, and under that there is no way to abolish it. I believe that the only power that can destroy slavery is the sword, and if the sword is once drawn no one can see the end."[44]

Douglas won the Senate contest in 1858 over Lincoln. Two years later, the split in the Democratic Party and in the nation, foreseen by Van Buren and Polk, finally became a reality. Territorial expansion, which had been the key to Jacksonian political power, became its undoing because each acquisition of additional soil rekindled the debate over slavery in increasingly violent and irreconcilable form. When the conflict finally took its ultimate form of secession and civil war, Stephen A. Douglas unconditionally supported the Union. The Democratic Party, which he had served and helped lead, suffered an eclipse from which it would not recover for a quarter of a century. Ironically, the recrudescence of the Democratic Party in 1876 would be under the leadership of Samuel Tilden, who as a young man in the 1840's had been a dedicated follower of Martin Van Buren.

[44] *Ibid.*, p. 47.

CHAPTER EIGHT

Henry Clay, Daniel Webster and the Whig Tradition

> "In the slave States the alternative is, that white men must govern the black, or the black the white. In several of these states the number of slaves is greater than that of the white population. An immediate abolition of slavery in them, as these ultra-abolitionists propose, would be followed by a desperate struggle for immediate ascendancy of the black race over the white race, or rather it would be followed by instantaneous collisions between the two races, which would break out into a civil war that would end in the extermination or subjugation of the one race or the other."
> —Henry Clay[1]

Henry Clay, Daniel Webster and John C. Calhoun dominated the American political scene during the crucial decades before the Civil War. As leaders of the Senate during an era characterized by weak Presidents, they shaped the critical debates over slavery, secession and the nature of the American polical system. The two great compromises over slavery of 1820 and 1850 which served to stave off disunion were primarily due to the statecraft of Clay.

These three men also symbolized the rising sectionalism that was a prelude to the Civil War. In the early phases of their careers, Clay and Calhoun were nationalists and warhawks, men who welcomed the War of 1812 as an opportunity for American territorial expansion westward and into Canada.

[1]Quoted from the *African Repository* for 1839, organ of the American Colonization Society. Alice Felt Tyler, *Freedom's Ferment* (Minneapolis, 1944), p. 479.

While Daniel Webster opposed the struggle with Great Britain, as did the New England Federalist faction with which he was politically allied, he later became a powerful and eloquent spokesman for an indivisible and expanding nation.

Calhoun was the spokesman for the South, Clay for the West, and Webster for the industrial and mercantile Northeast. Each man played at times a major role in the Executive Branch. Clay was Secretary of State under John Quincy Adams; Calhoun held that office under Tyler; Daniel Webster under Fillmore. Each was an aspirant to the Presidency, and Henry Clay was defeated for that office three times, losing by only a narrow popular margin in 1844. Clay and Webster were also the most important leaders of the Whig Party, which vied with the Jacksonian Democrats for power. Significantly, it was the Whig tradition which shaped Abraham Lincoln's political career and on several occasions Lincoln acknowledged his immense intellectual debt to Henry Clay.

As a political theorist, who held that the Constitution was an indissoluble compact, Webster transcended the sectional interests which he represented. The ingenious compromises on slavery which he devised or promoted and his elaboration of the "American System" gave Clay national stature. Calhoun was the intellectual equal and perhaps superior of Daniel Webster. His contributions to the ideology of slavery are sufficiently important and original to warrant our devoting an entire chapter to him.

Henry Clay

Emphasizing the "common man" theme which dominated American politics during the Jacksonian era, Henry Clay liked to talk about his humble origins and to exaggerate his youthful poverty and vicissitudes. When Henry was four, his father died in somewhat awkward financial circumstances, but rich enough to leave two slaves to each of his three sons. Clay's mother remarried almost immediately, and found herself the mistress of an estate with eighteen slaves and 464 acres of such excellent land that it was taxed at twice the average rate for the county.[2]

[2]Clement Eaton, *Henry Clay and the Art of American Politics* (Boston, 1957), pp. 6–7.

While a student at the University of Virginia, Clay attracted the notice of Chancellor George Wythe, who made him his secretary. Wythe favored gradual emancipation of the Negro and had lived up to his convictions by freeing his own Negroes and bequeathing his property to them.[3]

In 1797, after receiving his law degree, Clay left Virginia to find his fortune in Kentucky. While slavery was less suited to Kentucky than to the Deep South, "it was becoming entrenched, aided by the constitution of 1792, which allowed individuals to free their slaves but prohibited any general emancipation law."[4]

Clay arrived in the State when a constitutional convention was about to assemble to institute basic reforms. Under the pen name *Scaevola*, he urged gradual emancipation. "Can any humane man be happy and contented," he asked, "when he sees near thirty thousand of his fellow human beings around him deprived of all the rights which make life desirable, transferred like cattle. . . . husbands separated from wives, and children from parents?" Asserting that "all America acknowledges the existence of slavery to be an evil," he urged "a safe and cautious liberation of the blacks, similar to the system adopted in Pennsylvania and other States to the North."[5]

Personal exposure to the "peculiar institution" during these early years left its mark on Clay's life. A slave who had been prized by his owner because of his intelligence seized an axe and killed the overseer who was beating him. As prosecutor, Clay argued that a free man could have pleaded self-defense, but since the defendant was a slave, the act was murder. He secured a conviction and the slave was hanged. The Negro's conduct so impressed Clay that he resigned as prosecutor and "never failed to express his sorrow at the part he had played in this case."[5]

The Kentucky Constitutional Convention of 1799 rejected plans for gradual emancipation and, in the years that followed, Henry Clay did nothing to stir up the dormant issue. As his

[3]Bernard Mayo, *Henry Clay, Spokesman of the New West* (Boston, 1937), I, 29.
[4]*Ibid.*, p. 64.
[5]Carl Schurz, *Henry Clay* (Boston, 1887), I, 23.

fortunes rose he built up his plantation, *Ashland,* to a point where he owned sixty slaves. These Negroes he treated with paternalistic kindness. The slave quarters at *Ashland* were better than the shacks in the vicinity belonging to the poorer Whites. Clay made a conscientious effort to keep the families of his slaves intact, often allowing his Negroes to visit relatives in Virginia and Maryland.

When a Quaker urged him to free his slaves, Clay pointed out that at least half a dozen were too old to earn a living; others were too young to work, and still others would not accept freedom if it were offered them. "My slaves," he replied, "are as well fed and clad, look as sleek and hearty, and are quite as civil and respectful in their demeanor, and as little disposed to wound the feelings of any one as you are."[6]

Nevertheless, some ran away. In his prime, Clay had no qualms about having these truants hunted down; in old age, he became more tolerant. When his personal servant, Levi, escaped during Clay's visit to Buffalo, his master made no attempt to recapture him since "in a reversal of our conditions, I would have done the same thing."[7]

Colonization of Free Negroes

On December 28, 1816, Clay presided over the first meeting of the American Colonization Society. During its long existence, this organization would be able to list among its officers such distinguished American statesmen as James Madison, Andrew Jackson, Daniel Webster, Stephen A. Douglas, William H. Seward, Francis Scott Key, General Winfield Scott, Matthew Carey, Edward Everett and two Chief Justices of the United States, John Marshall and Roger B. Taney. The purpose of the organization was to colonize the free Negroes of the United States in Africa or any other suitable foreign area and to get Congress to appropriate the necessary funds so this could be accomplished.

"Introduced among us by violence, notoriously ignorant, degraded and miserable, mentally diseased, broken-spirited, acted upon by no motive to honourable exertions, scarcely

[6]Eaton, *Clay,* p. 120.
[7] *Ibid.*

reached in their debasement by the heavenly light," the free Negroes "wander unsettled and unbefriended through our land, or sit indolent, abject and sorrowful, by the streams which witness their captivity."[8] The Society proclaimed that the free Negro could not possibly compete with the white man and hence would be a perpetual pariah if he remained in the United States. According to Elias B. Caldwell, secretary of the Society, the Negro should be kept "in the lowest state of degradation and ignorance," since education would merely give him ambitions which he could not possibly realize.[9]

Presiding over the initial convention of this Society, Henry Clay described its purpose as a noble one, since it proposed to "rid our country of a useless and pernicious, if not dangerous, portion of its population." Transported to Africa, the American Negroes would serve as a civilizing leaven among the natives and would contribute to "the spreading of the arts of civilized life, and the possible redemption from ignorance and barbarism of a benighted quarter of the globe."[10]

Clay pointed out that two groups opposed the objectives of the American Colonization Society. The first desired immediate emancipation of the Negro and considered the Society "a scheme of the slave-holder to perpetuate slavery." The second considered slavery "a blessing" and feared the Society was plotting "to let loose on society all the slaves of the country, ignorant, uneducated, and incapable of appreciating the value, or enjoying the privileges of freedom."[11]

The answer to the second group was that the Society was engaged in colonizing free Negroes, not slaves. "What is the true nature of the evil of the existence of a portion of the African race in our population?" Clay asked. "It is not that there are *some,* but that there are so *many. . . .* who can never amalgamate with the great body of our population." Other countries had national and racial minorities, different in appearance and in abilities, but, due to "the smallness of their number," they were "incapable of disturbing the general tran-

---

[8]Leon F. Litwack,*North of Slavery: the Negro in the Free States, 1790-1860* (Chicago, 1961), p. 21, quoting official Society documents.
[9]*Ibid.,* p. 23.
[10]Wilson, *Slave,* I, 212.
[11]*The Life and Speeches of Henry Clay* (Philadelphia, 1860), I, pp. 268-69.

quillity. Here, on the contrary, the African part of our population bears so large a proportion to the residue, of European origin, as to create the most lively apprehension. . . ."[12]

Clay believed that African colonization, coupled with continued white immigration, would reduce the quantitative importance of Negroes in the American population. Since the white reproduction rate was, Clay believed, greater than the black, he looked forward to a time when the Negroes would dwindle to only 5 percent of the American population.

His preoccupation with the dangers caused by the Negro presence made Clay oppose the extension of the Missouri Compromise line to the Pacific Ocean. "Coming from a slave State," he told the Senate in 1850, "I owe it to myself, I owe it to truth, I owe it to the subject, to say that no earthly power could induce me to vote for a specific measure for the introduction of slavery where it had not before existed, either south or north of that line. While you reproach, and justly too, our British ancestors for the introduction of this institution on the continent of America, I am, for one, unwilling that the posterity of the present inhabitants of California and New Mexico shall reproach us for doing the same thing which we reproach Great Britain for doing to us."[13]

A year earlier, he had written a letter to Richard Pendell of New Orleans which expounded his views on slavery fully and candidly. He rejected the Aristotelian argument that slavery could be justified by the natural inferiority of the slaves to their masters. If this were so, "the wisest man in the world would have a right to make slaves of all the rest of mankind." Our superiority as white men, he thought, "would require us not to subjugate or deal unjustly with our fellow-men who are less blessed than we are, but to instruct, to improve, and to enlighten them."

He proposed a specific, and he hoped a practical, plan for emancipation. All slaves born after 1855 or 1860 should be free at the age of twenty-five on condition that they be colonized in Africa. This would give the slave States a third of a century, that is, until 1880 or 1885, to adjust to the disappearance of the

[12] *Ibid.*
[13] Wilson, *Slave,* II, 235–36.

peculiar institution. The mandatory coupling of emancipation and deportation would solve the free Negro problem.[14] Consistent with this attitude was his battle for more vigorous suppression of the African slave trade. Clay was not only appalled at the inhumanity of the Atlantic Passage; he viewed the African trade, insofar as it managed to persist illegally, as nullifying the work of the American Colonization Society.

The Fugitive Slave Issue

Part of the Compromise of 1850, which delineated the terms on which the territories seized from Mexico were to be divided between slavery and freedom, was a new and more stringent Fugitive Slave Act. This provided that anyone who could establish proof of ownership before a Federal Commissioner could seize a Negro and bring him back to a slave State. The accused was not entitled to a hearing or jury trial. Federal officers were empowered to call upon all citizens to help enforce the law and those who wilfully obstructed it were subject to fines and imprisonment. The obligation to deliver fugitive slaves to their owners was not merely a matter of state laws, but was incorporated in Clause 3, Section 2 of Article IV of the Constitution, which read:

"No Person held to Service or Labour in one State, under the Laws thereof, escaping into another, shall, in Consequence of any Law or Regulation therein, be discharged from such Service or Labour, but shall be delivered up on Claim of the Party to whom such Service or Labour may be due."

Nevertheless, the Abolitionists launched a concerted drive to nullify the operation of the Fugitive Slave Act by mob violence, a campaign which centered in Boston, where they were strongest. In February 1851, a colored waiter named Shadrach was arrested on a Federal warrant and a hearing was held to determine whether he was in fact a runaway slave and the property of John de Bree, the Virginia plaintiff. While the hearing was in progress, a mob of Negroes rescued Shadrach and he was spirited off to Canada.

Henry Clay denounced this action and demanded a full investigation: "By whom was this mob impelled onward?" he asked.

[14] *Ibid.,* pp. 176–77.

"By our own race? No, sir, but by negroes; by African descendants; by people who possess no part, as I contend, in our political
system; and the question which arises is, whether we shall have
law, and whether the majesty of the Government shall be
maintained or not; whether we shall have a Government of
white men or black men in the cities of this country." He denounced "that negro mob which dared to lay their sacrilegious
hands, in the sanctuary of justice, upon the very sword of justice itself, and to wave it over its officers and ministers." There
were guilty parties in high places "who instigated, incited, and
stimulated those poor, black, deluded mortals and miserable
wretches."[15]

Clay's indignation may seem, more than a century later, disproportionate to its cause. He recognized, however, that nothing enraged the South more than the nullification of the Fugitive Slave Act by organized mob action; that nothing was pola-
rizing the country more effectively into two warring camps,
and that nothing was more likely to bring about that secession
which he feared and which he was prepared to resist with the
full authority of the Federal Government.

As he approached death, which would come to him in 1852
during his seventy-fifth year, Henry Clay saw the "firegaping
wounds" of his "endangered and bleeding country," but enjoyed
the comforting illusion that the patchwork compromise he had
engineered two years before would save the nation from fratricidal conflict.

Daniel Webster

Unlike Henry Clay, Daniel Webster was a scholar, immensely learned in constitutional law, well-read in political
economy and a student of government who followed in the
tradition of James Harrington, John Locke, Edmund Burke,
Alexander Hamilton and John Adams. Where Clay was an im-
proviser and an empiricist, Webster was a philosopher. Where
Clay was clever, Webster was profound.

He believed that Harrington in his *Oceana* was the first man
to have "illustrated and expanded the principle" that property
is "the true basis and *measure* of power." Webster believed that

[15] *Congressional Globe,* 31 Congress, 2nd session, p. 597.

this principle, which had been perceived before Harrington, by Aristotle, Francis Bacon and Walter Raleigh, was profoundly true and that "our own immortal Revolution was undertaken, not to shake or plunder property, but to protect it."[16] Until 1820, Webster was a disciple of Adam Smith, believed in *laissez-faire,* and regarded the economic doctrines of mercantilism as fallacious.[17] In his middle years, Webster shifted from advocacy of free trade to support of protective tariffs. This may have reflected a basic change in his convictions or the simple fact that Massachusetts, which he represented, was becoming more important as a center of manufacturing industry (and therefore more protectionist) than one of shipping and international trade.

A friend of Associate Justice of the Supreme Court Joseph Story, Webster evolved a powerful neo-Federalist conception of the nature of the American governmental system. The people were sovereign. They had ordained the Constitution, which was an indissoluble contract. The Constitution was the supreme law of the land and operated directly on the individual citizen with no intermediate State sovereignty intervening.

Webster had little contact with slavery and little interest in the controversy. He would have preferred to have the Government have "nothing to do with slavery as it exists in the States."[18]

In 1835, Webster joined Henry Clay in opposing a request by President Jackson that legislation be passed imposing severe penalties on the dissemination of insurrectionary propaganda in the South, which might excite the slaves and lead to a servile war. The basis for his opposition was that it violated the guaranties of free speech incorporated in the First Amendment.[20]

Six years later, the brig *Creole* sailed from Richmond to New Orleans with 135 slaves aboard. A Negro named Madison Wash-

[16]Daniel Webster, *The Writings and Speeches of Daniel Webster* (Boston, 1903), III, 14–16. The exception to the principle was the state under military rule.
[17]*Ibid.,* pp. 118–22.
[18]Quoted by Richard N. Current, *Daniel Webster and the Rise of National Conservatism* (Boston, 1955), p. 98.
[20]Wilson, *Slave,* I, 342.

ington, who had won his own freedom in Canada and had now returned to liberate his wife, organized a mutiny in which a passenger was killed and two officers and ten members of the crew were wounded. The *Creole* was then taken to Nassau by the mutineers.

Webster, who was Secretary of State, informed the British Government, which had refused to deliver the mutineers to American authorities, that the case was one "calling loudly for redress." The brig had been on a "perfectly lawful" voyage, taking the property of an American citizen from one American port to another. The "mutineers and murderers," having taken the vessel to a British port, must be delivered by the British to the appropriate U.S. authorities for trial and punishment. While Webster's note won the praise of Calhoun, the British refused to deliver the offenders.

In 1837, Webster stated his strong objections to the annexation of Texas. The pledges made to the slaveowning States in the Constitution ought to be "fulfilled in the fulness of their spirit and to the exactness of their letter," but Texas "is likely to be a slaveholding country; and I frankly avow my unwillingness to do anything that shall extend the slavery of the African race on this continent, or add another slaveholding State to the Union."

He had enough vision to recognize the moral and emotional potential of the anti-slavery cause. It "has not only attracted attention as a question of politics, but it has struck a far deeper-toned chord," he declared in Boston in 1837. "It has arrested the religious feeling of the country; it has taken strong hold on the consciences of men. He is a rash man indeed, and little conversant with human nature, and especially has he a very erroneous estimate of the character of the people of this country, who supposes that a feeling of this kind is to be trifled with or despised."[21]

In 1847 Webster supported the Wilmot Proviso, barring slavery from any territory taken from Mexico as a result of the War, but excluding Texas, which had already been annexed, from consideration. "I understand that an imperative call is made on us to act now," Webster declared, "to take security

[21]James Ford Rhodes, *History of the United States* (New York, 1910), I, 72.

now, to make it certain now that no more slave States shall be added to the Union."[22]

In 1848, Webster delivered a compelling speech defending the exclusion of slavery from the territories. He asserted that slavery was not sanctioned by natural law, and existed only by local law. "And wherever that local law does not extend, property in persons does not exist. Well, Sir, what is now the demand on the part of our Southern friends? They say, 'We will carry our local laws with us wherever we go. We insist that Congress does us injustice unless it establishes in the territory in which we wish to go our own local law.' This demand I for one resist, and shall resist."[23]

Retreat from an Anti-Slavery Stance

During the great debate on the Compromise of 1850, the galleries waited anxiously for Daniel Webster to deliver what would be, it was hoped, one of his great orations. The impact of these speeches on the minds and emotions of the men of the age can scarcely be exaggerated. "Three or four times I thought my temples would burst with the gush of blood," George Ticknor wrote of his feelings on hearing Webster deliver his Plymouth oration. When Thomas Marshall of Kentucky heard Webster reply to Hayne, he "listened to one inspired, and finally thought he could see a halo around the orator's head. . . ."[24]

This particular oration began with an historical view of slavery. After stating that men "equally sincere and virtuous" could be found "on both sides" of the question, Webster made the somewhat trite observation that, at the time of the writing of the Constitution, both North and South were inclined to believe slavery a moral and political evil.

He then moved suddenly to entirely new ground and asserted that slavery had now become "the Christian institution, no evil, no scourge, but a great social, religious, and moral blessing. . . . The age of cotton became the golden age of our Southern brethren.[25] Webster asserted that "vast, illimitable Texas" had been turned over to slavery and that the Government, in his opinion,

[22]Wilson, *Slave,* II, 23–24.
[23]Webster, *Writings,* V, 309.
[24]Rhodes, *History,* I, 138.
[25]Wilson, *Slave,* II, 243.

was bound to divide Texas into four slave States as soon as possible. This proposal would have drastically changed the political balance of power in favor of the South.

He thought there was no point in voting for the exclusion of slavery in New Mexico and California because this would be merely "a taunt to our Southern brethren." Slavery was banned from these territories "by a law even superior to that which admits and sanctions it in Texas. I mean the law of nature, of physical geography, the law of the formation of the earth." He could not envisage the irrigated strips of land in California and New Mexico being sowed to diversified crops by gangs of African slaves.

The probable reason for this drastic shift in Webster's public views was Presidential ambition. He had come to the conclusion that the North was disunited and that "the South alone was in earnest."[26] He had been shunted aside in 1848. His last chance for the Presidency was the forthcoming 1852 elections, at which time he would be seventy years of age. He may have calculated that he could win Southern support by kind words concerning slavery without alienating his Northern political base. If so, it was an old man's miscalculation.

Webster returned to Boston to attack the militant Abolitionists and their "incessant efforts made for twenty years to pervert the public judgment." He said there was "an exaggerated sense of the evils of the reclamation of slaves." This was caused by "the incessant attrition of Abolition doctrine, Abolition presses and Abolition lectures upon the common mind." Every hour and every day, there was "the din and roll and rub-a-dub of Abolition presses and Abolition lectures."[27]

As the 1852 election approached, he spoke more intemperately. He characterized Syracuse, New York, as "that laboratory of Abolitionism, libel, and treason." He ridiculed "the higher law" of Seward, observing that "no common vision can discern it; no conscience, not transcendental and ecstatic, can feel it; the hearing of common men never listens to its high behests."[28]

[26] *Ibid.*, p. 245.
[27] *Ibid.*, p. 276.
[28] *Ibid.*, p. 361.

Despite all this, General Winfield Scott won the Whig nomination for the Presidency, with Daniel Webster a poor third to Millard Fillmore. He had, however, brought down upon his head the hate and condemnation of the Abolitionists. Whittier compared him to Satan and, two and a half years after his death, the Unitarian minister Theodore Parker took to his pulpit to heap down abuse upon Webster's memory.[29] Daniel Webster did not deserve this opprobrium. He had always disliked slavery, but he had believed that no plan could be imposed upon the South. "If any gentleman from the South shall propose a scheme, to be carried on by this government upon a large scale, for the transportation of free colored people to any colony or any place in the world, I should be quite disposed to incur almost any degree of expense to accomplish that object."[30]

To the Abolitionists, Daniel Webster was a miserable opportunist and even an instrument of the Devil because he did not feel passionately about slavery. He did, however, feel passionately about the United States. His great political purpose was to preserve and, if possible, to strengthen it; to consolidate the power of the Federal Government under the Constitution, and to make secession impossible. Whether this end was to be accomplished with slavery or without it was to Webster, as it was to Henry Clay and as it would be to Abraham Lincoln, a very secondary consideration.

[29]Walker Lewis (ed.), *Speak For Yourself, Daniel* (Boston, 1969), p. 407.
[30]*The Works of Daniel Webster* (Boston, 1851), V, 364.

CHAPTER NINE

Calhoun and Athenian Democracy

> It follows, from what has been stated, that it is a great and dangerous error to suppose that all people are equally entitled to liberty. It is a reward to be earned, not a blessing to be gratuitously lavished on all alike;—a reward reserved for the intelligent, the patriotic, the virtuous and deserving;—and not a boon to be bestowed on a people too ignorant, degraded and vicious, to be capable either of appreciating or of enjoying it.
>
> —John C. Calhoun, *Works,* I, 54.[1]

The year 1825 marks a turning-point in the political and intellectual history of the South. In that year James Monroe, after having served two terms, relinquished the Presidency to John Quincy Adams, thus terminating an uninterrupted twenty-four years of government by Thomas Jefferson and his two chosen successors. In the third of a century that was to elapse before the outbreak of the Civil War, leadership of the South would pass from the Virginia dynasty to more dynamic and aggressive spokesmen from the newer and more fertile cotton lands of the Black Belt.

Of these, John C. Calhoun of South Carolina towered above the rest in genius and iron determination, in breadth of outlook, in intellectual creativity and in his ability, not merely to argue a case, but to build a novel political philosophy. The successors to Calhoun, men who adopted his ideas with scarcely any original contributions of their own, were also primarily politicians

[1]The full title is R. K. Cralle (ed.), *Works of John C. Calhoun* (New York, 1851).

of the new cotton lands. They included Alexander H. Stephens, Robert Toombs and William Lowndes Yancey of Georgia, Judah P. Benjamin of Louisiana and, of course, Jefferson Davis of Mississippi.

To suggest that Virginians contributed nothing to the emerging political philosophy, which asserted that slavery was both necessary and a positive good when two races of widely disparate abilities occupied the same territory, would be false. John Taylor of Caroline County, Virginia, initiated this revaluation of moral concepts when he suggested that Jefferson's attacks on slavery were merely a reflection of the intellectual environment of the American and French Revolutions.[2] Professor Thomas Roderick Dew of the College of William and Mary was one of the first American intellectuals to defend slavery as a desirable institution. His 1833 work *An Essay in Favor of Slavery* had an enormous impact on the Southern mind. Finally, George Fitzhugh, the Richmond lawyer and writer, went beyond Calhoun to the extremist position that slavery is a more just and desirable relationship than wage labor even among white people.

Fitzhugh asserted that "the Cavaliers, Jacobites, and Huguenots of the south of England naturally hate, contemn, and despise the Puritans who settled the north. The former are master races, the latter a slave race, the descendants of the Saxon serfs."

He compared the slave and the free laborer in these terms:

> Slavery without domestic affection would be a curse, and so would marriage and parental authority. The free laborer is excluded from its holy and charmed circle. Shelterless, naked, and hungry, he is exposed to the bleak winds, the cold rains, and hot sun of heaven, with none that love him, none that care for him. His employer hates him because he asks high wages or joins strikes; his fellow-laborer hates him because he competes with him for employment . . . As a slave, he will be beloved and protected. Whilst free, he will be hated, despised, and persecuted.[3]

[2]John Taylor, *Arator* (1803), pp. 51–52.
[3]George Fitzhugh, *Sociology for the South, or the Failure of a Free Society* (Richmond, 1854). Fitzhugh also wrote *Cannibals All, or Slaves without Masters* (Richmond, 1856).

An economic revolution caused the new Southern imperialism and the displacement of the Jeffersonian philosophy. The
development of a modern cotton spinning and weaving industry in England, coupled with the invention of the cotton gin by
Eli Whitney, laid the foundations for the transformation of the
South into a monocultural agrarian society. Machine-made cotton textiles and clothes progressively supplanted home-made
woolens throughout Europe. As cotton textiles fell in price until
they were within reach of the masses, the demand for raw
cotton rose. During the decades before the Civil War, there was
a rapid increase in the cost of slaves since, with the African slave trade outlawed, cotton cultivation was expanding
faster than the slave labor force could be bred and raised to
working ages. The price of an able-bodied male slave for field
work was $350 to $500 in 1800 and double that twenty years
later.

Cotton cultivation, like sugar cane cultivation, involved an
enormous expenditure of hard, back-breaking labor. Unlike the
diversified family farming of the North and West, cotton
agriculture consisted primarily of the repetition of simple
manual operations, requiring physical strength, the ability to
work under intense heat, and practically no exercise of intelligence or judgment. Chopping and picking were operations
which could be performed by gang labor, in which entire families participated, and in which normal daily performance per
worker could be estimated with a fair degree of accuracy. All
of these characteristics made cotton cultivation well adapted
to Negro slave labor and shunned, wherever possible, by free
white labor. Thus, as the South became transformed from the
diversified agricultural economy of Jefferson's age to the cotton
monoculture of Calhoun's, Negro slavery ceased to appear as
an obsolete and morally obnoxious institution and seemed
rather to be the cornerstone of the entire Southern economy.
This transformation of economic fundamentals made a philosophical and ethical justification of slavery urgently needed as
a prop for the morale and self-respect of the slave-owning
class.

As the 19th Century advanced, the Southern Cotton Kingdom
acquired a peculiar dynamism of its own. Under the prevailing

methods of tillage, cotton quickly exhausted soils. Loss of soil fertility spread southward from Virginia to the Carolinas and westward to the Piedmont and beyond. The South opened up new lands to cotton to meet rising European demand. Planters from the exhausted lands of Virginia and the Carolinas moved westward with their slaves in search of better soil or else stayed behind and sold off the natural increase in their Negro population. Despite all efforts to encourage Negro reproduction, the demand for slave labor increased faster than the supply. The consequent increase in the cost of slave labor was accompanied by marked and significant improvements in the working conditions, diet, housing and medical care of the latter. Since Negroes were neither cheap nor easy to replace, it was to the masters' interest to keep them at peak working efficiency as long as possible.

The Southern theory of the dynamics of slavery was predicated on continuous expansion into new lands propitious for Negro labor. This expansion was putatively necessary to counteract falling soil fertility, to meet rising world demand for cotton, and to maintain the balance of power in Congress. As each new State was admitted to the Union, two new members were added to the Senate. As existing States increased in population, the balance in the House of Representatives changed. The basis of Southern political power was threatened by the torrent of European immigration into the free States of the North and the free States and territories of the West. The Southern power position was visibly menaced in the House of Representatives as the 1840's drew toward a close. Immigration had increased from 84,000 in 1840 to 370,000 in 1850. At this rate, immigration was adding 1½ percent per annum to the United States population and virtually the entire stream was directed toward free States.

The South's last power stronghold within the Union seemed to be the Senate, where representation was not based on population. Hence, it was no accident that the most able and brilliant political leaders of the South, its professional military men excepted, served as Senators. Even here, the South found itself in an impasse after the annexation of Texas. Within the territorial limits of the United States, there were no other present or prospective candidates for statehood which seemed climatically propitious for Negro slavery or likely to request admission as slave States. In desperation, as the crisis of secession and civil strife approached, the political leaders of the South sought to expand slavery by purchase, subversion or conquest of potential slave lands in the West Indies, Mexico and Central America.

Calhoun and the Inequality of Man

That admirable commentator on American political thought, Vernon Louis Parrington, considered Calhoun "the greatest figure" in the long controversy over slavery, the intellectual superior of Henry Clay and Daniel Webster, "the one outstanding political thinker in a period singularly barren and uncreative," a man of tenacious logic and "apostolic zeal," a pervasive influence on his age, "the master political mind of the South," and its uncrowned king.[4]

After this unstinted praise, Parrington made the extraordinary comment: "Born and bred in South Carolina, he was enveloped from infancy in the mesh of southern provincialisms." Actually, Calhoun was less provincial than most of his contemporaries. He spent two years at Yale, where he graduated with distinction and was elected to Phi Beta Kappa. After studying law in Connecticut for another year and a half, Calhoun entered politics, where he served as Congressman, Senator, Secretary of War (in which post his record was outstanding), Vice President of the United States, and Secretary of State. He lived in Washington as much as in South Carolina and travelled all over the United States.

The owner of anywhere from 30 to 90 slaves, Calhoun was generally conceded to be a kind and just master. He believed that every planter should be "the parent as well as the *master* of his Slaves; that is, let the Slaves be made to do their duty as well as to eat, drink and sleep; let morality and industry be taught them, and the Planter will have reason to be satisfied; he will always obtain seven or eight per cent upon the value of his Slaves; and need never be compelled to the distressing alter-

[4]Parrington, *Main Currents,* II, 69.

native of parting with them unless he allows them by overindulgence to waste his substance."[5]

Calhoun refused to separate slave families. He once freed a Negro shoemaker who with his family went North, where, as a free Negro, he starved. Returning to the plantation, the shoemaker begged Calhoun to take him back into slavery, where his wants and those of his family would be satisfied. Calhoun obliged. The incident made a deep impression on him and fortified his conviction that the natural state of the Negro was slavery.

Thomas Clemson, Calhoun's son-in-law, decided he could make money by selling his plantation and renting out his slave labor force, then returning to his native Pennsylvania. Deeply shocked, Calhoun replied that this would mean mistreatment and abuse of the Negores. "The object of him who hires is generally to make the most he can out of them, without regard to their comfort or health, and usually to the utter neglect of the children and the sick." Rather than have Clemson rent out his Negroes in this fashion, Calhoun would buy them himself.[6]

Even when the planters were just, kindly and good managers, Calhoun recognized that they were perched on the rim of a volcano. "We are surrounded by invisible dangers, against which nothing can protect us, but our foresight and energy." The obstacle to concord was "the diversity of the races," a difficulty which "no power on earth can overcome."

Calhoun rejected Jefferson's statement in the Declaration of Independence that "all men are created equal," stating that "there is not a word of truth in it." Strictly speaking, they were not created men, but infants. Infants and children are subordinated to their parents; wives to their husbands. When they grow to manhood, their inequality persists and may even be intensified. The poor are not equal to the rich, the weak to the strong, the stupid to the intelligent, or, Calhoun added, the black to the white.

[5]Quoted in Margaret L. Coit, *John C. Calhoun, American Portrait* (Boston, 1950), p. 286.
[6]Coit, *Calhoun*, p. 298.

As he put the matter in his most important political statement, *A Disquisition on Government:*

That they are united to a certain extent,—and that equality of citizens, in the eyes of the law, is essential to liberty in a popular government is conceded. But to go further, and make equality of *condition* essential to liberty, would be to destroy both liberty and progress. The reason is, that inequality of condition, while it is a necessary consequence of liberty, is, at the same time, indispensable to progress. In order to understand why this is so, it is necessary to bear in mind, that the main spring to progress is, the desire of individuals to better their condition; and that the strongest impulse which can be given to it is, to leave individuals free to exert themselves in the manner they may deem best for that purpose, as far at least as it can be done consistently with the ends for which government is ordained,—and to secure to all the fruits of their exertions. Now, as individuals differ greatly from each other, in intelligence, sagacity, energy, perseverance, skill, habits of industry and economy, physical power, position and opportunity,—the necessary effect of leaving all free to exert themselves to better their condition, must be a corresponding inequality between those who may possess these qualities and those who may be deficient in them. The only means by which this result can be prevented are, either to impose such restrictions on the exertions of those who may possess them in a high degree, as will place them on a level with those who do not; or to deprive them of the fruits of their exertions. But to impose such restrictions on them would be destructive of liberty,—while, to deprive them of the fruits of their exertions, would be to destroy the desire of bettering their condition. It is, indeed, this inequality of condition between the front and rear ranks, in the march of progress, which gives so strong an impulse to the former to maintain their position, and to the latter to press forward into their files. This gives to progress its greatest impulse. To force the front rank back to the rear, or attempt to push forward the rear into line with the front, by the interposition of the government, would put an end to the impulse, and effectually arrest the march of progress.[7]

Thus far, Calhoun was merely stating, forcefully, logically and without any of those oratorical embellishments which his eloquent opponent, Daniel Webster affected,[8] the fundamental

[7]Calhoun, *Works,* I, 55–56.
[8]And which make Webster seldom read by modern Americans.

conservative attitude on the advantages of free competition. The paragraph just quoted could have been written by Calhoun's fellow Scot, Adam Smith. But, having said this, Calhoun immediately moved on to new ground:

> These great and dangerous errors have their origin in the prevalent opinion that all men are born free and equal;—than which nothing can be more unfounded and false. It rests upon the assumption of a fact, which is contrary to universal observation, in whatever light it may be regarded. It is, indeed, difficult to explain how an opinion so destitute of all sound reason, ever could have been so extensively entertained, unless we regard it as being confounded with another, which has some semblance of truth;—but which, when properly understood, is not less false and dangerous. I refer to the assertion, that all men are equal in the state of nature; meaning, by a state of nature, a state of individuality, supposed to have existed prior to the social and political state; and in which men lived apart and independent of each other ... But such a state is purely hypothetical. It never did, nor can exist; as it is inconsistent with the preservation and perpetuation of the race. ... Instead of being the natural state of man, it is, of all conceivable states, the most opposed to his nature—most repugnant to his feelings and most incompatible with his wants. His natural state is, the social and political—the one for which his Creator made him, and the only one in which he can preserve and protect his race.[9]

In this same brilliant essay, Calhoun discussed the relationship between liberty and security. Of the two, the latter was the more important, because security was essential to survival, liberty merely to progress. A society can survive without progress, but it cannot progress without survival. As Calhoun put it:

> Liberty, then, when forced on a people unfit for it, would, instead of a blessing, be a curse; as it would, in its reaction, lead directly to anarchy,—the greatest of all curses. No people, indeed, can long enjoy more liberty than that to which their situation and advanced intelligence and morals fairly entitle them. If more than this be allowed, they must soon fall into confusion and disorder,—to be followed, if not by anarchy and despotism, by a change to a form of government more simple and absolute; and,

[9] *Ibid.,* pp. 57–59.

therefore, better suited to their condition. And hence, although it may be true that a people may not have as much liberty as they are fairly entitled to, and are capable of enjoying,—yet the reverse is unquestionably true,—that no people can long possess more than they are fairly entitled to.

Liberty, indeed, though among the greatest blessings, is not so great as that of protection; inasmuch, as the end of the former is in the progress and improvement of the race,—while that of the latter is its preservation and perpetuation. And hence, when the two come into conflict, liberty must and ever ought, to yield to protection; as the existence of the race is of greater moment than its improvement."[10]

These general principles constitute the foundation for Calhoun's views on slavery and the Negro, but it is worth noting that they apply to much larger problems and issues.[11] The analysis of the relationship between liberty and security, together with the *a priori* argument for the primacy of the latter, sound as if they had been written for the education of those Twentieth Century liberals who believe that unlimited tolerance of subversion is compatible with national survival. Calhoun's remarks about the transition from abused liberty to anarchy or dictatorship seem equally pertinent.

Slavery as a Positive Good

Thus far, Calhoun has jettisoned the ideology of natural rights, the Jeffersonian hypothesis of man's natural equality, the fiction of the social contract, and the political philosophy deriving from man in a state of nature. Having done this, he has argued that security must always take priority over freedom, because survival is more important than progress; that only peoples with intelligence and character deserve freedom and can profit from it, and that, when it is given to the unintelligent and characterless, they are not benefited but wronged, because freedom in their hands will lead to anarchy or despotism. He has defended the position that the inequality of man is a fundamental law of nature and a precondition of progress and that

---

[10] *Ibid.,* pp. 54–55.
[11] Calhoun's constitutional doctrine of the "concurrent majority," while it may be his most original and significant intellectual contribution, is not discussed here, because we believe it more relevant to his views on nullification than to his opinions concerning slavery.

those social reformers who try to equalize man's state deprive the most capable members of society of their incentive to excel and thus condemn society to stagnation.

In these matters, Calhoun spoke as a conservative. "I aim not at change or revolution," he declared in 1848 when discussing the issue of slavery in Oregon.

> My object is to preserve. I am thoroughly conservative in my politics. I wish to maintain things as I found them established. I am satisfied with them, and am of the opinion that they cannot be changed for the better. I hold it to be difficult to get a good government, and still more difficult to preserve it, and as I believe a good government to be the greatest of earthly blessings, I would be adverse to the overthrow of ours, even if I thought it greatly inferior to what I do, in the hope of establishing a better. Thus thinking, my sincere desire is to preserve the Union.[12]

Like most Americans of the day, Calhoun believed the Negro to be mentally and morally inferior. Seizing on statistics derived from the Census of 1840, the accuracy of which was dubious, Calhoun replied to a formal British request that slavery be outlawed in Texas with the assertion that "in all instances in which the States have changed the former relation between the two races, the condition of the African, instead of being improved, has become worse. They have invariably sunk into vice and pauperism, accompanied by the bodily and mental inflictions incident thereto—deafness, blindness, insanity, and idiocy—to a degree without example." By contrast, in the slave States, the Negroes had shown improvement in "intelligence, and morals." Calhoun added that Britain's action "under the plausible name of the abolition of slavery" would either destroy the Negro race or relegate it to "vice and wretchedness."[13]

In 1842, Calhoun succeeded in excluding Negroes from the Navy except as cooks, stewards and servants and defeating a proposal that they be recruited for service in "unhealthy climates." Calhoun asserted that it was wrong "to bring those who have to sustain the honor and glory of the country down to a

[12]Quoted in Gerald M. Capers, *John C. Calhoun—Opportunist* (Gainesville, 1960), p. 242.
[13]Quoted in Litwack, *Slavery*, p. 43.

footing of the negro race—to be degraded by being mingled and mixed up with that inferior race."[14]

In a more formal and considered defense of slavery, Calhoun observed,

> In the present state of civilization, where two races of different origin, and distinguished by color, and other physical differences, as well as intellectual, are brought together, the relation now existing in the slave-holding States between the two, is, instead of an evil, a positive good. . . . There has never yet existed a wealthy and civilized society in which one portion of the community did not, in the point of fact, live on the labor of the other. . . . I fearlessly assert that the existing relation between the two races in the South, against which these blind fanatics are waging war, forms the most solid and durable foundation on which to rear free and stable political institutions.[15]

Calhoun's vision of the South was based on Athenian democracy as he understood it. At the time of Pericles, Athens had had 43,000 citizens, who alone were entitled to vote and discharge political functions, 28,500 *metics,* or resident aliens, and 115,-000 slaves. A century and a half later, Demetrius of Phalerum took a census of the city and counted only 21,000 citizens, 10,000 *metics,* and 400,000 slaves.[16] The presence of this large slave class to do menial and manual work gave the citizens leisure to cultivate their minds, defend their city and help guide its policies.

Calhoun accepted Aristotle's views concerning the distinction between natural and artificial slaves and the social necessity of keeping the former in a state of bondage. Just as Aristotle believed that servitude was beneficial to the natural slave, because the man who was merely an instrument needed a directing brain, so Calhoun deemed slavery beneficial to the Negro as a school in which he could advance from barbarism toward civilization.

In Plato's ideal society, depicted in *The Republic,* the population was distributed on the basis of ability among four great

[14] *Ibid.,* p. 33.
[15] Calhoun, *Works,* II, 631–32.
[16] A. W. Gomme, *The Population of Athens in the Fifth and Fourth Centuries B. C.* (New York, 1933), pp. 21, 26, 47; Will Durant, *The Life of Greece* (New York, 1939), pp. 91, 95, 150, 160–61, 173, 254–55, 561.

classes: the guardians, who ruled the city; the warriors, who defended it; the merchants and artisans, who provided it with goods and services; and the slaves, who did the unskilled menial work. The existence of a slave class, in Calhoun's view, gave the white population the leisure necessary for cultural and political development.

Moreover, a slave society was, not an arena of class conflict, but a community. The whites were unified by a common interest and harmony. The slaves were cared for by responsible masters, creating a reciprocal relationship of interdependence and trust, in contrast to the harsh, impersonal relationship of the capitalist labor market. Here, as elsewhere, Calhoun at times appears to be a Marxist in reverse. His strictures against the irresponsibility of employers toward their free laborers are similar to those leveled by Marxian socialists. His comments concerning the impersonality and fundamental irresponsibility of the wage contract, as it existed under mid-Nineteenth Century capitalism, are reminiscent of Marx's discussion of "commodity fetishism" in *Capital.* [17] From all this, Marx derived the solution of social revolution; Calhoun, that of slavery.

Unlike Jefferson, Calhoun believed that the ownership of slaves trained the white people of the South in self-government and the government of others. Men so educated would appreciate the blessings of liberty and be willing to sacrifice their comforts and risk their lives to defend their freedom. This appraisal of the Southern martial spirit would be vindicated in the Civil War.

In the free society of the North, there was an incessant struggle between the haves and the have-nots. Since both classes were citizens, the region was faced, not only with incessant economic class war, but with a sort of electoral politics, which was also class war under a thin disguise.

"The Southern States," Calhoun wrote, "are an aggregate, in fact, of communities, not of individuals. Every plantation is a little community, with the master at its head, who concentrates in himself the united interests of capital and labor, of which he

[17]Karl Marx, *Capital,* (Chicago, 1921), Volume I, Part I, Chapter I, Section 4: "The Fetichism of Commodities and the Secret thereof."

is the common representative. These small communities in the aggregate make the State, in all whose action, labor, and capital is equally represented and perfectly harmonized. Hence the harmony, the union, the stability of that section, which is rarely disturbed, except through the action of their Government. The blessing of this state of things extends beyond the limits of the South. It makes that section the balance of the system; the great, conservative power which prevents other portions, less fortunately constituted, from rushing into conflict."[18]

On the basis of this somewhat idealized picture of Southern harmony and Northern discord, Calhoun hinted at a grand strategy to save both the South and the Union. His concept was an alliance between the South and the propertied classes of the North, based on the guarantee of slavery below the Mason and Dixon Line and stability above it. The South was permanently secure against revolution because her black proletariat were not citizens. The North, on the contrary, would, "with the increase of its population and wealth, be subject to all the agitation and conflicts growing out of the divisions of. . . . capital and labor. . . ." Because of the "conservative nature" of slavery, its permanence in the South would prevent class war there and provide the propertied classes of the North with a stable and powerful ally.[19]

Chattel Slavery or Wage Slavery

During the four years Calhoun lived in New England as a student, he probably saw "the paupers of the Town. . . . sold at auction to those who keep them cheapest. . . ." For these paupers were "slaves as long as they lived."[20] He knew that Alexander Hamilton had championed child labor as a means of keeping minors out of mischief and that he had ordered small looms from England for the use of child workers. In the Providence area, entire families above the age of five often worked twelve to fourteen hours a day in the mills. England, according to Lord Ashley's 1842 report, worked over five thousand white women underground in her coal mines where, half-naked and in rags, they were harnessed with leather straps to the coal

[18]Calhoun, *Works*, III, 180.
[19]Capers, *Calhoun*, p. 243.
[20]Thomas L. Nichols, *Forty Years of American Life*. (London, 1864), I, 60; II, 125. Quoted in Coit, *Calhoun*, p. 40.

cars, which they dragged all day for a starvation wage, crawling on all fours.[21] After describing how these women butted the coal cars with their balding heads and how their children "harnessed like brutes. . . . tugged and strained in the bowels of the earth" for sixteen hours a day, Sarah M. Maury concluded: "The sole advantage possessed by the white Slaves of Europe. . . . is that they have permission to change each naked, hungry and intolerable bondage for a worse."[22] Thomas Carlyle put the distinction succinctly: "Free labor means work or starve. Slave labor means work or be flogged."

Having observed some of these conditions and read about others, Calhoun was perhaps understandably unimpressed by those Abolitionist orators who bled for the wrongs suffered by the enslaved Negroes in the South, but were often unconcerned about the bestial oppression of women and children of their own race nearer to home. Calhoun saw the social order as inevitably based on arrangements between an owning class and a propertyless working class, in which the former utilized a variety of coercive devices to compel the latter to labor for it. "I hold," he wrote,

that there never has yet existed a wealthy and civilized society in which one portion of the community did not, in point of fact, live on the labour of the other. The devices to accomplish this are almost innumerable, from the brute force and gross superstition of ancient times to the subtle and artful contrivances of modern times. I might well challenge a comparison between them and the more direct, simple and patriarchal mode by which the labour of the African race is, among us, employed. I may say with truth that in few countries is so much left to the share of the labourer, and so little exacted from him; or where there is more kind attention paid to him in sickness or in the infirmities of age.[23]

To what extent was Calhoun's comparison objective and factual? To what extent was it mere special pleading in favor of the peculiar institution? One uncontested fact lends force to Calhoun's assertion that the conditions of the Negro slave were

[21]Arthur Styron, *The Cast-Iron Man* (New York, 1935), p. 376.
[22]Sarah M. Maury, *The Statesmen of America* (Philadelphia, 1847), p. 365. Coit, *Calhoun*, p. 301.
[23]Styron, *Cast-Iron*, p. 375.

better than those of unskilled white labor. Throughout the
South, it was customary to employ Irish gangs in digging irriga-
tion ditches and draining swamps, work that was not only
unusually hard and dangerous, but which exposed the laborers
to malaria and a variety of gastroenteritic diseases. When
asked the reason for this preference, a planter told that eminent observer of slavery in the South, Frederick L. Olmsted:
"It's dangerous work and a negro's life is too valuable to be
risked at it. If a negro dies it is a considerable loss you know."
W. H. Russell, the London *Times* correspondent in Washington
during the Civil War, speculated about the vast number of
"poor Hibernians (who) have been consumed and buried in
these Louisianian swamps, leaving their earnings to the dram-
shop keeper and the contractor, and the results of their toil to
the planter."[24]

To attempt a comparison between the real wages and living
conditions of Negro slaves and free white labor would be statis-
tically arduous and inconclusive. The significant comparison is
between the condition of free Negroes and slaves since,
whether slave or free, the black man would generally command lower wages and worse working conditions than the
white man.

Between 1850 and 1860, according to the Census, the slave
population increased by 29 percent and the free Negro population by only 12 percent. In both cases, the preponderant part of
the increase was caused by the excess of births over deaths, the
increment through immigration[25] being nugatory.

Contemporary records in those Northern cities with good
birth and death statistics reveal a fairly uniform pattern of
high mortality among the free Negroes. In Boston, during 1855–
1859 inclusive, Negro deaths exceeded Negro births by a bit less
than two to one; in Philadelphia in 1860, free Negro deaths were
double the number of births.[26]

[24]v. Ulrich B. Phillips, *American Negro Slavery* (Baton Rouge, 1966), pp.
301–03.
[25]In the case of the slave population, immigration was caused by the illegal
African trade; in the case of the free Negroes, by manumission and escape
North. The two latter factors represented simultaneously an emigration of
slaves.
[26]*1860 Census of the United States,* pp. 7–8.

In his classic study *The Health of Slaves on Southern Plantations,* Postell reviews testimony of contemporary physicians to the effect that the Negro slave received "good care, wholesome diet, prompt medical attention, and restraint from dissipations which were injurious to his health" and was "healthier in the main than the whites." Tuberculosis, cancer, scrofula, and syphilis were described as rare among plantation slaves. Yet in the *post-bellum* period the tuberculosis rate among Negroes was twice that of whites.[27] Postell's examination of numerous plantation records convinced him that white and Negro mortality in the same areas was about equal. The slave infant mortality rate in the plantations studied averaged 153 per thousand. By comparison, *as late as 1915,* the infant mortality rate was 163 among Massachusetts Negroes, 185 among Pennsylvania Blacks and 192 for the colored people of New York State. Despite the lapse of over a half-century during which considerable advances had occurred in both medical science and public health, infant death rates among free Negroes were substantially higher than those which had prevailed under slavery. This evidence suggests that Calhoun's appraisal of the material advantages of Negro slavery over Negro freedom may have been well grounded in the evidence.

Calhoun achieved what few men have. He created a logical, comprehensive and self-contained system of political philosophy. This justified slavery for the Negro within a much broader context of history and sociology. Yet, as a political achievement, Calhoun's work was merely the harbinger of catastrophe for his beloved South. Its repudiation of the dominant doctrines of human equality and natural rights was emotionally unacceptable to the North. Once the Southern States were irrevocably committed to Calhoun's philosophy of aristocracy, of the natural inequality of men, of the inevitability of class oppression, of the institution of slavery as a positive good and of the expansion of slavery as a virtual necessity, the coming of the Civil War was made both more probable and more imminent.

[27]William Dosite Postell, *The Health of Slaves on Southern Plantations* (Baton Rouge, 1951), p. 143.

CHAPTER TEN

The Abolitionists and the Negro

> The black color of the body, the wooly hair, the thick lips, and other peculiarities of the African, forms so striking a contrast to the Caucasian race, that they may be distinguished at a glance. . . .They are branded by the hand of nature with a perpetual mark of disgrace.
>
> —William Lloyd Garrison in *The Liberator*, January 22, 1831. [1]

> I have observed that when the subject of acting out our profound principles in treating men irrespective of color is discussed heat is always produced. I anticipate that the battle is to be fought here, and if ever there is a split in our ranks it will arise from collision on this point.
>
> —Lewis Tappan, after a meeting of the Executive Committee of the American Anti-Slavery Society in April 1836 at which a member had threatened to resign if abolition meant social intercourse between Whites and Blacks. [2]

With the possible exception of Salmon P. Chase, Lincoln's Secretary of the Treasury, none of the Abolitionists had sufficient political stature to warrant considering him as a statesmen. Yet they were a major source of the agitation which led to the Civil War. In terms of sheer bulk, their writings constitute what is probably the most extensive collection of material on the American Negro during this period. The victory of the

[1] Quoted in Litwack, *Slavery*, p. 224.
[2] *Diary of Lewis Tappan*, quoted in *ibid.*, pp. 217–18.

Union cause and the abolition of slavery gave greater *ex post facto* importance to the writings of Garrison, Phillips and the others than they were believed to have at the time.

The arguments of the Abolitionists against slavery tend to be repetitious. The gap between the principles they espoused and the conduct of some of them toward the Negro, as the quotation from Tappan suggests, provide an interesting sidelight. Within this movement of revolt, there were conflicts of viewpoint, strategy, and tactics.

William Lloyd Garrison

The anti-slavery movement had roots that stretched back in time to Benjamin Franklin and to his predecessors in colonial times. In the 1830s, however, as Louis Filler has observed, "Abolition seemed to burst upon the public."[3] One of the reasons for this renewed awareness was the debates over slavery in the conventions which were assembled to rewrite the constitutions of Virginia and other States. A second factor was the Nat Turner slave insurrection in Virginia. Finally, and most important, was William Lloyd Garrison's decision to launch his paper, the *Liberator,* on January 1, 1831.

The son of an alcoholic sea captain and a mother of exceptional beauty and inflexible moral principles, Garrison had been a largely self-educated apprentice printer. The weekly which he started at the age of twenty-five would continue publication for the next thirty-five years, going out of existence only after slavery had been abolished by the Thirteenth Amendment.

Garrison moved to capitalize on existing discontent. To a friend he wrote of "perilous times" ahead. "So infuriated are the whites (against the Negroes) . . . since the Virginia and North Carolina insurrection that the most trifling causes may lead to a war of extermination."[4]

The South reacted with fury to Garrison's attacks. Attempts were made to arrest anyone caught distributing the *Liberator.*

[3]Louis Filler, *The Crusade Against Slavery 1830–1860* (New York, 1960), p. 142; and John F. Hume, *The Abolitionists, Together with Personal Memories of the Struggle for Human Rights* (New York, 1905), Chapter VII.

[4]John L. Thomas, *The Liberator: William Lloyd Garrison A Biography* (Boston, 1963), p. 138.

In an obvious suggestion that its editor be kidnaped, the Georgia Legislature offered five thousand dollars "to be paid to any person or persons, who shall arrest, bring to trial and prosecute to conviction, under the laws of this State, the editor or publisher of a certain paper called the *Liberator.*"[5] Attacked for the "severity" of his language, Garrison replied, "I shall be as harsh as truth, and as uncompromising as justice. . . . I am in earnest—I will not equivocate—I will not excuse—I will not retreat a single inch—and I will be heard."

Through Garrison's efforts, an active anti-slavery society was organized in New England. In his attacks on slavery as morally wrong, Garrison used natural rights arguments that had been advanced long before by Tom Paine and others. "The right to enjoy liberty is inalienable. To invade it is to usurp the prerogative of Jehovah. Every man has a right to his own body—to the products of his own labor—to the protection of law—and to the common advantage of society."[6]

Moving to the question of means, Garrison argued that the Abolitionists should shun the use of force and physical compulsion. "Ours shall be only as the opposition of moral purity to political corruption—the destruction of error by the potency of truth—the overthrow of prejudice by the power of love—and the abolition of slavery by the spirit of repentence."[7]

Garrison's moralistic approach and his avoidance of political action culminated in his anarchistic position, which split the anti-slavery movement. By 1844, he had reached the conclusion that the Constitution was the main support of slavery and hence "a covenant with death and an agreement with hell."[8] This belief precluded orderly participation in American party politics and in 1840 Garrison opposed formation of an anti-slavery party.

Even in the initial phases of his activity, Garrison faced difficulties. He realized that it was not enough to label the slaveowners "hard hearted incorrigible sinners." Some plan to deal

---

[5]Quoted in *Ibid.*

[6]*Selections from the Writings and Speeches of William Lloyd Garrison* (Boston, 1852), p. 68.

[7]Quoted in *Ibid.*

[8]While much of Garrison's literary reputation rests on this phrase, it was borrowed from *Isaiah.*

with the situation was needed. With no plan of his own, Garrison began a violent attack on the one alternative which had won the support of many distinguished Americans—the idea of colonization.

Garrison's most comprehensive argument against colonization was contained in a 244-page pamphlet, entitled *Thoughts on African Colonization.* While Garrison claimed it was written with "unbiassed mind," John L. Thomas noted in his sympathetic and authoritative biography: "In his resolve to ruin the Colonization Society whatever the cost, Garrison did not scruple to use dishonest methods. His promise to discuss the Society as a whole counted for nothing. Individual opinions of its members he treated as official declarations of policy; he held the society responsible for all the editorial views of the *African Repository* (the official publication of the Society.) But his most serious editorial transgression was the sin of quoting out of context."[9]

The main thrust of Garrison's polemic was against the view put forward by the Colonization Society that "Nature . . . has raised up impassable barriers between the races."[10]

> I understand by this expression," he replied, "that the blacks are of a different species from ourselves, so that all attempts to generate offspring between us and them must prove as abortive, as between a man and a beast. It is a law of Nature that the lion shall not beget the lamb, or the leopard the bear. Now the planters at the south have clearly demonstrated, that an amalgamation with their slaves is not only possible, but a matter of course, and eminently productive. It neither ends in abortion nor produces monsters. In truth, it is often so difficult in the slave States to distinguish between the fruits of this intercourse and the children of white parents, that witnesses are summoned at court to solve the problem! Talk of the barriers of Nature, when the land

[9]Thomas, *Liberator,* p. 148.
[10]William Lloyd Garrison, *Thoughts on African Colonization* (Boston, 1832), pp. 141–7, reprinted in George M. Frederickson (ed.), *William Lloyd Garrison* (Englewood Cliffs, N.J., 1968), p. 35. During his last visit to the United States Lafayette expressed great surprise at the extent of recent amalgamation of the races in the slave states. "He said that on his first visit nearly all the colored people in Virginia were black, but that now mulattoes appeared to be in the majority." Ralph Korngold, *Two Friends of Man, The Story of William Lloyd Garrison and Wendell Phillips and Their Relationship with Abraham Lincoln* (Boston, 1950), p. 68.

swarms with living refutation of the statement! Happy indeed it would be for many a female slave, if such a barrier could exist during the period of her servitude to protect her from the lust of her master![11]

Garrison's language was so inflammatory that even his fellow Abolitionists expressed concern. Samuel J. May wrote him that "You have gone too far. . . .Your language has been too severe—your censures too indiscriminate. I fear you have already injured greatly a cause for which, I doubt not, you are ready to sacrifice every thing but your hope of Heaven."[12]

Garrison pointed out that in England, France and Spain, and in many other countries, "persons of color maintain as high a rank and are treated as honorably as any other class of the inhabitants, in despite [sic] of the 'impassable barriers of Nature.' " He decried the idea which he attributed to the Colonization Society "that the American people can never be as republican in their feelings and practices as Frenchmen, Spaniards or Englishmen! Nay, that *religion* itself cannot subdue their malignant prejudices, or induce them to treat their dark skinned brethren in accordance with their professions or republicanism!"[13]

The New England Abolitionist simply could not believe that Americans were "willing thus to be held up as tyrants and hypocrites for ever," or that they would be "less magnanimous and just than the populace of Europe." The answer was not colonization, but immediate abolition.[14]

The Colonization Society, Garrison charged, "is unfriendly to the improvement of the free people of color while they remain in the United States." Thus,

The Society prevents the education of this class in the most insidious and effectual manner, by constantly asserting that they must always be a degraded people in this country, and that the cultivation of their minds will avail them nothing. Who does not readily perceive that the prevalence of this opinion must at once paralyze every effort for their improvement? For it would be a

[11]Frederickson, *Garrison,* p. 35.
[12]*Ibid.*
[13]*Ibid.*
[14]*Ibid.*

waste of time and means, and unpardonable folly, for us to attempt the accomplishment of an impossible work—of that which we know will result in disappointment. Every discriminating and candid mind must see and acknowledge, that, to perpetuate their ignorance, it is only necessary to make the belief prevalent that they 'must be for ever debased, for ever useless, for ever an inferior race,' and their thralldom is sure."[15]

In searching the pages of *The African Repository*, Garrison claimed that he could not find "any hint that the prejudice which is so prevalent against them is unmanly and sinful, or any evidence of contrition for past injustice, or any remonstrance or entreaty with a view to a change of public sentiment, or any symptoms of moral indignation at such unchristian and anti-republican treatment."[16] Instead, he found everywhere "inculcated" a "hatred and contempt" for the Negro.

The American Colonization Society was "responsible for their debasement and misery; for as it numbers among its supporters the most influential men in our country, and boasts of having the approbation of an overwhelming majority of the wise and good whose examples are laws, it is able, were it willing, to effect a radical change in public sentiment—nay, it is at the present time public sentiment itself."[17]

But, on the contrary, "though it has done much, and may do more, (all that it can it will do,) to depress, impoverish and dispirit the free people of color, and to strengthen and influence mutual antipathies, it is the purpose of God, I am fully persuaded, to humble the pride of the American people by rendering the expulsion of our colored countrymen utterly impracticable, and the necessity for their admission to equal rights imperative."[18]

Exuding confidence, Garrison believed that, "As neither mountains of prejudice, nor the massy shackles of law and of public opinion, have been able to keep them down to a level with slaves, I confidently anticipate their exaltation among ourselves. Through the vista of time,—a short distance only,—I see them here, not in Africa, not bowed to the earth, or derided

[15] *Ibid.*, p. 36.
[16] *Ibid.*, p. 37.
[17] *Ibid.*
[18] *Ibid.*

and persecuted as at present, not with a downcast air or an irresolute step, but standing erect as men destined heavenward, unembarrassed, untrammelled, with none to molest or make them afraid."[19]

As the anti-slavery movement gained momentum, rifts began to develop within it. It is doubtful that Wendell Phillips was correct when he said that Garrison "began, inspired, and largely controlled" the whole Abolitionist movement from its inception to its demise, but he certainly was its dominant figure.[20] His rigid personality made it difficult, however, for others to work closely with him for any great length of time. A second, and probably more important factor was Garrison's moralistic approach, which led him to condemn the Constitution and eschew any political solution to the problem. Thus, by the 1850s, Frederick Douglass and many of the other Abolitionist leaders had broken with Garrison because they believed that the movement must become active in the political arena if anything was ever going to be done about freeing the slaves.

Wendell Phillips

The most famous of all the Abolitionist orators was Wendell Phillips, a member of the Boston aristocracy. He was among those who broke with Garrison over political action. Phillips believed that the right to vote would be an important forward step for the Negro, while the editor of the *Liberator* felt that this was a matter of minor importance.

Phillips' arguments against slavery were essentially the same as those of Garrison. Since he placed such great emphasis on Negro suffrage, Phillips did much of his political work in the years immediately following the Civil War, at a time when many of the other Abolitionists had retired from the scene.

In 1866, Phillips was disgusted over the fact that Congress was debating Reconstruction and the civil rights of the Negro without considering legislating Negro suffrage. He wrote Thaddeus Stevens: "I see the report of the Reconstruction Committee. It is a total and fatal surrender. The South carries off

[19] *Ibid.*
[20] Russel B. Nye, *William Lloyd Garrison and the Humanitarian Reformers* (Boston, 1955), p. 204.

enough of the victory to enable her to control the nation, mold its policy and shape its legislation for a dozen years to come. Twenty years of admiring trust in your anti-slavery devotion must be my apology for urging you to protest against this suicidal step. It is not necessary. The country is ready for its duty. It needs only leaders. Do not let the Republican Party desert its post. Or, if that must be, let the statesmen, the 'practical statesmen' of the nation be true to their duty."[21]

It is difficult to find any Black Republican who wished to see the South punished any more than did Phillips. In one of his most famous phrases, he said in a speech before the American Anti-Slavery Society shortly after writing to Stevens, "The national sword must never be sheathed. South Carolina shall never be shut up like China or Japan against civilization. The doctrine of States Rights, which meant a dungeon for white men to make victims of black men in is exploded forever.—This is the new dispensation. This is the New Testament, 1860 is the blank leaf between the old and the new."[22]

For Phillips the Negro Revolution was only beginning. Thus as early as 1855 he had proclaimed: "The best thing to be learned from these struggles is, how to prepare for another." Phillips "should never think Massachusetts a State fit to live in, until he saw one man, at least, as black as the ace of spades, a graduate of Harvard College. (Cheers) . . . When they had high schools and colleges to which all classes and colors were admitted on equal terms, then he should think Massachusetts was indeed the noblest representative of the principles that planted her."[23]

In stressing his concern for the rights of the Negro he did not hesitate to criticize the views of colleagues in the anti-slavery movement. To the Negroes he expressed his disagreement, "Mr. Sumner . . . warns you colored men not 'to band together in a hostile camp, and keep alive the separation of races'! The Negro, robbed, tortured, murdered, trodden under foot, defenseless in resisting submission—who has the heart to charge him with an iota of the guilt of 'keeping alive the separation of the

---

[21]Quoted in Irving H. Bartlett, *Wendell Phillips, Brahmin Radical* (Boston, 1961), pp. 300–01.
[22]*Ibid.*
[23]Quoted in Litwack, *Slavery,* p. 149.

races'? Surely this lamb has never shown any hate, or any undue prejudice, against the wolf."[24]

Like Garrison, Phillips attacked those who wished to colonize
the Negro. "Colonize the blacks! . . . We need the blacks even
more than they need us. They know every inlet, the pathway of
every wood, the whole country is mapped at night in their instinct. And they are inevitably on our side, ready as well as
skilled to aid: the only element the South has which belongs to
the nineteenth century. Aside from justice, the Union needs the
blacks."[25]

In a footnote in *Wendell Phillips, Orator and Agitator*, published in 1909, Lorenzo Sears cites W.F. Poole, "Anti-Slavery
Opinions Before 1800," as stating "I am not aware that Wendell
Phillips or William Lloyd Garrison ever claimed that the Negro
race was equal in its capacity for improvement to the white
race." Sears himself then added, "This should be borne in mind
in view of charges often made against the two agitators as
contending for equality of the two races in all respects. Freedom and citizenship were what they demanded for the blacks
rather than social commingling."[26] In the light of what we have
quoted above from the writings of Garrison and Phillips, these
assessments are untenable.

Frederick Douglass

In many ways the most fascinating of all the Abolitionists
was a Negro; the escaped slave and acknowledged leader of the
Negroes in America, Frederick Douglass. Douglass was a man
of great courage who, while a slave, turned and thrashed a
notoriously brutal overseer. After a daring escape North, he
began his long process of self-education. Beginning first as a
speaker on slavery, the ex-slave formed a strong firm friendship with Garrison. In 1845 he published the *Narrative of the
Life of Frederick Douglass,* and several years later, upon re-

---

[24]Louis Filler (ed.), *Wendell Phillips, on Civil Rights and Freedom* (New
York, 1965), p. xxv.

[25]*Ibid.*

[26]Reprinted (New York, 1967), p. 29. A biased biography in favor of Phillips,
but which contains interesting bibliographical notes, taking to task such pro-
Southern writers as Avery Craven, is Oscar Sherwin's *Prophet of Liberty; The
Life and Times of Wendell Phillips* (New York, 1958).

turning from England, began publishing the *North Star,* which later became the official organ of the Liberty party. In the 1850s Douglass became aware of the inadequacy of the "moral-suasionist approach" of Garrison. He joined the political Abolitionists, eventually ending up in the Republican Party. Considerable emphasis has been given by historians to the pioneer role of Booker T. Washington in stressing the need for vocational training of the Negro. Yet, though he is frequently thought of as a radical, Douglass urged this course of action forty years before Washington's famous Atlanta address.

Speaking candidly to his people, Douglass noted, "Three things are notoriously true of us as a people. These are POVERTY, IGNORANCE, AND DEGRADATION. . . . These constitute the social disease of the Free Colored people in the United States.

"To deliver them from this triple malady, is to improve and elevate them, by which I mean simply to put them on an equal footing with their fellow-countrymen in the sacred right to *'Life, Liberty* and the pursuit of happiness.' "[27]

In order to achieve this, Douglass maintained, "I am for no fancied or artificial elevation, but only ask fair play." The immediate need was not

high schools and colleges. Such institutions are, in my judgment, beyond our immediate occasions, and are not adapted to our present most pressing wants. High schools and colleges are excellent institutions, and will, in due season, be greatly subservient to our progress; but they are the result, as well as they are the demand of a point of progress, which we, as a people, have not yet attained. Accustomed, as we have been, to the rougher and harder modes of living, and of gaining a livelihood, we cannot, and we ought not to hope that, in a single leap from our low condition, we can reach that of *Ministers, Lawyers, Doctors, Editors, Merchants,* etc. These will, doubtless, be attained by us; but will only be, when we have patiently and laboriously, and I may add successfully, mastered and passed through the intermediate gradation of agriculture and the mechanical arts. [28]

[27] *Proceedings of the Colored National Convention Held in Rochester, July 6th, 7th and 8th, 1853,* reprinted in Benjamin Quarles (ed.), *Frederick Douglass* (Englewood Cliffs, 1968), p. 51.
[28] *Ibid.,* pp. 51–2.

There were already more colleges open to the Negroes in the free States than they could make use of. Few could use a classical education. Some had gone into the ministry, "but you need not be told that an educated people is needed to sustain an educated ministry. There must be a certain amount of cultivation among the people to sustain such a ministry. At present, we have not that cultivation amongst us; and therefore, we value, in the preacher, strong lungs, rather than high learning." Although there were some Negro lawyers they found it difficult to get work. If they were men of real ability (and Douglass cited several cases), they simply left the country.[29]

On the whole, agriculture was not the answer, "because it is almost impossible to get colored men to go on the land." This was because of "our want of self-reliance. Slavery more than all things else, robs its victims of self-reliance. To go into the western wilderness, and there to lay the foundation of future society, requires more of that important quality than a life of slavery has left us. This may sound strange to you, coming as it does from a colored man; but I am dealing with the facts, and these never accommodate themselves to the feelings or wishes of any."[30]

As to other solutions, there was little hope that the Negro would leave the country even if it were desirable. "This black man—unlike the Indian—loves civilization. He does not make very great progress in civilization himself but he likes to be in the midst of it, and prefers to share its most galling evils, to encountering barbarism. . . . Individuals emigrate—nations never."[31]

The answer was to build an "Industrial College" in which to develop the mechanical arts. The Negro could then show the white man what he could accomplish:

The fact that we make no show of our ability is held conclusive proof of our inability to make any, hence all the indifference and contempt with which incapacity is regarded, fall upon us, and that too, when we have no means of disproving the infamous opinion of our natural inferiority. I have during the last dozen

[29] *Ibid.*, pp. 52–3.
[30] *Ibid.*, pp. 53–4.
[31] *Ibid.*, pp. 55.

years denied before the Americans that we are an inferior race; but this has been done by arguments based upon admitted principles rather than by the presentation of facts. . . . The most telling, the most killing refutation of slavery, is the presentation of an industrious, enterprising, thrifty, and intelligent black population.[32]

Nowhere was Douglass's realistic attitude toward life any more evident than in his assessment of Lincoln's views about the Negro. In an address given on the eleventh anniversary of the President's death at a memorial statue being dedicated in his honor, Douglass demonstrated a better understanding of Lincoln's outlook than have many modern historians. "Lincoln," Douglass held, "was not . . . either our man or our model. In his interests, in his associations, in his habits of thought, and in his prejudices, he was a white man."[33]

Douglass believed that Lincoln

was preeminently the white man's President, entirely devoted to the welfare of the white man. He was ready and willing at any time during the first years of his Administration to deny, postpone, and sacrifice the rights of humanity in the colored people to promote the welfare of the white people of this country. . . . He came into the Presidential chair upon one principle alone, namely, opposition to the extension of slavery. . . . He was ready to execute all the supposed guarantees of the United States Constitution in favor of the slave system anywhere inside the slave states. . . . The race to which we belong were not the special objects of his consideration.[34]

Yet Douglass was grateful for what Lincoln had done. However haltingly and unwillingly, the President had moved toward freeing the Negroes. "Viewed from the genuine abolition ground," he concluded, "Mr. Lincoln seemed tardy, cold, dull, and indifferent; but measuring him by the sentiment of his country, a sentiment he was bound as a statesman to consult, he was swift, zealous, radical, and determined."[35]

[32] *Ibid.*, pp. 55–7.
[33] *Oration Delivered on the Occasion of the Unveiling of the Freedmen's Monument in Memory of Abraham Lincoln*, In Lincoln Park, Washington, D.C., April 14, 1876, reprinted in *Ibid.*, p. 74.
[34] *Ibid.*
[35] *Ibid.*, p. 78.

Hinton R. Helper

There were several Southerners who turned from the role of slaveowner to that of Abolitionist. The most notable of these were Cassius Marcellus Clay and James Gillespie Birney, the candidate for President of the Liberty Party in 1840. While both men were active in the politics of the slave question during this period, neither contributed anything original to the debate.[36] By far the most intriguing of the Southern Abolitionists was Hinton Rowan Helper, who combined opposition to slavery with strong hostility toward the Negro.

In *The Impending Crisis of the South; How to Meet It,* Helper attacked the "oligarchy of slave holders." Though the book sold well in the North after its publication in 1857, where many came to think of Helper as a friend of the Negro, it was little read in the South, for whose masses it was intended.

Through the massive use of statistical tables, Helper sought to show that slavery had impoverished the South. Since the 1790s the South had fallen steadily behind the North.[37] Abolition of slavery was necessary because it would free the white yeomanry from their degradation by the planter oligarchy.

During the Civil War, Helper served as U.S. Consul in Buenos Aires. He returned to find that Reconstruction spelled the opposite of his hopes. Negroes were given choice government jobs and the poor whites remained where they had always been, near the bottom. Helper began writing again, turning out three books in three years, arguing against what was being done.

In *Nojoque, A Question for a Continent* (1867), he stated his belief that "No Slave nor Would-be Slave, No Negro nor Mulatto, No Chinaman nor unnative Indian, No Black nor Bi-colored Individual of whatever Name or Nationality" ought to be allowed to "find Domicile anywhere within the Boundaries of the United States."[38]

In over a hundred pages, Helper showed that throughout his-

[36] See, for example, Betty Fladeland, *James Gillespie Birney, Slaveholder to Abolitionist* (Ithaca, 1955), and David Smily, *The Lion of White Hall, The Life of Cassius Marcellus Clay* (Madison, 1962).

[37] Hinton R. Helper, *The Impending Crisis of the South; How to Meet It* (New York, 1860), pp. 28–32.

[38] Quoted in Hugh C. Bailey, *Hinton Rowan Helper, Abolitionist-Racist* (University, Alabama, 1965), p. 135.

tory black had been thought of as "A Thing of Ugliness, Disease and Death . . . a most hateable thing."[39] From his sojourn in Latin America, he drew the conclusion that the poverty of that area was due to its extensive population of "black and bi-colored negroes, Indians, and hybrids."[40] Citing Jefferson and Lincoln among others, he drew up a list of the unsightly physical characteristics which he associated with the Negro. Helper noted that Dr. David Livingstone, the well known missionary in Africa, had found no science among the Negroes. Their great concern was with the "wants of the stomach," nor was there evidence in East or West Africa of workshops or of any intellectual activity.[41]

Despite his obvious dislike of the Negro, Helper did not believe he should be mistreated. A policy of segregation, coupled with colonization, he thought, would be the most appropriate solution to the American race problem.

Religiously inspired Midwestern Abolitionists, such as Charles G. Finney, Lewis Tappan and Theodore Weld, had essentially the same beliefs concerning slavery and the Negro as Garrison and Phillips. The Abolitionists were agreed in their hatred of slavery, but not in their reasons for hatred. Some accepted the Negro as a full equal; others looked upon him as an inferior to be helped; still others felt antipathy toward him and wished him segregated or colonized outside the United States.

[39] *Ibid.*
[40] *Ibid.*, p. 137.
[41] *Ibid.*, pp. 137–42.

CHAPTER ELEVEN

Confederate Leaders on the Negro and Slavery

> My object is simply to bring to your mind the great truth—
> that without an increase of African slaves from abroad, you
> may not expect or look for many more slave States.
> —Alexander H. Stephens to the Georgia Legislature,
> July 2, 1859.

The leaders of the Confederacy lacked stature as philosophers of history or of politics. To the extent that they made intellectual contributions to the topics of slavery and the role of the Negro in American society, they did so primarily as lawyers and Constitutional historians. None had the culture of a John Adams or a Thomas Jefferson. Not one could equal John C. Calhoun in breadth of vision or intellectual power. This was not perhaps so much a failing of the Confederacy, as one of the times. With the exception of Abraham Lincoln, the spokesmen for the Union cause were also deficient in philosophical depth, originality and the capacity to see issues in a larger frame of reference than the controversies of the hour.

Of the Confederate leaders, Jefferson Davis was pre-eminent in authority. As early as the 1850s he inherited the mantle of John C. Calhoun and emerged as the major spokesman for the slave society of the South. Of Scotch-Irish, English and Welsh stock, Davis was austere, humorless, intellectually disciplined, imbued with some of the doctrinaire habits of mind character-

istic of his Southern Puritan heritage and with the virtues and
grace of the planter aristocracy to which he belonged. Inflexible, persevering and reluctant to entertain the possibility that
he might be mistaken, Davis was a man of considerable cultivation. A West Point graduate, he served with distinction and bril-
liance in the Mexican War. After four years in the United
States Senate, Davis resigned at the age of 43 and retired to his
plantation. He was cajoled into serving as Secretary of War in
the Pierce Administration, where he exercised a powerful personal influence over a weak President who admired and loved
him.[1] Despite the fact that he would have preferred command
of the Southern armed forces in the field, he was chosen unanimously as President of the Confederacy.

From the outset of his political career, Davis extolled slavery
as a positive good and as a necessary institution wherever the
White and Black races coexisted. Thus on July 12, 1848, Senator
Davis urged that the territorial government of Oregon permit
the introduction of slaves, not because the peculiar institution
might strike roots there, but as a fundamental Constitutional
right.

"Compare the slaves in the Southern States with recently
imported Africans as seen in the West Indies," Davis observed,

> and who can fail to be struck with the increased improvement of
> the race, whether physically, morally, or intellectually consid-
> ered? Compare our slaves with the free blacks of the Northern
> States, and you will find the one contented, well provided for in
> all their physical wants, and steadily improving, in their moral
> condition; the other miserable, impoverished, loathesome for the
> deformity and disease which follow after penury and vice, cover-
> ing the records of the criminal courts, and filling the penitentia-
> ries. Mark the hostility to caste, the social degradation which
> excludes the able from employment of profit and trust, and
> leaves the helpless to want and neglect. Then turn to the condi-
> tion of this race in the States of the South, and view them in the
> relation of slaves. There, no hostility exists against them—the
> master is the natural protector of his slaves, and public opinion,
> common feeling, mere interest would not allow him to neglect
> his wants.

[1]Rhodes, *History,* (New York, 1910), I, 390, 438.

Davis asked rhetorically whether "the sorrow, the suffering, the crime" so visibly prevalent among the free Negroes of the North should be attributed to the hostility of the White majority or to the unfitness of the Negroes for freedom. "Does the condition of St. Domingo, or Jamaica give higher evidence? Or, do the recent atrocities in Martinique encourage better hopes?" As for the permanence of the institution of chattel slavery, he called this a problem "which must bring its own solution. Leave natural causes to their full effect, and when the time shall arrive at which emancipation is proper, those most interested will be most anxious to effect it."[2]

If Jefferson Davis seemed to idealize the relationships prevailing between Southern masters and their slaves, the picture was not an inaccurate one as applied to his own conduct. Vernon Louis Parrington, a source generally hostile to the slavocracy, characterized Davis as "kindly and humane" and a master who "treated his dependents with singular consideration," adding: "He set up a curious little democracy amongst the slaves of his plantation, and his negroes were devoted to him with rare loyalty."[3]

As the conflict between North and South became more acute, Davis' views hardened. He referred to slavery as "established by decree of Almighty God" and declared that "through the portal of slavery alone have the descendants of the graceless son of Noah ever entered the temple of civilization."[4] The justification of chattel slavery in terms of the curse of Canaan seemed to imply that it was to be a permanent affliction.

In the 1850s, Davis was vigilant and energetic in seeking to expand the frontiers of slavery by means of expansion into the Caribbean and elsewhere in Latin America. In 1851, Narcisso López, a Cuban adventurer, offered him command of a military expedition to liberate Cuba from Spanish rule. Davis refused, believing that command of a filibustering expedition was incompatible with his role as United States Senator, and recommended that Robert E. Lee serve in his stead. Three years later, Jefferson Davis became "the ruling spirit"[5] in a cabal

---

[2]Hudson Stroude, *Jefferson Davis* (New York, 1955), I, 203–204.
[3]Parrington, *Main Currents*, II, 66.
[4]*Congressional Globe*, XXII, 153.
[5]Rhodes, *History*, II, 28.

to force Congress to declare war on Spain on somewhat flimsy grounds[6] so that Cuba might be annexed and carved into slave states.

In the 1850s Jefferson Davis supported the increasingly strident Southern demand to reopen the African slave trade. He believed that it was not in Mississippi's interest to have more slaves, but that this did not apply to Texas or to other territories or states which might be acquired south of the Rio Grande. He urged the acquisition of Cuba, where the slave trade was still legal, and added to the usual reasons "the importance of the island of Cuba to the Southern States if formed into a separate confederacy."[7] On another occasion, he predicted that the South would secede if Seward, Chase, Lincoln or any other "Abolitionist" were elected President. In the summer of 1859, Jefferson Davis told Southern audiences that "there is not probably an intelligent mind among our own citizens who doubts either the moral or the legal right of the institution of African slavery, as it exists in our country." He added that the Supreme Court in the Dred Scott decision "has decided the issue in our favor" and, though "fanatics rail," its judgment commands "the respect and obedience of every citizen of the United States."[8]

Once installed as President of the Confederacy, Jefferson Davis took a somewhat different tack. The African slave trade was outlawed by the Confederate Constitution, primarily as a means of getting diplomatic recognition in Europe and support in the Border States and in the North. In his history of the Confederacy, Davis calls slavery not the real issue, but a red herring. After refusing "to be drawn into any discussion of the merits or demerits of slavery as an ethical or even as a political question" since this would "divert attention from the genuine issues involved," Davis observes:

"As a mere historical fact, we have seen that African servitude among us—confessedly the mildest and most humane of

---

[6]The pretext was that the cargo of the American merchantman *Black Warrior* had been confiscated by the Havana authorities because she had no authority to carry freight into that port and had not listed it on her manifest.

[7]Jefferson Davis, speech of July 6, 1859 to the Democratic State Convention of Mississippi.

[8]*Ibid.*

all institutions to which the name 'slavery' has been applied—existed in all the original States, and that it was recognized and protected in the fourth article of the Constitution." It was abolished in the North for climatic and economic, not moral, reasons, and Northern ships continued to monopolize the African slave trade.

Men differed in their views as to the abstract question of its right or wrong, but for two generations after the Revolution, there was no geographical line of demarkation for such differences . . . Mr. Jefferson, a Southern man, the founder of the Democratic party, and the vindicator of State rights—was in theory a consistent enemy to every form of slavery. The Southern States took the lead in prohibiting the slave-trade, and, as we have seen, one of them (Georgia) was the first State to incorporate such a prohibition in her organic Constitution. Eleven years after the agitation on the Missouri question, when the subject first took a sectional shape, the abolition of slavery was proposed and earnestly debated in the Virginia Legislature, and its advocates were so near the accomplishment of their purpose, that a declaration in its favor was defeated only by a small majority, and that on the ground of expediency. At a still later period, Abolitionist lecturers and teachers were mobbed, assaulted, and threatened with tar and feathers in New York, Pennsylvania, Massachusetts, New Hampshire, Connecticut and other States. One of them (Lovejoy) was actually killed by a mob in Illinois as late as 1837.

These facts prove incontestably that the sectional hostility which exhibited itself in 1820 . . . was not the consequence of any difference on the abstract question of slavery. It was the off-spring of sectional rivalry and political ambition." It "happened, however," that the "demarkation of sectional interests coincided exactly or very nearly with that dividing the States in which Negro servitude existed from those in which it had been abolished.[9]

Jefferson Davis advocated secession on familiar Constitutional grounds. He defended slavery on the pragmatic basis that it worked, in his opinion, to the advantage of both races. He was not interested in social contract theory, nor did he follow other Confederate statesmen in reviving the Aristotelian doctrine of the natural slave.

[9]Jefferson Davis, *The Rise and Fall of the Confederate Government* (New York, 1958), I, 78–79.

Thus, "under the mild and genial climate of the Southern States and the increasing care and attention for the well-being and comfort of the laboring class, dictated alike by interest and humanity,[9] the African slaves had augmented in number from about 600,000 at the date of the adoption of the constitutional compact, to upward of 4,000,000. In moral and social condition they had been elevated from brutal savages into docile, intelligent, and civilized agricultural laborers, and supplied not only with bodily comforts but with careful religious instruction." Supervised by "a superior race," their labor was directed both to improve their own status and to clear the wilderness and build a prosperous South.[10]

Like many Southern leaders, Jefferson Davis believed that racial hatred was rampant in the North and that the Northern solution of emancipation would lead to oppression and genocide on a frightful scale. He castigated Lincoln's decision to arm Negro slaves and incorporate them in the Union armies as an incitement to servile insurrection and race war. He also criticized the practice as a crime against the Negroes:

> Nor has less unrelenting warfare been waged by these pretended friends of human rights and liberties against the unfortunate Negroes. Wherever the enemy have been able to gain access they have forced into the ranks of their army every able-bodied man that they could seize, and have either left the aged, the women, and the children to perish by starvation, or have gathered them into camps where they have been wasted by a frightful mortality. Without clothing or shelter, often without food, incapable without supervision of taking the most ordinary precautions against disease, these helpless dependents, accustomed to have their wants supplied by the foresight of their masters, are being rapidly exterminated wherever brought in contact with the invaders. By the Northern man, on whose deep-rooted prejudices no kindly restraining influence is exercised,

[9]It was true that the economic conditions of Negro slaves in the South improved enormously during the last three decades of slavery. But one of the reasons for this improvement was the outlawry of the African slave trade, which had raised the price of slave labor. Had Jefferson Davis succeeded in getting the African slave trade legalized, living conditions for Negroes in the South would have fallen as their supply increased and their price fell.

[10]Allan Nevins (ed.), *The Messages and Papers of Jefferson Davis and the Confederacy Including Diplomatic Correspondence 1861–1865* (New York, 1966), I, 68.

they are treated with aversion and neglect. There is little hazard in predicting that in all localities where the enemy have gained a temporary foothold the Negroes, who under our care increased sixfold in number since their importation into the colonies by Great Britain, will have been reduced by mortality during the war to no more than one-half their previous number.[11]

This prediction turned out to be an exaggeration. The Negro population of the South, which had increased by 22 percent between 1850 and 1860, increased by 8 percent during the war decade 1860 to 1870. During the last forty years of slavery (1820–1860), the Negro population of the South increased two and a half times; during the next forty years (1860–1900), it barely failed to double.[12]

Robert E. Lee

The Commander-in-Chief of the Confederate States Army had misgivings concerning the ethics and expediency of slavery. If he led the forces of the Confederacy, it was not because of any love for the peculiar institution, but because he considered his allegiance to the Commonwealth of Virginia more compelling than his loyalty to the United States.

On December 27, 1856 Lee wrote his wife, condemning Northern Abolitionists who "must also be aware, that their object is both unlawful & entirely foreign to them & their duty; for which they are irresponsible & unaccountable; & Can only be accomplished by *them* through the agency of a Civil & Servile war." He continued:

> In this enlightened age, there are few I believe, but what will acknowledge, that slavery as an institution, is a moral & political evil in any Country. It is useless to expatiate on its disadvantages. I think it however a greater evil to the white than to the black race, & while my feelings are strongly enlisted in behalf of the latter, my sympathies are more strong for the former. The blacks are immeasurably better off here than in Africa, morally, socially & physically. The painful discipline they are undergoing, is necessary for their instruction as a race, & I hope will prepare & lead them to better things. How long their subjugation may be

[11]*Ibid.,* p. 380.
[12]U.S. Bureau of the Census, *Historical Statistics of the United States 1789–1945,* (Washington, 1949), Series B, 48–71.

necessary is known & ordered by a wise Merciful Providence. Their emancipation will sooner result from the mild & melting influence of Christianity, than the storms & Tempest of fiery Controversy.

After continuing his speculations concerning the role of Providence in eventual emancipation of the Blacks, Lee closed with a parting shot at Northern Abolitionists: "Is it not strange that the descendants of those pilgrim fathers who Crossed the Atlantic to preserve their own freedom of opinion, have always proved themselves intolerant of the Spiritual liberty of others?"[13]

On December 21, 1862, Lee again wrote his wife, instructing her to free those of his slaves who desired their freedom. Eight days later he executed a deed manumitting those Custis slaves whose names he could recall. A considerate and kind master, Lee never flogged any of his 63 Negroes. Since there was not enough work for them, he had some farmed out. On one of these occasions, two ran away, were recaptured and sent by Lee to the southern part of Virginia.[14]

After the War, when Lee was named President of Washington College, the New York *Independent* branded him as a man "who broke his solemn oath of allegiance to the United States, who imbrued his hands in the blood of his country's noblest men, for the purpose of perpetuating human slavery" and who was, therefore, not "fitted to be a teacher to young men." It added the gratuitous lie that "slaves found on his plantation at Arlington averred that he had treated them with atrocious cruelty."[15]

The following year, Lee discussed the lies and malicious misrepresentations of the Northern press with Dr. Leyburn. He was indignant at the charge that the South had fought to "perpetuate slavery." As Leyburn recalled it: "He said it was not true. He declared that, for himself, he had emancipated most of his slaves years before the war, and had sent to Liberia those that were willing to go; that the latter were writing back most

[13]Douglas Southall Freeman, *R. E. Lee, A Biography* (New York, 1935), I, 372–73.
[14]Freeman, *Lee,* I, 390.
[15]*Ibid.,* IV, 351.

affectionate letters to him, some of which he received through
the lines during the war. He said, also, as an evidence that the
colored people did not consider him hostile to their race, that
during this visit to Baltimore some of them who had known him
when he was stationed there had come up in the most affectionate manner and put their hands into the carriage window to
shake hands with him. They would hardly have received him
in this way, he thought, had they looked upon him as fresh from
a war intended for their oppression and injury.

" 'So far,' said Lee, 'from engaging in a war to perpetuate
slavery, I am rejoiced that slavery is abolished. I believe it will
be greatly for the interests of the South. So fully am I satisfied
of this, as regards Virginia especially, that I would cheerfully
have lost all I have lost by the war, and have suffered all I have
suffered, to have this object attained.' "[16]

Alexander H. Stephens

Alexander Hamilton Stephens, the Vice President of the
Confederacy, was probably the outstanding intellectual among
the political leaders of the insurgent South and certainly a man
with a clearer comprehension of the dangers latent in the drift
toward secession than his colleagues. Small, frail, with black,
smoldering eyes, Stephens never knew a day without pain, and,
probably because of illness, never married. He was an orphan
who had known poverty and had risen from a $6-a-month coun-
try law practice to become the most eloquent spokesman of the
South. His personal magnetism, character and intellectual
gifts made him admired and loved by men who strongly disapproved of his fundamental beliefs. It was not remarkable that
Jefferson Davis should call him "the little pale star from
Georgia," but it was less predictable that the aged former President and implacable foe of slavery, John Quincy Adams, should
express his friendship and esteem for Stephens in verse.[17]

Despite the fact that it was destined to expand the frontiers
of slavery, Alexander H. Stephens opposed the Mexican War.

[16] *Ibid.,* IV, 400–01.
[17]   "As strangers in this hall we met;
                       "But now with one united heart;
                       "Whate'er of life awaits us yet,
                       "In cordial friendship let us part."

Although it had "lasted upwards of eight months, at a cost of many millions of dollars and the sacrifice of many valuable lives," he said, "no man can tell for what object it is prosecuted." He charged President Polk with having provoked the conflict to carry out "secret designs." He added: "To suppress inquiry, and silence all opposition to conduct so monstrous, an executive ukase has been sent forth, strongly intimating, if not clearly threatening, the charge of treason, against all who may dare to call in question the wisdom or propriety of his measure." Stephens then asked whether "the free people of this country" would be "so easily awed by the arrogance of power." After an allusion to the decapitation of Charles I, he declared: "There are some things more to be dreaded than the loss of a throne, or even the loss of a head—amongst which may be named the anathema of a nation's curse, and the infamy that usually follows it."[18]

Stephens' fellow Congressman, Abraham Lincoln, was vastly moved by this speech and wrote his young law partner, Billy Herndon: "I just take up my pen to say that Mr. Stephens, of Georgia, a little slim, pale-faced, consumptive man, with a voice like Logan's, has just concluded the best speech, of an hour's length, I ever heard. My old,[19] withered, dry eyes, are full of tears yet."[20]

Lincoln's admiration for Stephens was reciprocated and the latter recalled that he had been "as intimate with Mr. Lincoln as with any other man" in that Congress with the possible exception of Robert Toombs of Georgia.[21] During the Civil War, Lincoln sought to utilize his friendship with Alexander Stephens as a bridge to peace negotiations with the Confederate authorities.

Stephens' political career was crippled by obscure ailments, described by contemporary biographers as "bilious fevers," "nephritic calculus" and "dyspeptic horribles."[22] He was at

[18]Carl Sandburg, *Abraham Lincoln, The Prairie Years* (New York, 1926), I, 377–78.
[19]Letter of February 2, 1848. Lincoln was a few days short of 39; Stephens was three years younger.
[20]Sandburg, *Prairie Years,* I, 388.
[21]*Ibid.,* p. 381.
[22]Henry Cleveland, *Alexander H. Stephens in Public and Private* (Philadelphia, 1866), p. 97.

times bedridden and unable to walk about his own house. A man of medium height, Stephens' weight fluctuated between 80 pounds when he was most ill, to about 100 when he was comparatively healthy.[23] At all times, he seems to have been plagued by racking headaches.

Having opposed the Mexican War, Stephens also opposed annexation of Mexican territory. He hoped that the United States was not driven by "an unholy lust of dominion and the spread of empire." He hoped America would be wise enough to avoid "that wild career of military prowess which has been the bane of so many nations which have gone before us, and has been the destruction of all former republics." He was "no enemy to the enlargement of our boundaries, when it can be properly done." But he held that free peoples dare not "enlarge the circuit of their extent by force of arms," since in flouting the free institutions of their neighbors, they jeopardize their own. On a purely practical level, he foresaw "incalculable troubles and difficulties" in absorbing Mexico's polyglot and polyethnic population. "What will be done with the people themselves? Are they to be made citizens? Spaniards, Indians, Mestizoes, Mulattoes, Negroes, and all?"[24]

One of Stephens' main reasons for opposing the War with Mexico had been his belief that it would contribute to the disruption of the United States. A consistent opponent of secession, he wrote a fellow Georgian, J. Henly Smith, before the 1860 elections to allay the alarmist appraisals then sweeping the South of the effect of a Lincoln election. He would not consider Lincoln's victory "sufficient cause . . . to warrant a disruption—particularly as his election will be the result if it occurs at all of the folly and madness of our own people." If, "without cause," the people of the South "destroy the present Government, the best in the world, what hopes have I that they would not bring untold hardships upon the people in their efforts to give us one of their own modeling?"[25]

---

[23]He was five feet, ten inches tall. He grew two inches after he was admitted to the bar at the age of 22, and cut his last tooth at the age of 27.

[24]Alexander H. Stephens, "Speech on the Territorial Bill (Clayton Compromise)", House of Representatives, August 7, 1848. Cleveland, *Stephens*, pp. 329–30, 331.

[25]Sandburg, *Prairie Years*, I, 378–79.

In a letter to Samuel R. Glenn of Washington, D.C., Stephens expressed the hope that "our rights may be maintained and our wrongs redressed in the Union." Secession was more probable. He viewed the prospect with "great apprehension." After the dissolution of the United States, "At the North, I feel confident anarchy will soon ensue; and whether we shall be better off at the South, will depend upon many things . . . Revolutions are much easier started than controlled, and the men that begin them, even for the best purposes and objects, seldom end them."[26]

On November 30, 1860 Stephens wrote a Massachusetts friend, George T. Curtis: "The times are indeed perilous, and nothing but the prompt and most energetic action on the part of the patriots in all sections of the country can save the Republic."[27] With increasing gloom, he wrote Glenn: "We are now in the midst of a revolution. That may be acted upon as a fixed, irrevocable fact. It is bootless to argue the causes that produced it, or whether it be a good or bad thing in itself. The former will be the task of the historian. The latter is a problem that the future alone can solve."[28]

On November 14 Stephens delivered a speech to the Georgia Legislature opposing secession and urging that the Union be maintained. This attracted the attention of President-elect Lincoln, who was quietly attempting to establish contacts in the South that might stave off the disruption of the United States. Lincoln requested a revised copy of the address in a letter which did not reach Stephens for two weeks. Stephens replied on November 30, telling Lincoln:

"Personally I am not your enemy—far from it—and however widely we may differ politically, yet I trust we both have an earnest desire to preserve and maintain the Union of the States, if it can be done upon the principles and in furtherance of the objects for which it was formed." There had always been differences of opinion concerning the morality of slavery among American political men, Stephens observed, just as there had always been differences of religious conviction.

[26]November 25, 1860, Cleveland, *Stephens*, p. 162.
[27]*Ibid.*, p. 159.
[28]February 6, 1861, *ibid.*, p. 161.

Washington, Jefferson and other Presidents had been anti-slavery, but this had not jeopardized the nation's existence. "We at the South do think African slavery, as it exists with us, both morally and politically right. This opinion is founded upon the inferiority of the black race. You, however, and perhaps a majority of the North, think it wrong. Admit the difference of opinion."

The new and dangerous ingredient in the political crisis was that Lincoln headed a political party which had as its leading objective, to place "nearly half the States under the ban of public opinion and national condemnation." When political parties are formed, "not from reason or any sense of justice, but from fanaticism," then "there is no telling where their impulses or passions may drive them."[29]

A word spoken by President-elect Lincoln now to allay the passions and fears of the South and curb the fanatical zeal of the Abolitionists might save the Union. "Nor can the Union under the Constitution be maintained by force. The Union was formed by the consent of independent sovereign States . . . Force may perpetuate a Union. That depends upon the contingencies of war. But such a Union would not be the Union of the Constitution."[30]

Upon receipt of this letter, Lincoln replied in a communication dated December 22, 1860 and marked *"for your own eye only."*

"Do the people of the South really entertain fears that a Republican Administration would, *directly or indirectly,* interfere with their slaves, or with them, about their slaves?" Lincoln asked. "If they do, I wish to assure you, as once a friend, and still, I hope, not an enemy, that there is no cause for such fears.

"The South would be in no more danger in this respect than it was in the days of Washington."

Lincoln realized that this was not enough, that Stephens wanted the President to make some major concession, such as endorsing the Crittenden compromise, and this he was not prepared to do.

[29]Alexander H. Stephens to Abraham Lincoln, *ibid.,* pp. 150–154.
[30]*Ibid.*

"I suppose, however, this does not meet the case," Lincoln continued. "You think slavery is *right* and ought to be extended, while we think it is wrong and ought to be restricted. That I suppose is the rub. It certainly is the only substantial difference between us."[31]

Stephens on Negro Slavery

"I am no defender of slavery in the abstract," Stephens said in a speech delivered in Texas in 1845, "Liberty always had charms for me, and I would prefer to see all the sons and daughters of Adam's family in the full enjoyment of the rights set forth in the Declaration of American Independence, if a stern decree of the Almighty did not in some cases interfere and prevent."[32]

Stephens based his defense of slavery on a single principle—the inferiority of the Negro race. "Pythagoras, Plato and Aristotle, the greatest philosophers of antiquity, directed their minds to the systems of government, and the proper constitution of a State," he observed. "The republican form was the ideal model of each. They all saw the necessity of some sort of gradation in the elements of its composition; but their systems failed, because they violated nature in making the subordinate class of the same race. Subordination is the normal condition of the Negro. This great truth, that such was the normal condition of any race, was not recognized in their theories; and hence their machinery, in practice, could not work."[33]

The sentences just quoted indicate the degree to which the mind and intellectual horizon of the Southern statesman had shrunk between the time of Jefferson and the Civil War. Stephens' version of Greek political thought on slavery is inaccurate: It is in fact misinformation clothed in spurious learning. If Pythagoras wrote about slavery and the state, neither his writings nor their content survive. According to tradition, he sought to establish a communistic aristocracy at Crotona in Sicily and was murdered in consequence by the democratic faction. Since neither Plato nor Aristotle attempted to establish

[31] *Ibid.*, p. 150.
[32] *Ibid.*, p. 125.
[33] Alexander H. Stephens, Speech at Augusta, Georgia, on his retirement from Congress, July 2, 1859, in *ibid.*, p. 127.

city-states based on their doctrines, speculation concerning the reasons for their failure seems pointless. Finally, in his discussion of the "natural slave," Aristotle touched on national and racial differences when he contrasted Greeks and barbarians.

At a time when the Abolitionist tide was rising internationally, Stephens, in common with many other Southern leaders, believed it was receding. Thirty years previous, Virginia had been on the verge of abolishing slavery. "Now, no such sentiment is to be found there." Twenty years ago, Wilberforce's agitation had borne fruit in emancipation of the slaves in the British West Indies. "That experiment has most signally failed" and, to replace the manumitted Negro slaves, coolies were being imported into the islands from Asia. "Carlyle, the greatest thinker of England, has repudiated the folly of abolitionism; and the London *Times* followed not far behind him. The world is growing wiser, and upon no subject more rapidly than that of the proper status of the Negro." He believed that in 1859 there were "more thinking men at the North" who approved of slavery "socially, morally and politically" than there had been in the South thirty years previous.

Stephens recognized that Jefferson, Madison and almost all the great political leaders of the South during the formative era of the American Republic had opposed slavery. But he believed them to have been wrong. He agreed with the anti-slavery Senator from New York, William H. Seward, who was soon to become Lincoln's Secretary of State, that the issue was one of "the 'higher law,' the laws of the Creator, as manifested in His words and His revelations." It would not do to defend slavery on utilitarian grounds as providing "the greatest good for the greatest number." On the contrary, "If slavery, as it exists with us, is not the best for the African, constituted and made as he is; if it does not best promote his welfare and happiness, socially, morally, and politically, as well as that of his master, it ought to be abolished."

The higher law, as Stephens saw it, was an order in nature, involving gradation and subordination:

We see it in the heavens above, in the greater and lesser lights, in the stars that differ from each other in magnitude and lustre;

we see it in the earth below, in the vegetable and animal king-doms, ranging from stateliest trees of the forests to the rudest mosses and ferns; from the magnolia grandiflora gloriosa, the rose and the japonica, down to the most uncouth flower we tread under foot; from the hugest monster of life in the air, on the land, or in the ocean, to the smallest *animalcule* to be found in them all, we see similar distinctions and gradation in the races of men, from the highest to the lowest type. These are mysteries in crea-tion which are not for us to explain.[34]

This biological justification for Negro slavery was delivered less than six months before Charles Darwin revolutionized the science of biology with the publication of his *Origin of Species*. Stephens' views were derived in large part from Louis Agassiz, the Swiss naturalist who dominated the life sciences in Amer-ica from his chair at Harvard. Agassiz believed that all living creatures had been created by divine act and that they con-stituted a hierarchic order. As early as 1850, Agassiz had ob-served that the Bible does not refer to human beings in the Americas, the Arctic, Japan or various other regions and that Adam and Eve were the first human beings "to which the white race is distinctly referred." Since Genesis did not mention the creation of non-white peoples, they must have arisen inde-pendently and in some other fashion. Racial differences had existed as far back as recorded history and it must, therefore, be assumed that these differences were not caused by variations of habitat, but resulted from separate acts of creation.[35]

Agassiz also asserted that it was "mock philosophy and mock philanthropy to assume that all races have the same abilities and enjoy the same powers, and show the same natural disposi-tions." He found Mongolians "obsequious" and Negroes so "sub-missive" that they had made no progress since the age of the Pharaohs.[36]

[34] *Ibid.*, p. 128.
[35] The view that racial differences preceded the appearance of *homo sapiens* has been advanced more recently, and on considerably stronger scientific grounds, by Franz Weidenreich (1873-1948) and by Carleton S. Coon, *The Origin of Races* (New York, 1952).
[36] Louis Agassiz, "The Diversity of Origin of the Human Race," *Christian Examiner*, July 1850. v. H. R. Hays, *From Ape to Angel* (New York, 1958), p. 239.

Reasoning from these somewhat abstract premises, Stephens reached the conclusion that it was essential to the security of the South that the African slave trade be reopened. In his farewell speech of July 2, 1859 he retreated from the stand he had taken during the Mexican War and urged that the United States expand territorially toward "Chihuahua, Sonora, and other parts of Mexico—to Cuba, and even to Central America." Of these potential acquisitions, "the most important to the whole country is Cuba." The natural path of empire was along a north-south rather than an east-west axis, because the former would further diversify the agriculture and resources of the nation. As yet, "We embrace no portion of the tropics." He opposed paying Spain thirty or forty million dollars for Cuba. It would be better to repeal the laws against filibustering expeditions so that Americans could land on the island and seize it. Similarly, he had expressed his entire sympathy with the filibustering expedition of William Walker in Nicaragua in 1858, because its purpose was to enable the United States to absorb that Central American Republic as a slave state.[37]

Nevertheless, it was useless to

expect to see many of the territories come into the Union as slave States, *unless we have an increase of African stock.* The law of population will prevent. We have not the people. Boundaries by rivers or mountains, do not make States. It takes people to make States; *and it requires people of the African race to make slave States.* This requires no argument; and I very much question whether, with our present stock of that population, we can furnish the requisite number to secure more than the four States to come out of Texas in the present territories of the Union. To look for, or expect many more, is to look in vain, without a foreign supply. . . My object is simply to bring clearly to your mind the great truth—that without an increase of African slaves from abroad, you may not expect or look for many more slave States. If the policy of this country, settled in its early history, of prohibiting further importations or immigrations of this class of population, is to be adhered to, the race of competition between us and our brethren of the North, in the colonization of new States, which heretofore has been so well maintained by us, will soon have to be abandoned.[38]

[37]Letter of January 3, 1858. v. Rhodes, *History,* II, 290.
[38]Cleveland, *Stephens,* pp. 646–647. Emphasis supplied.

Throughout the 1850s, there was a severe shortage of slave labor in the South with consequent rising labor costs in the Cotton Belt and a type of exploitative farming that wasted soil resources. One Southerner estimated that Texas alone could absorb six million Negroes. The agitation for the revival of the African slave trade was strongest in the Deep South and the new Western slave areas, weakest in the old cotton regions of the Southeastern Seaboard, where the sale of surplus Negroes to the newer Western and Southern areas was made increasingly profitable by supply scarcity and high prices. Such organs of slave-based agriculture as *De Bow's Review* argued that revival of the African trade would spread ownership of Negroes "more generally among the people" and narrow the economic gap between the large planters and the small farmers. Every white man in the South should own at least one Negro. If the small farmers had slaves of their own, they would not have to have their children work in the fields "when they should either be at school or at play." Furthermore, "We do not wish to see the white man of the South act as a boot-black, a cook, a waiter, or as one of a gang of laborers in the sugar and cotton fields."[39]

Nevertheless, it is odd that a man of Stephens's political acumen should not have realized that the goal of reopening the African slave trade was in conflict with his other great purpose, that of avoiding secession. The North might have accepted a spatially restricted slaveholding society, in fact, Lincoln specifically so pledged his Administration, but it would be far less tolerant of a slave system with an unlimited dynamic of expansion. Resumption of the African trade would have alienated the South from Great Britain and Western Europe. It would have awakened strong anxieties among the people of the Border States and perhaps also among the yeomen of the South. Northern sympathizers of the South were often powerfully motivated by dislike and hatred of the Negro. They feared that emancipation of the Blacks would result in their dispersion from the Southern plantations into Northern communities where they were not wanted. These negrophobes might well

[39]Quoted from *De Bow's Review* (1858) and the *Texas State Gazette* (1859), in Stampp, *Peculiar Institution,* pp. 274–275.

have found the prospect of an unlimited African slave trade hideous because of its fateful implications for the future population of the United States.

The lack of foresight on this matter of such Confederate leaders as Jefferson Davis, Alexander H. Stephens, Judah P. Benjamin and Robert Toombs seems astonishing. All, at one time or another, argued in favor of revival of the African trade. While Jefferson had foreseen that every addition to the Negro population made the American race problem more insoluble for future generations, the Southern leaders of the 1850s were blinded to the potential long-range implications of their policy by visions of an Athenian democracy in the South. The prospect of the population of the United States becoming ethnically similar to that of present-day Brazil does not seem to have distressed them.

Despite Stephens' intransigent attitude on slavery and the slave trade, Lincoln regarded him as a moderate and met with him on a U.S. vessel anchored near Fort Monroe in February 1865 to discuss means of bringing the conflict to an end. According to Stephens' account, he suggested to Lincoln, that a restoration of the Union without further bloodshed could be attained by the North and the Confederacy joining forces to assert the Monroe Doctrine by driving the Emperor Maximilian and his armies out of Mexico. Lincoln replied that hostilities could not be terminated until the South pledged its immediate return to the Union. The conversation turned toward slavery. As Stephens remembered it:

> He [Lincoln] said it was not his intention in the beginning to interfere with Slavery in the States; that he never would have done it, if he had not been compelled by necessity to do it, to maintain the Union; that the subject presented many difficult and perplexing questions to him: that he had hesitated for some time, and had resorted to this measure, only when driven to it by public necessity; that he had been in favor of the General Government prohibiting the extension of Slavery into the Territories, but did not think that the Government possessed power over the Subject in the States, except as a war measure; and that he had always himself been in favor of emancipation, but not immediate emancipation, even by the States.[40]

[40]Stroude, *Davis,* II, 985–86.

Stephens was one of the first of the Confederate leaders to realize that the war was lost and one of the first to come to terms with the new order. Once his goal of a great slave empire had been irretrievably shattered, he turned toward the attainable and realistic objective of a return to law and orderly government. On February 22, 1866 he addressed the Georgia Legislature, pointing out that the South had just gone through a drastic social revolution and must recognize that fact:

> One of the results of the war is a total change in our whole internal polity. Our former social fabric has been entirely subverted. Like those convulsions in nature which break up old incrustations, the war has wrought a new epoch in our political existence . . . Slavery, as it was called, or the *status* of the black race, their subordination to the white, upon which all our institutions rested, is abolished forever, not only in Georgia, but throughout the limits of the United States. This change should be received and accepted as an irrevocable fact.

He urged that the new system be given "a fair and just trial." This required "great changes in our former laws" applying to the Negro and that the latter be given "ample and full protection" so that the former slaves "may stand equal before the law, in the possession and enjoyment of all rights of person, liberty and property." The South owed this to the Negroes. "They cultivated your fields, ministered to your personal wants and comforts, nursed and reared your children; and even in the hour of danger and peril they were, in the main, true to you and yours. To them we owe a debt of gratitude as well as acts of kindness. This should also be done because they are poor, untutored, uninformed; many of them helpless, liable to be imposed upon, and need it. Legislation should ever look to the protection of the weak against the strong."[41]

Since Stephens had always regarded chattel slavery as an institution to elevate and improve the Negro, there was no fundamental inconsistency between his *ante-bellum* and his *post-bellum* stances. He remained actuated by a sense of *noblesse oblige.*

The Negro had made great progress in America and "the

[41]Cleveland, *Stephens,* pp. 812–813.

present generation" was "far above their savage progeni-
tors . . ." This proved that improvement was possible. Legislation should remove "all obstacles, if there be any," to their
physical, intellectual, and moral advance. "Channels of education should be opened up to them." They must be put to school
because the danger to society of a free Negro population
"reared in ignorance, depravity, and vice" was incalculable.

He then cited some remarks of the Reverend Henry Ward
Beecher, a leading Northern Abolitionist. Beecher feared "the
most terrible conflict of classes" unless the working class was
educated and imbued with Christian principles. "We are told by
zealous and fanatical individuals that all men are equal,"
Beecher continued. "We know better. They are not equal . . .
Now, as in all times, the strong go to the top, the weak go to the
bottom. It's natural, right and cannot be helped." This process,
however, must lead to class strife and social revolution unless
education and love dominate the minds of the lower classes.

Stephens expressed his agreement with this prognosis, given
"the fearful antagonism of classes" in the North. The two
classes in the South "are as distinct as races of men can be. The
one is of the highest type of humanity, the other of the lowest."
As for the future, he found it "dark and impenetrable." He
would not arouse false hopes. "Whether the great barrier of
races which the Creator has placed between this, our inferior
class and ourselves, shall prevent a success of the experiment
now on trial . . . let the future, under the dispensations of Providence, decide."

Alexander H. Stephens survived the ordeal of Reconstruction
and the Compromise of 1877. In a symposium published in the
North American Review in 1879, he and two other former
Confederate leaders, Wade Hampton and L. Q. C. Lamar,
agreed "not only that the disfranchisement of the freeman was
impossible, but that even if it were possible the South would not
desire it."[42]

Neither Stephens nor the other leaders of the Confederacy
ever abandoned their view that the Negro race was morally and
intellectually inferior to the Caucasian. Like other Southern

[42]C. Vann Woodward, *The Strange Career of Jim Crow,* New York, 1956, p. 34.

spokesmen, Stephens had always had a patriarchal and paternalistic attitude toward the Blacks and had regarded slavery as a school in the rudiments of civilization. With the social conditions of the South irrevocably changed in a drastic manner, he was prepared to accept and even to welcome the gradual extension of rights to the Negro as he acquired the ability to exercise them intelligently.

CHAPTER TWELVE

Abraham Lincoln: The House Dividing

> I have said that the separation of the races is the only perfect
> preventive of amalgamation . . . Such separation, if ever
> effected at all, must be effected by colonization . . . Let us be
> brought to believe it is morally right, and, at the same time
> favorable to, or, at least, not against, our interest, to transfer
> the African to his native clime, and we shall find a way to do
> it, however great the task may be.
> —Abraham Lincoln, Speech of June 26, 1857.

Not even Jefferson has had his views on slavery, the Negro and
the strategy of emancipation as grossly misrepresented as has
Abraham Lincoln. The folk image of Lincoln as the Great
Emancipator, the indefatiguable fighter for Negro freedom and
the friend and protector of the oppressed colored masses is so
irresistibly attractive to the mythmakers and romanticizers of
American history that it has obscured and supplanted the factual record. A glaring instance of the displacement of truth by
legend is the statement made by Lincoln's most poetic biographer, the late Carl Sandburg, in a television interview in
November 1957, that if Lincoln were President at that time, he
would be planning civil rights strategy in daily White House
conferences with the leaders of the N.A.A.C.P. All one can reply
is that this is not the way Lincoln behaved while alive.

The truth is more complicated than the legend. Throughout
his life, Lincoln repudiated slavery on moral grounds, but he
did not believe that he had the Constitutional power to abolish

it. His antagonism to slavery was sufficiently secondary for him to be willing to commit the United States Government to perpetuate it rather than risk dismemberment of the nation. His repudiation of chattel slavery was not accompanied by any admiration for its victims. Following in the footsteps of Thomas Jefferson and Henry Clay, Lincoln believed that the Negro was an unassimilable element in American life. He believed that the Negro presence had caused the Civil War. He neither desired nor advocated that the manumitted slaves be given the rights of American citizens. If freed, he held, they should be removed in their entirety to some more congenial country. He opposed social equality for Negroes and regarded sexual mixture of the two races as a calamity.

Lincoln's dogged, energetic and relentless support of colonization and deportation schemes, some of them impractical, others proposed by shady promoters and swindlers, has been portrayed by some historians as an aberration of slight importance. This misses the vital point that Lincoln's solution to the Negro problem throughout all, or nearly all, of his political life was based on the proposition that freedom must be coupled with the removal of the black population from American territory. His views in this matter exactly paralleled those of Thomas Jefferson. During the last year of his life, Lincoln probably abandoned his efforts to achieve the total deportation of American Negroes, but this change if it actually occurred seems to have been, not a reversal of his fundamental convictions, but a recognition that the opportunity to achieve this solution had slipped away.

Lincoln acknowledged his intellectual debt to Jefferson in his Cooper Union Address of February 27, 1860, the oration that gave him recognized national stature and won for him the Republican nomination for the Presidency. In the days when public schools had a modicum of academic standards, practically every American high school student had read *about* the Cooper Union speech. Many even recalled its eloquent closing assertion: "Let us have faith that right makes might; and in that faith let us to the end, dare to do our duty as we understand it." But very few, even in those earlier days, actually read the speech and noted what it proposed.

Lincoln characterized slavery as "an evil not to be extended, but to be tolerated and protected only because of and insofar as its actual presence among us makes that toleration and protection a necessity." He then urged that emancipation be gradual and that it be accompanied by removal of the slaves, when freed, to some other country. "In the language of Mr. Jefferson, uttered many years ago, 'it is still in our power to direct the process of emancipation and deportation peaceably, and in such slow degrees, as that the evil will wear off insensibly and their places be, *pari passu*, filled up by free white laborers. If, on the contrary, it is left to force itself on, human nature must shudder at the prospect held up.' "[1]

He also acknowledged his intellectual debt to Henry Clay. Toward the close of 1864, some five months before his assassination, Lincoln urged James S. Rollins, a representative from a slave district in Missouri and one of the largest slaveowners in the nation, to support the Thirteenth Amendment. The grounds suggested for this action were expediency: Border State backing of the Amendment would convince the South that it could no longer hope for aid from that quarter and would thus help bring the war to a close at "the earliest possible date." As Rollins recollected it, Lincoln told him: "You and I were old whigs, both of us followers of that great statesman, Henry Clay, and *I tell you I never had an opinion upon the subject of slavery in my life that I did not get from him.*"[2]

Early Attitudes toward Slavery

An imperishable episode in the Lincoln legend is that of the New Orleans slave market. Twenty-two-year-old Abe Lincoln went to that city on a flatboat and saw a "vigorous and comely" mulatto girl handled like a mare by the slave auctioneer. This aroused an implacable hatred of slavery in Lincoln's soul and he swore: "If I ever get a chance to hit that thing, I'll hit it hard."

The source is John Hanks, who went with Lincoln part of the way, but got off before New Orleans and hence was no eyewitness. Hanks told it to Billy Herndon thirty-five years later, but

[1]Lincoln's quotation is from Jefferson's *Autobiography*.
[2]J. G. Randall and Richard N. Current, *Lincoln the President, Last Full Measure* (New York, 1955), p. 309.

Herndon, who had been Lincoln's law partner, was an Abolitionist with a drinking problem whose veracity was questionable. Moreover, in his 1860 autobiography, Lincoln does not
mention the episode. Since the 1860 document was put together
for campaign purposes, the omission is not conclusive. The
pledge to "hit it hard" thus belongs in the penumbra area of
perhapses.[3]

In 1841, Lincoln made a trip with his good friend, Joshua
Speed, by steamboat down the Ohio. He wrote Speed fourteen
years later that "ten or a dozen slaves, shackled together with
irons" were aboard and that the "sight was a continual torment
to me." Yet at the time of the episode, he had written Speed's
sister, Mary, in very different terms. The letter described the
slaves "strung together like so many fish upon a trot line," as
being taken from their Kentucky homes to be sold down river
where slavery was believed to be at its harshest and facing
permanent separation from their families and friends. Despite
this, Lincoln observed, "they were the most cheerful and apparently happy creatures on board."[4]

Passing from this twilight zone between history and legend
to the record, there are a few definite statements that can be
made about Lincoln's early attitudes toward slavery and the
Negro.

During the twenty-five years that he practiced law in Illinois,
Lincoln handled several cases involving Negroes, largely because he had gained a reputation as a cheap lawyer who sometimes charged five-dollar fees.

In 1840, Lincoln won a breach of contract suit, involving the
services of Nance, a colored woman, who was alleged to be an
indentured servant. He argued successfully that she must be
considered free under the Northwest Ordinance of 1787 and the
Illinois Constitution unless proved to be a slave.

Five years later, Lincoln represented Robert Matson, a Kentucky planter, in a somewhat malodorous slave-catching case.
Matson had sent his favorite mulatto slave, Jane, and her four
children to Illinois to do seasonal work for him. State law per-

[3]Richard N. Current, *The Lincoln Nobody Knows* (New York, 1958), pp. 215–
17.
[4]*Ibid.*, pp. 214–16.

mitted this provided the Negroes did not remain in Illinois continuously for an entire year. When Jane had been in Illinois without interruption for two years, she ran afoul of Matson's housekeeper, who prevailed on him to sell her South, together with her four children, one of whom had blue eyes and red hair. Feeling against Matson ran high in the state. Ten armed Abolitionists patrolled the court house, ready to seize Jane and her family by force and take them to safety in the event of an adverse decision. Lincoln argued that the crucial point was that his client had not *intentionally* allowed Jane and her children to remain in Illinois beyond the allotted time. He lost the case and the Negroes were declared free and sent to Liberia.[5]

In February 1837, the Illinois Legislature passed a resolution deploring the existence of slavery, but followed this with a tirade against Abolitionist agitation and the assertion that "The right of property in slaves, is sacred." Lincoln and Dan Stone protested. They asserted their belief that "The institution of slavery is founded on both injustice and bad policy; but that the promulgation of Abolitionist doctrine tends rather to increase than to abate its evils."[6] They added their conviction that Congress had no power to interfere with slavery in the States, adding that it had power to regulate it in the District of Columbia, but ought not to do so unless so requested by the inhabitants.

During his brief career in Congress, Lincoln twice voted against resolutions ordering committees of the House to report bills abolishing the slave trade in the District of Columbia. He opposed a bill against slavery in the nation's capital, but advanced a plan of his own in January 1849 which would have freed all children born to slave mothers in the District after January 1, 1850, with full compensation to their owners, and would also have indemnified masters who were willing to free their slaves. The bill would become law only after approval by majority vote in a referendum of free District residents. Lest

[5]Benjamin Quarles, *Lincoln and the Negro* (New York, 1962), pp. 21–27. This book by a prominent Negro historian is a rich repository of esoteric information, but its judgments are sometimes unsophisticated. Quarles, for example, accepts the New Orleans slave auction story without any reservations.
[6]Roy R. Basler (Editor), *The Collected Works of Abraham Lincoln*, (New Brunswick, 1953), I, 74–75.

the nation's capital become a lodestone and sanctuary for Negro runaways, Lincoln added provisions requiring the municipal authorities in Washington and Georgetown to arrest and return to their masters all such fugitives without delay.[7] The infants born into freedom after January 1, 1850 were to "owe reasonable service as apprentices" to their former owners until they reached an age which Lincoln left blank in the draft bill.[8] This measure, which could scarcely be described as a radical one, was abandoned by Lincoln because it lacked support in Congress.

The Lincoln-Douglas Debates

As early as 1854, Lincoln challenged the "squatter sovereignty" doctrine of Stephen A. Douglas, the brilliant and politically formidable Senator from Illinois and recognized contender for the Presidency. In an effort to avoid both exacerbation of the slavery conflict and secession and civil war, Douglas had introduced a bill in January 1854 for the organization of the territories of Kansas and Nebraska which became law in May of that year. This measure repealed the Missouri Compromise and established the general principle that the people of "any State or Territory" were "free to form and regulate their domestic institutions in their own way, subject only to the Constitution of the United States."

Douglas was a strong nationalist, a believer in the indissoluble union of the States and in manifest destiny and an opponent of the expansion of slavery. "Let each State mind its own business and let its neighbors alone," he declared in one of the 1858 debates with Lincoln. "[If] we will stand by that principle," then, "This republic can exist forever divided into free and slave States . . . Stand by that great principle and we can go on as we have done, increasing in wealth, in population, in power, and in all the elements of greatness, until we shall be the admiration and terror of the world, . . . until we make this continent one ocean-bound republic."[9]

Lincoln launched his attack on the "squatter sovereignty"

---

[7]Quarles, *Lincoln,* pp. 29–30.
[8]Basley, *Works,* II, 20–21.
[9]Stephen A. Douglas, speech of October 13, 1858 at Quincy, Illinois.

doctrine from the moment of its promulgation, basing his strategy on the assertion and reiteration of abstract principles and deduced conclusions. On September 26, 1854 he stated that the basic issue was whether the Negro was or was not a man. If he was not, "Then it is no business of ours whether he is enslaved upon soil which belongs to us, any more than it is our business to trouble ourselves about the oyster-trade, cranberry-trade, or any other legitimate traffic carried on by the people in territory owned by the Government." But if he *was* a man, "Then there is not even the shadow of popular sovereignty in allowing the first settlers upon such soil to decide whether it shall be right in all future time to hold men in bondage there."[10]

A month later, Abraham Lincoln made an important statement, defining his attitudes toward slavery and the reasons for his moral repudiation of the institution. He hated the *"declared* indifference, but as I must think, covert *real* zeal for the spread of slavery" because of "the monstrous injustice of slavery itself." This moral indifference "deprives our republican example of its just influence in the world—enables the enemies of free institutions, with plausibility, to taunt us as hypocrites—causes the real friends of freedom to doubt our sincerity, and especially because it forces so many really good men amongst ourselves into an open war with the very fundamental principles of civil liberty—criticizing the Declaration of Independence, and insisting that there is no right principle of action but *self-interest."*[11]

He had no prejudice against the Southern people. "If slavery did not exist amongst them, they would not introduce it. If it did now exist amongst us, we should not instantly give it up." When they say they are no more responsible for the origin of slavery than Northerners, "I acknowledge the fact." He understood and appreciated the Southern view that it was very difficult to get rid of slavery. He, himself, had no panacea and frankly admitted as much:

"If all earthly power were given me, I should not know what to do, as to the existing institution. My first impulse would be to free all the slaves, and send them to Liberia,—to their own

[10]Basler, *Works,* II, 239.
[11]*Ibid.,* p. 255.

native land. But a moment's reflection would convince me, that whatever of high hope, (as I think there is) there may be in this, in the long run, its sudden execution is impossible. If they were all landed there in a day, they would all perish in the next ten days; and there are not surplus shipping and surplus money enough in the world to carry them there in many times ten days."

What were the alternatives? What interim solution was there while a gradual and orderly program of colonization was being carried into effect?

"What then? Free them all, and keep them among us as underlings? Is it quite certain that this betters their condition? I think I would not hold one in slavery, at any rate; yet the point is not clear enough for me to denounce people upon."

What Lincoln was saying here was that he conceded, or half-conceded, the Southern point that the free Negroes, living as miserable outcasts and despised pariahs in both North and South, were perhaps worse off than the slaves. He next turned to the Abolitionist solution of full equality:

> *What then? Free them, and make them politically and socially our equals? My own feelings will not admit of this; and if mine would, we well know that those of the great mass of white people will not. Whether this feeling accords with justice and sound judgment, is not the sole question, if indeed, it is any part of it. A universal feeling, whether well or ill-founded, can not be safely disregarded. We can not then make them equals.* It does seem to me that systems of gradual emancipation might be adopted; but for their tardiness in this, I will not undertake to judge our brethren of the south.[12]

Lincoln added that, when Southerners reminded him of their rights under the Constitution to have their fugitive slaves apprehended and returned to them, he conceded these rights, "not grudgingly, but fully, and fairly." He didn't think that the Fugitive Slave legislation was "any more likely to carry a free man into slavery, than our ordinary criminal laws are to hang an innocent one." This admission, however, "furnishes no more

---

[12]*Ibid.* The quotation from this speech, delivered at Springfield, Illinois on October 16, 1854 is uninterrupted, but our commentary has broken it into paragraphs. Emphasis supplied.

excuse for permitting slavery to go into our own free territory, than it would for reviving the African slave trade by law."

On June 26, 1857 he returned to the subject and to his persistent and deeply-calculated attack on Stephen A. Douglas, his principal rival for political leadership in Illinois. He now considered the inflammable and passion-saturated issues of miscegenation and social equality.

"There is a natural disgust in the minds of nearly all white people," Lincoln observed, "to the idea of an indiscriminate amalgamation of the white and black races; and Judge Douglas evidently is basing his chief hope, upon the chances of being able to appropriate the benefit of this disgust to himself." Douglas's political prospects, Lincoln alleged, were contingent on being able to show that the Republicans were advocates of social equality between the races.

> He finds the Republicans insisting that the Declaration of Independence includes ALL men, black as well as white; and forthwith he boldly denies that it includes negroes at all, and proceeds to argue gravely that all who contend it does, do so only because they want to vote, and eat, and sleep, and marry with negroes! He will have it that they cannot be consistent else. Now I protest against that counterfeit logic which concludes that, because I do not want a black woman for a *slave* I must necessarily want her for a *wife*. I need not have her for either, I can just leave her alone. In some respects she certainly is not my equal; but in her natural right to eat the bread she earns with her own hands without asking leave of any one else, she is my equal, and the equal of all others.[13]

Reverting to the issue of race mixing, Lincoln turned the argument against his opponent and claimed that Douglas' solution would promote this putative evil:

> But Judge Douglas is especially horrified at the thought of the mixing blood by the white and black races: agreed for once—a

[13] *Ibid.,* p. 405. Speech of June 26, 1857. The point that his disinterest in a Negro woman for his slave did not imply a craving for her as his wife evidently pleased the crowd, for Lincoln used it again and again in his polemics with Douglas. Much of the content and even phrasing of these speeches of the late 1850's is taken from the writings of Henry Clay. The contrast between equal abilities and equal rights was made by Thomas Jefferson.

thousand times agreed. There are white men enough to marry all
the white women, and black men enough to marry all the black
women; and so let them be married. On this point we fully agree
with the Judge; and when he shall show that his policy is better
adapted to prevent amalgamation than ours we shall drop ours
and adopt his. Let us see. In 1850 there were in the United States
405,751 mulattoes. Very few of these are the offspring of whites
and *free* blacks; nearly all have sprung from black *slaves* and
white masters. A separation of the races is the only perfect preventive of amalgamation, but as an immediate separation is impossible the next best thing is to *keep* them apart *where* they are
not already together. If white and black people never get together in Kansas, they will never mix blood in Kansas. That is at
least one self-evident truth. A few free colored persons may get
into the free States, in any event; but their number is too insignificant to amount to much in the way of mixing blood... In New
Hampshire, the state which goes farthest towards equality between the races,[14] there are just 184 Mulattoes, while there are
in Virginia—how many do you think? 79,775, being 23,426 more
than in all the free States together."[15] (A reason for there being
incomparably more mulattoes in Virginia than in New Hampshire which Lincoln did not mention, since it was not a good
debating point, was that Virginia had incomparably more
Negroes.)

Lincoln proceeded to argue that slavery and forced concubin-
age produced "nine tenths of all the mulattoes." He believed
that total separation of the races, through colonization, was the
only permanent cure for race-mixing. While the Republican
Party was not formally on record in its platform as advocating
colonization, he could say that "A very large proportion of its
members are for it."

Illinois in 1858 had some of the rough and raw characteristics
of the frontier which had by then swept beyond it toward the
Pacific. Lacking such sophisticated means of enjoying leisure
as viewing soap operas and television comics, the country
folk and townsmen of the state had not yet absorbed the
art of divorcing recreation from the use of their minds. Hence
crowds as large as 20,000 swarmed into county seats to hear
Lincoln and Douglas, the two rival candidates for the Senate

---

[14]Lincoln was mistaken. Only Maine gave Negroes full civil rights. New
Hampshire let them vote, but kept them out of the militia.
[15]*Ibid.*, pp. 407–08.

from Illinois, debate the great issues of the day.

The central issue was whether slavery should be irrevocably banned from all territories of the United States, as Lincoln demanded, or whether the question should be left to the voters in these territories, as Douglas asserted. In the seven debates, the discussion ranged over the peripheral and ancillary aspects of this area of dispute and enabled both contestants to repeat and rephrase their ideas on the topic.

On August 21, 1858 Lincoln again denied that he had ever advocated "perfect social and political equality with the negro" and added that any logic which imputed that idea to him was "but a specious and fantastic arrangement of words, by which a man can prove a horse chestnut to be a chestnut horse." He believed that the Negro was entitled to "all the natural rights enumerated in the Declaration of Independence, the right to life, liberty and the pursuit of happiness." But he also agreed with Judge Douglas that the Negro "is not my equal in many respects—certainly not in color, perhaps not in moral or intellectual endowment."

Lincoln emphasized that he did not wish to destroy slavery in the Southern States, that he did not favor social equality, and that he believed in white supremacy:

> I will say here, while upon this subject, that *I have no purpose directly or indirectly to interfere with the institution of slavery in the States where it exists,* I believe I have no lawful right to do so, and *I have no inclination to do so. I have no purpose to introduce social and political equality between the white and the black race. There is a physical difference between the two, which in my judgment will probably forever forbid their living together upon the footing of perfect equality, and inasmuch as it becomes a necessity that there must be a difference, I, as well as Judge Douglas, am in favor of the race to which I belong having the superior position.* [16]

On another occasion, Lincoln challenged Chief Justice Taney's decision that Negroes could never be citizens of the United States. "Now my opinion is that the different states have the power to make a negro a citizen under the Constitution of the United States if they choose. The Dred Scott decision

[16] *Ibid.,* III, 16.

decides that they have not that power. *If the State of Illinois had that power, I should be opposed to the exercise of it."* [17] The fourth debate was at Charleston, Illinois, on September eighteenth. Lincoln repeated what he had said about opposing social and political equality, adding: "I am not nor ever have been in favor of making voters or jurors of negroes, nor of qualifying them to hold office." He reiterated his advocacy of white supremacy and his skepticism concerning the coexistence of the two races in the United States. On the issue of miscegenation, he told a guffawing crowd: "I have never had the least apprehension that I or my friends would marry negroes if there were no law to keep them from it." [18]

Moral Crisis or Red Herring?

What were the real underlying issues of substance in the Lincoln-Douglas debates? Were there any? Pro-Southern revisionists, led by the distinguished Civil War expert and Professor Emeritus at Chicago, Avery Craven, have argued that Lincoln's inflexible insistence on a moral principle precipitated an avoidable war and plunged the nation into the tragedy of sectional schism:

> The danger of slave extension, on which the party was founded, was over. And by 1858 even Republican leaders understood this fact. Some said the party had fulfilled its mission and should join with Stephen A. Douglas in the formation of a new party for wider sectional and national ends. Some talked of a 'broad base' by which the Republicans could attack the old Southern Whigs. But Abraham Lincoln, in his 'House Divided' speech, prevented himself and his party from being thrust aside by a desperate appeal to old moral formulations. Though *his* own policy and that of 'Judge' Douglas gave identical results, the latter was not born of moral conviction. And until the issue was conceived in terms of 'the eternal struggle between two principles—right and wrong throughout the world', the fight must go on. *That is why a man who was willing to save the Union at the cost of a bloody civil war, even with slavery untouched, would not save it by a compromise which yielded party principle but which did not sacrifice a single material thing.* [19]

[17] *Ibid.*, p. 179. Emphasis supplied.
[18] *Ibid.*, p. 146.
[19] Avery Craven, "Coming of the War between the States: an Interpretation," in *An Historian and the Civil War* (Chicago, 1964), p. 42.

Had slavery, in short, reached its own natural frontiers by 1860? Westward lay country unsuited for the great traditional staples of slave agriculture—sugar, cotton and tobacco. The bloody political battles to decide whether the soil of Kansas and Nebraska were to be slave or free seem retrospectively super-fluous in the light of the cold economic fact that the 1860 Census reported a total of exactly 17 slaves in the two territories.

The expansion of slavery southward through seizure of land from Spain or from Latin American republics would almost certainly have been unacceptable to the people and Congress of the United States. Slavery in the South faced slow strangulation from eroding soils and rising labor costs. The solution, urged by Southern diehards, that the African slave trade be reopened, was not even favored, it would seem, by a majority of the people of the South.

It seemed to many dispassionate observers that slavery had no economic future and was destined to die of anemia within a generation or so. Thus, Daniel Webster thought the furor over the extension of slavery to the territories "mere abstraction" since the limits of plantation slavery had already been irrevocably set by "an ordinance of nature."[20]

Against this viewpoint, Richard N. Current, one of the best of the historians of the Civil War, argues that slavery need not have been confined to the plantation agriculture of the South. The recent history of Nazi and Soviet labor camps reveals that forced labor can be applied to mining, construction and even certain forms of manufacturing.[21] Writing from a Marxist viewpoint, Eugene D. Genovese ably marshals evidence that such Southern expansionists as De Bow were thinking seriously, and perhaps realistically, about the expansion of slavery to exploit the mineral resources of Mexico and the American West.[22] In the history of Europe, Negro slaves were employed primarily in tropical and semi-tropical agriculture, as in the sugar plantations of Cyprus of the Fourteenth Century, owned by Italian entrepreneurs and worked by Negro slave gangs. Yet, as late as 1785, some Negro slaves were being imported into

[20]Current, *Lincoln*, pp. 94–103.
[21]*Ibid.*, p. 99.
[22]Eugene D. Genovese, *The Political Economy of Slavery* (New York, 1965), pp. 256–260.

Portugal to work in the mines[23] and the much vaunted medieval Negro kingdom of Ghana owed much of its prosperity to slave labor in the salt mines of Taghaza.[24]

Nevertheless, there are several reasons for rejecting the analyses of Current and Genovese and concluding that, by the late 1850s, the prospects for expansion of the slave-owning economy of the South were dim. One of these reasons was the limited applicability of Negro slave labor because of its low productivity and appalling inefficiency. Slave labor was concentrated in the production of the basic plantation crops, where operations were routinized and unskilled and required the application of a large amount of muscle, but only a rudimentary input of intelligence. Genovese has accumulated a great deal of evidence concerning the unproductiveness of Southern slave labor, which he attributes to lack of incentive and education, rather than to low intelligence.

Thus, throughout the ante-bellum period, the South failed to develop a viable livestock agriculture, partly due to "the brutal and careless treatment that slaves accorded livestock."[25] Crude and heavy farm implements were used, but even these were habitually broken and left in disrepair. Maintenance of equipment, repairs, household industry and skilled labor in general had to be assigned to paid white workmen.[26] "The harsh treatment that slaves gave equipment shocked travelers and other contemporaries, and neglect of tools figured prominently among the reasons given for punishing Negroes," Genovese observed.[27] Even in Virginia, which was in advance of the Deep South in agricultural techniques, the slave plantations discarded the "Yankee hoe," which slaves habitually broke, in favor of the "nigger hoe," which weighed about three times as much.

A basic principle of the slave economy, Karl Marx noted, is "only to employ the rudest and heaviest instruments and such as are difficult to damage owing to their sheer clumsiness." In

[23]Davis, *Slavery,* pp. 42, 45.
[24]Daniel Chu and Elliott Skinner, *A Glorious Age in Africa* (New York, 1965), pp. 32–35.
[25]Genovese, *Economy,* p. 110.
[26]*Ibid.,* pp. 52–53.
[27]*Ibid.,* p. 55.

the slave-states bordering on the Gulf of Mexico, down to the date of the civil war, ploughs constructed on old Chinese models, which turned up the soil like a hog or a mole, instead of making furrows, were alone to be found. Marx then quoted Olmsted:

> So too when I ask why mules are so universally substituted for horses on the farm, the first reason given, and confessedly the most conclusive one, is that horses cannot bear the treatment that they always must get from the negroes; horses are always soon foundered or crippled by them, while mules will bear cudgelling, or lose a meal or two now and then, and not be materially injured, and they do not take cold or get sick, if neglected or overworked. But I do not need to go further than the window of the room in which I am writing, to see at almost any time, treatment of cattle that would ensure the immediate discharge of the driver by almost any farmer owning them in the North.[28]

Thus, a major obstacle to the extension of the slave economy to factories and temperate crops was the lack of responsibility, skill, forethought or intelligence in the black labor force. Unskilled gang labor, closely supervised by white foremen, would have been possible in some of the Western mines—the successful employment of hundreds of thousands of Bantu pick-and-shovel workers in the gold mines of the Rand in South Africa proves this—but it is difficult to conceive of a flourishing wheat agriculture or textile industry based on Negro slave labor. Moreover, in the Southern states, the Negro enjoyed some competitive advantage by his ability to toil in intense heat. In some of the Northern states, he would have been climatically at a disadvantage.[29]

A more fatal obstacle to the expansion of slavery was that the South had already lost its demographic competition with the North. Southern leaders were clearly aware of this fact. Under the Douglas principle of squatter sovereignty, the new territories would inevitably have been settled primarily by newcomers of Northern origin and these men would have established

[28]Marx, *Capital,* I, 219–220, footnote.
[29]P. F. Iampietro, R. F. Goldman, E. R. Buskirk and D. E. Bass, "Response of Negro and white males to cold," *Journal of Applied Physiology,* XIV (1959), 5, 798–803.

territorial governments which excluded slavery. The only way such Southern leaders as Alexander H. Stephens saw of avoiding both demographic defeat and its political consequences (that of making the slave States an increasingly small minority in Congress) was to reopen the African slave trade. That gambit, however, was politically impossible.

Thus, we are driven to the provisional conclusion that the struggle over slavery between Lincoln and Douglas did not save the territories for free settlers, since they would inevitably have been free in any event. What the struggle and its outcome did achieve was to formulate and strongly enunciate an inflexible moral stand. The South considered this a condemnation of its history and its institutions. It reacted to rising Abolitionist zeal and increasingly fervent moral exhortations against slavery by restricting freedom of speech and of the press in Dixie, constricting itself into its own narrow ideological cocoon, giving free rein to the most radical apologists of chattel slavery— those who demanded reopening the African slave trade— and denouncing Northern "interference" with the peculiar institution. The opinions of the nation on the great subject of slavery were becoming polarized and, with this polarization, the extremists in both camps came to the forefront like the froth on an angry sea. The reciprocal interaction of these two bands of extremists, in the forms of invective, agitation, propaganda and moralistic cant, reinforced the intransigence of each, if such reinforcement was necessary. Thus, the avoidable war became the irrepressible conflict.

Yet it would be unfair to conclude that Lincoln deliberately risked disunion and war because of a fanatical attitude. Few Northerners were more understanding of the South, more ready to indemnify Southern slaveowners for their financial loss in the event of emancipation, more willing to enforce the fugitive slave laws, less starry-eyed about the Negro's potential role in American society once freed or more anxious to rid the country of its black and mulatto population.

Lincoln asserted that legislating freedom in the territories was important to white Americans. During the debates with Douglas, the *Clinton Central Transcript* for July 30, 1858 summarized his views as follows: "But for the sake of millions of the free laborers of the north,—for the sake of the poor white man of the South, and for the sake of the eternal prosperity of the Union, he was opposed to slavery extending one inch beyond its present limits."[30]

Almost immediately after Lincoln's inauguration, Charles S. Morehead, a former Governor of Kentucky, came to see him. Morehead argued that the laws of nature would prevent the extension of slavery into the hard country of New Mexico or the cold lands of the Northern territories. Hence, why risk secession and war by insisting on legislation that was unnecessary? Lincoln replied merely that he was committed on the subject.[31] At about the same time, Lincoln wrote his Republican friend, J. T. Hale, who also urged compromise:

"We are told in advance the government shall be broken up unless we surrender to those we have beaten, before we take the offices. In this they are either attempting to play upon us or they are in dead earnest. Either way, if we surrender, it is the end of us and of the government. They will repeat the experiment upon us *ad libitum.*"[32]

This was a persuasive argument, but it ignored a crucial fact of which Lincoln was keenly aware. The South was not a monolithic force for evil, determined to outmaneuver and blackmail the Republican Administration into making concession after concession until the aggrandizement of slavery was assured. It no doubt contained some politicians of this sort, as did the North. Yet influential political leaders of the South were prepared to seize upon any compromise offered by Lincoln, not for purposes of blackmail, but to dissuade their States from leaving the Union.

Polemicists and logicians sometimes become entangled in their own rhetoric. They cease believing in what they know and come to believe only in the logic of what they have asserted.

[30]Basler, *Works,* II, 626–27.
[31]Carl Sandburg, *Abraham Lincoln, The War Years* (New York, 1939), I, 95.
[32]*Ibid.,* p. 28.

CHAPTER THIRTEEN

Lincoln: The Ambivalent Emancipator

See our present condition—the country engaged in war!—our white men cutting one another's throats, none knowing how far it will extend; and then consider what we know to be the truth. But for your race among us there could not be war, although many men engaged on either side do not care for you one way or the other. Nevertheless, I repeat, without the institution of Slavery and the colored race as a basis, the war could not have an existence.

—Abraham Lincoln, *Address on Colonization to a Deputation of Negroes*, August 14, 1862.[1]

As the Civil War gathered momentum, Union generals who favored Abolitionism began to liberate runaway slaves and put them to work for the Army. As early as May 1861, General Benjamin F. Butler, who had been a lawyer in civilian life, began to free slaves as "contraband of war" and within a few months had about a thousand under his military control. When Butler requested instructions from Washington, Secretary of War Simon Cameron approved his employment of the Negroes as a war measure, but left their final disposition an open question.

In August, Congress declared that slaves used by their masters in the service of the Confederacy were to be confiscated. The following year, an even stronger confiscation act was passed which made the slaves of all persons in rebellion

---

[1] *New York Tribune*, August 15, 1862. Basler, *Works*, V, 372.

"forever free" regardless of whether or not they were working for the Confederate armed forces. Lincoln considered vetoing the second of these laws, as he viewed it in the nature of a bill of attainder, but chose to compromise by signing the measure and failing to enforce it.[2]

Some of the more conservative generals refused to accept fugitive slaves as contraband of war, among them General Henry W. Halleck. As late as May 1861, General George B. McClellan, commanding the Department of the Ohio, issued orders to his forces to "suppress all attempts at Negro insurrection."[3] Whether the moderate and circumspect attitude of these two officers on the Negro question influenced their subsequent military careers is an open question, but both were favored by Lincoln. McClellan was promoted to General in Chief of the Union armies in 1861, but was demoted, under radical pressure and because Lincoln believed that he "had the slows," to the command of the Army of the Potomac. Upon McClellan's transfer to this field command, General Halleck was advanced from command of the Department of Missouri to General in Chief.

General John C. Frémont, who had been the unsuccessful Republican candidate for the Presidency in 1856, used his position as commanding general of the Department of the West to proclaim martial law in Missouri on August 30, 1861, decree the confiscation of all rebel property and the freedom of all slaves belonging to rebel masters.

Lincoln promptly repudiated Frémont's proclamation and publicly reversed similar action by General David Hunter, commanding officer of the Department of the South, as "altogether void." His reasons for refusing to allow hotheaded subordinate officers to legislate the future condition of the slaves by military fiat were both those of principle and of expediency. As he explained the matter in a "private & confidential" letter to Orville H. Browning:

> If the General needs them (slaves), he can seize them, and use them; but when the need is past, it is not for him to fix their permanent future condition. That must be settled according to laws made by law-makers, and not by military proclamations.

[2]Current, *Lincoln,* p. 221.
[3]Quarles, *Lincoln,* p. 70.

The proclamation in the point in question is simply 'dictatorship.' It assumes that the general may do *anything* he pleases—confiscate the lands and free the slaves of *loyal* people, as well as of disloyal ones . . . But I cannot assume this reckless position; nor allow others to assume it on my responsibility. You speak of it as being the only means of *saving* the government. On the contrary, it is itself the surrender of the government. Can it be pretended that it is any longer the government of the U.S.—any government of Constitution and laws,—wherein a General, or a President, may make permanent rules of property by proclamation?[4]

So much for the principle of the thing. As for expediency, the Kentucky Legislature, upon learning of Frémont's action, had refused to take any steps to support the War; Kentucky volunteers had laid down their arms and disbanded; there was some danger, Lincoln asserted, that the arms furnished Kentucky to fight the Confederacy would be used against the Union unless this and similar actions by zealot generals were rescinded. The reaction of Kentucky was shared by other Border States, and the attitude of the Border States was the key to victory or defeat in the military struggle.[5]

Having made it abundantly clear that the great issue of emancipation would not be settled by the whims, desires or preconceptions of officers in the field, Lincoln formulated his own plan for the gradual extinction of chattel slavery. It contained five basic principles. The first was that emancipation must be by action of the States and not the Federal Government, since slavery was a "domestic" institution recognized by the Constitution. Second, the slaveowners must be given full and fair compensation for their loss. Third, the Federal Government should assist the States in meeting the financial burden of compensation through grants in aid. Fourth, the process of emancipation need not be precipitate and the States should be permitted to delay the completion of the process of enfranchisement until 1900. Fifth, the slaves, when freed, must be persuaded to leave the country and must be colonized beyond the territorial limits of the United States.[6]

[4]Basler, *Works,* IV, 531–32. Letter dated September 22, 1861.
[5]*Ibid.,* p. 532.
[6]Current, *Lincoln,* pp. 221–22.

The Dream of Negro Colonization

In his First Annual Message to Congress, Lincoln recommended that slaves emancipated by the Southern and Border States and free Negroes, if they so desired, be assisted by Congress in their emigration to "a climate congenial to them." This colonization scheme, Lincoln recognized, "may involve the acquiring of territory, and also the appropriation of money beyond that to be expended in the territorial acquisition." There was no doubt that the United States could constitutionally acquire foreign soil; she had been doing so for the past sixty years.

He thought the expediency of adopting this or some similar colonization scheme amounted to "absolute necessity," without which "the government itself cannot be perpetuated." Lincoln than added that "the war continues" and, in considering means of bringing it to a close, he was concerned that the conflict "shall not degenerate into a violent and remorseless revolutionary struggle."[7] This was an oblique allusion to the possible implications for race war of emancipating Negro masses at a time when the United States was split by fratricidal struggle.

Schemes for colonization gained momentum as slaves were freed in the course of military operations and as the free Negroes of the North became increasingly exposed to the sort of violent antagonism by the white population that was to erupt in the New York draft riots of 1863. As early as the 1850s, a group of Negro leaders had begun to urge emigration to Haiti or Central America. James Redpath, a white newspaperman and radical, who had been born in Great Britain, played a leading role in this venture. After three trips to Haiti in 1859 and 1860 for Horace Greeley's anti-slavery newspaper, *The New York Tribune,* Redpath became an enthusiastic propagandist for Negro colonization of the Black Republic. A new Haitian President, Fabre Geffrard, eagerly espoused Redpath's plan for development of the island's resources through American Negro colonization. In this lush, fertile tropical paradise, Redpath believed, American Negroes would be able to prove their ability to build as flourishing and civilized a society as any other race.

Appointed "General Agent of the Haytian Bureau of Emigra-

[7]Basler, *Works,* V, 48. Speech of December 3, 1861.

tion" and given $20,000 by the Haitian Government, Redpath opened up recruiting offices in Boston, formed a committee of leading Negro citizens, and offered prospective colonists $15 each toward passage expenses, and cheap land on generous credit when they arrived.[8]

Haiti was a land, Redpath wrote, "where the Black and the man of color are undisputed lords ... where neither laws, nor prejudice, nor historical memories press cruelly on persons of African descent; where the people whom America degrades and drives from her are rulers, judges, and generals, ... authors, artists, and legislators."[9]

Although Liberia was one of the few countries which welcomed American Negro colonists, Lincoln decided to concentrate his efforts on Central America and the West Indies. He believed that Liberia was too remote from world sea lanes and had too unhealthy a climate to be a suitable new home for black Americans. The cost of transporting the Negro population across the South Atlantic and resettling them in West Africa would be exhorbitant. Moreover, Negroes would be more willing to try emigration to a country on this side of the Atlantic, from which they could return to the United States without too much difficulty if the experiment failed.[10]

As early as the summer of 1861, Lincoln was investigating a plan to settle American Negroes voluntarily in the Chiriqui province of Panama, then part of the Republic of Colombia. The proposal came from Ambrose W. Thompson, the moving force in a group of promoters and speculators called the Chiriqui Improvement Company. Thompson's proposition was that freed Negroes be sent to the Chiriqui land grant to mine its supposedly rich coal deposits and to settle there. The Federal Government should put up the money and the Navy buy the coal.

In August 1861 Gideon Welles, Secretary of the Navy, wrote Lincoln that he lacked "the time necessary to investigate the subject of the proposed Chiriqui contract" and hence any arrangement concluded should be "by some officer other than

[8]James M. McPherson, *The Negro's Civil War*, (New York, 1965), p. 78.
[9]*Ibid.*
[10]Quarles, *Lincoln*, p. 111.

myself." In November Francis P. Blair, former member of Andrew Jackson's "Kitchen Cabinet" and self-appointed advisor to Presidents, recommended to Lincoln that the U.S. Minister to Venezuela be sent to Chiriqui for an on-the-spot investigation of the plan. Travel orders were cut for Ambrose Thompson, son of the promoter, to take the Minister, Henry T. Blow, to Chiriqui in a naval vessel, but the trip did not materialize. As the year approached its close, Secretary of the Treasury Salmon P. Chase wrote Lincoln that he had "given the Chiriqui business all the consideration I could today; and am much impressed by the prospects it offers." Chase was not ready for a final verdict, but would study the matter further on his return from New York.[11]

Diplomatic recognition of the Negro republics of Liberia and Haiti had been witheld in deference to Southern prejudices, but in December 1861 Lincoln observed that he was "unable to discern" any valid reason for this discriminatory omission. In April of the following year, the Senate authorized diplomatic recognition by a four-to-one majority and Lincoln promptly named an American envoy to Haiti.

When the State Department announced that a Negro could not be received as a diplomatic representative from either country, Redpath told Lincoln that President Geffrard was willing to send a white man to represent his country if this would save the President embarrassment. "You can tell the President of Hayti," Lincoln rejoined, "that I shan't tear my shirt if he sends a nigger here."[12]

In April 1862 the House of Representatives appointed a Select Committee on Emancipation and Colonization to examine the various programs and proposals for Negro emigration and settlement. The District Emancipation Act, passed in the same month, appropriated $100,000 "to be expended under the direction of the President of the United States, to aid in the colonization and settlement of such free persons of African descent now residing in said District, including those liberated by this act, as may desire to emigrate to the Republic of Hayti or Liberia, or such other country beyond the limits of the United

[11]Basler, *Works,* V, 3, footnote 1.
[12]Sandburg, *War Years,* I, 578; Quarles, *Lincoln,* pp. 99–100.

States as the President may determine." Two months later, Congress appropriated another half-million dollars for the emancipation and colonization of the slaves of the nation's capital. Simultaneously, the Select Committee reported that the emancipated Negroes had no future in this country, as they would always be remembered as slaves "by the changeless color of the Ethiope's skin." Once settled in the American tropics, however, they could make a major contribution, since "Our American negroes surpass in skill and intelligence all the other colored of the world."[13]

Now that he had the support of Congress and an initial appropriation of $600,000, Lincoln decided to publicize colonization as effectively as he could. He appointed the Reverend James Mitchell as Commissioner of Emigration in the Department of the Interior and gave Mitchell the responsibility for arranging to have a committee of Negroes meet Lincoln in the White House to discuss the future of their race in America. This meeting, which was the first occasion on which Negroes met an American President to discuss an issue of public policy, took place on August 14, 1862 and was widely publicized by the Administration. At this meeting, Lincoln expressed his views on the Negro more fully and freely than on any other occasion. Hence, we give the most complete and accurate account of Lincoln's words available, that of the *New York Tribune* for August 15, 1862:[14]

Lincoln's Address to a Negro Delegation

This afternoon the President of the United States gave audience to a Committee of colored men at the White House. They were introduced by the Rev. J. Mitchell, Commissioner of Emigration. E. M. Thomas, the Chairman, remarked that they were there by invitation to hear what the Executive had to say to them. Having all been seated, the President, after a few preliminary observations, informed them that a sum of money had been appropriated by Congress, and placed at his disposition for the purpose of aiding the colonization in some country of the people, or a portion of them, of African descent, thereby making it his duty,

[13] *Ibid.,* pp. 109–10.
[14] Basler, *Works,* V, 370–75.

as it had for a long time been his inclination, to favor that cause; and why, he asked, should the people of your race be colonized, and where? Why should they leave this country? This is, perhaps, the first question for proper consideration. You and we are different races. We have between us a broader difference than exists between almost any other two races. Whether it is right or wrong I need not discuss, but this physical difference is a great disadvantage to us both, as I think your race suffers very greatly, many of them by living among us, while ours suffers from your presence. In a word we suffer on each side. If this is admitted, it affords a reason at least why we should be separated. You here are freemen I suppose.

A VOICE: Yes, sir.

The President.—Perhaps you have long been free, or all your lives. Your race are suffering, in my judgment, the greatest wrong inflicted on any people. But even when you cease to be slaves, you are yet far removed from being placed on an equality with the white race. You are cut off from many of the advantages which the other race enjoy. The aspiration of men is to enjoy equality with the best when free, but on this broad continent not a single man of your race is made the equal of a single man of ours. Go where you are treated the best, and the ban is still upon you.

I do not propose to discuss this, but to present it as a fact with which we have to deal. I cannot alter it if I would. It is a fact about which we all think and feel alike, I and you. We look to our condition, owing to the existence of the two races on this continent. I need not recount to you the effects upon white men growing out of the institution of Slavery. I believe in its general evil effects on the white race. See our present condition—the country engaged in war!—our white men cutting one another's throats, none knowing how far it will extend; and then consider what we know to be the truth. But for your race among us there could not be war, although many men engaged on either side do not care for you one way or the other. Nevertheless, I repeat, without the institution of Slavery and the colored race as a basis, the war could not have an existence.

It is better for us both, therefore, to be separated. I know that there are free men among you, who even if they could better their condition are not as much inclined to go out of the country as those, who being slaves could obtain their freedom on this condition. I suppose one of the principal difficulties in the way of colonization is that the free colored man cannot see that his comfort would be advanced by it. You may believe you can live in Washington or elsewhere in the United States the remainder of your life (as easily), perhaps more so than you can in any foreign country, and hence you may come to the conclusion that you have nothing to do with the idea of going to a foreign country. This is (I speak in no unkind sense) an extremely selfish view of the case.

But you ought to do something to help those who are not so fortunate as yourselves. There is an unwillingness on the part of our people harsh as it may be, for you free colored people to remain with us. Now if you could give a start to white people, you would open a wide door for many to be made free. If we deal with those who are not free at the beginning, and whose intellects are clouded by Slavery, we have very poor materials to start with. If intelligent colored men, such as are before me, would move in this matter, much might be accomplished. It is exceedingly important that we have men at the beginning capable of thinking as white men, and not those who have been systematically oppressed.

There is much to encourage you. For the sake of your race you should sacrifice something of your present comfort for the purpose of being as grand in that respect as the white people. It is a cheerful thought throughout life that something can be done to ameliorate the condition of those who have been subject to the hard usage of the world. It is difficult to make a man miserable while he feels he is worthy of himself, and claims kindred to the great God who made him. In the American Revolutionary war sacrifices were made by men engaged in it; but they were cheered by the future. Gen. Washington himself endured greater physical hardships than if he had remained a British subject. Yet he was a happy man, because he was engaged in benefiting his race— something for the children of his neighbors, having none of his own.

The colony of Liberia has been in existence a long time. In a certain sense it is a success. The old President of Liberia, Roberts, has just been with me—the first time I ever saw him. He says they have within the bounds of that colony between 300,000 and 400,000 people, or more than in some of our old States, such as Rhode Island or Delaware, or in some of our newer States, and less than in some of our larger ones. They are not all American colonists, or their descendants. Something less than 12,000 have been sent thither from this country. Many of the original settlers have died, yet, like people elsewhere, their offspring outnumber those deceased.

The question is if the colored people are persuaded to go anywhere, why not there? One reason for an unwillingness to do so is that some of you would rather remain within reach of the country of your nativity. I do not know how much attachment you may have toward our race. It does not strike me that you have the greatest reason to love them. But still you are attached to them at all events.

The place I am thinking about having for a colony is in Central America. It is nearer to us than Liberia—not much more than one-fourth as far as Liberia, and within seven days' run by steamers. Unlike Liberia it is on a great line of travel—it is a highway. The country is a very excellent one for any people, and with great natural resources and advantages, and especially because of the similarity of climate with your native land—thus being suited to your physical condition.

The particular place I have in view is to be a great highway from the Atlantic or Caribbean Sea to the Pacific Ocean, and this particular place has all the advantages for a colony. On both sides there are harbors among the finest in the world. Again, there is evidence of very rich coal mines. A certain amount of coal is valuable in any country, and there may be more than enough for the wants of the country. Why I attach so much importance to coal is, it will afford an opportunity to the inhabitants for immediate employment till they get ready to settle permanently in their homes.

If you take colonists where there is no good landing, there is a bad show; and so where there is nothing to cultivate, and of which to make a farm. But if something is started so you can get your daily bread as soon as you reach there, it is a great advantage. Coal land is the best thing I know of with which to commence an enterprise.

To return, you have been talked to upon this subject, and told that a speculation is intended by gentlemen, who have an interest in the country, including the coal mines. We have been mistaken all our lives if we do not know whites as well as blacks look to their self-interest. Unless among those deficient of intellect everybody you trade with makes something. You meet with these things here as elsewhere.

If such persons have what will be an advantage to them, the question is whether it cannot be made of advantage to you. You are intelligent, and know that success does not as much depend on external help as on self-reliance. Much, therefore, depends on yourselves. As to the coal mines, I think I see the means available for your self-reliance.

I shall, if I get a sufficient number of you engaged, have provisions made that you shall not be wronged. If you will engage in the enterprise I will spend some of the money intrusted to me. I am not sure you will succeed. The Government may lose the money, but we cannot succeed unless we try; but we think, with care, we can succeed.

The political affairs in Central America are not in quite as satisfactory condition as I wish. There are contending factions in that quarter; but it is true all the factions are agreed alike on the subject of colonization, and want it, and are more generous than we are here. To your colored race they have no objection. Besides, I would endeavor to have you made equals, and have the best assurance that you should be the equals of the best.

The practical thing I want to ascertain is whether I can get a number of able-bodied men, with their wives and children, who are willing to go, when I present evidence of encouragement and protection. Could I get a hundred tolerably intelligent men, with their wives and children, to 'cut their own fodder', so to speak? Can I have fifty? If I could find twenty-five able-bodied men, with a mixture of women and children, good things in the family relation, I think I could make a successful commencement.

I want you to let me know whether this can be done or not. This is the practical part of my wish to see you. These are subjects of very great importance, worthy of a month's study, (instead) of a speech delivered in an hour. I ask you then to consider seriously not pertaining to yourselves merely, nor for your race, and ours, for the present time, but as one of the things, if successfully managed, for the good of mankind—not confined to the present generation, but as

"From age to age descends the lay,
"To millions yet to be,
"Till far its echoes roll away,
"Into eternity."

The above is merely given as the substance of the President's remarks.

The Chairman of the delegation briefly replied that 'they would hold a consultation and in a short time give an answer.' The President said: 'Take your full time—no hurry at all.' The delegation then withdrew.

Reactions to the Colonization Plan

Lincoln made his proposal against a background of preponderant white support for Negro colonization and a minority movement of Blacks in favor of settlement elsewhere. In 1854, Negro delegates from eleven States had met in Cleveland for the National Emigration Convention of the Colored People. Under the leadership of such race politicians as Martin R. Delany, the assembly had denounced the "disappointment, discouragement and degradation" which Blacks were forced to endure in the United States and had recommended that

Negroes go to the West Indies or Latin America where they could live as equals and in dignity. It was significant that the Convention should assert that Negroes had little in common with Anglo-Saxons and that they possessed "inherent traits" and "native characteristics" which would enable "the black race" to "instruct the world" in ethics, metaphysics, jurisprudence and the natural sciences.[15]

Among white Americans, all but a handful of those who opposed slavery favored colonization. William H. Seward, the Abolitionist statesman who would serve as Lincoln's Secretary of State, was a member of the American Colonization Society. As late as 1860, Seward deemed the American Negro "a foreign and feeble element, like the Indians, incapable of assimilation . . . a pitiful exotic unwisely and unnecessarily transplanted into our fields, and which it is unprofitable to cultivate at the cost of the desolation of the native vineyard."[16] Harriet Beecher Stowe, whose *Uncle Tom's Cabin* did so much to stir up the fratricidal hate that precipitated the Civil War, had George Harris depart at the close of the novel to *"my country, —my chosen, my glorious Africa!"*[17] If such Abolitionists as Senator (and later Vice President) Henry Wilson were cool toward colonization and recommended that the Negro be granted full citizenship, this attitude was often due to a conviction that the Blacks presented no threat to white supremacy. Thus Wilson explicitly stated his disbelief "in the mental or the intellectual equality of the African race with this proud and domineering white race of ours."[18]

If a minority of Negro leaders considered colonization the only way the American black man could escape from bondage in the South and pariah status in the North, the reaction of the mass of free Negroes was much less than enthusiastic. The peak year for Negro emigration to Haiti was 1860 in which more than 600 Blacks took advantage of President Geffrard's invitation. The *Anglo-African* Magazine described the Negro republic in glowing terms; skilled free Negroes, some of whom had accumulated considerable property, emigrated from the

[15]Litwack, *Slavery,* pp. 258–260.
[16]*Ibid.,* p. 271.
[17]*Ibid.,* p. 255.
[18]*Ibid.,* pp. 271–72.

South, and a regular steamship line soon plied between New Orleans and Port-au-Prince. By the close of 1861, some 1,200 American Negroes had left for Haiti.[19]

Most of those who settled in the new promised land reported that the pledges made them by the Haitian authorities were being flouted, that they lived under miserable conditions and that "they were in danger of becoming slaves to men of their own color."[20] One of those who returned bitterly disillusioned reported in October 1861: "Hayti is not the place for a colored American unless he is a capitalist, and it is utter folly for a poor man to go there and expect to make money, *or even procure as decent a living there as can be easily obtained here.*"[21] As late as 1862, over two hundred California Negroes petitioned Congress to be colonized "in some country in which their color will not be a badge of degradation,"[22] but the adverse reports from the victims of the Haitian colonization scheme were spreading like wildfire through the free Negro urban communities of the East and South and whatever enthusiasm may have previously existed for emigration was rapidly vanishing.

The White supporters of colonization, by contrast, gathered strength and cohesion in the wake of John Brown's raid and in the ominous light of the impending Civil War. An influential group within the Republican Party, including the Blairs and a few Border State Senators, concluded as early as 1858 that an energetic and constructive approach to colonization might not merely solve the race problem in America, but reassure the South. Two years before the Civil War, Representative Francis P. Blair, Jr. urged Congress to acquire territory in Central or South America to which Negroes, "a class of men who are worse than useless to us," might be deported.[23]

Widely publicized though they were, Lincoln's proposals for colonization in Central America to the Negro delegation of August 14, 1862 encountered reactions ranging from indifference to hostility among organized American Negro groups. Frederick Douglass charged the President with furnishing "a

[19]Quarles, *Lincoln*, p. 119.
[20]*Ibid.*, p. 120.
[21]McPherson, *Negro's*, p. 88. Emphasis supplied.
[22]Litwack, *Slavery*, p. 262.
[23]*Ibid.*, p. 272.

weapon to all the ignorant and base" so they could "commit all kinds of violence and outrage upon the colored people" and then added the charge of hypocrisy.[24] Prominent free Negroes attacked Lincoln in the press; meetings of Blacks in Long Island, Philadelphia and elsewhere joined the protest; indignation was even expressed at the idea that free Negroes should mine coal in Central America.[25]

Despite this unfavorable reaction, Lincoln went ahead with his plans. In the summer of 1862, the President appointed Senator Samuel Clarke Pomeroy as United States Colonization Agent to recruit Negro emigrants and arrange their transportation. Pomeroy published an open letter "to the free colored people of the United States" which praised the climate and economic opportunities for Negro settlers in the two-million-acre Thompson Chiriqui concession in Panama. The core of the plan was that the United States would supply Thompson with the settlers he needed to develop the natural resources of his concession and in return Thompson would sell the Navy coal at half prevailing prices.[26] Senator Pomeroy proceeded energetically with his operation and by October 1862 had chartered a ship, bought the needed equipment and recruited some five hundred Negro colonists for the great adventure.

Misfortune, however, continued to hound Lincoln's efforts. Joseph Henry, America's most distinguished physicist, analyzed coal samples from Chiriqui for the Smithsonian Institution and found them worthless. On August 30, a fortnight after Lincoln's White House appeal to the free Negroes, a Cabinet meeting was held to discuss the Panama project. The majority recommended that the plan be given up, but the press gleaned "that the President does not desire to have the matter abandoned."[27]

The death blow to the plan was the unwillingness of Central and South American Republics to accept Negro immigration. A negrophile historian has represented this reluctance as Latin American protest "against any Yankee effort to establish a colony in Central America,"[28] but the root of the objection was,

[24] *Douglass' Monthly,* September 1862, pp. 707–708.
[25] Quarles, *Lincoln,* p. 118.
[26] McPherson, *Negro's,* p. 95.
[27] *Cincinnati Daily Gazette,* August 30, 1862.
[28] McPherson, *Negro's,* p. 96.

not the North American presence, but the race of the proposed colonists. As Lincoln sorrowfully put the matter in his Annual Message to Congress of December 1, 1862:

> Applications have been made to me by many free Americans of African descent to favor their emigration, with a view to such colonization as was contemplated in recent acts of Congress. Other parties, at home and abroad—some from interested motives, others upon patriotic considerations, and still others influenced by philanthropic sentiments—have suggested similar measures; while, on the other hand, several of the Spanish-American republics have protested against the sending of such colonies to their respective territories. Under these circumstances, I have declined to move any such colony to any state, without first obtaining the consent of its government, with an agreement on its part to receive and protect such emigrants in all the rights of freemen, and I have, at the same time, offered to the several states situated within the tropics, or having colonies there, to negotiate with them, subject to the advice and consent of the Senate, to favor the voluntary emigration of persons of that class to their respective territories, upon conditions which shall be equal, just, and humane. *Liberia and Hayti are, as yet, the only countries to which colonists of African descent from here, could go with certainty of being received and adopted as citizens;* and I regret to say such persons, contemplating colonization, do not seem so willing to migrate to those countries, as to some others, nor so willing as I think their interest demands. I believe, however, opinion among them, in this respect, is improving; and that, ere long, there will be an augmented, and considerable migration to both these countries, from the United States.[29]

In the teeth of Latin American governmental opposition, Lincoln reluctantly abandoned the Chiriqui project, one that might conceivably have been economically viable even without commercially valuable coal deposits. The President was now faced with hard obstacles that may have appealed to his sense of irony. Despite the strident Abolitionist propaganda about the miserable economic, social and educational conditions of American Negroes, whether as chattel slaves or as nominally free pariahs, a large majority of these outcasts seemingly preferred life in the United States to life elsewhere. Judging by the reports of returnees from Haiti, the simple reason for this pref-

[29]Basler, *Works*, V, 520–21. Emphasis supplied.

erence was that they lived better in their American land of bondage. The Spanish American republics were unwilling to accept free Negroes as settlers. They were welcome, however, in Liberia and Haiti, the only two states on the surface of the earth where black men ruled. Yet, as Lincoln reluctantly conceded, those American Negroes who were prepared to accept colonization, were less willing to move into states ruled by men of their own color than to the Spanish American republics where Negroes occupied a socially subordinate position. Under these conditions, a less determined man would probably have abandoned the entire colonization solution as chimeric. Lincoln's reaction was to turn his gaze toward Haiti.

Emancipation Proclamation Interlude

According to James C. Welling, editor of the *National Intelligencer,* Lincoln told Edward Stanly, the pro-slavery Southerner he had appointed military governor of the occupied North Carolina coast, that the Emancipation Proclamation "had become a civil necessity to prevent the Radicals from openly embarrassing the government in the conduct of the war."[30]

The preliminary announcement declared that, after January 1, 1863, all slaves in States still in rebellion would be deemed free. The final Proclamation exempted the slaves in the Border States and those in portions of the South occupied by Union forces. Lincoln estimated the measure would free only 200,000 of the nation's four million slaves. Cynics observed that the President was offering freedom to those Negroes beyond his reach and keeping in bondage those subject to his control.[31]

There was no inconsistency between the programs of limited emancipation and colonization. As in Jefferson's thinking, the two measures were inextricably intertwined. Believing the Negro to be unfit for American citizenship and an indigestible element in American society, Lincoln coupled emancipation with colonization or deportation.

Accordingly, the Preliminary Emancipation Proclamation of

[30]Current, *Lincoln,* p. 227.
[31]*Ibid.,* pp. 227–28.

September 22, 1862 added the phrase, "The effort to colonize persons of African descent, with their consent, upon this continent or elsewhere, with the previously obtained consent of the Governments existing there, will be continued."[32] The clause "with their consent" was not in the original Lincoln draft, but was inserted at the insistence of Secretary of State Seward.

In his eloquent Annual Message to Congress of December 1, 1862, Lincoln urged his listeners to act with the consciousness of their great historic responsibility in words which generations of American school children have memorized:

"Fellow-citizens, *we* cannot escape history. We of this Congress and this administration, will be remembered in spite of ourselves. The fiery trial through which we pass, will light us down in honor or dishonor, to the latest generation." What is not always recollected is that these resounding phrases were a preliminary to the advocacy of *deportation* of American-born Negroes to foreign countries willing to accept them. The word *deportation*, which Lincoln used instead of the customary *colonization*, suggests that he was prepared to remove all Negroes from the United States regardless of their wishes.[33]

In this same message, Lincoln offered fair compensation in the form of United States bonds to those States agreeing to emancipate their slaves. Negroes freed "by the chances of the war" were to be "forever free," but their owners would be entitled to the same compensation as slaveowners in States abolishing slavery.

The Île-à-Vaches Fiasco

Lincoln's last effort at Latin American colonization of Negroes was in Île-à-Vaches (Cow Island) off the coast of Haiti. A promoter named Bernard Kock had approached Lincoln as early as October 1862, stating that he had a long-term lease of this island and offering to colonize American Negroes there. He claimed that he could settle up to five thousand in a healthy, snake-free area, providing them with homes, steady employment, churches with New England ministers and schools with

---

[32]Basler, *Works,* V, 434.
[33]This point is made by Current, *Lincoln,* p. 228.

New England teachers.[34] The President delegated the ever-hopeful Pomeroy to investigate Kock and his claims, a mistake because Pomeroy too often reported what Lincoln wanted to hear. Edward Bates, the Attorney General, sized up Kock as an "errant humbug" and "charlatan adventurer."[35] Nevertheless, Lincoln signed an agreement with Kock on December 31, 1862, providing for the settling of 5,000 American Negroes on Cow Island at a cost to the Government of $50 a head.

Bernard Kock raised capital in New York and over four hundred Negroes were shipped to Cow Island, where they immediately began to suffer from bad housing, lack of the promised jobs, the greed and corruption of Haitian officials, and the autocratic manners of Kock. Reports of the fiasco filtered back to Washington and, on April 16, 1863, Lincoln issued a proclamation canceling his contract with Kock on the lawyer-like grounds that the Seal of the United States had not been affixed to the document, adding that he would not affix it for "considerations, by me deemed sufficient."[36] In March 1864, the government-chartered *Marcia C. Day* brought 368 survivors of the colonization ordeal back to the United States. About a hundred Negro settlers had died or been lost in the operation.

The Black Republic of Texas

Despite the collapse of the Cow Island venture, Lincoln persisted with his purpose. At some date early in 1863, the President approached Lucius E. Chittenden, the Register of the Treasury, with a strange proposal. As Chittenden recalled the episode:

> During one of his welcome visits to my office, the President seemed to be buried in thought over some subject of great interest. After long reflection, he abruptly exclaimed that he wanted to ask me a question.
>
> 'Do you know any energetic contractor?' he inquired; 'one who would be willing to take a large contract attended with some risk?'
>
> 'I know New England contractors,' I replied, 'who would not be

[34]Quarles, *Lincoln*, p. 113.
[35]Randall and Current, *Lincoln*, p. 140.
[36]Basler, *Works*, VI, 178–79.

frightened by the magnitude or risk of any contract. The element of prospective profit is the only one that would interest them. If there was a fair prospect of profit, they would not hesitate to contract to suppress the Rebellion in ninety days.'

'There will be profit and reputation in the contract I may propose,' said the President. 'It is to remove the whole colored race of the slave States into Texas. If you have any acquaintaince who would take that contract, I would like to see him.'

'I know a man, who would take that contract and perform it,' I replied. 'I would be willing to put you into communication with him, so that you might form your own opinion about him.'

By the President's direction, I requested John Bradley, a well-known Vermonter to come to Washington. He was at my office the morning after I sent the telegram to him. I declined to give him any hint of the purpose of my invitation, but took him directly to the President. When I presented him I said: 'Here, Mr. President, is the contractor whom I named to you yesterday.'

I left them together. Two hours later Mr. Bradley returned to my office overflowing with admiration for the President and enthusiasm for his proposed work. 'The proposition is,' he said, 'to remove the whole colored race into Texas, there to establish a republic of their own. The subject has political bearings of which I am no judge, and upon which the President has not yet made up his mind. But I have shown him that it is practicable. I will undertake to remove them all within a year.'[37]

The background of this Texas plan remains obscure. The careful reader will have noted that Chittenden reported the President as proposing that Texas be reserved for the Negroes of the slave States, whereas Bradley understood that the program was to apply to the entire colored population of the nation. The Bradley version seems *prima facie* more plausible since rounding up the Negroes in the Confederate States and resettling them in Texas would depend on military operations and be work that could be done more easily by the Army than by a private contractor. There is no indication of whether the free Negroes were to be cajoled into migrating to Texas or herded there against their will. Nor does the record reveal how the project was to be financed or what Constitutional authority the President was prepared to invoke for the ceding of Texas to the Blacks.

[37]Hume, *Abolitionists,* pp. 134–135, quoting L. E. Chittenden, *Recollections of President Lincoln.*

Lincoln the Realist

As Union armies cut deep into the heartland of the Confederacy, hundreds of thousands of slaves won their freedom by attaching themselves to the Northern forces. It became increasingly impractical to remove these Negroes to prospective colonization areas. The pace of emancipation, one dictated by military operations, would have outstripped colonization and deportation to Latin America even if the Haitian and Panamanian schemes had been less unprepossessing.

Lincoln adapted his thinking to the new situation. Recognizing that incorporation of the freedmen into American society in one form or another was inevitable, even though it was a necessity which he deplored, he wavered between conservative and radical expressions of opinion. Thus, in a letter to James S. Wadsworth of January 1864, he began by recognizing that, if he granted "universal amnesty" in return for a "loyal and cheerful submission on the part of the South," he could not "avoid exacting in return universal suffrage, or, at least, suffrage on the basis of intelligence and military service." He would consider it his "religious duty" to serve as "the nation's guardian of these people, who have so heroically vindicated their manhood on the battle-field, where, in assisting to save the life of the Republic, they have demonstrated in blood their right to the ballot ... The restoration of the Rebel States to the Union must rest upon the principle of civil and political equality of both races; and it must be sealed by general amnesty."[38] It is unlikely that Lincoln would have written Wadsworth a merely political letter, one designed to achieve a practical purpose and to mask his true opinions, for he had great respect for the "self-sacrificing patriotism" of this Union general and was deeply moved when Wadsworth was killed in action at the battle of the Wilderness in May 1864.

Two months after his letter to General Wadsworth, Lincoln wrote more circumspectly to Michael Hahn, congratulating him on his election as Governor of Louisiana and adding:

"Now you are about to have a Convention which, among other things, will probably define the elective franchise. I

[38]Basler, *Works*, VII, 101.

barely suggest for your private consideration, whether some of the colored people may not be let in—as, for instance, the very intelligent, and especially those who have fought gallantly in our ranks. They would probably help, in some trying time to come, to keep the jewel of liberty within the family of freedom. But this is only a suggestion, not to the public, but to you alone."[39]

In April 1864, Lincoln wrote Albert G. Hodges of Frankfort, Kentucky, stating that he had always believed slavery to be morally evil, but that, when he was elected President of the United States, he took an oath to support the Constitution and he had lived up to that oath without subterfuge or reservation. He had no right to use his office to advance his private moral judgments. Therefore, he had been prepared to abolish slavery if that were the only way to preserve the Union or to perpetuate slavery if that were the only way. He had moved toward emancipation because military necessity and the needs of the Union required it. Lincoln did not "claim to have controlled events, but confess(ed) plainly that events have controlled me."[40]

As the War moved toward its now visible conclusion, Lincoln opened the White House to Negro visitors as no other American President had. He permitted colored school children in the District of Columbia to celebrate the Fourth of July 1864 on the White House lawns. He invited such prominent Negro leaders as Frederick Douglass to the White House and, on one occasion, when guards tried to hustle him out, intervened and announced to his guests, "Here comes my friend, Douglass." In his discussions with Lincoln, Douglass reminisced, "I was impressed with his entire freedom from popular prejudice against the colored race." On one occasion in 1864, when a Negro delegation requested that the wages of Negro workers for the Government be raised to equal those of Whites, Lincoln summarized the matter: "Well, gentlemen, you wish the pay of 'Cuffie' raised." When a brash member of the delegation objected to the word *Cuffie,* Lincoln replied:

"I stand corrected, young man, but you must know I am by birth a Southerner and in our section that term is applied with-

[39]Basler, *Works,* VII, 243.
[40]*Ibid.,* p. 282.

out any idea of an offensive nature. I will, however, at the earliest possible moment do all in my power to accede to your request." A month later, Lincoln had the War Department equalize the pay of Negro and white laborers.[41]

Lincoln was approached by conciliators who urged that he offer some concession to the South on the issue of slavery as a means of ending the bloodshed. In a letter to Charles D. Robinson, dated August 17, 1864, Lincoln replied that it would be immoral for him to re-enslave men whose freedom he had promised. "As matter of morals, could such treachery by any possibility, escape the curses of Heaven, or of any good man?" Moreover, the mere announcement of such an intent would dry up the recruitment of Negro soldiers and to that extent weaken the Union and strengthen the Confederacy.

"In addition to what I have said, allow me to remind you that no one, having control of the rebel armies, or, in fact, having any influence whatever in the rebellion, has offered, or intimated a willingness to, a restoration of the Union, in any event, or on any condition whatever. Let it be constantly borne in mind that no such offer has been made or intimated. Shall we be weak enough to allow the enemy to distract us with an abstract question which he himself refuses to present as a practical one? . . . If Jefferson Davis wishes, for himself, or for the benefit of his friends at the North, to know what I would do if he were to offer peace and re-union, saying nothing about slavery, let him try me."[42]

On March 4, 1865, one month and ten days before his assassination, Lincoln delivered his Second Inaugural Address. This brief and eloquent document was a far cry from his previous offers to save the Union at the cost of perpetuating slavery and from his repeated statements that Southern slaveowners were, not moral lepers, but the products of circumstance. With Old Testament eloquence, he stated: "It may seem strange that any men should dare to ask a just God's assistance in wringing their bread from the sweat of other men's faces; but let us judge not that we be not judged." Slavery was a moral enormity. He prayed that the War might quickly end. "Yet, if God wills that it continue, until all the wealth piled by the bond-man's two

[41]Randall and Current, *Lincoln,* pp. 317–320.
[42]Basler, *Works,* VII, 500–01.

hundred and fifty years of unrequited toil shall be sunk, and until every drop of blood drawn by the lash, shall be paid by another drawn with the sword, as was said three thousand years ago, so still it must be said, 'the judgments of the Lord, are true and righteous altogether.' "[43] Immediately after this somewhat bloodthirsty reference to Divine vengeance came the immortal sentence which begins with the words, "With malice toward none."

While Lincoln seemed to be in the process of being swept by the tide of events toward a moralistic view of the War and the acceptance of the *post-bellum* Negro as a full-fledged American citizen with the same civic rights as the white man, there were indications of his hard substratum of skeptical realism. At some time in April 1865, the month of his assassination, Lincoln had a conference with Benjamin F. Butler in which he expressed his fear of a race war in the South if the freed slaves who had become Union soldiers went back there. They would "be but little better off with their masters than they were before, and yet they will be free men." As Butler recalled the conversation, Lincoln then said that he feared "a race war" which would be all the more bloody "because we have taught these men how to fight." Remembering the John Brown raid and its Northern financial agents, Lincoln predicted that there would always be Northerners who would support the Southern Negroes in armed struggles against the white people of the South if the former believed the Blacks were being oppressed. As Butler recalled it, Lincoln then reverted to his old solution of colonization of Negro soldiers. Butler made the countersuggestion that they be employed on a canal digging project outside the territorial limits of the United States. Lincoln liked the idea and asked Butler to discuss its diplomatic aspects with Secretary of State Seward, who then told Butler that he knew of the President's anxiety about race war in the South and had heard him express his concern on several occasions.[44]

---

[43] *Ibid.*, VIII, 332–33.

[44] Benjamin F. Butler, *Autobiography and Personal Reminiscences of Major-General Benjamin F. Butler: Butler's Book* (Boston, 1892) pp. 903–07. Quoted by Herman Belz, *Reconstructing the Union* (Ithaca, 1969), p. 282. Although Butler's reputation for veracity is not of the best, Belz, whose volume was awarded the Albert J. Beveridge Memorial prize, accepts the truth of this episode as entirely consistent with Lincoln's thoughts and actions.

Thus, Lincoln achieved his most important purpose, that of saving the Union. He failed to achieve the gradual and compensated emancipation he desired and failed even more signally to remove the Negroes from United States soil and thus prevent them from becoming full-fledged American citizens.

Ironically, the Reluctant Emancipator would go down in history as the Great Emancipator. The advocate of race separation and White supremacy would become the harbinger of a nascent multiracial American democracy which a century after his death would seem to some observers not to have solved, but to have exacerbated, its racial problems.

CHAPTER FOURTEEN

Reconstruction—The Age of Wrath

> The punishment of traitors has been wholly ignored by a treacherous Executive and by a sluggish Congress. . . . To this issue I desire to devote the small remnant of my life. . . .
> —Thaddeus Stevens, speech in the House of Representatives, March 17, 1867.[1]

> I look upon as being opposed to the fundamental principles of this Government and as now laboring to destroy them, Thaddeus Stevens, Charles Sumner, and Wendell Phillips.
> —Andrew Johnson, speech from the White House portico on Washington's Birthday, February 22, 1866.[2]

The small band of determined men who led the Reconstruction Revolution in the aftermath of the Civil War tended to have certain emotional and intellectual characteristics in common which set them apart from the mass of American politicians.

Most had been advocates of other unpopular causes and reforms. Charles Sumner, Thaddeus Stevens and Salmon P. Chase all opposed the death penalty for nonpolitical crimes other than murder. Chase denounced the practice of compelling military prisoners to wear plates marked "thief" and that of confining them by ball and chain. Hannibal Hamlin of Maine, Lincoln's first Vice President, favored the abolition of

[1] *Congressional Globe,* March 19, 1867, p. 204. Quoted in Fawn M. Brodie, *Thaddeus Stevens: Scourge of the South* (New York, 1959), p. 306.
[2] Quoted in Claude G. Bowers, *The Tragic Era: The Revolution after Lincoln* (New York, 1929), p. 104.

flogging in the Navy. Henry Wilson, another radical who would
serve as Vice President, Ben Wade, General Ben Butler and
William H. Seward, Lincoln's Secretary of State, all worked for,
or quietly sympathized with, women's suffrage. They tended to
oppose discrimination against religious and racial minorities,
Ben Wade's championship of the Chinese against persecution
in California being a case in point.[3]

To infer that they were tolerant and reasonable men would
do violence to the evidence. Senator Charles Sumner had a
flirtation with the anti-foreign, anti-Catholic Know Nothing
movement. Henry Wilson was not only one of its principal leaders, but a "notorious Jew-hater."[4] Thaddeus Stevens' virulence
was not directed exclusively at the upper classes of the South.
Blackballed when he sought membership in the Masons, Stevens retaliated by becoming the Pennsylvania leader of the
anti-masonic movement and fanned the flames of intolerance
against Freemasonry for years. "This feeble band of lowly rep-
tiles," he charged, drank wine from human skulls and swore to
keep each other's secrets, "murder and treason not excepted."
Masonry was "a base-born issue of a foreign sire. . . . a pros-
tituted harlot," a secret conclave which "binds the mind in
darkness."[5] Stevens' violent hatred of this movement was
based, not only on personal vanity but on the European tradition that Freemasonry was a secret organization composed of
members of an aristocracy and social elite interested in political power.

There was a somewhat irreligious cast to the Reconstruction
movement. Charles Sumner held "vaguely Unitarian views."[6]
Ben Wade's political career was hobbled by the prevalent belief
that his religion was "nothing to speak of" and his faith in
spiritualism did not reassure his constituents.[7] As for Stevens,
he accepted the Calvinist doctrine that man is inherently evil,
but rejected most of the rest. Concerning ministers, he once

[3]H. L. Trefousse, *Benjamin Franklin Wade* (New York, 1963), pp. 119, 312.
[4]Lawrence H. Fuchs, *The Political Behavior of American Jews* (Glencoe, 1956), p. 33.
[5]Brodie, *Stevens*, p. 41.
[6]David Donald, *Charles Sumner and the Coming of the Civil War* (New York, 1960), p. 18.
[7]Trefousse, *Wade*, pp. 125, 93.

observed, "these reverend parasites do more to make infidels than all the writings of Hume, Voltaire, and Paine."[8]

Many of these new leaders were self-made men who had risen from poverty, resented the upper classes from which they were excluded, and were crude in manners, deficient in education, and uncertain of their own worth. Ben Wade, a poor farmboy who had hired himself out as a cattle drover, was notorious for insolence and vulgarity, a supposed friend of the Negro who always used the term "nigger." Had President Andrew Johnson been found guilty at his impeachment trial, Wade would have succeeded him and James G. Blaine predicted that the impeachment would fail since the Congress "would rather have a President than that scalawag, Ben Wade."[9] As for Henry Wilson, he came from such a poor background that he had been apprenticed to a farmer from the age of ten to twenty-one. He had received practically no formal education. Thaddeus Stevens was the son of an incompetent farmer and part-time shoemaker and wrestler who became an alcoholic, deserted his wife and children, and was killed in the War of 1812. As in the case of Henry Wilson, whatever Stevens achieved he attained by his own efforts.

Thaddeus Stevens, Apostle of Hate

The most able, implacable and mysterious of the Reconstruction radicals was Thaddeus Stevens, the originator of the Fourteenth Amendment, the chief prosecutor of President Andrew Johnson during the latter's impeachment trial, the proponent of indefinite military occupation of the South and the champion of the confiscation of Southern white landed property for distribution among the enfranchised Negroes.

James G. Randall, the distinguished Lincoln biographer, called Stevens "vindictive" and "malignant," an "apostle of proscription and hate" and a "madman." He added the epithet "Caliban," a reference to the fact that Thaddeus Stevens, like his elder brother, had been deformed from birth.[10] George M. Drake, a Southern editor and contemporary of Stevens, called

[8]Speech to the House of Representatives, June 10, 1850. Brodie, *Stevens*, p. 55.
[9]Bowers, *Tragic Era*, p. 159.
[10]Unlike Stevens, the misbegotten monster of *The Tempest* was a loutish clod of sub-human intelligence.

his clubfoot "hell's seal of deformity. . . . fixed in his mother's womb." The popular belief of the time was that congenital deformity was the mark of demonic possession or satanic character.

Richard N. Current, one of the outstanding living Lincoln scholars, believes that Stevens' public career was motivated not by principle but by "frustrated personal ambitions." Appraising his contributions to Reconstruction shortly after his death, The *New York Times* called him "the Evil Genius of the Republican Party" and a "defiant, despotic" leader. As for his intemperate Southern critics, they coined such ingenious epithets for Stevens as "atrabilious sansculotte." He had, and still has, to be sure, a few admirers. These included the incurably sentimental Carl Sandburg; the Negro communist historian W. E. Burghardt Du Bois; Ignatius Donnelly, the Populist politician and author of sadistic, eschatological novels; and Ralph Korngold, a Stevens biographer who also admired Robespierre.[11]

The underlying motivations for the monumental and malignant hatred that served as the mainspring for Thaddeus Stevens' political activities must remain a mystery. Fawn M. Brodie, his most perceptive biographer, had drawn attention to the fact that his political life was clouded by suspicions and scandals, of which the charge that he was Talleyrand's bastard was the least damaging.[12] Stevens' business dealings were sharp to a point approaching fraud; he was probably corruptly implicated in the Credit Mobilier scandal, but escaped detection during his lifetime. More significant in terms of his passionately defensive but ambivalent attitude toward Negroes was the fact that he was publicly accused of having impregnated "a small negro woman, servant of Mr. Hersh," in Gettysburg in 1824 and, when she was within a month of giving birth, of having drowned her and her unborn child. A possible motivation would have been fear that the child would be born with a

[11]Ralph Korngold, *Thaddeus Stevens, a Being Darkly Wise and Rudely Great* (New York, 1955).

[12]Both Talleyrand and Stevens were gamblers, had clubfeet, and had relations with mulatto women. Moreover, Talleyrand did sire distinguished bastards, notably Eugene Delacroix. However, to perpetrate a bad pun, the periods of Talleyrand's sojourn in the United States and Thaddeus Stevens' conception do not tally.

clubfoot, making it virtually impossible for Stevens to deny paternity and blighting his political career. The evidence against Stevens is inconclusive.[13]

Attitudes toward the Negro

"I do not know," Stevens said in Congress in January 1864, "that I shall ever come across men of dark color of the same intelligence as white men. I have seen some that I thought not much inferior to most of us."[14]

This presumptive mental inferiority did not, however, affect the Negro's right to the same legal protection as the white man.

"I am for negro suffrage in every rebel State," Stevens declared. "If it be just, it should not be denied; if it be necessary, it should be adopted; if it be a punishment to traitors, they deserve it."

He conceded that this meant "negro equality" in the sense that "every man, no matter what his race or color; every earthly being who has an immortal soul, has an equal right to justice, honesty, and fair play with every other man; and the law should secure him those rights. . . . This doctrine does not mean that a negro shall sit on the same seat or eat at the same table with a white man. That is a matter of taste which every man must decide for himself."[15]

He opposed the slogan of "a white man's government" on the grounds that it differed from slavery only in degree.

"If equal privileges were granted to all," he added, "I should not expect any but white men to be elected to office for long ages to come. The prejudice engendered by slavery would not soon permit merit to be preferred to color. But it would still be beneficial to the weaker races. In a country where political divisions will always exist, their power, joined with just white men, would greatly modify, if it did not entirely prevent, the injustice of majorities." These remarks were made in Congress in December 1865 and they proved poor prophecy. The Recon-

[13]The view that Stevens was too civilized to commit this sort of brutal murder seems implausible. When in college, one of his pranks involved stealing a cow and killing it with an axe. For the Gettysburg episode, see Brodie, *Stevens,* pp. 35–48.

[14]*Ibid.,* p. 193.

[15]*Congressional Globe,* 39th Congress, 2nd Session, I, 252.

struction legislatures in most Southern States would have large
Negro minorities; in Louisiana the races would be equally divided in the constitutional convention; in South Carolina, there
would be 76 Blacks to only 48 Whites.

Although Thaddeus Stevens insisted that he be buried in a
racially mixed cemetery, he contributed to schemes for Negro
colonization outside the United States during the Civil War.
Recognizing that the Chiriqui project in Panama was
thoroughly unsound, he nevertheless thought that emancipated slaves in the District of Columbia might be persuaded
to emigrate to Haiti.[16]

The dominant note in Stevens' attitude toward the Negro was
that regardless of whether he equaled the white man in intelligence or not he was entitled to the same rights and privileges
at law and under the Constitution. Stevens was the dominant
force behind the Fourteenth Amendment. He fostered Negro
schools under the Freedmen's Bureau. While he personally favored integration and left funds in his will for a racially
desegregated orphan asylum, he voiced no public objection to
educational segregation.

Stevens had a strong personal reason for his ardent championship of the cause of the Negro. During the last twenty years
of his life he lived with his housekeeper Lydia Smith, a light
mulatto, who had been beautiful as a young woman. Toward
the end of his life he shocked Jonathan Blanchard, an Abolitionist preacher who had visited him to persuade him to repent
his sins, by admitting his liaison obliquely. The form of the
confession was to compare his conduct with that of Richard M.
Johnson of Kentucky, who had served as Vice President under
Van Buren. Johnson had lived openly with Julia Chinn, his
mulatto housekeeper, had produced two daughters by her, educated them, attempted to introduce them into society, and married them off to white men. When Julia died, Johnson began an
affair with another slave girl of mixed blood. When she ran
away with an Indian lover, Johnson had her pursued, caught,
and sold South. He then made the runaway's sixteen-year-old
sister his mistress and lived with her openly.

"Johnson's slaveholding sanctioned his vices," Stevens told

[16]Hans L. Trefousse, *The Radical Republicans* (New York, 1969), p. 30.

Blanchard, "so that a family of mulatto children did not prevent his being the idol of the negro-hating democratic party. . . . and Vice President of the United States." By contrast, he, Stevens, with three times Johnson's ability, could not even be elected to the Senate or appointed to a Cabinet post.[17]

The Malignant Revolutionary

If Stevens defended the Negro's right to equal treatment under the law partly for personal reasons, he also considered the Negro a weapon with which he could vent his destructive impulses on the defeated white South. As early as May 2, 1864, he warned the House against generous treatment of the vanquished: "Where does such doctrine lead you? It leads you into subjection to traitors and their Northern allies."[18]

Stevens demanded that treason be made odious. He believed that for years to come the Southern states must be ruled by Congress as "conquered provinces." Afterwards they might be admitted as territories and, as such, "learn the principles of freedom and eat the fruit of foul rebellion." He would admit them into the Union as States if, and only if, there was assurance of "the perpetual ascendancy" of the Republican Party.

Anticipating that some Congressmen might be shocked at his plan to impose a one-party dictatorship on a free country, Stevens continued: "Do you avow the party purpose? exclaims some horror-stricken demagogue. I do. For I believe, on my conscience, that on the continued ascendancy of that party depends the safety of this great nation." Unless the Negro vote in the South were manipulated to deprive the Whites of political power, "you will be the perpetual vassal of the freetrade, irritated, revengeful South." As for the Negroes in the Northern States, they did not constitute a political problem because there were few of them and because such States as Ohio denied them the franchise.

Stevens sought to justify his dictatorial propensities with a bizarre theory of American government: "In this country the whole sovereignty rests with the people. . . . Though the President is Commander-in-Chief, Congress is his commander; and,

[17]Brodie, *Stevens,* pp. 90–91.
[18]Korngold, *Stevens,* p. 238.

God willing, he shall obey. He and his minions shall learn that this is not a Government of kings and satraps, but a Government of the people and that Congress is the people."

As a Constitutional lawyer of some ability Stevens knew that this doctrine was preposterous. He expounded it because he was a revolutionary in an era when Congress was the radical organ of revolutionary change. The legislative bodies in three French and two Russian revolutions have played similar roles. Stevens and his fellow leaders of Radical Reconstruction were prepared to fight for the unlimited aggrandizement of Congress because they were addicted to authoritarian solutions and preferred naked power to the niceties of the law.

In pursuing his objective, the destruction of the social order in the prostrate South, Stevens succeeded in imposing a 3 percent tax on cotton at a time when the South was suffering from the ruinous competition of Indian and Egyptian staples, which had been brought into production during the years of blockade and Civil War. He capped this with a high tariff, designed to aid in the destruction of the agriculture and commerce of the defeated Confederate States.

Stevens proposed unsuccessfully that all estates of rebels and rebel sympathizers worth $5,000 or more be confiscated and divided into forty-acre farms, one for each Negro family. Marxist and pseudo-Marxist historians have hailed this proposal that Southern agriculture be reduced to a subsistence basis as the height of revolutionary statesmanship. Had the plan been adopted, the probable result would have been a prolongation of the dire poverty which the South suffered after Appomattox, the retrogression of agriculture to something approaching the techniques of present-day Haiti, and an accentuation of racial strife in the South. There is little reason to believe that the Negroes would have kept their forty-acres-and-a-mule allotment. It seems probable that Stevens devised this scheme less for the benefit of the freedmen than for further vengeance on the aristocratic society of the white South which he hated and perhaps secretly envied.

Stevens was the only member of Congress who applauded the execution of Emperor Maximilian in Mexico. "To treat an enemy with compassion meant a blunting of his hatred," Fawn M. Brodie wrote. "And for Thaddeus Stevens hatred was an energizing force."[19]

He argued that "the forgiveness of the gospel" should apply to personal relationships only and not to the conduct of governments. "Gentlemen mistake, therefore, when they make these appeals to us in the name of humanity. They, sir, who while preaching this doctrine are hugging and caressing those whose hands are red with the blood of our and their murdered kinsmen, are covering themselves with indelible stains which all the waters of the Nile cannot wash out."

Thaddeus Stevens was a true revolutionary nihilist. The mainsprings of his hatred are, at this distance in time, impenetrable. A psychiatrist might be tempted to speculate on the fact that his known liaisons were not with women of his own class primarily but with those far beneath him. The fact that he chose a mulatto woman for his life companion, rather than a white woman of the upper classes whom he would not have had to camouflage as his housekeeper, and who could have aided his immense political ambitions, has intrigued all of his biographers. To attribute this choice to an overwhelming passion or romantic infatuation would be to display ignorance of Stevens' character. Some will regard Stevens' choice of Lydia Smith as symbolic of his lifelong desire to champion the oppressed. Others will wonder whether it did not denote a lack of self-esteem so overwhelming that he felt incapable of a satisfactory relationship with a woman who was his intellectual equal and social equal or superior.

Stevens' indignation over the wrongs inflicted upon slaves and freedmen served as a moral justification for the release of massive hostility and rancor. The ordinary criminal of the sociopathic sort vents his hatred in action because it pleases him; the political fanatic espouses an ideology, whether religious or political, because he often needs a moral justification for the destructive activity necessary to him. The compulsion to devote one's life to acts of hostility in the political sphere and to justify this nihilist conduct on lofty grounds is probably the hallmark

[19]Brodie, *Stevens*, p. 307.

of every true revolutionary from Savonarola to Luther and from Hitler to Stalin.[20] It is no accident that so many of the leaders of the Reconstruction movement were, in one way or another, psychic cripples, tormented by their own fears and hatreds.

Charles Sumner

Descended from a distinguished New England family, reasonably well-to-do, educated at Harvard, lionized when he traveled in Europe, a man of learning, education and charm, Charles Sumner had little visibly in common with such men as Thaddeus Stevens. In addition to the other gifts which nature and fortune had showered upon him, he was handsome, distinguished, well over six feet tall and endowed with unusual physical strength.

The first discordant note is his relationship with women. He "fell in love" with eligible unmarried women, but nothing ever came of it. The only females he spoke of as entirely suitable were those who were unattainable because they were happily married. In 1842, when he was thirty-one years old, he wrote a friend that his wife would have to be educated, intelligent and probably rich, but that women of that sort inspired in him "a certain awe, and a sense of (their) superiority, which makes me. . . . anxious to subside into my own inferiority."[21]

When he was in his middle fifties this cold, pompous, theatrical and uncertain man married a young widow, who gained from the union great social position and the reflected light of immense power. The relationship was an almost immediate and notorious fiasco, so much so that the young widow started a flagrantly public affair with a Prussian attaché, then deserted Sumner and went to Europe until he divorced her.

Humorless, pedantic, always immaculately dressed and groomed, he "thought of himself as an American Cicero," and delivered speeches with "polished rhetoric, chaste diction" and

[20]The American Revolution of 1776 does not fit into this unattractive pattern. The leaders of that movement were not destructive by internal necessity, but reformers who resisted specific abuses and advocated specific constructive changes.

[21]Donald, Sumner, p. 91.

"rounded periods," which he had previously committed to memory.[22] Henry Adams, who was not on the whole an uncharitable observer, thought him a "pathological study" and that his mind "had reached the calm of water which receives and reflects images without absorbing them; it contained nothing but itself."[23] According to another contemporary, he had no patience with due process of law when it interfered with his objectives and showed an "absolute disregard of constitutional restraints."[24] He loved mankind, but not men; "his sympathies were for races—too lofty to descend to persons."[25]

Sumner on the Negro

On his way through Maryland in 1834, Charles Sumner, then twenty-three years old, first saw slaves. "My worst preconception of their appearance and ignorance did not fall as low as their actual stupidity," he wrote his family. "They appear to be nothing more than moving masses of flesh, unendowed with anything of intelligence above the brutes. I have now an idea of the blight upon that part of the country in which they live."[26]

In 1852, Sumner, then a freshman Senator from Massachusetts, delivered his so-called Freedom National speech, a studied oration, lasting three and three-quarters hours, which rested on the historically untenable argument that, since the Constitution did not explicitly mention slavery, it did not recognize its existence and, therefore, by natural law, all slaves were free. The speech was a rehash of ten years of Abolitionist propaganda and even Wendell Phillips thought it almost devoid of intellectual originality.

In this oration, Sumner declared that just as "a blade of grass would not grow where the horse of Attila had trod," so would "no true prosperity spring up in the foot-prints of the slave." He hoped that eventually the "profane assumption of race" would vanish, but stressed that he did not wish "to change human

[22]Bowers, *Tragic Era,* p. 335.
[23]Henry Adams, *The Education of Henry Adams* (New York, 1906), pp. 251–52.
[24]George F. Hoar, *Autobiography* (New York, 1903), I, 214.
[25]Hugh McCulloch, *Men and Measures* (New York, 1888), p. 234.
[26]Donald, *Sumner,* p. 29.

nature, or to force an individual into relations of life for which
he is not morally, intellectually, and socially adapted." Nor
should one assume "that a race, degraded for long generations
under the iron heel of bondage, can be taught at once all the
political duties of an American citizen." While he assumed that
most Negroes, once liberated, would prefer to remain in the
United States, Sumner was interested in plans "for opening our
neighboring tropical lands to the colonization of people of the
African race." Frederick Douglass complained that Sumner
had failed to recognize "the entire manhood and social equality
of the colored people" in this peroration.[27]

On another occasion, Sumner declared:

"If the African race be inferior, as is alleged, then it is the
unquestionable duty of a Christian Civilization to lift it from its
degradation, not by the bludgeon and the chain. . . . but by a
generous charity."[28]

During the beginnings of secession in December 1860, Sumner seemingly forgot about the outrages, real or imaginary,
inflicted upon the slaves in his delight at the departure of
Southern States from the Union. He foresaw bloody slave insurrection and hoped to watch the Southern slaveowners "rush
upon their destiny." He wrote Samuel Gridley Howe on December 16th:

"The difficulties in the way of the *seceders* are so great that
I fear we shall not get rid of them *long enough.* My desire is
that 4 or 5 should go out *long enough* to be completely humbled
and chastened and to leave us in the control of the Government."[29]

Other Reconstruction Radicals had ambivalent or over-
whelmingly negative attitudes toward the Negro. Charles
Francis Adams, the brother of Henry and Brooks, thought the
Negroes a "terrible inert mass of domesticated barbarism."[30]
Professor Louis Agassiz of Harvard, the leading naturalist in
America and one of the foremost in the world, observed: "While
Egypt and Carthage grew into powerful empires and attained
a high state of civilization; while in Babylon, Syria, and Greece

---

[27] *Ibid.*, pp. 236–37.
[28] *Ibid.*, p. 356.
[29] *Ibid.*, p. 368.
[30] *Atlantic Monthly,* April 1861.

were developed the highest culture of antiquity, the negro race groped in barbarism and *never originated a regular organization among themselves.* "[31]

General Sherman wrote Chief Justice Salmon Chase in May 1865: "To give all loyal negroes the same status as white voters will revive the war. . . . I have never heard a negro ask for that and I think it would be his ruin." At about the same time, General Schofield wrote Grant from the South about the "absolute unfitness of the negroes as a class" and their belief that freedom means "they are to live in idleness and be fed by the Government." Even the iron-handed Governor Oliver P. Morton, who had implacably crushed the copperhead movement in his native Indiana, said that it was "impossible to conceive of instantly admitting this mass of ignorance to the ballot." The 25,000 free Negroes in Indiana were denied the ballot, the right to testify in court, or to send their children to public schools. "With what face," Morton pertinently asked, "can Indiana go to Congress and insist on the right of suffrage to the Negroes of the South?"

Even Ralph Waldo Emerson believed that "the degradation of that black race" had not occurred "without sin." The veteran Abolitionist leader William Lloyd Garrison observed: "Chattels personal may be instantly translated into freemen, but when were they ever taken at the same time to the ballot-box, and invested with all political rights and immunities?" Uncouth old Ben Wade complained to his wife in 1873 about the servant problem: "For mere Nigger power it will cost over $500 a year. I wish that we could get a white woman of the English or Northern European breed. I am sick and tired of Niggers."[32] With his usual candor, Thaddeus Stevens commented privately: "In my county, there are fifteen hundred escaped slaves. If they are a specimen of the negroes of the south, they are not qualified to vote."[33]

As early as 1838, William H. Seward had opposed property qualifications for White voters. As far as Negro aspirants for the franchise were concerned, he was "not prepared to say,

[31]Louis Agassiz to Samuel Gridley Howe, August 1863. Emphasis in the original.

[32]Trefousse, *Wade,* p. 312.

[33]W. W. Holden, *Memoirs of W. W. Holden* (Durham, N.C., 1911), pp. 85, 166.

having in view the actual condition of that race, that no test ought to exist." Twenty-two years later, on the eve of the Civil War, Sumner described the Negro to a political rally as "a foreign and feeble element like the Indians, incapable of assimilation. . . . a pitiful exotic unwisely and unnecessarily transplanted into our fields, and which it is unprofitable to cultivate at the cost of the native vineyard." As for Henry Wilson, he saw no reason to fear granting the Negro education and citizenship since he denied "the mental or the intellectual equality of the African race with this proud and domineering white race of ours."[34]

Discordant Voices—James Pike

James Shepherd Pike, a Maine Republican, was a zealous anti-slavery writer for Horace Greeley's *New York Tribune.* Serving as Minister to the Netherlands during the entire Civil War, Pike returned to Washington to side with the Radical Republicans. Disillusioned, he toured the South and published *The Prostrate South: South Carolina under Negro Government* in 1873, a book that almost instantly became the classic indictment of misrule in the defeated South by coalitions of carpetbaggers, scalawags and Negroes. While the political power which Pike wielded was negligible, his ideas are of interest both because of their originality and because they bare to the light a facet of the Reconstruction mentality which has generally been hidden.

Pike's hatred of the slave-holding aristocracy of the South was largely based on his conviction that it had brought Africans into the American Republic who, because of their "fecundity," could never be "rooted out." As early as 1853, he vehemently opposed Southern plans for the annexation of Cuba because we did not want territory filled "with black, mixed, degraded and ignorant, or inferior races." He wanted to free the Negroes and give them the West Indies so that America could rid itself of their "burden and hindrance." Fearing that the Antilles would not be sufficient, Pike was prepared to throw in American territory on the Gulf of Mexico.

As Chairman of the Resolutions Committee of the Republi-

[34]Litwack, *North,* pp. 87–88, 271–72.

can National Convention of 1857, Pike drafted the resolution on the Negro which was unanimously adopted: "That the natural increase of the white race on this continent demands the widest possible area for its expansion, and thus requires the confinement of the degrading character and influence of African slavery to the narrowest limits."[35]

With slavery eventually extinguished, he asserted, "the ignorant and servile race will not and cannot be emancipated and raised to the enjoyment of equal civil rights with the dominant and intelligent race; they will be driven out." This process might be "cruel and un-christian," but it was necessary.[36]

During the Civil War, Pike supported Lincoln's colonization schemes and sounded out the Dutch Government on its interest in importing Negro laborers from the United States. He worked out indenture arrangements with the Dutch authorities by which free Negroes might be shipped to the insalubrious colony of Surinam on the northern coast of South America.

During the secession crisis, Pike had urged a "peacable separation" and the surrender of "the Gulf States to the Black race, and the Whites who as yet rule that race." In July 1862, Pike elaborated his own scheme for settling the struggle. Colonization of the Negroes in foreign countries would be the best solution, but it was impractical. Therefore, the United States should "carve out a portion of the country, embracing some states East of the Mississippi & South of the Potomac & Ohio, as few as may be, and surrender it to the blacks, and such of the whites as desire to go with them." Early in 1863, he wrote a pessimistic letter to William Pitt Fessenden, the Republican Senator from Maine, which regretted the slow and bloody course of the War and concluded with the statement that he "should have no tears to shed over the making of a negro pen of the rest of the South & withdrawing our jurisdiction over it."[37]

For Radicals such as Pike, who hated the South for having caused or perpetuated the Negro presence in the United States, the *post-bellum* efforts to incorporate the Blacks into Ameri-

[35]Robert Franklin Durden, *James Shepherd Pike*, (Durham, 1957), p. 31.
[36]*Ibid.*, p. 32.
[37]*Ibid.*, pp. 41, 93–95.

can society seemed an unmitigated tragedy. Pike and others veered to a pro-Southern stand, expatiated on the utter incapacity of the Negroes to participate constructively in the legislatures of the South, and supported the new subordinated status imposed upon the Negro in the former Confederate area. It was consistent with their fundamental motivation that they should prefer the presence of the Negro in the South as a segregated half-citizen, possessed of only rudimentary civil rights, to his ubiquitous presence throughout the nation as an equal.

The Reconstruction Revolution

At the end of 1865, four Southern States had been reconstructed under the liberal Lincoln plan by White voters who swore loyalty to the Union. When Congress convened, Thaddeus Stevens and the Republican caucus ordered the clerks of House and Senate to omit the Southern States when reading the roll call. This procedure was sustained by a simple majority vote, the Southern representatives not voting, and the duly elected Southern Congressmen were thus denied their seats.

In the summer of 1866, the powerful Joint Committee on Reconstruction, dominated by Stevens, declared the Southern States dead and mere occupied territory. Congress, not the President, had authority to administer the conquered area. Martial law was extended to violations of civil rights under a bill which Navy Secretary Gideon Welles called "a terrific engine. . . . a governmental monstrosity." Johnson vetoed the measure as unconstitutional.

The Fourteenth Amendment passed both Houses on June 13, 1866. It pronounced Negroes citizens of the United States and provided that no State might "abridge" their "privileges and immunities" or deprive them "of life, liberty or property, without due process of law; nor deny to any person within its jurisdiction the equal protection of the laws." It said nothing about the right to vote.

In the 1866 elections, the Radicals triumphed. The result was three military reconstruction acts in 1867 and a fourth in 1868. These acts divided the South into military districts under generals appointed by the President. Provisional governments could be overruled by the military and civilians could be tried by martial law. Seceded States were allowed to call constitutional conventions and to draw up new basic charters. The voters eligible to select delegates to these conventions were the Negroes and those Whites who were not disfranchised as former rebels or rebel supporters. Congress could then accept or reject the new States as it pleased. President Johnson vetoed this measure as unconstitutional, but an enraged radical Congress overruled his veto.

The culminating Reconstruction measure was the Fifteenth Amendment, providing that "the right of citizens of the United States to vote shall not be denied or abridged . . . on account of race, color, or previous condition of servitude." It was passed by Congress in 1869 and declared ratified by 1870.

The Reconstruction State governments in the South have been depicted as incredibly corrupt and incompetent. Yet they introduced needed reforms, established free public schools for both races, modified excessively severe penal systems, created needed social services, and gave women rights they had not previously possessed.

The tide was ebbing by 1870 and it had run out seven years later. It was somewhat incongruous that these strange and somewhat twisted Reconstruction revolutionaries should have taken such gigantic strides to suppress American democratic institutions in the name of popular sovereignty. They curbed freedom of speech and of the press, substituted martial law for due process, rigged elections, disfranchised the majority of Southern Whites, and almost destroyed the independence of the Executive Branch. When the Supreme Court, under a Republican Chief Justice, limited the scope of martial law, Stevens' reaction was a proposal to strip the Court of its entire appellate jurisdiction.[38] The Radicals could proceed along this course because they had little respect for the Constitution. They were the intellectual heirs of William Lloyd Garrison who had characterized that instrument as "a covenant with death and an agreement with hell."

Few of the Radical leaders had any affection or respect for

[38] *ex parte Milligan,* 4 Wallace 2 (1866).

the Negro. Charles Sumner was sincere in his struggle for equal rights. Thaddeus Stevens combined his identification with the submerged Negroes with his thirst for the destruction of the existing power elite. Others merely used the ideology of equal rights as a means toward centralizing political power and thus establishing the indefinite and untrammeled rule of themselves and of their faction.

CHAPTER FIFTEEN

Decades of Disillusionment, 1870-1900

> Every State that seceded from the Union was a Democratic State. . . . Every man that endeavored to tear the old flag from the heaven it enriches was a Democrat. Every man that tried to destroy the Nation was a Democrat. . . . Every man that shot down Union soldiers was a Democrat. . . . The man that assassinated Abraham Lincoln was a Democrat. . . . Every man that raised bloodhounds to pursue human beings was a Democrat. Every man that clutched from shrinking, shuddering, crouching mothers babes from their breasts and sold them into slavery was a Democrat. . . . Every man that tried to spread smallpox and yellow fever in the North . . . was a Democrat. Soldiers, every scar you have on your heroic bodies was given you by a Democrat. . . . Yes, the question is, 'Shall the solid South, a unified South, unified by assassination and murder, a South solidified by the shotgun—shall the solid South with the aid of a divided North control this great and splendid country?'
> —Robert G. Ingersoll, Speech at Indianapolis, Republican Presidential Campaign of 1876.[1]

From the inauguration of Ulysses S. Grant in 1869 to the assassination of President McKinley in 1901, the political leadership of the nation was weak and mediocre. With few exceptions, the dominant political figures of the day were men of deficient education and character, of commonplace minds and of few original ideas.

During the earlier part of this era at least, the Republican

[1]Quoted in Bowers, *Tragic Era*, p. 492.

leadership included men who combined the profession of lofty moral principles with pecuniary rapacity. Thus, in the Crédit Mobilier railroad scandals, those accused of bribe-taking included James A. Garfield, a future President of the United States; Schuyler Colfax, a former Speaker of the House and, at the moment, Vice President of the United States; Henry Wilson, who would succeed Colfax in the Vice Presidency; James G. Blaine, Speaker of the House and for twenty years the dominant figure in the Republican Party; Congressman John Bingham, who had been one of the managers of the impeachment of President Johnson; Senator Patterson of New Hampshire, and George S. Boutwell, who had played a sinister role in the investigation of the Lincoln assassination and was, at the time he was accused, Secretary of the Treasury.

With the exception of Patterson, who was an unadulterated corruptionist, these men were all leaders of the radical faction. They pursued punitive and relentless policies toward the defeated South, disfranchising the White majority and imposing military rule. Professing deep concern for the Negroes of the South, they enforced the right of the newly enfranchised slaves to vote as a means of perpetuating Republican majorities in both Houses. When the President sought to exercise his normal constitutional powers, they attempted to remove him by impeachment. These men were engaged in transforming the Federal Government from a delicate balance of three coordinate branches into a Congressional dictatorship, armed with overriding powers that dwarfed both the Executive Branch and the States.

James G. Blaine

The most important of these men in terms of power was James G. Blaine. Chauncey M. Depew thought that Blaine's name "will rank with Lincoln's."[2] No other man, wrote one of his biographers, "has had a following so devoted, so blind, so passionate, and so persistent. . . . Before five successive conventions of his party his name came as a candidate for the Presidency. When he could have been elected he was defeated for

[2]David Saville Muzzey, *James G. Blaine, A Political Idol of Other Days* (Port Washington, 1934), p. 492.

the nomination, defeated by machinations and against the will of the majority of his party. When he was nominated he was defeated at the polls by chance and accident. When he could have been both nominated and elected he declined the nomination." Yet in summing up Blaine's achievements, his biographer observed drily: "No other man in our annals has filled so large a space and left it so empty."[3]

Blaine supported President Johnson for the first year of the latter's Administration. He considered it "illiberal and narrow-minded" of the Radicals to attempt to close the doors of West Point to loyal Southern candidates and he rejected Thaddeus Stevens' view that "the entire population of the Southern States are alien enemies."[4] By late 1866, however, he had moved into the more powerful radical camp and demanded full Negro suffrage in the South: "You must protect the loyal man in the South by the gift of free suffrage—the most far-sighted provision against social disorder, the surest guarantee for peace, prosperity and public justice."[5]

He did not share the hates of the radical leaders or their fanaticism. When his biographer, Charles Edward Russell, states that Blaine "stood at Stevens' right hand," he exaggerates and does his subject injustice.[6] Blaine clashed with Thaddeus Stevens on such crucial issues as the indefinite prolongation of military rule in the South, which the latter advocated.[7]

Blaine had been publicly accused of corruption in the Crédit Mobilier affair in 1872. Four years later, with the Republican convention soon to meet and nominate a Presidential candidate, Blaine rose in the House to deliver one of his great orations. The occasion was a bill to remove all civil disabilities imposed on Southerners who had supported the Confederacy. Blaine's amendment was to exclude Jefferson Davis from the provisions of the bill. His reason, he said, was not that Davis had been "the head and front of the Rebellion," since that fact made him no more guilty than others. The objection was that

[3]Charles Edward Russell, *Blaine of Maine, His Life and Times* (New York, 1931), pp. 431–32.
[4]Quoting Blaine, not Stevens.
[5]Muzzey, *Blaine*, p. 53.
[6]Russell, *Blaine*, p. 149.
[7]Bowers, *Tragic Era*, p. 154.

Davis was responsible for the horrors of the Confederate prisoner-of-war camp at Andersonville.

". . . Neither the deeds of the Duke of Alva in the Low Countries, nor the Massacre of St. Bartholemew, nor the thumbscrews and engines of torture in the Spanish Inquisition begin to compare in atrocity with the hideous crime of Andersonville," Blaine told the House. His peroration continued with these clauses:

> "Parched with thirst and mad with hunger; racked with pain or prostrated with the weakness of dissolution; with naked limbs and matted hair; filthy with smoke and mud; soiled with the very excrement from which their weakness would not permit them to escape; eaten by the gnawing worms which their own wounds had engendered; with no bed but the earth; no covering save the cloud or the sky; these men, these heroes, born in the images of God, thus crouching and writhing in their terrible torture and calculated barbarity, stand forth in history as a monument of the surpassing horrors of Andersonville as it shall be seen and read in all future time, realizing in the studied torments of their prison house the ideal of Dante's Inferno and Milton's Hell."[8]

There was little of exaggeration in these charges. The crimes committed against the 35,000 Union prisoners of war at Andersonville were hideous. Moreover, when high officials of the Confederate States Army had exposed conditions there to President Davis and requested the removal of the camp commandant, General Winder, Davis had reacted by promoting Winder to be Commissioner General of all Confederate prisons. Until the end of his life, Blaine insisted that his denunciation of Jefferson Davis had been motivated by a desire for justice and not for the Republican nomination. The reaction of some of his contemporaries was more cynical and Blaine was accused "of raking up again the embers of dead hate" during the centennial year of American independence.[9]

In 1879, Blaine demanded in the Senate that the United States unilaterally abrogate its treaty with China and exclude further Chinese immigration. Since it cost $50 to transport an Ameri-

---

[8] *Congressional Record*, 44th Cong., 1st Sess., p. 325. Russell, *Blaine*, pp. 267–69.

[9] Muzzey, *Blaine*, p. 79.

can from Omaha to San Francisco and only $30 to ship a coolie to California from Shanghai, continued free immigration meant that "our laborers of the Pacific coast" would be "reduced to the servile standards of the coolies." The "white citizenry" was "threatened with a social degradation worse than the South had ever feared under the rule of the Negro. Law and order could be maintained in California only by the intervention of the military arm five years hence if their immigration were allowed to continue." Wherever free and servile labor were placed in competition, the former was dragged down to the level of the latter. "It has been tried against the African slave in the South; it has been tried against the peons in Mexico and Peru; it has been tried against the Chinaman in California. The universal result is the same. The lower strata pull down the upper, the upper never elevate the lower."[10]

Blaine finally got his chance to run for President in 1884. His nomination was the signal for a massive desertion of Mugwumps, including some of the outstanding intellectuals of the country, to the Cleveland banner. Under the leadership of E. L. Godkin, editor of the *Nation,* three columns of letters appeared in the *New York Times,* opposing Blaine because of his dubious financial operations, his opportunism and his Anglophobia. These letters were signed by Carl Schurz, Henry Ward Beecher, Charles F. Adams, Jr., President Charles Eliot of Harvard and most of the Harvard faculty.[11]

As a Presidential candidate, Blaine decided to forget about the plight of the Negro and approach those White Southerners who favored high tariffs and were in the Old Whig tradition. The South, he said, needed "capital and occupation, not controversy." With the rise of Southern industry, manufacturers below the Mason-Dixon line who voted Democratic were using their votes to "destroy their own future."[12]

Blaine tried this new approach in West Virginia, where the development of coal mining and railroads made it seem promising. October elections in that State went against him and

[10] *Congressional Record,* 45th Cong, 3d Sess, pp. 1299, 1303. Muzzey, *Blaine,* p. 153.

[11] Kelley, *Transatlantic Persuasion,* p. 301.

[12] Stanley P. Hirshson, *Farewell to the Bloody Shirt* (Bloomington, 1962), p. 24.

Blaine again flaunted the bloody shirt. A Democratic victory in November, he asserted, "would be as if the dead Stuarts were recalled to the throne of England, as if the Bourbons should be invited to administer the government of the French Republic, as though the Florentine Dukes should be called back and empowered to govern the great Kingdom of Italy."[13]

Unfortunately for Blaine, the Mulligan letters were printed and broadcast during the campaign. These purported to show that, while a Congressman, Blaine had taken bribes to help an Arkansas railroad get a land grant. He lost support among New York Irish voters by failing to rebuke one of his clerical supporters who had branded the Democrats the party of "Rum, Romanism, and Rebellion."

Blaine lost the election by the narrow margin of about 60,000 votes in almost ten million cast. The electoral count was 219 to 182. The loser attributed his defeat to the machinations of the South and the disfranchisement of Negroes below the Mason-Dixon Line. Since the electoral vote was proportionate to population and since Southern Negroes were denied the ballot, he argued, the vote of one former Rebel equaled that of two loyal Union men. The Northern Mugwump press, which included such distinguished organs as the *Nation* and *Harper's Weekly*, commented that, regardless of the logic of Blaine's complaint, the existing electoral structure had saved the country from four years of "this remarkable demagogue" and had prevented him from exercising his "varied powers of mischief" from the White House.[14]

As a pioneer advocate of Pan Americanism and a spokesman for the expansion of American power to Hawaii and Samoa, Blaine has a claim on his country's memory and on its gratitude. Yet, all in all, he was a reflection of the political mediocrity of his age.

Samuel J. Tilden

Of the political figures of the age, Samuel J. Tilden stands isolated from the rest by his immeasurable superiority of intellect and character. "Perhaps no other Democratic leader has

[13] *Ibid.*, p. 126.
[14] *Ibid.*, p. 131.

ever so closely resembled Jefferson in the quality of his philosophy and in his personal tastes," wrote Claude G. Bowers, who judged men and events from the double perspective of historian and leader of the Democratic Party. "In intellect, character, capacity," Bowers added, "Tilden suffered nothing in comparison with any one who has ever held the Presidency."[15]

A frail, precocious boy, Tilden steeped himself in the political philosophy of Thomas Jefferson and the economics of Adam Smith. Before reaching manhood, he benefited from long discussions with Martin Van Buren and Chancellor Kent, who regarded him as a protégé of enormous promise. A Jacksonian and a Democrat, Tilden was repelled by the Calvinist morality and fanaticism of the New England mind as represented by Abolitionism, the religious zeal of the "burned-over district" of New York State, hatred of Catholicism, and at times the militant, God-defying atheism of anti-slavery zealots such as Robert G. Ingersoll.[16]

While he was not of Dutch descent, Tilden lived near Kinderhoek and was exposed to the *patroon* tradition, one which was fundamentally aristocratic, tolerant, opposed to concentration of political power. He trained himself deliberately for the highest public office much as members of the British aristocracy did during his time. A man who disliked crowds, who had few close friends, Tilden was reticent and retiring, a lawyer of the conference table rather than the courtroom, and a political leader who appealed to the mind rather than the emotions. Probably because of poor health he never married. Yet he was vigorous enough to lead the Democratic Party for a quarter of a century and, at the same time, accumulate one of the largest fortunes in America.

Tilden viewed the history of the United States in terms of a continuing struggle between two opposing philosophies, the Hamiltonian and the Jeffersonian. He was unalterably opposed

---

[15]Bowers, *Tragic Era*, p. 488.
[16]The "burned-over district" in western New York experienced religious revivals in the 1830s and 1840s. Believing they were in direct contact with God, that the Second Coming was imminent and that no compromise with sin was possible, the participants in this movement hated slavery and wanted a theocratic government. Most were originally New England Congregationalists who had converted to Presbyterianism. Born in New York State, Ingersoll was the son of a Congregationalist minister.

to the Federalist system, which he regarded as a movement by entrenched wealth to perpetuate its power, oppress the working classes and stifle progress by the establishment of monopolies supported and enforced by government. The Federalist movement was a drive toward centralization of political power, through the legislative rather than the executive branch, in which the diversity of American institutions and the freedom of the individual were stifled.

As a twenty-four-year-old law student, Tilden told an overflow audience of Jacksonian Democrats in New York City that the wealthy were

> an organized class which acts in phalanx and operates through all the ramifications in society; concentrating property in monopolies and perpetuities, and binding it to political power,— it has established an aristocracy more potent, more permanent, and more oppressive than any other which has ever existed. Such at this moment is practically the ruling power in nearly every civilized nation. . . . Monopolies overspread the land, paralyzing individual effort and exhausting the life-blood of the body politic. The burden of the gigantic machinery of State, the Church establishment, the pauper system, and the national debt, crushes the laboring classes, on whom exclusively it is made to fall. . . .
>
> Where the avaricious few have so controlled legislation as to concentrate and perpetuate property in themselves, it is natural they should seek to exclude from political power all who have no 'stake in society,' and that they should regard the plundered masses as hostile to such 'rights of property' and such a 'social order.' . . . But where society is constructed on just principles, such apprehensions are visionary and absurd. . . . The masses never were prone to disorder. All history repels the calumny. Still more absurd is it to suppose them disloyal to our peculiar institutions. Our social system is the only one which has ever secured their rights, and cannot be changed except at their expense. In European society the few hold the State; in ours the many.[17]

As a young man, Tilden was strongly opposed to the extension of slavery. To allow "its blighting presence" in lands taken from Mexico, which had outlawed human bondage, "would be the greatest opprobrium of our age" and would "cover

[17]John Bigelow (ed.), *The Writings and Speeches of Samuel J. Tilden* (New York, 1885), I, 82, 86.

with shame" those who believe in free institutions.[18]
These views were not predicated on any admiration for the
Negro, but were based on principle and the desire to reserve the
West for white labor. Tilden detested Abolitionists and fought
to deny the vote to the free Negroes of New York State.[19] In this
as in other matters, his approach was unemotional. Thus, he
strongly approved the purposes of the American Social Science
Association, founded in 1865, and told its members that he believed "the complex phenomena of society, its grand tides of
movement, its successions of changes, growth and decay of
populations, mortality, pauperism, crime" could be "analyzed,
studied, and reduced to formulas."[20]

On October 30, 1860 Tilden wrote a remarkable letter to William Kent. This communication, which runs to about forty
printed pages, was designed to prevent Abraham Lincoln's election and was published in the *New York Evening Post.* Our
forefathers, he wrote, having been driven to revolution by the
centralizing tendencies of George III, "said to be 'the most honest man in his own dominions,' " decided to establish a government on very different principles.

> They foresaw that a single government, exercising all the pow-
> ers of society over the people destined to occupy so vast a region
> as the United States, and embracing the elements of such diversi-
> ties of interest, industry, opinion, habits, and manners, would be
> intolerable to bear and impossible to continue. They therefore
> largely adopted the federative idea in the mixed system which
> they established; and vesting only the powers appertaining to our
> foreign relations and to certain specified common objects of a
> domestic nature in a federative agency, *they left the great re-
> siduary mass of governmental functions to the several States.*[21]

Tilden continued with the point that sectionalism had always
been involved in American party politics, but had been kept
within manageable limits. The controversy over slavery involved "relations which constitute a whole system of industry"

---

[18]Alexander Clarence Flick, *Samuel Jones Tilden, A Study in Political
Sagacity* (Port Washington, 1939), p. 85.
[19]Kelley, *Transatlantic Persuasion,* p. 269.
[20]*Ibid.,* p. 275.
[21]Bigelow, *Writings,* I, 290–91. Emphasis supplied.

for fifteen States, which determine their economic pattern and exports, involve three billion dollars of property and four million Negroes. The existence of "a social order" is at stake. When this Southern social order is threatened, the dominant race in the South feels "a pervading sense of danger to the life of every human being and the honor of every woman."[22]

It would be strange, Tilden thought, "if this immense and powerful popular machinery (of extremist propaganda), swaying the State governments of both sections, which has been employed for five years in dividing the country geographically, had not cloven down between the masses of the people in the two sections a chasm deeper and wider and more difficult to close up than ever existed before."[23]

The two sides were at the brink of secession and war. Tilden stated, "The immense presumption that the Southern people understand the effects upon themselves of the Republican organization and policy better than the Republicans do; that, at all events, the nearly unanimous judgment of fifteen great communities ought to be respected; and that their judgment as to the establishment over them of any affirmative measures exclusively affecting themselves ought to be conclusive."[24]

Tilden then turned to Seward's doctrine of the "higher law," that since slavery was immoral it should be combated by any means permitted under the Constitution. This arid, aprioristic approach to politics went completely against Tilden's grain. He replied that the Founding Fathers had been right and wise in their decision to leave the issue of slavery to the States. "If the wisdom collected from the experience of the world in regard to government is to be relied on, the distribution of powers they adopted was the best; the depository of the trust of working out the problem of the superior and subject races within the States, if not perfect, was the safest which the nature of the case admitted."[25]

Tilden then turned to Abraham Lincoln's solution of confining slavery to the area in which it was then lawful and not permitting its extension to the territories. This was, of course,

[22] *Ibid.*, pp. 292–93.
[23] *Ibid.*, p. 297.
[24] *Ibid.*, p. 298.
[25] *Ibid.*, p. 306.

the view that Tilden had himself adopted twenty years previously, but his opinion had changed.

In the first place, there was no danger to the North from any further extension of slavery because, through "geographical causes," Southern emigration was turned "to the southwest," operating to deflect "the element of slavery and to carry that to the southwest."[26] Actually, with the expansion and prosperity of cotton agriculture, slaves were being moved from such places as St. Louis, which were unsuitable for their employment, to the Cotton Belt.

Tilden believed that the Lincoln policy would, in the long run, have certain predictable and dire results. Lacking new fertile lands and faced with diminishing soil fertility and a continuing natural increase of the Negro population, "Will not the master be forced, by the necessity of self-preservation upon a struggle to over-work and under-feed the slave, until, failing to make the products of labor meet the cost of subsisting the laborer, he succumbs, and the social and industrial systems topple in common ruin? Has not philanthropy run mad when it proposes to work out the liberation of the slave by. . . . starv(ing) him into freedom?"[27]

As this process accelerated, the ruined planters would move to free States and free territories, leaving their slaves behind because they would not be allowed to bring them with them. The ultimate effect would be to "convert our sister States into negro governments." Americans would then have to ask themselves this question:

"Would it not, on the whole, be better to let the black man go to the tropics as best he may, bond or free, so that, if at last we come to dissolve our Union, the dissolution may be only with the black republics of the tropics, and we may at least retain the original thirteen that fought the battle of our independence, and the riparian States that control the navigation of the Mississippi, with white men for the governing power?"[28]

After Lincoln's election, Tilden used his influence to try to dissuade the new Chief Executive from war. He thought that

26 *Ibid.*, p. 309.
27 *Ibid.*, pp. 312–13.
28 *Ibid.*, p. 313.

Lincoln, "a frank, genial, warm-hearted man," was bound to take "conservative views," once he understood that "the cotton States are far more unanimous for secession than our fathers were when they made our Revolution."[29] He also attempted to influence Jefferson Davis to moderation through intermediaries. When War broke out, Tilden sided with the Union.

On March 11, 1868 Tilden gave a major speech before the Democratic State Convention at Albany in which he arraigned the radicals for their vengeful reconstruction policy toward the South. Here, as in his letter to William Kent, the underlying theme was the continuing conflict between Jeffersonian democracy and Hamiltonian autocracy.

He said he would not inquire into the causes of the Civil War. "When at last we brought the contest to a successful issue, and especially when the voluntary extinction of slavery declared— what moral and material causes had already made certain— that our Northern systems of society and industry are to prevail in every part of this continent which shall be occupied by us, I hoped that we might speedily restore the peoples of the revolted States to their true relations to the Union; and then that we might at once begin to deal with the administrative questions which the war had cast upon us."

The most urgent of these questions was centralization:

> The reaction against the heresy of secession, the public necessities during a great war, the lead throughout all that struggle of a party always imbued with false ideas of government and with obsolete notions of political economy, and always dominated over by class interests, had created for the time an overwhelming tendency to centralism. All our administrative systems had become buried under a fungus-growth which was smothering all trade and sucking out the vitality of all the industries of the country.[30]

Faced with this situation,

> A magnanimous policy would not only have completed the pacification of the country, but would have effected a reconciliation between the Republican party and the white race in the South.

[29]Flick, *Tilden*, pp. 128–29.
[30]Bigelow, *Writings*, I, 396–97.

Every circumstance favored such a result. The Republican party possessed all the powers of the government, and held sway over every motive of gratitude, fear, or interest. The Southern people had become thoroughly weary of the contest; more than half of them had been originally opposed to entering into it, and had done so only when nothing was left to them but to choose on which side they would fight. . . . The mass yearned to come back to what was left of their birthright. On the surrender of General Lee every hostile sword fell, and the abolition of slavery was yielded with universal alacrity.

All that was necessary to heal the bleeding wounds of the country and to allow its languishing industries to revive, was that the Republican party—which boasts its great moral ideas and its philanthropy—should rise to the moral elevation of an ordinary pugilist, and cease to strike its adversary after he was down.[31]

The Republican Party, however,

could not change its own nature. . . . Even a large demagogue might have been a national benefaction. But two hundred small demagogues—not one of them able to extend his vision beyond the horizon of one Congressional district, nor having much moral sway over the opinion of his constituency—found it easier and safer to stimulate the hatreds left by the war, and the provincial passions which led to the war, than to act with the wise moderation of a comprehensive statesman, or even the prudent liberality of a conqueror.[32]

Thus, "The Republican party resolved to establish negro supremacy in the ten States in order to gain for itself the representation of those States in Congress. . . ." The prize was twenty Senators and fifty Representatives. But to subordinate four and a half million Southern Whites to three million Southern Negroes meant "to obliterate every vestige of local authority" and that "a bayonet had to be set up to supervise and control every local organization. The military dictatorship had to be extended to the remotest ramifications of human society."[33]

Tilden then characterized the new ruling class of the South in these words:

[31] *Ibid.*, pp. 397–98.
[32] *Ibid.*, pp. 397–99.
[33] *Ibid.*, p. 400.

These three millions of negroes—three fourths of the adult population of whom are field-hands who have been worked in gangs on the plantations, and are immeasurably inferior to the free blacks whom we know in the North, who have never even had the education which might be acquired in the support of themselves or in the conduct of any business, and who, of all their race, have made the least advance from the original barbarism of their ancestors—have been organized in compact masses to form the ruling power in these ten States. They have been dissociated from their natural relations to the intelligence, humanity, virtue, and piety of the white race, set up in complete antagonism to the whole white race, for the purpose of being put over the white race. . . .[34]

The main agency of this revolution was "the Freedman's Bureau," which was "partly an eleemosynary establishment which dispenses alms to the liberated slaves and assumes to be their friend and protector. It is to a large extent a job for its dependents and their speculative associates. But in its principal character it is a political machine to organize and manage the three millions of negroes."[35]

Reconstruction rule, Tilden pointed out, had destroyed that local democracy in the South which is the cornerstone of free institutions. It had fettered free trade and free enterprise in favor of mercantilist monopolies of a stultefying sort. It flouted Jefferson's belief that "The concentration of legislative, executive, and judicial powers in the same hands is precisely the definition of despotic government." Tilden again quoted Jefferson as asserting, "An elective despotism was not the government we fought for."

Tilden hoped that "the renovation of the South" might occur through continuing natural increase of the White population and the combination of low Negro birth rates and Black emigration to the tropics. "The admission of the inferior races into our political system" he thought, "is simply a question of quantity." As a separate people, Negroes could never "maintain such a government as ours." The experiment of free governments based on racially mixed peoples had failed throughout Latin America.[36]

[34]*Ibid.*, p. 401.
[35]*Ibid.*, pp. 401–02.
[36]*Ibid.*, pp. 414–15.

Tilden thought there was gross inconsistency in demanding five years' residence before an immigrant "from the most highly civilized nations of Europe, belonging to a race perfected by many centuries of culture" can attain citizenship and the right to vote, while giving the franchise instantly to "the descendant of a barbarian from Africa."

Place of birth was irrelevant. "A man born in the land of our ancestors may become, in every essential characteristic, a native here almost immediately. A man descended from an African may be, after the lapse of centuries, still an alien."

The Negro could only develop in cooperation with, and under the tutelage of, the white men of the South. Whether this element could be absorbed into the stream of American society was essentially a question of "how much of so evil a dilution can we afford."[37]

Races, Tilden believed, "have a growth and culture as well as individuals. What a race has been many centuries in accumulating, is often appropriated and developed in an individual life, in the ascent from the humblest origin to the highest attainments of the species. Our accessions are drawn from races which have lived under essentially the same climatic influences with ourselves, which have attained the highest civilization and made the largest progress in the arts and industries of mankind. They are attracted here by their aspirations for civil liberty or for the improvement of their personal condition; and every aspiration ennobles."[38] By contrast, the Africans were brought to America against their will and without any urge on their part for a more advanced society.

Tilden seldom returned to these themes. His custom was to think long and carefully on a large subject and then express his ideas on the matter fully in a single document. Having done so, he seldom repeated himself.

In 1876, Tilden ran for President of the United States against the Republican standard bearer, Rutherford B. Hayes, an honest nonentity. Tilden had a plurality of 250,000 votes out of a total of slightly over eight million. Fraud was charged in four States, three of them Southern. If all these States were swung to the Republican column, Hayes would have a majority of one

37 *Ibid.*, p. 415.
38 *Ibid.*, pp. 412–13.

vote in the Electoral College and be given the Presidency. Congress set up an electoral commission which sent its agents to the disputed States. Men such as James A. Garfield, the politician tinged by the Crédit Mobilier scandals who would himself occupy the Presidency, went to the South and cajoled Republican victories out of thin air.

On the basis of his pledge to restore self-government in the South and abandon the old radical policies of vengeance and military rule, Rutherford B. Hayes was certified the winner. Three other factors contributed to this somewhat dishonorable triumph. The Republicans dangled the prospect of government support for a transcontinental railroad that would pass through Texas before Southern eyes, a scheme which Tilden would have opposed as contrary to his *laissez-faire* beliefs. Behind the scenes stood the massive presence of the U.S. Army, which would in all probability move wherever ordered by the President, General Ulysses S. Grant. Finally, Tilden was tired and in failing health. Thus, Hayes earned the unique distinction of having become President of the United States by fraud.

Dominican Interlude and Godkin

In his last message to Congress, delivered December 5, 1876, President Grant defended one of his pet projects, the purchase and annexation of Santo Domingo[39] in these terms:

> The emancipated race of the South would have found there a congenial home where their civil rights would not be disputed, and where their labor would be much sought after. The poorest among them could have found the means to go. Thus, in cases of great oppression and cruelty, such as has been practiced upon them in many places within the last eleven years, whole communities would have found refuge in Santo Domingo. I do not suppose the whole race would have gone, nor is it desirable that they shall go. Their labor is desirable—indispensable, almost—where they now are, but the possession of this territory would have left the negro master of the situation by enabling him to demand his rights at home on pain of seeking them elsewhere.[40]

[39]The Dominican Republic.
[40]Hirshson, *Bloody Shirt,* p. 64.

Grant's annexation plan was by no means universally popular. Carl Schurz, the German veteran of the liberal revolutions of 1848, who had started his American political career as an Abolitionist and a radical, was dismayed. The United States could not afford to acquire a tropical empire. In refusing to admit the territories thus acquired to citizenship, we would be false to our democratic heritage; in doing so, we would destroy the homogeneity and viability of the Republic. There was no single instance in history of a tropical people maintaining itself as a self-governing society. These peoples had "neither language, nor habits, nor opinions or ways of thinking; nay, not even a code of morals" in common with Americans. They "cannot even be reached by our teachings, for they will not understand or appreciate them."

In the specific case of Santo Domingo, "Fancy ten or twelve tropical States added to the Southern States we already possess; fancy the Senators and Representatives of ten or twelve millions of tropical people, people of the Latin race mixed with Indian and African blood; . . . fancy them sitting in the Halls of Congress, throwing the weight of their intelligence, their morality, their political notions and habits, their prejudices and passions, into the scale of the destinies of this Republic. . . ."[41]

Holding these views concerning race, Schurz would oppose all American territorial expansion in the Caribbean or the Pacific for the rest of his life. Becoming progressively disillusioned with the progress of the emancipated slaves, he doubted the capacity of the American Negro for self-government and concluded that the South must be ruled by its white citizens.

Another opponent of the Dominican adventure was E. L. Godkin, who had come to the United States in 1850, founded the *Nation* in 1865 and become "the voice of the Mugwumps, exerting an extraordinary influence on the opinions of the educated, professional and reforming classes."[42] In William James' opinion, "Godkin's was certainly the towering influence in all thought concerning public affairs, and indirectly his influence

---

[41]Robert L. Beisner, *Twelve Against Empire, The Anti-Imperialists, 1898–1900* (New York, 1968), pp. 23–24.
[42]Kelley, *Transatlantic Persuasion*, p. 299.

has certainly been more pervasive than that of any other writer of the generation." By origin an Irish Protestant, Godkin was, in Theodore Roosevelt's judgment, "a malignant and dishonest liar," afflicted with "a species of moral myopia, complicated with intellectual strabismus."[43]

Godkin was violently opposed to the annexation of Santo Domingo because it would admit "200,000 ignorant Catholic Spanish negroes" and be followed by the acquisition of Haiti, which would be even worse. We would be told, he wrote in 1868, that "art, science, and literature will be the better for it; the prairie breezes sigh for it; the lonely loon of the Northern lakes cries for it. In the name of our common humanity, then open the door to this dusky daughter of the sun-kissed seas, and let her take her seat in her golden robes among her frost-crowned sisters of the continent."[44]

Godkin opposed all territorial aggrandizement in Latin America. He referred to Mexicans as "greasers" and feared Cuban acquisition because it would incorporate people no more capable of understanding "our religion, manners, political traditions and habits of thought" than "the king of Dahomey."[45] He deplored the acquisition of Hawaii because, in his opinion, it meant the incorporation of "alien, inferior, and mongrel races to our nationality."[46]

These racial views he naturally extended to the Southern Negro. Opposing Henry Cabot Lodge's 1890 "force bill," which was designed to ensure the Negro franchise guaranteed by the Fifteenth Amendment through Federal investigatory machinery, Godkin asked: "What would be the effect on southern society of *not* suppressing the Negro vote?" The "ignorance with which the South has to contend surpasses the ignorance with which any other popular government has had to contend."[47] His practical proposal was that Congress establish a national literacy test as a prerequisite to the franchise. This should be applied forthwith to all new immigrants and all Negroes; then to all new voters; finally, after a year's grace, so

[43]Beisner, *Twelve*, p. 56.
[44]*Ibid.*, p. 72.
[45]*Ibid.*, p. 73.
[46]*Ibid.*, p. 76.
[47]Hirshson, *Bloody Shirt*, p. 216.

foreigners could learn the language, to everybody.[48]

A new colonization plan was to settle Southern Negroes in the Northern States, a venture in which the egregious Garfield was prominent. Frederick L. Douglass, the pre-eminent Negro political and intellectual leader of the day, opposed the scheme primarily because it was "an untimely concession to the idea that white people and colored people cannot live together in peace and prosperity unless the whites are a majority and control the legislation and hold the offices of the States." He also thought that the plan would be attacked "on the ground that these people, so ignorant and helpless, have been imported for the purpose of making the North solid by outvoting intelligent white Northern citizens."[49]

Meanwhile, Northern political and intellectual leaders were tiring of the incessant "bloody shirt" denunciations of the South, were wearying of the Negro's plight, and were voicing increasing skepticism about the Negro's innate capacity. Even Horace Greeley would write privately in 1868 about "the colored rabble of the South." Lord Bryce would characterize the American Negro as "affectionate, docile, pliable, submissive," as showing the "childishness" and "lack of selfcontrol" of "primitive peoples," as fluent in language, but without "capacity for abstract thinking, for scientific inquiry, or for any kind of invention." He was also devoid of "foresight. . . . heedless and unthrifty, easily elated and depressed, with little tenacity or purpose, and but a feeble will to better his condition."[50]

Even Charles Sumner attacked Blaine for continuing to wave the bloody shirt and Horace Greeley asked: "Fellow citizens, are we never to be done with this? . . . You cannot afford to teach a part of your country to hate you, to feel that your success, your greatness is identical with their humiliation. . . . The war is ended, let us again be fellow countrymen, and forget that we have been enemies."[51]

---

[48]John G. Sproat, *"The Best Men": Liberal Reformers in the Gilded Age* (New York, 1968), p. 253.

[49]Hirshson, *Bloody Shirt,* p. 72.

[50]James Bryce, *The American Commonwealth* (New York, 1910), II, 517–18, 546–47, 552–55.

[51]September 19, 1872. Paul H. Buck, *The Road to Reunion: 1865–1900* (Boston, 1937), pp. 92–93.

Little Men

The Compromise of 1877 re-established White rule in the South. For the next half-century, the Negro question would cease to agitate Congress to any large extent. The future of the Negro would be determined mainly by the States in which he lived and, if he lived in the South, he would remain subordinate to the White majority. The rights guaranteed him by the Fourteenth and Fifteenth Amendments would there exist as much in the breach as in the observance. His progress would be largely determined by such slow, nonpolitical processes as education, internal migration northward, the growth of an industrial demand for his labor and the slow revival of the prostrate agriculture of the South.[52]

For this reason, the Presidents of the period from 1876 to 1900 had little of consequence to say concerning the Negro. Their lack of intellectual stature and, in some instances of character as well, contributed to make their utterances less than memorable.

Informed that he had lost the 1876 election, Rutherford B. Hayes declared: "I don't care for myself; and the party, yes, and the country, too, can stand it, but I do care for the poor colored men of the South. . . . the colored man's fate will be worse than when he was in slavery, with a humane master to look after his interests. That is the only reason I regret the news as it is."[53] This pious declaration did not prevent Hayes from making a deal with the white South by which he abandoned all attempts to assert the Negro right to the franchise or to civic equality. His attitude toward the Negro and the South was almost totally opportunistic. Thus, late in the 1876 campaign, he wrote Blaine:

"Our strong ground is the dread of a solid South, *rebel rule,* etc., etc. I hope you will make these topics prominent in your speeches. *It leads people away from 'hard times,' which is our deadliest foe."*[54]

[52]The disruption of the *pre-bellum* plantations with their comparatively advanced farming methods and their displacement by subsistence tenant farms had led to a steady decline in agricultural productivity. (Buck, *Road,* p. 146.) Had Thaddeus Stevens had his way and put through his 40-acres-and-a-mule plan, the wreckage would have been catastrophic.

[53]Hirshson, *Bloody Shirt,* pp. 24–25.

[54]Matthew Josephson, *The Politicos* (New York, 1938), pp. 223–24. (Emphasis supplied by Josephson.)

Hayes was succeeded by James Garfield, a former college president who believed that education was the key to the advancement of the Negro in the South and to his acquiring the capacity to assert those political rights guaranteed him by the Constitution. When Garfield was assassinated, he was succeeded by Chester A. Arthur, a New York machine politician, who had little to say about the Negro problem other than that colored applicants "pestered" him for government jobs.

Blaine's defeat in 1884 ended a quarter of a century of unbroken Republican rule and brought Grover Cleveland into the White House. Some Negroes feared that they would be re-enslaved,[55] but the only major change was to bring former Confederate leaders into the Cabinet and to strengthen the influence of the South. Cleveland's two Presidential terms were separated by a four-year interregnum during which Benjamin Harrison, a Republican, was President. Harrison appealed for cooperation between Negroes and Whites in the South. He pledged himself not to appoint ignorant Negroes or Whites to office merely because they were Republicans, but to prefer capable Southern Democrats, who favored high tariffs.[56]

During the Harrison Administration, Republican control of both Houses of Congress made it seem expedient to introduce legislation to enforce the Negro's Constitutional right to vote in those Southern States where it was denied. Henry Cabot Lodge introduced the so-called "force bill" in 1890, providing for Federal inspection of Negro disfranchisement. "If, as I have heard it stated in this chamber," Senator Lodge observed,

"Southern elections are perfectly fair, and the black man goes carolling to the voting place by the side of his employer, seeking to cast his vote for those whose interests are identical with his own, then sir, it is the duty of the United States Government to uncover this pleasing picture and display it to the country so that confidence may be restored, and no man suspect that Southern elections are open to criticism."[57]

[55]Allan Nevins, *Grover Cleveland, A Study in Courage* (New York, 1962), p. 188.
[56]Hirshson, *Bloody Shirt*, p. 165.
[57]*Ibid.*, pp. 212–13.

Lodge's bill was subjected to filibuster, then buried because of a political deal on silver coinage. It was defeated fundamentally because the public was tired of pro-Negro agitation and wanted a return to normal relations between North and South. The intellectual leaders of the day had deserted the radicals and egalitarians. As Hirshson put the matter:

> "The Mugwumps also played a major role in the story. They reasoned that the Negro was inferior and uneducated; that his ignorance made him an easy prey for voracious and unscrupulous machine politicians; that Reconstruction had proven the folly of colored rule; and that measures like the Force bill would unduly increase the authority of the central government at the expense of local and state authorities."[58]

Booker T. Washington

Like the two other principal political leaders of the American Negro people, Booker T. Washington was of mixed blood, his mother having been a slave and his father an unknown White man.[59] At the age of twenty-five, he founded and became the first president of Tuskegee Institute in Alabama, which was designed to train Negro teachers and which emphasized construction work, agriculture and industrial training. Fourteen years later, Washington gave an address at the opening of the Cotton States and International Exposition at Atlanta, which was received with tumultuous applause, gave him a worldwide reputation, and made him the acknowledged spokesman for the Negro people of the United States. His autobiography *Up from Slavery* (1901) further consolidated his reputation. Theodore Roosevelt sought his advice on race problems and characterized him in private correspondence as "a genius such as does not arise in a generation." Andrew Carnegie supported Tuskegee and called Washington "one of the most wonderful men living or who has ever lived."[60]

The basis of Washington's philosophy was that the progress

---

[58] *Ibid.*, p. 252.

[59] Frederick Douglass was the son of a white man and a slave; W. E. Burghardt Du Bois was a mixture of Negro, French and Dutch. v. Harold R. Isaacs, *The New World of Negro Americans* (London, 1963), p. 214.

[60] E. L. Thornbrough (ed.), *Booker T. Washington* (Englewood Cliffs, 1969), p. 17.

of the Negro depended on his economic advancement. He took a hard, realistic view of the condition of his people and urged them to concentrate on simple, attainable objectives. It was more important that they learn trades than that they produce college graduates and professionals. They must be taught thrift and the dignity of labor, rather than concentrate on "the ornamental gewgaws of life." He believed that once the Negroes acquired property, paid taxes and became people of economic substance, they would be respected by the White race.

Uncompromising in his condemnation of lynching, Booker T. Washington was more pliable on other issues. In 1898, he wrote: "The Negro agrees with you that it is necessary to the salvation of the south that restriction be placed upon the ballot," but he urged that the educational and property qualifications for the franchise be the same for the two races.[61] The Negro would advance only through cooperation with the white people of the South. "The wisest among my race," he told his White audience at Atlanta, "understand that the agitation of questions of social equality is the extremest folly."

Washington rose to prominence during a period of Negro subordination and deprivation of Constitutional rights, an age which was disillusioned with the promises of Reconstruction and increasingly skeptical of the Negro's inherent ability and intelligence. The prevalence of lynching, often accompanied by hideous brutality and torture, cast a sombre shadow over the colored race. Working to advance his people under these difficult conditions, Booker T. Washington preserved at least a facade of optimism.

Where the Populists of the 1890s had sought an alliance between the poor Whites and the Negro masses based on economic and class demands, Booker T. Washington regarded the rednecks of the South as an uncouth and brutalized element and the Negro's worst enemy. He believed that the Negro had been helped and protected by the patrician South and that his natural alliance was with the cultivated upper classes.

A result of slavery, he asserted, "was to bring to the surface in the life of the stronger race two qualities or sets of qualities, one good and the other bad, one which tended to degrade the

[61] *Ibid.,* p. 13.

Negro and the other to lift him up and civilize him. These two sets of qualities eventually became embodied in two types or classes of individuals.

> One of these was known as the 'poor whites'; the other was the Southern aristocracy. It was from the ranks of the 'poor whites' that the majority of the overseers, the men who performed all the brutal and degrading work connected with slavery were drawn. It was this class that was most injured by the effects of slavery; and it was but natural, perhaps, that the men of this class should have come to have the most bitter hatred of the black man. . . .
>
> On the other hand, members of the old Southern families were brought in the daily lives of their homes into intimate human relationship with the black people about them, and, as a consequence, grew to feel a deep sympathy with and responsibility for the slaves under their care. Many of these people deplored the system in which they found themselves fatally entangled. Many of them freed their slaves, and many more would gladly have done so if they had felt that freedom would have solved the problem which the system of slavery created. I have always felt that the best and truest friend of the Negro in freedom has been that Southern white man who, in slavery days, gained an intimate and personal acquaintance with the Negro in the way I have described.[62]

In recent decades, Booker T. Washington's reputation has been tarnished by the charge of "Uncle Tomism" and he has been depicted as a force for appeasement and surrender. His view that the Southern Negro should seek the support of the White upper classes has been considered anathema by Marxists and other social revolutionaries. Yet Washington's conclusion that the main force for brutality, hatred and irrational repression in Southern race relations was the poor whites has been echoed by authoritative sociologists and historians.

[62] *Ibid.*, p. 31. From an article by Booker T. Washington in *World's Work*, January 1911.

CHAPTER SIXTEEN

Populists, Progressives and Radicals

The white tenant lives adjoining the colored tenant. Their houses are almost equally destitute of comforts. Their living is confined to bare necessities. They are equally burdened with heavy taxes. They pay the same high rent for gullied and impoverished land.

They pay the same enormous prices for farm supplies. Christmas finds them both without any satisfactory return for a year's toil. Dull and heavy and unhappy, they both start the plows again when 'New Year's' passes.

Now the People's Party says to these two men, 'You are kept apart that you may be separately fleeced of your earnings. You are made to hate each other because upon that hatred is rested the keystone of the arch of financial despotism which enslaves you both. You are deceived and blinded that you may not see how this race antagonism perpetuates a monetary system which beggars both.

—Thomas E. Watson, "The Negro Question in the South" (1892).[1]

With the exception of Theodore Roosevelt and Robert Marion LaFollette, the leaders and spokesmen of the Populist, Progressive and other radical movements could not be termed statesmen without stretching the definition of that word exorbitantly. Most of those who wielded power of one sort or another were better endowed with emotional fervor than with political wisdom and were driven more by intense antipathies and destructive urges than by the desire for constructive achievement. Many were rabble rousers of scanty education and Himalayan prejudices. The intellectuals of these movements

[1] *Arena,* VI (September, 1892), pp. 540–550. Reprinted in John Anthony Scott (ed.), *Living Documents in American History.* (New York, 1968), II, 384–95.

were not statesmen because they were primarily thinkers and writers on political subjects rather than shapers of events. Yet some consideration of the thoughts of these leaders on the issues of slavery and the Negro seems essential to a rounded picture, for they influenced the stream of events and reflected powerful political and social undercurrents.

Since this is not a political history of American radical movements, we propose to follow Richard Hofstadter in using the term *Populism* to cover, not merely the People's Party, but its predecessor Greenback and Grange movements. In terms of ideological characteristics, Populism was not merely a mode of organized political expression, but a mood and an attitude of mind. It covers a broad spectrum of movements, ideas and writings, characterized, to a greater or lesser extent, by common views and preconceptions about American society. Among these was the conviction that history was a conspiracy of rich against poor; of idlers and parasites against productive businessmen, farmers and workers; of bloodsucking finance capital against creative agricultural and agrarian capital; of sinister, subtle, sophisticated English and Jewish manipulators of world power against simple, upright American ordinary folk. The Populists tended to believe that the two great political parties of their country were a sham, essentially identical, both corrupt tools of the interests, engaged in loud but spurious battles as a means of diverting the attention of productive America from the fact that it had been deprived of its political birthright. Other ingredients in the peculiar witches' brew of the Populist *Weltanschauung* were a yearning for a bygone American golden age, in which the nation had been a community of productive citizens without the glaring contrasts between wealth and poverty so conspicuous at the turn of the Nineteenth Century; an immense oversimplification of political problems; a utopian faith in a potential future of uninterrupted harmony and plenty, coupled with a Doomsday fear of an onrushing final crisis of mankind; a distrust of the educated and power elite, and a trusting faith in the instinctive virtue and good sense of the common man. Above all, the Populists believed that the key to economic well-being was monetary manipulation and that the hard times and debt-ridden status of the masses were the result of a deflationary conspiracy of the bankers and gold lords.[2]

"It is a struggle between the robbers and the robbed" was the way Sockless Jerry Simpson, one of the leading spellbinders of the movement, put it. "There are but two sides in the conflict that is being waged in this country today," a Populist manifesto asserted. On the one side are the allied hosts of the monopolies, the money power, great trusts and railroad corporations, who seek the enactment of laws to benefit them and impoverish the people. On the other are the farmers, laborers, merchants, and all other people who produce wealth and bear the burdens of taxation. . . . Between these two there is no middle ground."[3]

Strangely enough, the irrationality of their conspirative theory of history and the falsity of some of their other underlying premises did not prevent the Populists from proposing practical steps of reform which were, to a great extent, moderate and necessary. In retrospect, the dispassionate observer must conclude that their monetary proposals were more constructive than the deflationary policies pursued by the Cleveland and Harrison Administrations.

The Populists held no consistent or uniform views concerning the status and future of the Negro. In 1895 Mary E. Lease, a lawyer, lecturer and unsuccessful Populist candidate for the U. S. Senate, wrote a book with the modest title, *The Problem of Civilization Solved*, which had considerable influence in radical circles. Mrs. Lease asserted that the civilization of Europe and the Americas stood on the brink of the abyss, faced by the two dire alternatives of a world controlled by anarchistic terror or a Russian total dispotism. Her solution was to "relieve the congested centers of the world's population of half their inhabitants and provide Free Homes for half of mankind" by engineering "the most stupendous migration of races the world had ever known." The tropical areas of both hemispheres were to be colonized by Negroes and Orientals who would serve as "tillers of the soil" under white masters. "Through all the vicissitudes of time," she wrote, "the Caucasian has arisen to the moral and intellectual supremacy of the world, until now this

[2]Richard Hofstadter, *The Age of Reform* (New York, 1963), pp. 60–93.
[3]Quoted in *Ibid.*, pp. 64–65.

favored race is fitted for the *Stewardship of the Earth and Emancipation from Manual Labor.*"[4] As for the under-races, the proposed new order would save them from their present condition of appalling misery and permit them to earn a livelihood on virgin soil and under the intelligent and benevolent direction of their white masters. They would therefore "hail with joy" a revolution in their economic condition, which would also bring them the blessings of Christianity.

The geopolitical thinking of this remarkable book was that the United States, allied with the Teutonic and Latin peoples, should annex Canada and the West Indies, dominate the rest of Latin America, and colonize the vacant lands to the South of her borders with a surplus white population which would be engaged in directing "vast swarms of Asiatics as laborers for the plantations." This expanded American empire would serve as a barrier against aggressive Russian authoritarianism and the machinations of Great Britain, which Mrs. Lease, like most good Populists, hated and feared.

Tom Watson: Metamorphosis of a Populist

Thomas Edward Watson (1856–1922) was probably the outstanding Populist leader of the South and, on the national scene, second only to William Jennings Bryan, who was not strictly speaking a Populist but shared many Populist ideas and attitudes. Watson's childhood was spent in rural Georgia during the harsh and bitter years of Reconstruction. Born on a large plantation with 1,372 acres and 45 slaves according to the 1860 Census, Tom Watson was hurled into poverty and insecurity by the shattering of the Confederacy, the emancipation of the slaves, and the punitive policies pursued toward the defeated South.

Little is known of his youth except that it was unhappy. Treatment by his parents which Watson deemed capricious and unjust seems to have twisted him into a man with strong paranoid tendencies. His adult life was disfigured by morbid suspicions and violent hates. The targets of his animosity changed from time to time, but its intensity never diminished. Unlike most people with paranoid tendencies, Watson had a clear-eyed recognition of his own disorder. In an eloquent letter to his

[4]Summarized in *ibid.*, pp. 83–85.

wife, written when he was 26 years old, Watson appraised his
character structure and vulnerabilities:

> Had I been trained in this manner, a very different man would
> be sitting here tonight. . . . On my heart there would not be the
> scar which many a trial has left there; and my memory would be
> rid of many a bitter recollection. I have imagined enemies where
> there were none: been tortured by indignities which were crea-
> tures of my own fancy, and have magnified the gloom of every
> reverse. . . .
> The better part of me is poisoned. A mistaken training leaves
> a trace from which there is no escape. Between the warp and
> woof of my life its busy shuttle will carry the black thread till the
> loom stops.
> Had I been firmly governed and not with fitful harshness: had
> I not been abused, ridiculed, mocked and scorned there would be
> sunshine where now is shadow. I could have joined in the com-
> panionship of the world, shared its loves, laughs, friendships and
> aspirations. As it is I stand where my boyhood put me, fed by my
> own thoughts, led by my own hopes, scourged by my own trou-
> bles.
> A sensitive spirit wounded by those who should have nurtured,
> sees all things in a false color, is proud of its own isolation,
> magnifies its defects, is unfitted for the intercourse of the world
> and as far as the necessities will allow retires within itself and
> imagines that all others are more fortunate, more deserving and
> more happy. Words fail to describe such a misfortune. A presence
> that poisons every joy, stains every beauty, checks every impulse.
> A shadow that follows like a hungry wolf. . . .[5]

By his early thirties Watson had managed to recoup his family's ruined fortunes and was worth $30,585, a large sum in im-
poverished post-bellum rural Georgia. In another four years his
income as a lawyer was exceeded by only two country lawyers
in the State, Robert Toombs, who had been a Confederate Briga-
dier General, and Benjamin H. Hill, who had been a Confederate Senator.[6]
Elected to Congress in 1891, Tom Watson distinguished him-

---

[5]Quoted in C. Vann Woodward, *Tom Watson, Agrarian Rebel* (New York,
1963), pp. 17–18. A poem Tom Watson wrote when he was fourteen ends with
the couplet:

"Yes, hated of all, hating all,
"I'll tread life's journey till I fall."
[6]*Ibid.,* p. 47.

self by attacking Georgia's vicious penal system, under which convicts were leased by the State, some of them for as long as twenty years, to private persons and corporations with practically no safeguards. "Here may be seen a group of penal institutions, the worst in the country by every evidence of their own setting forth: cruel, brutalizing, deadly; chaining, flogging, shooting, drowning, killing by exhaustion and exposure," wrote the novelist George W. Cable after an extensive probe of convict leasing in the South. In Georgia, 90 percent of the victims were Negroes.[7]

Watson abandoned the Democratic Party and declared himself a Populist. He supported an eight-hour day for labor and declared that it was a purpose of his Party to "make lynch law odious to the people."[8] He spoke frequently on the same platform with Negroes, nominated a Negro for the Party's state executive committee, and asked: "Tell me the use of educating these people as citizens if they are never to exercise the rights of citizens."[9]

Watson ridiculed "those writers who tediously wade through census reports to prove that the Negro is disappearing." The contrary was the case. "The truth is that the 'black belts' in the South are getting blacker. The race is mixing less than it ever did. Mulattoes are less common (in proportion) than during the times of slavery. Miscegenation is further off (thank God) than ever. Neither the blacks nor the whites have any relish for it. Both have a pride of race which is commendable. . . ."[10]

The problems and interests of the poor White and Black men of the South were the same. But just as the White South would never join the Republican Party, so the Black South would never join the Democratic Party. The solution, according to Watson, was for them to unite forces in the People's Party.

> Cannot these two men act together in peace when the ballot of the one is a vital benefit to the other? Will not political friendship be born of the necessity and the hope which is common to both?

[7] *Ibid.*, p. 106.
[8] C. Vann Woodward, *The Strange Career of Jim Crow* (New York, 1957), p. 44.
[9] Woodward, *Watson*, p. 221.
[10] Scott, *Documents*, p. 387.

Will not race bitterness disappear before this common suffering and this mutual desire to escape it? Will not each of these citizens feel more kindly for the other when the vote of each defends the home of both?[11]

As for the fear of "Negro supremacy," Watson observed: "The question of social equality does not enter into the calculation at all. That is a thing each citizen decides for himself."[12]

During the 1892 campaign a Negro Populist minister who had barnstormed the State in support of the Party was threatened with lynching and found refuge in Tom Watson's house. Watson issued a call and two thousand armed White supporters, some of whom had to ride all night, surrounded the house and protected its occupant for two days and nights.

Again and again, Watson was defeated by a Negro vote which was brought behind the Democratic slate by means of bribery, intimidation or simply fraud. At the 1904 convention of the People's Party, at a time when it had become moribund and its electoral chances were hopeless, Watson was nominated for President. Four years later, he capitulated to the by now dominant segregationist mood of the South and in 1908 ran for public office as the only candidate "standing squarely for *White Supremacy.*" In his house organ, *Watson's Jeffersonian Magazine,* the aging politician wrote about *"the superiority of the Aryan"* and the "HIDEOUS, OMINOUS, NATIONAL MENACE" of Black domination.[13]

As his paranoid condition deteriorated, Watson became obsessed with sexual hallucinations. He wrote articles on Catholicism with titles such as: "The Murder of Babes," "The Sinister Portent of Negro Priests," "How the Confession is Used by Priests to Ruin Women" and "One of the Priests Who Raped a Catholic Woman in a Catholic Church." He asserted: "The Romanists are trying to put me in the penitentiary, *because I quoted* FROM ONE OF THEIR DIABOLICAL BOOKS."[14]

He opposed the political ambitions of Woodrow Wilson, a Southerner who would impose almost total segregation of the

[11]*Ibid.,* p. 391.
[12]*Ibid.,* p. 395.
[13]Woodward, *Watson,* p. 402.
[14]*Ibid.,* p. 425.

races in Washington departments as President, on the grounds that he was *"ravenously fond of the negro"* and had "SENT BOOKER WASHINGTON A MESSAGE OF CONDOLENCE AND CONFIDENCE WHEN THAT COON WAS CAUGHT AT A WHITE WOMAN'S BEDROOM, AND WAS DESERVEDLY BEATEN FOR IT."[15]

When a young Atlanta Jew, Leo M. Frank, was unjustly accused of, and tried for, the murder of Mary Phagan, a young factory hand, Watson devoted his journalistic abilities to propagating the sort of antisemitism which depicted the Jew as sexually superior to the Gentile and which Julius Streicher would later popularize under the Nazis. Frank was a "Sodomite," "a lascivious pervert, guilty of the crime that caused the Almighty to blast the Cities of the plain." He was "the typical young libertine Jew" with "an utter contempt for the law and a ravenous appetite for the forbidden fruit—a lustful eagerness enhanced by the racial novelty of the girl of the uncircumcized." He appealed to his redneck readers for a lynching, asking *"How much longer is the innocent blood of little Mary Phagan to cry in vain to Heaven for vengeance?"*[16] When a mob acted on these exhortations and took Frank from custody and lynched him, Watson exulted: *"The next Leo Frank case in Georgia will never reach the Courthouse."*[17]

"Lynch law is a good sign," Watson proclaimed, *"It shows that a sense of justice yet lives among the people."* He would no more hesitate to kill a Negro rapist than to shoot a mad dog.

Watson's decision to abandon the political strategy of racial cooperation against the established Democratic machine was a rational one. The Negro vote was being so effectively dragooned against the Populists as to spoil their chances in Georgia. The sentiment of the poor Whites was strongly segregationist and a deal between moderate Populists and the Establishment was feasible on the basis of common acceptance of segregation and White supremacy.

The lunatic way in which Watson made his political *volte face,* his tirades against the successful leaders and statesmen

[15] *Ibid.,* pp. 426–27.
[16] *Ibid.,* pp. 440–41.
[17] *Ibid.,* p. 443.

whom he envied, his insane attacks on Catholics and Jews and his perverted hallucinations about their sexual activities—all these were symptoms of a progressive physical and mental degeneration of which Watson, in his more lucid moments, was aware.[18]

When Watson died in 1924, the well-meaning leader of the American Socialist Party, Eugene Victor Debs, wrote his widow: "He was a great man, a heroic soul who fought the power of evil his whole life long in the interest of the common people, and they loved and honored him."[19]

A political leader who had feasted on the rhetoric of destruction for most of his adult life and nurtured himself on the imagery of Apocalypse, Debs was evidently unable to distinguish between a "great man" and a paranoid schizophrenic.

The verdict of C. Vann Woodward, Watson's able biographer, was more judicious:

"If Watson had any hand in launching the new organization, no record has been found that reveals it. Yet if any mortal man may be credited (as no one man rightly may be) with releasing the forces of human malice and ignorance and prejudice, which the Klan merely mobilized, that man was Thomas E. Watson."[20]

William Jennings Bryan

While never a Populist, William Jennings Bryan was endorsed as the Presidential candidate of the People's Party in 1896 and thus ran on that ticket as well as serving as Democratic standard bearer. His Populist running-mate incidentally was Tom Watson.

During his long and voluble political life, Bryan made few statements concerning race. He considered restrictions on Negro suffrage "justified on the ground that civilization has a right to preserve itself "[21] and he believed in segregation of the two races. During the 1924 Democratic Party Convention, Bryan spoke against a motion to denounce the Ku Klux Klan

---

[18] *Ibid.*, p. 444.
[19] *Ibid.*, p. 486.
[20] *Ibid.*, p. 450.
[21] George Brown Tindall, *The Emergence of the New South, 1913–1945.* (Baton Rouge, 1967), p. 165.

specifically and by name. Before hostile, Tammany-packed galleries, he told the New York gathering that "it requires more courage to fight the Republican Party than it does to fight the Ku Klux Klan." He was instrumental in persuading the convention to reject the motion of censure by one vote.[22]

As early as the 1897 campaign, Bryan had to assure a Jewish audience that the fact that he favored free coining of silver did not mean that he was anti-Semitic.[23] A quarter of a century later he was suspected of intolerance toward Jews and Catholics and given the sobriquet "the greatest Klansman of them all." The charge was without substance. He joined over a hundred eminent Americans, among them former Presidents William Howard Taft and Woodrow Wilson, in protesting Henry Ford's defamatory articles in the *Dearborn Independent* against Jews. Bryan refused to support Ford's Presidential aspirations because of the latter's anti-Semitism, denounced the *Protocols of the Learned Elders of Zion* as a forgery and added that it was a libel on "one of the greatest races in history."[24] Bryan served on the American Committee on the Rights of Religious Minorities and often spoke out in defense of both Jews and Catholics. He shared the widely held belief that Negroes were inferior to Caucasians, but he was not a Nativist in any sense of the word.

The Progressives and the Negro

The Progressive Party of 1912 wished for major reforms in American life, but deliberately avoided any sweeping commitment to Negro causes. The men who founded and guided the new political party were, to a large extent, heirs of the Abolitionists, a group of men who had expected miraculous results to follow upon emancipation of the Negro and who had been bitterly disappointed. Thus Lyman Abbott, a young Congregationalist clergyman, had served the freedmen with high hopes and great expectations immediately after the Civil War and called for total integration. A generation later he reminisced:

[22]Arthur M. Schlesinger, Jr., *The Age of Roosevelt: The Crisis of the Old Order* (Boston, 1957) p. 99.
[23]Hofstadter, *Reform*, p. 80.
[24]Lawrence W. Levine, *Defender of the Faith: William Jennings Bryan: The Last Decade 1915–1925.* (New York, 1965), pp. 257–58.

"Men of that generation blundered egregiously, and brought upon the country, especially the South, and most of all upon the negro race, tragic disaster of their blundering."[25] Editor of the *Outlook* and an associate of Roosevelt at the time of the Progressive campaign of 1912, Abbott now asserted that Negroes were inferior, that miscegenation should at all costs be prevented and that the problem should be left in the hands of the White South.

Carl Schurz was, as we have already seen, another voice of disillusion from the ranks of the erstwhile Abolitionist zealots. Professor Edward A. Ross of the University of Wisconsin Sociology Department, a muckraker and fellow traveler of the Populists, shuddered at the new immigration from southern and eastern Europe, demanded that America assume an "uncompromising attitude toward lower races" and branded the Negro an inferior.

Professor John R. Commons, the liberal historian of the American labor movement, found the Negroes "indolent and fickle." Josiah Royce of Harvard, one of the leading American philosophers of the day, rejected the dogmatic theorizing about racial superiority and inferiority of Lothrop Stoddard and Madison Grant on the grounds that it was unscientific and unproven. He held, however, that the Negro would remain primitive "for reasons which are not merely due to circumstance but which are quite innate in his mental constitution."[26] Even Ray Stannard Baker, the pro-labor muckraker who had exposed oppression of the Negro in a series of articles, primarily in the *American* Magazine, entitled *Following the Color Line,* concluded that much though the Negro suffered from coexistence with the Southern White man, the latter "with his higher cultivation, his keener sensibilities, his memories of departed glory had suffered far more."[27]

A more significant and more interesting example was

[25]Lyman Abbott, *Reminiscences* (Boston, 1915), p. 235.
[26]David W. Southern, *The Malignant Heritage: Yankee Progressives and the Negro Question, 1901–1914* (Chicago, 1968), pp. 50–51. We have drawn heavily on this admirable study which was given the William P. Lyons Masters Essay Award in 1967.
[27]Ray Stannard Baker, *Following the Color Line* (New York, 1908), p. 293. Quoted in Southern, *Heritage,* p. 42.

Charles Francis Adams, Jr., an opponent of slavery who had been a young Union Army officer in the Civil War and was brother to Henry and Brooks Adams. A trip to sub-Saharan Africa in 1906 shocked him out of his preconceptions and "the scales fell from [his] eyes." Writing in the *Century* Magazine, Adams pondered the lessons of his African visit and the "awful corollary" posed by the presence of ten million Negroes in the United States, an unassimilable element, in his opinion, which could neither be expelled nor incorporated in the social and political organism. The race problem could not be solved "in utter ignorance of ethnological law." It must be approached, not with good intentions and religious precepts, but in "more of a scientific spirit." Since free societies must consist of "homogeneous equals," Adams asserted, the Negro could not be accepted as a citizen and probably was not even entitled to equality under the law.[28]

Herbert Croly and Walter Weyl

Theodore Roosevelt endorsed Herbert Croly's *The Promise of American Life* and Walter Weyl's *The New Democracy* as the true books of progressivism.[29] Both writers were founding editors of the *New Republic.* While they agreed as to the need for fundamental reforms in the American social, economic and political fabric, Croly was an exponent of nationalism and the principle of empire, whereas Weyl leaned more toward a Jeffersonian view, was more of a pacifist and an internationalist.

Roosevelt's conceptions of geopolitics and strategy had been profoundly influenced by Alfred Thayer Mahan's magnificent exposition of the role of sea power in history.[30] Croly's powerful enunciation of an American nationalism, which was to solidify the country through a program of social reform, curbing the

[28]Southern, *Ibid.,* p. 39.

[29]Charles Forcey, *The Crossroads of Liberalism: Croly, Weyl, Lippmann and the Progressive Era, 1900–1925* (New York, 1961, p. 139). Croly's and Weyl's books were published by Macmillan in 1909 and 1912 respectively. Weyl was the father of one of the authors of the present volume.

[30]Alfred Thayer Mahan, *The Influence of Sea Power upon History 1660–1783* (Boston, 1890).

abuses of corporate power and asserting American power internationally, gave Theodore Roosevelt the political philosophy he needed, but the book appeared too late to influence his policies as President. In a review of Croly's *magnum opus* in the January 1911 *Outlook*, Roosevelt called it "the most powerful and illuminating study of our national conditions which has appeared in many years."[31]

Croly regarded slavery as a "disease" and an institution incompatible with American principles. Yet he had little admiration for the Negro and considered the Abolitionists blind fanatics whose zeal for abstract principles nearly tore the nation asunder. "In their devotion to their adopted cause," he wrote, 'They lost all sense of proportion, all balance of judgment, and all justice of perception; and their narrowness and want of balance is in itself a sufficient indication that they were possessed of a half, instead of a whole, truth."

Croly continued:

> The fact that the Abolitionists were disinterested and for a while persecuted men should not prevent the present generation from putting a just estimate on their work. While they redeemed the honor of their country by assuming a grave and hard national responsibility, they sought to meet that responsibility in a way that would have destroyed their country. The Abolitionists, no less than the Southerners, were tearing at the fabric of American nationality. They did it, no doubt, in the name of democracy; but of all perverted conceptions of democracy, one of the most perverted and dangerous is that which identifies it exclusively with a system of natural rights. Such a conception of democracy is in its effect inevitably revolutionary, and merely loosens the social and national bond. In the present instance they were betrayed into one of the worst possible sins against the national bond—into the sin of doing a gross personal injustice to a large group of their fellow-countrymen. Inasmuch as the Southerners were willfully violating a Divine law, they became in the eyes of the Abolitionists, not merely misguided, but wicked men; and the Abolitionists did not scruple to speak of them as unclean beasts, who were fattening on the fruits of an iniquitous institution. But such an inference was palpably false. The Southern slave owners were not unclean beasts; and any theory which

[31]Forcey, *Crossroads*, p. 139.

justified such an inference must be erroneous. They were, for the most part, estimable if somewhat quick-tempered gentlemen, who did much to mitigate the evils of negro servitude, and who were on the whole liked rather than disliked by their bondsmen. They were right, moreover, in believing that the negroes were a race possessed of moral and intellectual qualities inferior to those of the white men: and, however much they overworked their conviction of negro inferiority, they could clearly see that the Abolitionists were applying a narrow and perverted political theory to a complicated and delicate set of economic and social conditions.[32]

Walter Weyl's attitude toward the Negro was more sympathetic, ambivalent and optimistic. "That the most indigent among Americans are not the leaders of democracy may be seen from a consideration of the status of the Negro," he wrote in 1912. "... The race is too poor, weak, ignorant, and disunited to make effective protest. For the most part it constitutes—through fault of circumstances—an inert mass, which could perhaps be more readily used, both industrially and politically for the prevention of democracy than for its attainment. While the Negro is rapidly progressing, while the future may well bring forth a prosperous, intelligent, united, and politically intrenched colored population, the role of the Negro in our progress towards democracy will for the time being remain wholly subordinate."[33]

In discussing the controversy between the economic approach to Negro progress of Booker T. Washington and the militant activism of W. E. Burghardt Du Bois, Weyl tended to side with the former. He thought it

probable that the present democratic movement, uneasily recognizing this danger in its rear, will move forward, leaving the problem of Negro suffrage to one side. It is a sign of disillusionment. We look at the Negro vote in Philadelphia and Cincinnati, and wonder whether it is worth while to lay aside other problems to secure a Negro vote in Atlanta and Charleston. Thus it happens that men, animated by a spirit analogous to that which freed the slaves, are seeking to ignore the problem of Negro

[32]Herbert Croly, *The Promise of American Life* (New York, 1909), pp. 80–8
[33]Walter E. Weyl, *The New Democracy*, (New York, 1912), p. 180.

disenfranchisement. Even the Socialist party, which is a defender of desperate causes, seems to avoid the problem.[34]

Weyl considered that the issue of Negro franchise could be tabled "if we can honestly believe that the denial to the Negro of the vote is advantageous, not only to us, but to him." This did not mean that the Negro could be offered merely "a subhuman or a subcivilized life." Weyl added prophetically:

> For as he grows, the Negro, if he be not given, will take. . . .
> There may arise a Negro consciousness, a dark sense of outraged
> racial dignity. There may come a stirring of a rebellious spirit
> among ten, or, as it soon will be, of twenty or thirty million black
> folk. We cannot hope forever to sit quietly at the feast of life and
> let the black man serve. We cannot build upon an assumed supe-
> riority over these black men, who are humble to-day, but who
> to-morrow may be imperious, exigent, and proudly race-con-
> scious.[35]

In the long run, Weyl believed, it would be impossible to make the Negro "a thing without rights, a permanent semieman-cipated slave, a headless, strong-armed worker ... Whether we love the Negro or hate him, we are, and shall continue to be, tied to him."[36]

The propinquity of the two races in America was an historic fact, a condition that could not be unravelled. But it was not a happy condition. Weyl wrote:

> If today our ten million American Negroes resided, not in the
> United States, but in a contiguous territory, asking for admission
> into the Union, it is extremely improbable that the mass of white
> men would permit the annexation. We might very well feel that,
> however engaging many of the qualities of the Negroes are, and
> however much the present bitter racial antagonism may be al-
> layed, it would be the part of folly to lay aside our own problems
> to take up new problems of racial adjustment. For the Negro's
> sake as well as for our own, we should prefer to stay apart.[37]

[34] *Ibid.*, p. 343.
[35] *Ibid.*, pp. 343–44.
[36] *Ibid.*, p. 345.
[37] *Ibid.*, pp. 345–46.

Karl Marx on the Negro

The widespread belief that Karl Marx and Friedrich Engels, the founders of modern socialism, believed in the equality of human races is so much nonsense. Marx considered race one of the forces shaping history. He did not propose to deal with it simply because it lay outside the dialectics of capitalist development and the cataclysmic coming of socialism which was his primary area of interest. As a young man he wrote:

> The first premise of all human history is of course the existence of living human individuals. The first fact to be established is therefore the physical organization of these individuals and their consequent relation to the rest of nature. We cannot here, of course, go into either the physical characteristics of men themselves or the natural conditions found by men—the geological, oro-hydrographical, climatic and other conditions. All historical work must start on the basis of these natural conditions and their modification in the course of history through the action of men.[38]

As revolutionary politicians, both Marx and Engels wrote about the Negro in sympathetic terms and supported the Northern cause in the American Civil War and Lincoln's emancipation measures. Their main interest seems to have been in a prolongation of the conflict which they hoped would deprive England of the raw cotton her textile mills needed and thus precipitate a crisis and perhaps lead to social revolution in Great Britain. Hence, Marx praised Lincoln publicly in his writings, while in a private letter to Engels he characterized his actions as "like the mean, pettifogging conditions which one lawyer puts to his opposing lawyer."[39]

The professed friendship of Marx and Engels for the Negro was also pure hypocrisy. Their secret attitude toward Africans was one of loathing and contempt. In their private correspondence, both Marx and Engels habitually used the English derogatory term "nigger" even though their correspondence

---

[38]Karl Marx, *Die Deutsche Ideologie* (1845–46). See *A Handbook of Marxism* (New York, 1935), pp. 210–11.

[39]Karl Marx to Friedrich Engels, London, October 29, 1862. *The Correspondence of Marx and Engels, 1846–1895* (New York, 1935), pp. 139–40.

was in German and the German word is the emotionally neutral *"Neger."*[40]

In a letter dated July 30, 1862—in other words contemporary with Marx's pro-Lincoln and pro-Emancipation articles in the *New York Daily Tribune*—Marx called his brilliant rival for the leadership of the German socialist movement, Ferdinand Lassalle, "the Jewish Nigger, Lassalle." He added the following comment:

> It is now entirely clear to me that, as his cranial structure and hair type prove, Lassalle is descended from the Negroes who joined Moses' flight from Egypt (that is, assuming his mother, or his paternal grandmother, did not cross with a *nigger*). Now this union of Jewry and Germanism with the negro-like basic substance must necessarily result in a remarkable product. The officiousness of the fellow is also *nigger-like.*[41]

Four years later, Marx wrote Engels to announce his discovery of a book by P. Trémaux which he hailed as "much more important and rewarding than Darwin."[42] Trémaux's great discovery was that "the common Negro type is a degeneration of a much higher type."[43]

Engels was deeply offended by Trémaux's theory that soil and climate can alter races. He wrote that "stories about the nigger, Santa Maria, and the transformation of white men into Negroes are a farce," adding that, if the theory had been correct, "we Rhinelanders" would have become "idiots and niggers a long time ago."[44]

The Socialist Party's "Lynchable Human Degenerates"

Between 1901 when it was founded and 1912, the year of its greatest strength, the American Socialist Party grew from less

[40]Zygmund Dobbs, *Red Intrigue and Race Turmoil* (New York, 1958). Dobbs is one of the few sources of the Marx-Engels private correspondence in English. The Library of Congress Edition, of which Dobbs made photocopies, can rarely be found complete in public libraries, since industrious disciples habitually mutilate these letters, cutting out portions which are incompatible with the Communist Party line. The letters quoted here are from the Dobbs photocopies.

[41]Marx to Engels, July 30, 1862.

[42]Marx to Engels, August 7, 1866.

[43]*Ibid.*

[44]Engels to Marx, October 2, 1866.

than 10,000 to 150,000 dues-paying members. At the peak of its power, the Party polled 900,000 votes and elected over two thousand public officials.[45] It lost ground in the 1916 elections; regained much of its strength with Eugene V. Debs as its standard bearer in the 1920 contest; and, during the next two decades, under the respected but ineffectual leadership of Norman Thomas, sank into political insignificance.

The American Socialist Party was split on the Negro question, as on other issues, between a Left Wing and a Right Wing, with a vacillating Center generally wielding the balance of power. Under such magnetic leaders as Eugene V. Debs and Big Bill Haywood, the Left tended to support the Industrial Workers of the World (I.W.W.) as against the craft unions of the American Federation of Labor (A.F. of L.) and to espouse proletarian revolution as against reform. Led by practical politicians such as Victor L. Berger of Wisconsin and Morris Hillquit of New York, the Right Wing stressed gradual reforms, clean city government and conventional trade union tactics. On the whole, the Right appealed to skilled workers, farmers and middle-class elements and was in the broad tradition of other indigenous American movements of protest from the Grangers to the Populists and the Progressives. Despite the fact that its two principal leaders, Berger and Hillquit, were Jews, the Right Wing was based preponderantly on native-born American stock from the older immigration streams and its strength was concentrated outside of New York City.

The revolutionary Left Wing, under Debs and Haywood, was essentially an incongruous coalition of urban intellectuals, workers from the newer immigration streams who had imbibed Marxist or anarcho-syndicalist doctrines of class war from European sources and the mass of unskilled and semiskilled workers that followed the harvests, logged in the Western forests or mined coal and metal ore.

The Left shared Marx's public views on the Negro; the Right was hostile to them. On September 14, 1901, the *Social Democratic Herald* characterized Negroes as inferior, depraved de-

[45]Ira Kipnis, *The American Socialist Movement, 1897–1912* (New York, 1968), p. 422.

generates who went "around raping women (and) children."[46]
In an article entitled "The Misfortune of the Negroes," published in the same organ on May 31, 1902, Victor L.
Berger observed: "There can be no doubt that the negroes and mulattoes constitute a lower race—and that the Caucasians and
indeed the Mongolians have the start on them in civilization by
many thousand years—so that negroes will find it difficult to
overtake them." Berger added, "The free contact with the
whites has led to further degeneration of the negroes."[47] White
girls who associated with Blacks were characterized in the socialist press as "depraved."[48]

Between 1901 and 1912, the Socialist Party adopted only one
resolution favorable to the Negro, an appeal for him to join the
movement, and this was carried only after repeated revisions
and motions to table. The platform of the Party in Louisiana
called for "the separation of the black and white races into
separate communities, each race to have charge of its own
affairs." This was justified on the grounds that race instincts
demanded segregation and that, without Jim Crow, socialist
ranks might be swamped by Blacks who had nowhere else to go
politically.[49]

In 1903, the Socialist Party was taken to task by the Second
International for its indifference to the rampant mob violence
against Negroes. The Socialist National Quorum replied that
only the abolition of capitalism and the victory of socialism
could prevent the procreation and production of "lynchable
human degenerates."[50] This extraordinary response seems to
have satisfied the international socialist organization.

At the 1910 Socialist Party Congress, the Committee on Immigration called for the "unconditional exclusion" of Chinese and
Japanese on the grounds that they were politically backward
and because America was already afflicted with the Negro

---

[46]Philip S. Foner, *History of the Labor Movement in the United States* (New
York, 1964), III, 1900–1909, 381.
[47]*Ibid.*
[48]Kipnis, *Socialist,* pp. 131–132.
[49]*Ibid.,* p. 131.
[50]"Report of the Meeting of the National Quorum of the Socialist Party,
November, 1903," *The Chicago Socialist,* November 28, 1903. Kipnis, *Socialist,*
p. 132.

problem. A defender of the resolution argued that race differences are caused by evolution and that experience with the Negro indicated that white Socialists would be unable to work with Asiatics.

Kipnis summarized Right and Center attitudes toward the Negro in the early 1900s as based on the premise that "socialism was exclusively an economic movement and had nothing to do with social equality," adding:

> The party would insist that under socialism both Negro and white workers receive all they produced. But that did not mean that the two races would work in the same factories or even live in the same cities. Center and Right-wing Socialists explained that Negroes and whites did not want to associate. It was capitalism that forced them to live and work together. Socialism would solve the race question in the only possible manner—complete segregation.[51]

In the 1920s, when the Socialist Party was withering away, substantial defections to the Ku Klux Klan occurred. Seymour Martin Lipset has pointed out that Klan candidates drew their greatest strength in working-class districts. As for Victor L. Berger's bailiwick: "More interesting is the fact that a study of the Midwest Klan indicates that an 'impressive number of Milwaukee's Socialists also crossed the portals of the Klan. A successful Socialist candidate for the Wisconsin Supreme Court was an avowed member and supporter of the Klan; he replied to the Socialists who attacked him for this by citing the large number of Socialists in the Klan."[52] When one of the present writers was a teen-age Socialist organizer in the late 1920s, he would sometimes be embarrassed by a request that he address a closed meeting of reliable comrades, "all true Socialists and Klansmen."

The Left Wing of the Socialist Party accepted Negroes as equals. Although Debs delighted in telling Negro dialect stories and extolled Tom Watson, he was indignant at the impoverishment of the Negro and the harsh treatment he suffered. "The

[51] *Ibid.*
[52] Seymour Martin Lipset, "An Anatomy of the Klan," *Commentary* (October, 1965), pp. 74–83.

history of the Negro in the United States," he wrote, "is a history of crime without parallel." While condemning oppression of Negroes, he had no specific program for them. "We have nothing special to offer the Negro, and we cannot make separate appeals to all races. The Socialist Party is the party of the working class, regardless of color—the whole working class of the whole world."[53]

Big Bill Haywood, the revolutionary Socialist and leader of the I.W.W., worked actively and at considerable personal risk to obtain race integration. He achieved the unprecedented feat of integrating the trade unions of Louisiana. In Alexandria, he demanded that Black and White union workers sit down together and discuss their problems together. "If it is against the law, this is one time the law should be broken."[54]

Ever since he had witnessed a lynching, Haywood had been emotionally stirred by the insults and oppression suffered by the American Negro. He recollected that as a boy he had heard Pitchfork Ben Tillman, the South Carolina rabble-rouser, talk in Salt Lake City. A Negro sitting beside Haywood had asked the speaker a question:

> His reply was a ferocious and insulting attack, with reflections on the colored man's mother. He referred to his questioner as a 'saddle colored son of Satan,' and went on to tell him what his mother must have been for the Negro to have been the color he was; this because the Negro obviously was of mixed blood. I looked at the Negro and his pained expression caused me forever after to feel that he and his kind were the same as myself and other people. I saw him suffering the same resentment and anger that I should have suffered in his place. I saw him helpless to express this resentment and anger. I feel that Ben Tillman's lectures must have made many people feel as I did. It seemed to me that I could look right into the breast of old Tillman and see his heart that was rotten with hate.[55]

The Socialist Party was split and shattered after World War I by the repercussions of the October Revolution in Russia. It

[53]H. Wayne Morgan, *Eugene V. Debs: Socialist for President* (Syracuse, 1969), p. 124.
[54]Joseph R. Conlin, *Big Bill Haywood and the Radical Union Movement* (Syracuse, 1969), pp. 124–25.
[55]*Ibid.*, pp. 124–25.

fragmented into two separate, bitterly squabbling communist parties and the core that remained faithful to the Second International. Both the Socialist and the Communist parties accepted Negroes as equal members, repudiated segregation and renounced race prejudice of any sort. Under the leadership of Norman Thomas, the Socialists fought doggedly for equal treatment of all races within the trade unions, but this occurred at a time when the Party had long since ceased to be a mass movement of the American working class.

CHAPTER SEVENTEEN

Theodore Roosevelt and White Mastery

There is to me always something both pathetic and grimly ironic in the socialistic propaganda when coupled with the fact that as a working theory no Socialist party in this country could endure for twenty-four hours if, not as a matter of theory, but as a matter of practice, it applied its doctrines to black men and yellow men. Every real democrat in this country, every democrat who tries to put his democracy into practice. . . . acts and always must act on the perfectly sound (altho unacknowledged, and often hotly contested) belief that only certain peoples are fit for democracy. . . . In Haiti, absolute democracy has been at work for over a century, and really, my dear Mr. Willard, it is sad to think of your sentence of the function of democracy being 'Godlike as a maker of men,' and then to think of what democracy has done in Haiti. It would be far truer to say that its functions there had been 'devil-like'; than that its function there had been 'Godlike.' . . . I suppose that no one now seriously contends that during reconstruction days the negro majority in Mississippi and South Carolina acted wisely, or that it was possible to continue the government in the hands of that majority.
— Theodore Roosevelt, Letter to Charles Dwight Willard, April 28, 1911.[1]

In addition to being the first American President to deploy the nation's power effectively in the arena of world politics, Theodore Roosevelt was a man of prodigious energy, versatility and intellect. His mind ranged over a field which extended

[1]Elting E. Morison and John M. Blum (eds.), *The Letters of Theodore Roosevelt* (Cambridge, 1951–1954), 7, 254–55.

from the domain of the naturalist and explorer to that of the anthropologist and ethnologist to that of the politician and economist.[2] He was one of the most widely read of the American Presidents and the extent and excellence of his published writings would do credit to a man who considered this, and not politics, his life work. Robert Frost, the poet, thought him one "of our kind." To the critical intelligence of Van Wyck Brooks he was "a man of genius."[3] Where his fifth cousin, Franklin Delano Roosevelt, was a second-rate student at both Groton and Harvard, a law school student who failed to win his degree, and a man unacquainted with either literature or culture, Theodore Roosevelt was graduated Phi Beta Kappa from Harvard, succeeded in every intellectual undertaking he attempted, and combined unobtrusive but extensive learning with his dedication to the strenuous life.

Theodore Roosevelt's views on race are somewhat obscured by the fact that he used the term inexactly in a variety of senses and often confused *race* with nationality. In 1911 he reviewed Houston Stewart Chamberlain's *Foundations of the Nineteenth Century,* a book destined to be one of the Bibles of European political anti-Semitism and of the Nazi movement. While he found Chamberlain capable of "noble thought" and "brilliant lapses into sanity," Roosevelt characterized the work as "bedlamite passion and nonsanity." Concerning its thesis of the superiority of the Aryan race, he commented: "Aryan speech, yes; Aryan race—well, I am *very* doubtful."[4]

He believed that races, nations and peoples differed enormously in intelligence, character and ability. Some were fit for self-government, a few for world mastery, many were not even capable of running their own affairs. This was not a matter of color. "Democracy, with the clear instinct of race selfishness, saw the race foe," he observed in 1894 concerning the Chinese, adding that "his presence is ruinous to the white race." Though

[2]The naturalist who accompanied him on his 1909 African trip wrote: "I constantly felt while with him that I was in the presence of the foremost naturalist of our time, as indeed I was."

[3]William H. Harbaugh (ed.), *The Writings of Theodore Roosevelt* (Indianapolis, 1967), p. xviii.

[4]Howard K. Beale, *Theodore Roosevelt and the Rise of America to World Power* (New York, 1962), p. 42.

he recognized that the Japanese were similar to the Chinese "in blood and in culture," he considered them a "wonderful people. . . . quite as remarkable industrially as in warfare." Japan was destined to "take its place as a great civilized power of a formidable type."

He seems to have believed that the inability of certain races to govern themselves with order and freedom was due to institutional and historic conditions which might, in the long run, be changed. Yet there are other indications in his writings that he considered certain races simply ill-equipped by nature to meet the challenge of modern civilization. Whatever Roosevelt thought of a race as a whole, he judged individual members of that race as individuals and on their own merits. An example is to be found in a long letter he wrote Owen Wister on April 27, 1906:

"Now as to the Negroes! I entirely agree with you that as a race and in the main they are altogether inferior to the whites." Having said this, Roosevelt continued:

> I may add that my own personal belief is that the talk about the Negro having become worse since the Civil war is the veriest nonsense. He has on the whole become better. Among the Negroes of the South when slavery was abolished there was not one who stood as in any shape or way comparable to Booker Washington. Incidentally I may add that I do not know a white man of the South who is as good a man as Booker Washington today. You say you would not like to take orders from a Negro yourself. If you had played football in Harvard at any time during the last fifteen years you would have had to do so and you would not have minded it in the least; for during that time Lewis has been field captain and a coach.[5]

A cardinal element in Theodore Roosevelt's philosophy was that energetic, creative peoples with the ability to govern had overriding rights as against backward, uncreative, slothful and corrupt peoples. He denied emphatically that there was any analogy between his seizure of the Isthmus of Panama from Colombia without the latter's consent and the German violation of Belgian neutrality in 1915. The Belgians "were as 'su-

---

[5]Morison and Blum, *Letters,* V, 226–27.

perior' as the Germans" whereas the Colombians could be equated to "a group of Sicilian or Calabrian bandits. . . . You could no more make an agreement with the Colombians than you could nail currant jelly to the wall. . . . The Canal was for the benefit of the entire world. Should the blackmailing greed of the Bogotá ring stand in the way of civilization?"[6]

He thought that it was the duty of the United States and other civilized powers "to put down savagery and barbarism" and thus to free the peoples forced to live under these conditions. "Peace has come through the last century to large sections of the earth because the civilized races have spread over the earth's dark places." The presence of France in Algeria, England in the Sudan, Russia in Turkestan and the United States in the Philippines was a good thing for the peoples of these backward areas. It was our duty "to govern those islands in the interests of the islanders."[7]

In his 1896 history, *Winning of the West*, Roosevelt expressed his views concerning the pacification of areas inhabited by backward or savage people. It did not matter how the white man won the land. "It was all important that it should be won, for the benefit of civilization and in the interests of mankind. It is indeed a warped, perverse and silly morality which would forbid a course of conquest that has turned whole continents into the seats of mighty and flourishing civilized nations." It was a good thing that "the hard, energetic, practical men who do the rough pioneer work of civilization in barbarous lands, are not prone to false sentimentality." Wars against savages were both "the most ultimately righteous of all wars" and "the most terrible and inhuman." These were struggles

> where no pity is shown to non-combatants, where the weak are harried without ruth, and the vanquished maltreated with merciless ferocity. A sad and evil feature. . . . is that the whites, the representatives of civilization, sink almost to the level of their barbarous foes.

Yet this "vast and elemental" struggle was portentous for the future of the world. It made little difference whether France or

---

[6]Beale, *Roosevelt,* p. 46.
[7]*Ibid.,* p. 78.

Germany ruled Alsace and Lorraine. It was "of incalculable importance that America, Australia, and Siberia should pass out of the hands of their red, black, and yellow aboriginal owners, and become the heritage of the dominant world races."[8]

Roosevelt's Evaluation of the Negro

In 1889, Roosevelt wrote that slavery was "ethically abhorrent to all right-minded men," but "The presence of the negro is the real problem; slavery is merely the worst possible means of solving the problem." Those white men "who brought slaves from Africa" to the United States were "the worst foes, not only of humanity and civilization, but especially of the white race in America."[9]

As a result of his trip to Africa in 1909, Roosevelt's views concerning the Negro crystallized. He thought it probable that the Negroes and Australoids represented an earlier and more primitive species or subspecies of man, which had been ousted or exterminated from Eurasia. Probably, these types were "thrust southward into Africa, Tasmania, Australia, and remote forest tracts of Indo-Malaysia where, being such backward savages, they never developed anything remotely resembling a civilization"[10]

Roosevelt believed that strong European rule was necessary in Africa "to bring forward the natives, to train them, and above all to help them train themselves, so that they may advance in industry, in learning, in morality, in capacity for self-government." He was impatient of those who criticized missionaries since the latter, with all their shortcomings, had let a feeble light penetrate Stygian darkness.

> As soon as native African religions—practically none of which have hitherto evolved any substantial ethical basis—develop beyond the most primitive stage they tend, notably in middle and western Africa, to grow into malign creeds of unspeakable cruelty and immorality, with a bestial and revolting ritual and cere-

[8] Quoted *ibid.*, pp. 149–50.
[9] *Memorial Edition of the Works of Theodore Roosevelt*, Hermann Hagedorn, (ed.), (New York, 1923–1926), XI, 260–61.
[10] *Ibid.*, IV, 176 (1916). These and other quotations have been assembled in Archibald B. Roosevelt (ed.), *Theodore Roosevelt on Race—Riots—Reds—Crime* (West Sayville, 1968), p. 82.

monial. Even a poorly taught and imperfectly understood Christianity, with its underlying foundation of justice and mercy,
represents an immeasurable advance on such a creed.[11]

Roosevelt wrote about "ape-like, naked savages, who dwell in
the woods and prey on creatures not much wilder or lower than
themselves."[12] He noted how the white administrators in the
Congo Free State "organized the wild pagan tribes" and, after
each battle, "had to be on guard no less against the thousands
of cannibals in their own ranks than against the thousands of
cannibals in the hostile ranks, for, on whichever side they
fought, after every battle the warriors of the man-eating tribes
watched their chance to butcher the wounded indiscriminately
and to feast on the bodies of the slain."[13]

Despite "very dark spots" in the European conquest of Africa,
"On the whole the African regions which during the past century have seen the greatest cruelty, degradation, and suffering,
the greatest diminution of population, are those where native
control has been unchecked."[14] By contrast, where white rule
was established, the black population flourished, multiplied
and enjoyed the benefits of order and justice.

Roosevelt's vigorous and inquiring mind noted that the African Negro was one of the few races of man who had failed to
domesticate the beasts of his habitat. "The African buffalo is as
readily tamed as its Asiatic brother; the zebra was as suscepti-
ble of taming as the early wild horse and ass; the eland is
probably of all big ruminants the one that most readily lends
itself to domestication. But none of them were tamed until
tribes owning animals which had been tamed for ages appeared in Africa; and then the already-tamed animals were
accepted in their stead. The asses, cattle, sheep and goats of
Asia are now the domestic animals of the negroes."[15]

Observing "the sly, furtive human life of the wilderness" of

[11] Archibald Roosevelt, *Roosevelt,* p. 83. *Memorial Edition,* V, 362–63 (1909).
[12] Archibald Roosevelt, *Roosevelt,* p. 77; *Memorial Edition,* V, xxv–xxvi
(1910).
[13] Archibald Roosevelt, *Roosevelt,* p. 84; *Memorial Edition,* VII (1909).
[14] Archibald Roosevelt, *Roosevelt,* pp. 84–85; *Memorial Edition,* XVIII, 344
(1909).
[15] Archibald Roosevelt, *Roosevelt,* p. 81; *Memorial Edition,* IV, 156–57 (1916).
The South African writer Stuart Cloete has independently made the same point
concerning the failure of the African Negro to domesticate the zebra in conversations with one of the authors.

Africa, Roosevelt speculated that the Bushmen and Negroes of Africa, the Tasmanians and the Eskimos of the Eighteenth Century reproduced the life of European man in the Pleistocene Age. He suggested that "far-back ancestors of ours lived the same lives of suspicion and vigilant cunning among the beasts of the forest" as those led by the African Negroes of 1909. He believed that this implied a cultural lag in development of from 50,000 to 100,000 years.[16]

Holding these views concerning the Negro, Roosevelt regarded his presence in the United States as a misfortune and toleration of miscegenation as suicidal. In 1894, he wrote, "Democracy needs no more complete vindication for its existence than the fact that it has kept for the white race the best positions of the new world's surface, temperate America and Australia." Under aristocratical governments, Chinese immigration would have been encouraged just as "the slave-holding oligarchy" had previously encouraged the African slave trade. "The presence of the negro in our Southern States is a legacy from the time when we were ruled by a transoceanic aristocracy."[17]

Black slavery in the United States was "a grossly anachronistic and un-American form of evil." In Haiti, it was characterized by even more flagrant abuses; "yet, looking at the condition of that republic now, it may well be questioned whether it would not have been greatly to her benefit in the end to have had slavery continue a century or so longer."[18]

In 1905, Roosevelt wrote that "all reflecting men of both races are united in feeling that race purity must be maintained."[19] Four years later, he observed that it was "highly inadvisable" that peoples in different stages of civilization or with different types of civilization "shall be thrown into intimate contact. This is especially undesirable when there is a difference of both race and standard of living."[20]

Unlike most American statesmen of his era, Roosevelt be-

[16]Archibald Roosevelt, *Roosevelt*, pp. 77–78; *Memorial Edition*, IV, 138–40 (1916).

[17]Archibald Roosevelt, *Roosevelt*, p. 88; *Memorial Edition*, XIV, 245–46 (1894).

[18]Archibald Roosevelt, *Roosevelt*, p. 89; *Memorial Edition*, VIII, 117–18 (1887).

[19]Archibald Roosevelt, *Roosevelt*, p. 15; *Memorial Edition*, XVIII, 467 (1905).

[20]Archibald Roosevelt, *Roosevelt*, p. 15: *Memorial Edition*, XXII, 429 (1909).

lieved that race was more fundamental than nation, language or religious belief. He wrote in 1910:

"National unity is far more apt than race unity to be a fact to reckon with; until indeed we come to race differences as fundamental as those which divide from one another the half-dozen great ethnic divisions of mankind, when they become so important that differences of nationality, speech, and creed sink into littleness."[21]

Slavery and the Abolitionists

The one American statesman whom Theodore Roosevelt admired above all others was Abraham Lincoln. When the fifth volume of James Ford Rhodes' *History of the United States* appeared, the one covering 1864–1866, President Roosevelt wrote the author a letter of congratulation in which he compared the work to that of Macaulay.

"In this last volume I was immensely pleased with everything," the President wrote. "Perhaps I should bar one sentence —that in which you say that in no quarrel is the right all on one side, and the wrong all on the other. As regards the actual act of secession, the actual opening of the Civil War, I think the right was exclusively with the Union people, and the wrong exclusively with the secessionists; and indeed I do not know of another struggle in history in which this sharp division between right and wrong can be made in quite so clear-cut a manner." He added that he was "half southern," that his mother's kinfolk fought on the Confederate side and he was proud of them. Nevertheless, that cause was "wrong with a folly that amounted to madness, and with a perversity that amounted to wickedness."[22] Roosevelt's attitude of passionate righteousness concerning the Civil War had resulted, twenty years earlier, in his publicly comparing Jefferson Davis with Benedict Arnold and, when Davis wrote him a letter of protest, replying with uncharacteristic rudeness and requesting the former Confederate President to cease "any further communication whatever" with him.[23]

---

[21]Archibald Roosevelt, *Roosevelt*, p. 16: *Memorial Edition*, XXI, 174 (1917).
[22]Theodore Roosevelt to James Ford Rhodes, November 29, 1904, *personal.* Morison and Blum, *Letters*, IV, 1049.
[23]Theodore Roosevelt to Jefferson Davis, October 8, 1885. *Ibid.*, I, 93.

"The trouble I am having with the southern question—which, my dear sir, I beg you to believe I am painfully striving to meet, so far as in me lies, in the spirit of Abraham Lincoln," Roosevelt continued in his letter to Rhodes, "emphasizes the infinite damage done in reconstruction days by the unregenerate arrogance and shortsightedness of the southerners, and the doctrinaire folly of radicals like Sumner and Thaddeus Stevens. The more I study the Civil War and the time following it, the more I feel (as of course everyone feels) the towering greatness of Lincoln."

Rhodes replied in a letter defending the South. Roosevelt retorted:

"You say, quite properly, that you do not wonder that much bitterness still remains in the breasts of the southern people about the carpetbag negro regime. So it is not to be wondered at that in the late sixties much bitterness should have remained in the hearts of the northerners over the remembrance of the senseless folly and wickedness of the southerners in the early sixties." He said that he "heartily" agreed "that it was the presence of the negro which made the problem." Therefore, those people who "tried to break up this Union because they were not allowed to bring slavery and the negro into new territory" were guilty of "one of the worst deeds which history records."[24]

Roosevelt's violently emotional and moralistic condemnation of the leaders of the Confederacy was not primarily motivated by his moral repudiation of slavery, unambiguous as that repudiation was. For slavery was a dead issue. The supreme crime of the Southerners, in his opinion, was to have saddled the United States with the Negro presence in such numbers that it created a major, and to Roosevelt an almost insoluble, problem. Roosevelt's stress on race as the fundamental basis of human society; his belief in Anglo-Saxon superiority and in Negro inferiority, and his repudiation of social intercourse (and most emphatically of miscegenation) made the putative Southern offense seem a moral enormity.

Late in 1904 Henry Smith Pritchett, an astronomer who was President of the Massachusetts Institute of Technology, wrote President Roosevelt to suggest that the Fourteenth Amend-

[24]Theodore Roosevelt to James Ford Rhodes, February 20, 1905. *Ibid.,* IV, 1125.

ment should not be enforced and the Fifteenth Amendment should be repealed. He thought that the problem of the Negro should be left in the hands of the Southern States. This communication also represented the views of James Ford Rhodes. In his reply, the President stated:

> But while I agree with you fundamentally—that is, I agree with you that the principal hope of the negro must lie in the sense of justice and good will of the people of the South, and that the northern people can do little for him—yet I do not think that the conclusions you draw as to the action to follow can at this time be safely accepted. . . . I have always felt that the passage of the Fifteenth Amendment at the time it was passed was a mistake; but to admit this is very different from admitting that it is wise, even if it were practicable, now to repeal that amendment. The Fourteenth Amendment, Mr. Rhodes very properly commends, and I fail to see how any man can do otherwise than commend it. I again agree with you that, as conditions are now, at this time, it would do damage rather than good to press for its active enforcement by any means that Congress has at its command.[25]

The Fifteenth Amendment provides that no citizen shall have his right to vote abridged because of "race, color, or previous condition of servitude." Roosevelt pointed out that in heavily Negro districts in the South "any white man is allowed to vote, no matter how ignorant and degraded," but the Negro was totally disfranchised because of race alone. He called attention to the flagrant case of John Sharp Williams, the minority leader of the House, who was elected by a district which was 75 per cent Negro and in which no Negro was allowed to vote. "It is an outrage that this one white man should first be allowed to suppress the votes of the three black men, and then to cast them himself in order to make his own vote equal to that of four men in Mr. Cannon's district."[26] In conclusion, Roosevelt observed: "To acquiesce in this state of things because it is not possible at the time to attempt to change it

[25]Theodore Roosevelt to Henry Smith Pritchett, December 14, 1904. *Ibid.*, 1066–67.
[26]Joseph Gurney Cannon of North Carolina, the Republican majority leader of the House.

without doing damage is one thing. It is quite another thing to do anything which will seem formally to approve it."

Having summarily rejected the suggestion that he recommend repeal of the Fifteenth Amendment, Roosevelt turned to Pritchett's proposal "to throw upon the states themselves the responsibility for dealing with the negro, subject only to the criticism of the other states, of England, and of the civilized world."[27]

Speaking from bitter experience, Roosevelt said:

"If I had adopted such a policy in its entirety during the last two years, slavery would be at this moment re-established in the guise of peonage in portions of Mississippi, Alabama and Georgia." When the Southern States moved in that direction, Roosevelt intervened through action by United States district attorneys. "In each case I took a southerner, and usually a Democrat, as the agent through whom to work; and it is to these men—notably Judge Jones, whom I appointed in Alabama as a district judge—that the credit for the work is mainly due."

As for the appointment of Negroes to office, Pritchett had asserted that "not even the southerners demand the exclusion of the negro from office."

Roosevelt retorted:

"Unfortunately, you are mistaken. As a whole the southerners do demand, in effect, just precisely this: that is, the entire exclusion of negroes from office. Of course, their best men do not demand it; ... the better sentiment of the South has been with me, but it has been cowed and overborne by the violence of the men who seem to furnish almost all their leadership, alike in politics and in the press." Any intelligent Southerner would concede, Roosevelt added, that his appointees in the South were better men than those of President Cleveland "and a smaller percentage of them are negroes than was the case under Mr. McKinley."

He complained that the South had done nothing to meet him halfway. As for government jobs for Negroes:

"Of the very few negro appointments, most were to small post offices in the black belt in villages where there were only negroes, and where therefore a negro had to be appointed.

[27]Quoting Pritchett, not Roosevelt.

Lastly, I somewhat diminished the number of officeholders who were negroes; so that the proportion, which was insignificant even under McKinley, has been still further reduced. Not a colored man was appointed save after securing his endorsement by all the best white people of the vicinity."

He asked Pritchett to read this letter to James Ford Rhodes. After having read the fifth volume of Rhodes' *History* and the page proofs of the sixth volume that had been forwarded to him, Roosevelt was able to say:

> I am fundamentally in agreement with the view he takes of reconstruction. I want you to know that I fundamentally agree with your own purposes, and with your sense of what ought to be done. But I wish you both to realize that as far as I can see I have actually gone along the very lines you say should be followed; and that as far as I can see it is the southerners who *speaking only of the present* are to blame for present conditions. . . .
>
> What definite plan that has not been tried during these three years can you suggest? Congress is actually leaving alone the question of legislation to enforce the Fourteenth and Fifteenth Amendments. Congress is not passing and has not passed any law, and is not taking and has not taken any action, menacing in the slightest degree the South, or touching on the color question.

The next day, Roosevelt wrote Rhodes that as far as "the southern question" was concerned "I am at my wits' end what to do." In his letter to Rhodes, the President stressed the problem of government appointments and the Republican Party in the South:

> Four years ago Booker Washington and I discussed what ought to be done by a President to the South. We agreed that in the Gulf and South Atlantic States, where, unlike what is the case in Tennessee and North Carolina, there is no real Republican party organization which has any particular effect at the polls, the thing to do would be freely to recognize Democrats; to try to appoint men of the highest character—Republicans where they were available, Democrats where they were not; *and to appoint a very few colored men of high character—just enough to make it evident that they were not being entirely proscribed.*[28]

This is precisely the plan I have followed, and in the abstract

[28]Emphasis supplied.

every reputable southerner agrees that it is the right plan, while every reputable and intelligent southerner agrees that it has actually been put into practice in his district. And yet it has not prevented such coarse and malignant mendacity from the political and newspaper leaders of the South as to create a corresponding bitterness in the North—a bitterness which I am doing all in my power to allay, or at least to prevent from finding expression."[29]

In a letter to Charles Dwight Willard written some six years later, Roosevelt discussed the Negro problem in terms of the broad framework of democracy.

"The rule of the majority is good," he observed, "only if the majority has the will and the morality and the intelligence to do right; and the majority of the peoples of mankind are not yet in such shape that they can prosper under the very kind of rule which it is essential for us here in America to have, and under which alone *we* can prosper and bring ourselves to the highest point of developed usefulness."

He recommended that Willard read "what Lincoln said in his answer to Douglas to the real meaning of the Declaration of Independence, and in the comparison he makes in speaking of equality between himself and a negro,[30] and you will get exactly the idea of what I regard as the proper temper to approach these subjects." Zeal should not prevent a man from looking facts in the face, Roosevelt said, adding:

"I too am a dreamer of dreams; I hold the man worthless who is not a dreamer, who does not see visions; but I also hold him worthless unless in practical fashion he endeavors to shape his actions so that these dreams and visions can be partially realized, and shall not remain mere dreams and visions, or, what is worse still, shall not be turned into will-o'-the-wisps to lead struggling mankind to destruction."[31]

[29]Theodore Roosevelt to James Ford Rhodes, December 15, 1904. Morison and Blum, *Letters,* IV, 1072–73.

[30]"Now I protest against that counterfeit logic which concludes that, because I do not want a black woman for a *slave* I must necessarily want her for a *wife.* I need not have her for either, I can just leave her alone. In some respects she certainly is not my equal; but in her natural right to eat the bread she earns with her own hands without asking leave of any one else, she is my equal, and the equal of all others." Abraham Lincoln, Speech of June 26, 1857.

[31]Theodore Roosevelt to Charles Dwight Willard, April 28, 1911. Morison and Blum, *Letters*, VII, 256.

Haiti

In a letter to Ray Stannard Baker, he took issue with an article in which Baker regarded the Negro problem as part of the struggle "between the Few and the Many." Roosevelt replied:

> The question is one of race. This is not a matter of theory at all.
> All you have to do is to study the history of Haiti when it yielded
> to the influence of the French Revolution, and see what became
> of the Jacobite[32] or ultrademocratic movement after it had been
> tried for a year or two in that island. . . . To say that any trouble
> or any conflict in connection with the fearful deterioration of
> either Haiti or Liberia has anything whatever to do with the
> conflict between the Few and the Many is, my dear Mr. Baker,
> pure nonsense.[33]

In 1908, Roosevelt invited Sir Harry Hamilton Johnston, a distinguished Scottish explorer and administrator who knew as much about Central Africa as any living man, to come to the United States and spend a night at the White House.

"What I am seriously concerned with," he wrote,

> is the great problem which you discuss; the problem, or rather
> the group of many complex problems, which we mean when we
> speak of the Negro question. I do wish I could hear from you at
> length, of course best of all in personal conversation, about Lib-
> eria; and I very earnestly hope that if you get over here you will
> visit the other Negro Republic—Haiti. I should like a more sym-
> pathetic interpretation of Haiti than that of St. John's book.[34] It
> may be that he tells fundamentally the truth, but yet that he does
> not give this truth its proper relative value. That Haiti stands
> behind the ordinary tropical American republic, low tho some of
> these tropical American republics are, is, I believe, beyond ques-
> tion. But what I would like to know is, whether the falling back
> has literally been to the old West African level. It seems to me
> that if St. John had compared Haiti, not with its pretensions, not
> with civilized or semicivilized states, but with the savage states
> or low-grade barbaric states from which the ancestors of most of

[32]He meant Jacobin. The Jacobites were the supporters of James III, the Stuart Pretender to the British throne.
[33]Theodore Roosevelt to Ray Stannard Baker, June 3, 1908. Morison and Blum, *Letters*, VI, 1048.
[34]Spenser Buckingham St. John, *Hayti: or, The Black Republic* (London, 1884).

the Haitian Negroes originally came, we would have had better material on which to base judgment.[35]

He added that he believed in granting to Negroes "the largest amount of self-government which they can exercise," but had only "impatient contempt" for "ridiculous theorists" who wish to give "the most utterly undeveloped races of mankind a degree of self-government which only the very highest races have been able to exercise with any advantage."

One of the minor crises of the Roosevelt Administration occurred when three Negro regiments were implicated in storming through Brownsville, Texas, one night in August 1906, and firing shots which killed a civilian. Circumstantial evidence and the testimony of witnesses implicated colored soldiers, but interrogation of the troops resulted in "a conspiracy of silence." Since the men "appear to stand together in a determination to resist the detection of guilt," the Inspector-General of the Army ruled, "they should stand together when the penalty falls." President Roosevelt ordered all 160 men, six of them Medal of Honor winners, discharged "without honor" and "forever barred from re-enlistment." This harsh decision deprived professional soldiers of their pension rights and left some unemployed and destitute. An investigation by Senator Foraker of Ohio resulted in the reinstatement of fourteen of them.[36]

"I have been really depressed over the Brownsville (Texas) business," Roosevelt wrote Baker,

—not so much by the attitude of the colored troops themselves, altho that was sufficiently ominous, but by the attitude taken by the enormous majority of the colored people in regard to the matter. I had never really believed there was much justification for the claim of the Southern whites that the decent Negroes would actively or passively shield their own wrongdoers; or at least I had never realized the extent to which the statement was true; but this Brownsville business has given me the most serious concern on this very point. If they were white troops I do not

[35]Theodore Roosevelt to Sir Harry Hamilton Johnston, July 11, 1908. Morison and Blum, *Letters,* VI, 1125–26.
[36]G. Wallace Chessman, *Theodore Roosevelt and the Politics of Power* (Boston, 1969), pp. 145–46. Henry F. Pringle, *Theodore Roosevelt* (New York, 1931, 1956), pp. 322–27.

believe that at this moment any human being would be maintaining their innocence. . . . But as it is, with a few noted exceptions the colored people have made a fetish of the innocence of the troops and have been supporting in every way the political demagogs and visionary enthusiasts who have struck hands in the matter of their defense.[37]

In 1901, President Roosevelt invited the Negro leader, Booker T. Washington, to dinner at the White House. The Southern press was aroused to indignant fury. "When Mr. Roosevelt sits down to dinner with a Negro, he declares that the Negro is the social equal of the white man," the *New Orleans Times-Democrat* observed. In the editorial opinion of the *Memphis Scimitar*, it was "the most damnable outrage ever." Josephus Daniels, who would later become the bureaucratic superior of another Roosevelt also destined to occupy the White House,[38] thought the dinner was not "a precedent that will encourage Southern men to join hands with Mr. Roosevelt."[39]

Roosevelt was taken aback at the furore. The "idiot or vicious Bourbon element of the South," he wrote Curtis Guild, "is crazy because I had Booker T. Washington to dine. I shall have him to dine just as often as I please, exactly as I should have Eliot or Hadley."[40] He expressed amazement that the dinner had "not only become a national but an international affair," adding that it had seemed natural to "show Booker Washington a little ordinary courtesy, as I was consulting and advising with him on public policies of great importance."[41]

Years later, he commented that "all the tomfool mugwumps of the land, the *Evening Post* people, for example, hysterically applauded me. Yet as a matter of fact what I did was a mistake. It was misinterpreted by the white men of the South and by the black men of the South; and in the North, it had no effect, either good or bad."

[37]Theodore Roosevelt to Ray Stannard Baker, March 30, 1907. Morison and Blum, *Letters,* V, 634.
[38]Daniels would be Secretary of the Navy under Woodrow Wilson throughout World War I and Franklin Delano Roosevelt would serve as his Assistant Secretary. When FDR became President, he named Daniels Ambassador to Mexico.
[39]Pringle, *Roosevelt,* p. 175.
[40]Theodore Roosevelt to Curtis Guild, October 28, 1901. Morison and Blum, *Letters,* III, 184.
[41]Theodore Roosevelt to Philip Bathell Stewart, October 25, 1901. *Ibid.,* p. 182.

He thought that to try to explain or justify the act would merely compound the error. The invitation had been "a mistake because I assumed that the Southern whites were much further advanced intellectually and morally than was actually the case and because I made a similar mistaken assumption about the Southern blacks."[42] It was a mistake Roosevelt did not repeat. He never again invited a Negro to a meal at the White House.

Lynching

Roosevelt condemned lynching, a crime which was so prevalent that it seemed to stigmatize the American character, both publicly and privately. He did so in unambiguous terms; yet he believed that Negro behavior had contributed to exacerbating the epidemic of mob violence and sadism. In 1903, he wrote his Attorney General, Philander Chase Knox, refusing to commute or pardon Benjamin Hill, a white man who was under sentence of death for murdering his wife:

> We are now passing through an era of lawlessness in this country. Lynching has become very common, and where the victims are colored men it takes the inhuman aspect of putting to death by torture—usually by burning alive. Among the causes that have produced this outbreak of lynching—I say 'among them,' for I do not know how prominent it should be put among them—is, in my judgment, unquestionably the delays of the law, and the way in which clever criminal lawyers are able ofttimes to secure the acquittal, and almost always to secure long delays in the conviction, of men accused of offenses for which the penalty should be absolutely certain and the punishment as quick as possible. Every pardon of a murderer who should have been executed is to my mind just so much encouragement to lynching, just so much putting of a premium on lawlessness.[43]

A few weeks later, he wrote Governor Durbin of Indiana, congratulating him on having intervened decisively and courageously to end a three-day race riot.

Roosevelt expressed alarm at "the growth of lynching in this

[42]Theodore Roosevelt to Charles Grenfill Washburn, November 20, 1915. *Ibid.,* VIII, 981–82.
[43]Theodore Roosevelt to Philander Chase Knox, July 24, 1903. *Ibid.,* III, 528.

country" and "the peculiarly hideous forms so often taken by mob violence when colored men are the victims." He had no sympathy for the criminals. "Men who have been guilty of a crime like rape or murder should be visited with swift and certain punishment." They were entitled to a fair trial, but the guilty had forfeited all right to sympathy.

The evils of lynching were multiple. "There are certain hideous sights which when once seen can never be wholly erased from the mental retina. The mere fact of having seen them implies degradation. This is a thousandfold stronger when instead of merely seeing the deed, the man has participated in it. Whoever in any part of our country has ever taken part in lawlessly putting to death a criminal by the dreadful torture of fire must forever after have the awful spectacle of his own handiwork seared into his brain and soul. He can never again be the same man."

Even if lynching invariably punished the guilty, it would be evil. "Every violent man in the community is encouraged by every case of lynching in which the lynchers go unpunished to himself take the law into his own hands whenever it suits his own convenience. . . . The spirit of lawlessness grows with what it feeds on, and when mobs with impunity lynch criminals for one cause, they are certain to lynch real or alleged criminals for other causes. In the recent cases of lynching over three-fourths were not for rape at all, but for murder, attempted murder, and even less heinous offenses."

Having said this, Roosevelt turned to the case in which a Negro commits a hideous crime. Such a man

> not merely sins against humanity in inexpiable and unpardonable fashion, but sins particularly against his own race, and does them a wrong far greater than any white man can do them. Therefore, in such cases the colored people throughout the land should in every possible way show their belief that they, more than all others in the community, are horrified at the commission of such a crime and are peculiarly concerned in taking every possible measure to prevent its recurrence and to bring the criminal to immediate justice. The slightest lack of vigor either in denunciation of the crime or in bringing the criminal to justice is itself unpardonable.[44]

[44]Theodore Roosevelt to Winfield Taylor Durbin, August 6, 1903. *Ibid.,* III, 541–42.

This letter was released for publication. In retrospect, it seems to place more responsibility on the Negro community for passivity than the latter deserved. The Negroes were in effect excluded from the judiciary, the profession of law, police forces and juries. There was little they could do legally to secure the prompt apprehension and punishment of criminals. Given a situation in which the accused Negro, whether guilty or innocent, ran the risk of being slowly roasted to death by a rabid mob, the reluctance of black communities to denounce suspects to the authorities seemed understandable.

Nevertheless, Roosevelt reiterated this theme and made it clear that he was not only concerned but shocked at black solidarity with criminals of the Negro race. "Negroes too often band together to shelter their own criminals," he pointed out, "which action had an undoubted effect in helping to precipitate the hideous Atlanta race-riots. I condemn such attitude strongly, for I feel that it is fraught with the gravest danger to both races."[45]

Equal Rights, Unequal Abilities

"I have not been able to think out any solution of the terrible problem offered by the presence of the Negro on this continent," Roosevelt observed in 1901, "but of one thing I am sure, and that is that inasmuch as he is here and can neither be killed nor driven away, the only wise and honorable and Christian thing to do is treat each black man and each white man strictly on his merits as a man, giving him no more and no less than he shows himself worthy to have."[46]

On another occasion, he observed that he could not "treat mere color as a permanent bar to holding office" any more than creed or birthplace, but he would not consider it as "conferring a right to hold office" either.[47]

On one occasion, he referred to the Negroes as an example of "a perfectly stupid race."[48] He believed that their future lay in increasingly skilled manual work rather than in the professions. "Laziness and shiftlessness, these, and above all, vice and criminality of every kind, are evils more potent for harm to the

[45]Archibald Roosevelt, *Roosevelt*, p. 3; *Memorial Edition*, XXIV, 33–35 (1906).
[46]*Ibid.*, p. 13; XXIII, 192 (1901).
[47]*Ibid.*, p. 9; XXIII, 196 (1903).
[48]*Ibid.*, p. 12; XIV, 127–28 (1895).

black race than all acts of oppression of white men put together."[49]

He did not believe that one could legislate equality. "The negroes were formerly held in slavery," he wrote. "This was a wrong which legislation could remedy, and which could not be remedied except by legislation. Accordingly, they were set free by law. This having been done, many of their friends believed that in some way, by additional legislation, we could at once put them on an intellectual, social, and business equality with the whites. The effort has failed completely."[50]

The only people who could really help the Negroes were the white Southerners. "For nearly half a century, the Republican party has proceeded on the theory that the colored man in the South, in order to secure him his political rights, should be encouraged to antagonize the white man in the South; for nearly half a century the Democratic party has encouraged the white man of the South to trample on the colored man."[51]

Roosevelt did not believe that all Negroes were entitled to the vote. He believed, and this was very different, that race should not be a reason for their disfranchisement. Under the leadership of "practical, competent, high-minded white men," he hoped, the right to vote would be secured "to the negro who shows that he possesses the intelligence, integrity, and self-respect which justify such right of political expression in his white neighbor."[52]

The Negro and the Progressive Party

When Theodore Roosevelt accepted the nomination of the Progressive Party for President in 1912, he broke with the traditional Republican political pattern in the South. Instead of creating an impotent Negro party south of the Mason-Dixon line, he backed the exclusion of colored delegates to the Progressive Party convention from that area. The reasons for this stand were stated ably and at length in a letter to Julian La Rose Harris, son of Joel Chandler Harris, who had achieved popularity as author of the *Uncle Remus* dialect stories.

[49] *Ibid.,* p. 8; XVIII, 465 (1905).
[50] *Ibid.,* p. 6; XVI, 377 (1895).
[51] *Ibid.,* p. 2; XIX, 415 (1912).
[52] *Ibid.,* p. 7; XIX, 417–18 (1912).

"Henry Ward Beecher once said that the worst enemy of the colored man was the man who stirred up enmity between the white and colored men who have to live as neighbors," Roosevelt wrote. "In the South, the Democratic machine has sought to keep itself paramount by encouraging the hatred of the white man for the black; the Republican machine has sought to perpetuate itself by stirring up the black man against the white, and surely the time has come when we should understand the mischief in both courses, and should abandon them."

The Progressive Party, he pointed out, was enlisting "the best colored men" from the northern States in its ranks on equal terms with white men. Negro delegates were being chosen for the national convention from these States. By contrast, the Republican Party had resisted with all its strength his efforts as President to appoint Negroes to public office in the North. The Republican view had been that the colored man "should have office only in the South."

"For forty-five years the Republican Party has striven to build up in the Southern States in question a party based on the theory that the pyramid will unsupported stand permanently on its apex instead of on its base. For forty-five years the Republican Party has endeavored in these States to build up a party in which the negro should be dominant, a party consisting almost exclusively of negroes."

These Negroes represented nothing but themselves. They had no political power, because they were disfranchised by the dominant white majority. They were unworthy people "controlled by the promise of office or by means even more questionable" and were manipulated by machine politicians to control conventions.

The 1912 Chicago Republican Convention had split the Republican Party by choosing Taft, rather than Roosevelt, as its Presidential standard bearer. That choice and the consequent schism was "forced by those rotten-borough delegates from the South." In the North, the Negro delegates voted substantially as did their white neighbors. The Negro delegates from the South, however, "representing nothing but their own greed for money or office," were "overwhelmingly antiprogressive."

In conclusion, Roosevelt observed:

"We face certain actual facts, sad and unpleasant facts, but facts which must be faced if we are to dwell in the world of realities and not of shams. . . . It would be much worse than useless to try to build up the Progressive Party in these Southern States where there is no Republican Party, by appealing to the negroes or to the men who in the past have derived their sole standing from leading and manipulating the negroes." All this course could achieve would be "to create another impotent little corrupt faction of would-be officeholders, of delegates whose expenses to conventions had to be paid, and whose votes sometimes had to be bought." The alternative and constructive course was "by appealing to the best white men in the South, the men of justice and of vision as well as of strength and leadership, and by frankly putting the movement in their hands from the outset" to "create a situation by which the colored men of the South will ultimately get justice as it is not possible for them to get justice if we are to continue and perpetuate the present conditions."[53]

This realistic appeal not only fell on deaf ears, but alienated almost all Negro leaders, including even Booker T. Washington. Their reaction should have been predictable. Power in the Progressive Party and patronage jobs if it should win the election were more important than those long-range benefits to the entire Negro population of the South which Roosevelt envisaged. Theodore Roosevelt's realism and honesty cost him Negro support. The colored vote swung to Woodrow Wilson, who won the three-cornered election and, once inaugurated, pursued a policy of racial segregation and Negro exclusion in the Federal bureaucracy which Roosevelt would neither have advocated nor have tolerated.

[53]Theodore Roosevelt to Julian La Rose Harris, August 1, 1912. Morison and Blum, *Letters*, VII, 584–90.

CHAPTER EIGHTEEN

Taft, Wilson and the New Segregation

> The white men of the South were aroused by the mere instinct of self-preservation to rid themselves, by fair means or foul, of the intolerable burden of governments sustained by the votes of ignorant negroes and conducted in the interest of adventurers: governments whose incredible debts were incurred that thieves might be enriched, whose increasing loans and taxes went to no public use but into the pockets of party managers and corrupt contractors.
>
> —Woodrow Wilson, *A History of the American People.*[1]

The four somewhat uneventful years of the presidency of William Howard Taft (1909–1913) were marked by no revolutionary changes in policy toward the Negro. In his Inaugural Address, Taft declared that he would not appoint Negroes to Federal offices in the South where white people objected to them and this induced W. E. Burghardt Du Bois to withdraw his support from the Republican President.[2] According to the historian of the National Association for the Advancement of Colored People (NAACP), Taft made "sweeping changes by replacing deserving Negroes with lily-white Republicans" in Government jobs. Whether those eliminated were in fact "deserving" is, however, a matter of dispute: in Theodore Roosevelt's opinion, the beneficiaries of the Negro patronage machines were

[1](New York, 1903), V, 58.
[2]Charles Flint Kellogg *NAACP* (Baltimore, n.d.), I, 73, 155.

even less competent than those who reaped public sinecures from their white counterparts.

According to a partisan and at times inaccurate source, Taft recognized that the Fifteenth Amendment, prohibiting the abridgment of the right to vote by either the Federal Government or the States "on account of race, color, or previous condition of servitude," had not been generally enforced. He thought that state legislation in the South did not violate the Amendment and that the right of "intelligent and well to do" Negroes would be asserted, while the franchise would be "withheld only from the ignorant and irresponsible of both races."[3]

The fledgling NAACP, which had been organized less than a year before Taft's inauguration, asked the President to urge Congress to pass an anti-lynching law, but Taft replied that this was a matter which lay exclusively within the jurisdiction of the several States and that the Federal Government had no constitutional power to intervene.[4] In 1919, after he had retired from the Presidency, Taft made his personal sympathies quite clear by joining with 129 other eminent Americans in signing an NAACP-sponsored "Address to the Nation on Lynching."[5]

In a case of flagrant injustice against a Negro, Taft intervened at the instigation of Oswald Garrison Villard. An illiterate South Carolina Negro farm hand, named Pink Franklin, was sentenced to death for killing a white man when he and his family were attacked in their hut by nightriders. The President interceded with the State Governor and Franklin's sentence was commuted to life imprisonment.[6]

Taft at Biddle University

On May 20, 1909, the newly inaugurated President addressed a large and enthusiastic audience at Charlotte, North Carolina, during a speaking tour of the South. Immediately after the speech, Taft was driven to Biddle University, a Negro institution founded by the Presbyterian Church in 1867 and dedicated to industrial, literary and Bible studies. Here he addressed "a

[3]Rayford W. Logan, *The Negro in the United States* (New York, 1957), p. 65.
[4]Kellogg, *NAACP*, p. 211.
[5]*Ibid.*, pp. 234–35.
[6]*Ibid.*, pp. 60–61.

select audience of the colored race, considerably above the general level of intelligence."[7]

Taft told his audience that he never went South without expressing his "profound sympathy with the colored race, and.... earnest hope in the success of the struggle they are making." He was aware of "the troublous times" through which the Negro had passed, but believed:

> There is growing over the entire South a feeling due to the development of the economic conditions, that you will be a necessity for the prosperity of the South, if you will only do what you ought to do to make your race happy....
>
> You can demonstrate to the white men of the South by making yourself members of the community, that it is as much to their interest to treat you well as it is to your interest to have them treat you well.
>
> I don't want to minimize the importance of the political rights, but I do wish to emphasize the fact that those rights attend and follow economic and industrial success....

To an applauding audience, Taft referred to "the interest that your Southern white neighbors is [sic] taking in your welfare, your education, and your profit."

As a member of the James trust fund for industrial colored schools and a trustee of Hampton Institute, Taft said that he had "ground for hope," but understood the "agonized feeling, when the negro feels that the whole world is against him."

Taft's view was that the Negro's future in the South would be chiefly in agriculture:

"Your race is adopted [sic] to be a race of farmers first, and all the time. You have shown it in the start, by the way you have taken over the agriculture of the South, and you are going to justify it by improving the agriculture, under the influence of the industrial education, which this school and other schools are going to give you within the next three or four years."[8]

---

[7] *Souvenir of the President's Visit to Charlotte, North Carolina, May 20.* No author, publisher, date or pagination given. This rare contemporary document was made available to us through the courtesy of Professor A. H. George (Retired) of Johnson University, the successor to Biddle.

[8] The anonymous white editor, from whose hands we have this one and only version of Taft's speech, was as ignorant of the elementary rules of English grammar as he was of spelling.

In his brief history, *The Negro in the United States,* Professor Rayford W. Logan of Howard University reports Taft's thoughts as follows:

"He ridiculed the idea that the two races could live amicably together in the United States and argued that the only way to solve the race problem was to send Negroes out of the United States."[9]

This version shows such an unwillingness or incapacity to even approximate historical truth that it is perhaps worth while to give the pertinent text of President Taft's remarks:

> Now there are gentlemen, and I don't know but what there are some of your colored race, who say, 'Well, there is no hope for the negro in America; we must ship him out of the country. It is hopeless to have two races, white and black, and think that they can't [sic][10] live together.' Well, we have been living together fifty years, and just how are we going to stop, nobody yet has been able to explain. There are some statesmen that say it is impossible, and we must ship the negro away. I don't know where, perhaps to Africa, perhaps to a desert island. There are ten million of you and you are growing and perhaps in the next ten or fifteen years there may be fifteen million. (Applause). While these gentlemen are explaining, the problem of the moving is getting more and more difficult. It is an absurdity; it is chemerical [sic] to talk about any such remedy for what is called the race problem. The time is coming, in my judgment, when the business men of the South are going to recognize much more fully than they do today, the great advantage the South has in your presence on the soil.

Professor Logan's misrepresentations of Taft's views have gained some circulation and credence, despite the fact that there is no support for them in Taft's papers, the back files of the *New York Times,* or the text just quoted. A moderate on the race issue, who supported Negro educational foundations before attaining the Presidency and served on an NAACP committee after returning to private life,[11] Taft has been inaccurately depicted as a man who, like Jefferson, Madison and Lincoln, advocated deportation of the Negro people from the United States.

[9]Logan, *Negro,* p. 66.
[10]The maladroit editor must mean *can.*
[11]Kellogg, *NAACP,* p. 141.

Woodrow Wilson, American Historian

"On the whole," wrote W. E. Burghardt Du Bois, at the time the outstanding intellectual of the militant Negro movement, "We do not believe that Woodrow Wilson admires Negroes."[12] The occasion for this magnificent understatement was Wilson's nomination in 1912 as Presidential candidate of the Democratic Party.

Had Du Bois taken the trouble to read Wilson's five-volume *History of the American People,* he could have entertained few uncertainties concerning its author's appraisal of the Negro. For example, Wilson characterized the condition of the newly emancipated black men of the South in these eloquent words:

> They had the easy faith, the simplicity, the idle hopes, the inexperience of children. Their masterless, homeless freedom made them the more pitiable, the more dependent, because under slavery they had been shielded, the weak and incompetent with the strong and capable; had never learned independence or the rough buffets of freedom. It was a menace to society itself that the negroes should thus of a sudden be set free and left without tutelage or restraint ... The country filled with vagrants, looking for pleasure and gratuitous fortune. Idleness bred want, as always, and the vagrants turned thieves or importunate beggars. The tasks of ordinary labor stood untouched; the idlers grew insolent, dangerous; nights went anxiously by, for fear of riot and incendiary fire. It was imperatively necessary that something should be done, if only to bring order again and make the streets of the towns and the highways of the country-sides safe to those who went about their tasks. The southern legislatures, therefore, promptly undertook remedies of their own—such remedies as English legislators had been familiar with time out of mind.
>
> The vagrants, it was enacted, should be bound out to compulsory labor; and all who would not work must be treated as vagrants ... Minor negroes were to be put under masters by articles of apprenticeship. Negroes were forbidden, upon pain of arrest by a vigilant patrol, to be abroad after the ringing of the curfew at nine o'clock, without written permission from their employers. Fines were ordered for a numerous list of the more annoying minor offences likely to be committed by the freedmen, and it was directed that all those who could not pay the fines should be hired out to labor by judicial process ...

[12] *New York Age,* July 11, 1912.

There was nothing unprecedented in such legislation, even where it went farthest. The greater part of it was paralleled by statutes of labor and vagrancy still to be found on the statute books of several of the northern States. But it was impossible it should stand in the same light. The labor and vagrancy laws of Maine, Rhode Island, and Connecticut, which they most resembled, were uttered against a few tramps and beggars, here and there a runaway servant or apprentice, an occasional breach of duties regularly contracted for; while these new laws of the South were uttered against an entire race, but just now emancipated.[13]

The reason the North was unable to take a calmer and more rational view of the vagrancy laws of the defeated South, in Wilson's opinion, was that the passions of the War had created in Northern minds an unrealistic view of the Negro:

The negro had got a veritable apotheosis in the minds of northern men by the processes of the war. Those who had sent their sons to the field of battle to die in order that he might be free could but regard him as the innocent victim of circumstances; a creature who needed only liberty to make him a man; could but regard any further attempt on the part of his one-time masters to restrain him as mere vindictive defiance. They did not look into the facts: they let their sentiment and their sense of power dictate their thought and purpose.[14]

"Roving Knight Errants of the Klan"

Woodrow Wilson's appraisal of the Ku Klux Klan was not exactly what his liberal devotees and enthusiasts of "the new freedom" would have expected. After describing how "a little group of idle young men in the Tennessee village of Pulaski" formed "a secret club for the mere pleasure of association, for private amusement," which they called the *Kuklos* (Greek for *circle*), Wilson proceeded:

Secrecy and mystery were at the heart of the pranks they planned: secrecy with regard to the membership of their Circle, mystery with regard to the place and the objects of its meetings; and the mystery of disguise and of silent parade when the comrades rode abreast at night when the moon was up: a white mask,

[13]Wilson, *History*, V, 18–22.
[14]*Ibid.*, p. 22.

a tall cardboard hat, the figures of man and horse sheeted like a ghost, and the horses' feet muffled to move without sound of their approach. It was the delightful discovery of the thrill of awesome fear, the woeful looking for calamity that swept through the country-sides as they moved from place to place upon their silent visitations, coming no man could say whence, going upon no man knew what errand, that put thought of mischief into the minds of the frolicking comrades. It threw the negroes into a very ecstasy of panic to see these sheeted 'Ku Klux' move near them in the shrouded night; and their comic fear stimulated the lads who excited it to many an extravagant prank and mummery. No one knew or could discover who the masked players were; no one could say whether they meant serious or only innocent mischief; and the zest of the business lay in keeping the secret close.

Here was a very tempting and dangerous instrument of power for days of disorder and social upheaval, when law seemed set aside by the very government itself, and outsiders, adventurers, were in the seats of authority, the poor negroes, and white men without honor, their only partisans. Year by year the organization spread . . . until at last there had sprung into existence a great *Ku Klux Klan,* an 'Invisible Empire of the South.' bound together in loose organization, to protect the southern country from some of the ugliest hazards of a time of revolution."[15]

The objectives of the Klan, according to Wilson, were " 'to protect their people from indignities and wrongs; to succor the suffering, particularly the families of dead confederate soldiers'; to enforce what they conceived to be the real laws of their States 'and defend the constitution of the United States and all laws passed in conformity thereto.' "[16]

Woodrow Wilson conceded that violent elements committed excesses either as members of the Klan or using its name.

"It was impossible to keep such a power in hand," he wrote.

Sober men governed the counsels and moderated the plans of these roving knight errants; but it was lawless work at best. They had set themselves after the first year or two of mere mischievous frolic had passed, to right a disordered society through the power of fear. Men of hot passions who could not always be restrained carried their plans into effect. Reckless men, not of their order, malicious fellows of the baser sort who did not feel the compulsions of honor and who had private grudges to satisfy,

[15] *Ibid.,* pp. 59–60.
[16] *Ibid.,* pp. 61–62.

imitated their disguises and borrowed their methods . . . It became the chief object of the night-riding comrades to silence or
drive from the country the principal mischief-makers of the
reconstruction regime, whether white or black. The negroes
were generally easy enough to deal with: a thorough fright usually disposed them to make utter submission, resign their parts
in affairs, leave the country,—do anything their ghostly visitors
demanded. But white men were less tractable . . . Houses
were surrounded in the night and burned, and the inmates shot
as they fled, as in the dreadful days of border warfare. Men
were dragged from their houses and tarred and feathered. Some
who defied the vigilant visitors came mysteriously to some sudden death.[17]

Despite these indubitable evils and "brutal crimes," the future President looked on the movement with a certain amount
of sympathy, considered it a generally salutory force and one
led by men of honor and dedicated to good principles. "The Ku
Klux and those who masqueraded in their guise struck at first
only at those who made palpable mischief between the races or
set just laws aside to make themselves masters;" he observed
in one place, adding, "But their work grew under their hands,
and their zest for it."[18] At another point, Wilson commented:
"Those who loved mastery and adventure directed the work of
the Ku Klux."[19]

A Southerner by birth and breeding, whose youth had been
scarred by the outrages inflicted on the white South by carpetbaggers, scalawags and freedmen, Woodrow Wilson shared
most of the views of his region and his class on the subject of
the Negro. He believed him to be childlike and credulous, super-
stitious and cowardly, a political incompetent destined to be
manipulated by one white group or another. He approved
the South's most violent reactions to *post-bellum* military
rule—the vagrancy laws and the night-riding secret organizations of terror, investing the latter with an aura of knightly
adventure. The inescapable implication of Wilson's *History*
was that its author did not regard the Negro as an equal and did

[17] *Ibid.,* pp. 62–63.
[18] *Ibid.,* p. 64.
[19] *Ibid.,* p. 72.

not consider him entitled to political or social equality with the white man.

Segregation under President Wilson

As President of Princeton, Woodrow Wilson had used evasive tactics to successfully prevent Negro students from enrolling in the University at a time when most of the great Northern universities admitted them.[20] Moreover, it was believed that he "had failed to give recognition to coloured men while governor of New Jersey."[21] He drew the color line in all social relations, though he was not as adamant a segregationist as his Georgia-born wife.

Negroes were disturbed over the fact that Wilson's campaign manager was Josephus Daniels, a staunch advocate of white supremacy who had worked with the anti-Negro Red Shirts. During the 1912 Presidential campaign, Daniels expressed his views on the race question in his newspaper in the following terms:

> The South is solidly Democratic because of 'the realization that the subjection of the negro, politically, and the separation of the negro, socially, are paramount to all other considerations in the South short of the preservation of the Republic itself. And we shall recognize no emancipation, nor shall we proclaim any deliverer, that falls short of these essentials to the peace and the welfare of our part of the country.'[22]

Appointed Secretary of the Navy by Wilson, Daniels and his young Assistant Secretary, Franklin Delano Roosevelt, incurred the wrath of the NAACP by admitting Negroes only as "mess corpsmen" throughout World War I.[23]

Oswald Garrison Villard, publisher of the *Nation*, a leader of the NAACP and a grandson of William Lloyd Garrison, had met Wilson as early as 1895 and quarreled with him on his appraisal

[20]Arthur S. Link, *Wilson: The Road to the White House* (Princeton, 1947), p. 502.

[21]Ray Stannard Baker, *Woodrow Wilson, Life and Letters: Governor, 1910–1913,* (New York, 1931), p. 387.

[22]*Raleigh News and Observer,* October 1, 1912. Quoted in Link, *White House,* p. 501.

[23]Kellogg, *NAACP,* p. 248.

of the Abolitionists in his *History.* A close friendship developed in 1910 and Villard's *Evening Post* backed Wilson for Governor of New Jersey. During the 1912 presidential campaign, Villard met regularly with Wilson's campaign managers to plan strategy.[24]

Wilson told Villard that he would not appoint Negroes to Government jobs in the South because that would simply intensify racial animosity and that he would not support Federal anti-lynching legislation because it was unconstitutional. However, he would speak out against lynching.[25] He assured a delegation of Blacks that, if elected, he would "seek to be President of the whole nation and would know no differences of race or creed or section."

J. Milton Waldron, head of the Washington, D.C. branch of the NAACP, interviewed candidate Wilson and reported in a memorandum to his organization that the latter had committed himself to veto legislation hostile to Negroes, to administer the laws fairly, and not to discriminate in government employment on the basis of race. When Villard forwarded this memorandum to Wilson with the request that he be authorized to publish it, the Democratic standard-bearer expressed amazement and said that he had neither promised to veto laws objectionable to the Negroes nor said that he was in need of Negro support. Villard then drafted a policy statement on the race question, but Wilson refused to sign it and also refused to address an NAACP-sponsored mass meeting at Carnegie Hall. He did, however, write the Negro bishop, Alexander Walters, "to assure my coloured fellow citizens of my earnest wish to see justice done them in every matter, and no mere grudging justice, but justice executed with liberality and cordial good feeling." He pledged himself to "absolute fair dealing" and to aid in "advancing the interests of their race in the United States."[26]

Wilson got the largest vote any Democratic candidate for President had ever obtained. When he was elected, Negro spokesmen predicted that the New Freedom would inaugurate a renaissance for their race. "Mr. Wilson is in favor of the

[24] *Ibid.,* p. 157.
[25] *Ibid.*
[26] Baker, *Wilson,* pp. 387–88.

things which tend toward the uplift, improvement, and advancement of my people," Booker T. Washington declared, and at his hands we have nothing to fear."[27]
One of Villard's pet projects was a National Race Commission to conduct "a non-partisan, scientific study of the status of the Negro in the life of the nation, with particular reference to his economic situation." The Commission was to consist of five Northern Whites, five Southern Whites and five Negroes. It was to be financed by a grant of $50,000, which Villard hoped he would be able to get from Jacob Schiff or Julius Rosenwald (the Rockefeller and Carnegie funds being, in his opinion, too conservative to consider.) The purpose of private financing was to sidetrack Congress, which would predictably turn it down. In May 1912, two months after the Inauguration, Villard presented Wilson with the printed plan, touted it as a record of fifty years of progress since emancipation, and left the White House believing the President had agreed to go forward on the matter.

When Villard returned from a trip to Europe, however, he found that segregation was being introduced into government departments and that Wilson was unwilling to endorse the National Race Commission.

"It would be hard to make anyone understand the delicacy and difficulty of the situation I find existing here with regard to the colored people," Wilson wrote Villard. "You know my own disposition in the matter, I am sure, but I find myself absolutely blocked by the sentiment of Senators; not alone Senators from the South, by any means, but Senators from various parts of the country." Wilson concluded that "because of the feeling that there is some sort of indictment involved in the very inquiry itself, I feel it would be a blunder on my part to consent to name the commission."[28] Villard retorted that the time would come when Wilson would "find it necessary to go ahead and do what is right" without considering the mood of the Senate.

Meanwhile, a swarm of Negro Democratic politicians, among whom Bishop Alexander Walters was conspicuous, were urging the President to dismiss Negro Republican office-hold-

[27]Arthur S. Link, *Wilson: The New Freedom* (Princeton, 1956), p. 242.
[28]Baker, *Wilson*, pp. 222–23.

ers and promptly replace them with Democrats of the same
race.[29] Attorney General Burleson and Secretary of the Treasury McAdoo, who headed the only departments with substantial numbers of Negro employees, began to get rid of Black
Republican office-holders and to downgrade or demote even
those Negro employees who were under civil service.[30] This
was not entirely dictated by race prejudice. It was in part a
reaction to the widespread belief, one shared by Theodore
Roosevelt, that the Negro office-holders appointed by the
Republicans had been chosen for exclusively political reasons
and without regard to their competence.

With the President's approval, Secretary McAdoo planned to
make the Registry Division in the Treasury a 100-percent Negro unit of the Federal Government. This project was shipwrecked, however, when the Senate refused to confirm the appointment of Adam E. Patterson, a Negro, as Register.

Wilson determined to comply with his promise made as a
Presidential candidate not to put the Negroes "to any greater
political disadvantage than they had suffered under previous
Democratic Administrations." He realized that this meant to
Negro leaders that he "would not willingly take away from
them the minor offices which they had so long occupied in the
District."[31]

Segregating Government Employees

The subject of segregation of government employees first
came up at a Cabinet meeting on April 11, 1913. Albert Burleson, the Texas-born Postmaster General, complained of "intolerable" conditions in the Railway Mail Service, where Whites
not only had to work with Blacks but to use the same towels,
lavatories and drinking glasses. He announced that he planned
to institute race segregation in the Railway Mail Service gradually, while continuing the employment of Negroes where this
"would not be objectionable." He expressed the view that race
segregation would be an appropriate policy for the Government
as a whole. President Wilson commented that his chief desire

[29]Link, *New Freedom*, p. 242.
[30]*Ibid.*, pp. 248–49.
[31]Baker, *Wilson*, p. 224.

was to avoid friction in the departments and no opposition to Burleson's program was voiced.[32]

The President also favored segregating all Negro employees of the Government from their White counterparts. This step was not only in conformity with his personal preference for social separation of the races; he also believed it was in the interests of the Negroes themselves as it would relieve the virulent racial tension in the District and elsewhere in the nation. The drive for segregation had widespread public support which reflected a growing mood of disillusion with and antipathy toward the Negro. In the spring of 1913, bills were introduced in Congress to legislate race separation on Washington streetcars. There was a vociferous public demand to dismiss all Negro officeholders who were in a position to "boss white girls." One Wilson official declared: "There are no Government positions for negroes in the South. A negro's place is in the cornfield.[33]

Backed by an anti-Negro group in Congress, the National Democratic Fair Play Association protested that White girls in government departments were being "compelled to work alongside of a greasy, ill-smelling negro man or woman" and "to take dictation from, be subservient to, bear the ignominy and carry the disgrace of the taunts, sneers or insults of such negroes."[34]

It was estimated that 24,500 of the 490,000 workers in the Railway Mail Service were Negroes. The Fair Play Association asserted that integration in the service was driving away all decent Whites. Complaints were received about "low and criminal elements" among the colored employees. A White female employee of the Department of the Interior wrote: "I also worked for a dark-skinned, wooly-headed Negro. I then felt if a human would ever be justified in ever ending his existence I would then, for I was a Southern woman, my father a distinguished officer during the Civil War."[35]

When President Wilson suggested that by keeping workers of

---

[32]Kathleen Wolgemuth, "Woodrow Wilson and Federal Segregation," *Journal of Negro History,* XLIV, No. 2 (April, 1959), 158–59.
[33]Link, *New Freedom,* p. 246.
[34]*Ibid.*
[35]Wolgemuth, "Wilson," p. 159.

the two races separate in governmental departments he was assuaging racial tension, he was subjected to a barrage of protests from social workers, clergymen, Jewish spokesmen, liberals and others, who termed the drift toward segregation "cruel, unjust. . . . and a lamentable betrayal of democratic principles."[36] Bewildered by the fury and the lofty moral tone of the protest, the President replied that he believed segregation to be in the best interests of the Negroes themselves and that several Negro spokesmen approved of his measures.

"It is true that the segregation of the colored employees in the several departments was begun upon the initiative and at the suggestion of several of the heads of departments," Wilson wrote Villard,

> but as much in the interest of the negroes as for any other reason, with the approval of some of the most influential negroes I know, and with the idea that the friction, or rather the discontent and uneasiness, which had prevailed in many of the departments would thereby be removed. It is as far as possible from being a movement *against* the negroes. I sincerely believe it to be in their interest. And what distresses me about your letter is to find that you look at it in so different a light.[37]
>
> My own feeling is, by putting certain bureaus and sections of the service in the charge of negroes we are rendering them more safe in their possession of office and less likely to be discriminated against.[38]

On September 8, 1913 Wilson wrote H. A. Bridgman, the Negro editor of the *Congregationalist and Christian World,* to take personal responsibility for the drive toward race separation. "In reply to your kind letter of September 4th," the President observed, "I would say that I do approve of the segregation that is being attempted in several of the departments."[39] Wilson was subjected to pressure of an opposite sort from Southern members of Congress. While he presided over the extension of segregation from one department to another, he

---

[36]Link, *New Freedom,* p. 250.

[37]Villard requested the names of the Negroes who had approved the segregationist policies, promising that they would be "driven out of the communities in which they reside, or at least held up to the scorn of the race," but Wilson understandably refused to oblige. Villard to Wilson, September 18, 1913.

[38]Wilson to Villard, July 23, 1913. Baker, *Wilson,* p. 221.

[39]*Ibid.,* p. 223.

took seriously his obligation to serve as President of all the people and he refused to deny a qualified candidate public office because of his race. When he renominated Robert H. Terrell, an able Negro, to a judgeship in the District of Columbia, Senator Williams of Mississippi objected. Wilson replied somewhat weakly that he "could not avoid the nomination of Terrell," since there was "every reason to believe that he has not only performed his duties excellently, but that he has been the best judge of his rank in the District."[40]

The President also received protests over the appointment of Negroes to positions in which they wielded authority over white women. One such objection was voiced by Thomas Dixon, who had written the popular novel *The Clansman* in 1905 and held inflexible views on the race question.

"I do not think you know what is going on down here," Wilson wrote Dixon.

> We are handling the force of colored people who are now in the departments in just the way in which they ought to be handled. We are trying—and by degrees succeeding—a plan of concentration which will put them all together and will not in any one bureau mix the two races. . . . I am trying to handle these matters with the best judgment but in the spirit of the whole country, though with entire comprehension of the considerations which certainly do not need to be pointed out to me.[41]

Wilson's concentration plan, however, was not working. Negroes were not only being segregated, they were being eliminated. Negroes complained that when Wilson's plan to make the Registry Section in the Treasury entirely Negro was thwarted by congressional refusal to approve his colored nominee for section chief, the Registry Section became 60 percent White and only 40 percent Negro. In 1914, the Civil Service required that photographs of all candidates be submitted with their applications and this device was used, it was charged, to screen out Negroes.[42] Oswald Garrison Villard tried to get Charles W. Eliot, president of the Civil Service Reform League, president and subsequently president emeritus of Harvard Uni-

[40] *Ibid.*, p. 224.
[41] *Ibid.*, p. 222.
[42] Wolgemuth, "Wilson," pp. 160, 164.

versity, originator of The Five Foot Shelf, author of many
books, and a name to conjure with in turn-of-the-century
American culture, publicly to oppose the policy of firing Negro
employees who supposedly had civil service tenure. Eliot, however, refused, observing that in a democracy "civilized white
men" could not be comfortable working beside "barbarous
black men," particularly when the contacts might lead to miscegenation.[43]

Negro organizations of all sorts and the Negro press united
in their opposition to racial segregation in Government. The
vehemence of the protests from Negroes and liberals and Wilson's need for the continued support of such liberal-to-radical
luminaries as Villard made Wilson slacken his campaign and
even persuade McAdoo to rescind some of the measures the
latter had taken in the Treasury. These minor withdrawals
were merely tactical maneuvers, however, and, by the second
Wilson Administration, race segregation was a firm policy in
Washington offices and had been extended to the Senate lunch-
room and galleries.[44]

The Birth of a Nation

In 1915, Thomas Dixon cooperated with D. W. Griffith in pro-
ducing *The Birth of a Nation,* an epic motion picture on Reconstruction in the South based on Dixon's novel *The Clansman.*
The viewpoint of the film was strongly segregationist and predictably it aroused the angry protests of such Negro pressure
groups as the NAACP and the usual coterie of liberal social
workers and churchmen. The favorable picture of the Ku Klux
Klan, the strong statement of the wrongs suffered by the White
South and the derogatory depiction of the Negro during Reconstruction in *The Birth of a Nation* could not have disturbed
Woodrow Wilson, since this was precisely the viewpoint he had
adopted in his *History.*

Probably, Dixon had never read Wilson's description of the
condition of the South under Reconstruction. In any event, he
felt obliged to write Joseph P. Tumulty, the Secretary to the
President, on May 1, 1915:

[43]Eliot to Villard, November 11, 1913. Kellogg, *NAACP,* p. 172.
[44]Kellogg, *NAACP,* p. 172.

Of course, I didn't dare allow the President to know the *real big purpose back of my film—which was to revolutionize Northern sentiment by a presentation of history that would transform every man in my audience into a good Democrat!* And make no mistake about it—we are doing just that thing ... Every man who comes out of one of our theatres is a Southern partisan for life —except the members of Villard's Inter-Marriage Society who go there to knock.[45]

Dixon arranged for a private showing of *The Birth of a Nation* which President Wilson, Chief Justice of the United States Edward D. White and various Senators, Representatives and other Washington dignitaries attended. The political purpose was to stifle liberal and radical agitation against the motion picture by indicating that the leaders of the Government approved it. Wilson was apparently impressed and was quoted as saying that the film wrote "history with lightning."[46] Louisiana-born Chief Justice White, however, threatened to attack the picture publicly unless Dixon stopped telling people that he endorsed it. Tumulty thought the President should write "some sort of a letter showing that he did not approve the 'Birth of a Nation,' " but Wilson demurred on the grounds that to do so might seem to be yielding to the agitation stirred up by "that unspeakable fellow Tucker."[47] Three years later when the nation was at war, Wilson disapproved of showings of what he now called that "unfortunate production."[48]

Wilson never saw eye to eye with his liberal and radical supporters on the Negro issue, but succeeded, by skillful maneuvering and evasion, in avoiding a political rupture. The gathering storm clouds of World War I overshadowed the issue of the Negro's place in American society and Wilson's mind and energies were soon preoccupied by other issues.

[45]Quoted from the *Wilson Papers.* Link, *New Freedom,* p. 253, ftn. 39.
[46]According to Robert Moats Miller, "The Ku Klux Klan," in John Braeman, Robert H. Bremner and David Brody (eds.), *Change and Continuity in Twentieth-Century America: The 1920's.* (Columbus, 1968), p. 219.
[47]Wilson meant William Monroe Trotter, a Boston Negro editor and race leader, whom he had had thrown out of his office in November 1914 because he believed Trotter was trying to blackmail him. Link, *New Freedom,* p. 252.
[48]Woodrow Wilson to Joseph P. Tumulty, April 22, 1918.

CHAPTER NINETEEN

Warren Gamaliel Harding, Mediocrity and Moderation

> Men of both races may well stand uncompromisingly against every suggestion of social equality. Indeed, it would be helpful to have that word 'equality' eliminated from this consideration, to have it accepted on both sides that this is not a question of social equality, but a question of recognizing a fundamental, eternal, and inescapable difference.
>
> —Warren G. Harding, Speech at Birmingham, Alabama, October 26, 1921.

Shortly after Warren G. Harding was nominated as the Republican Party's standard-bearer at Chicago in 1920, Joseph P. Tumulty, private secretary to President Wilson, was approached by a stranger who showed him what purported to be documentary evidence that Harding had Negro blood. The stranger explained that this was campaign material and added that he thought the Democratic National Committee might be interested.

"The national Committee wouldn't touch it," Tumulty retorted.

"Why not?"

"Suppose Senator Harding is elected. What a terrible thing it would be for the country if it came out that we had a President alleged to be part Negro! I'll have nothing to do with it."[1]

---

[1] Samuel Hopkins Adams, *Incredible Era: The Life and Times of Warren Gamaliel Harding* (Boston, 1939), p. 181. The anecdote is based on Tumulty's statement to Adams.

The rumor that he was partly Negro had pursued Harding all of his adult life, poisoned his relationship with his father-in-law for many years, and impeded his rise on the ladder of political influence and power. Harding reacted with understandable anger and impotence. To deny the rumors would bring them out into the open and give them broader circulation and more general credence. He contented himself with assailing his tormentors in his newspaper, the *Marion* (Ohio) *Star*.[2] Harding once considered beating up the chief source of the report, Professor William Estabrook Chancellor of the College of Wooster in Wooster, Ohio, but political caution prevailed. His iron-willed wife, Florence Harding, flatly vetoed a suggestion that he repudiate the charge.[3]

The allegation that Harding was of mixed blood was based on a genealogy and research by Chancellor, a fanatic on the race question but by no means an ignoramus or an incompetent. William Estabrook Chancellor was a graduate of Amherst, where he had been class orator and had made Phi Beta Kappa. He then got his master's degree, studied at Harvard Law School, and completed his postgraduate education in Europe. He had taught history, sociology, political science, education and economics at reputable universities, among them Johns Hopkins, Northwestern, the University of Chicago and George Washington University. In *Who's Who in America* (1918–19 edition), he listed eighteen books he had written, one of them a two-volume history of the United States.

Although these accomplishments were by no means negligible, they did not make Dr. Chancellor a judicious or a dispassionate man. He did not know Harding and had no personal reason to dislike him, but his attitude was nevertheless paranoid. "A people threatened by contamination of the blood ought to care for the truth about its head man . . . .," Chancellor wrote. "Big, lazy, slouching, confused, ignorant, affable, yellow, and

---

[2] A sample is Harding's appraisal of a rival Marion, Ohio, newspaper publisher: "This Crawford, who works the temperance and pious racket for church support while his inebriate associate caters to saloon patronage . . . foams at the mouth whenever his sordid mind grasps anything done without his counsel; he rolls his eyes and straight evolves from his inner consciousness a double-twisted unadulterated, canvas-back lie that would make the devil blush." Adams, *Incredible Era*, p. 12.

[3] *Ibid.*, p. 185.

cringing like a negro butler to the great, such is the man who
has been used by Lodge, Smoot, Penrose, Knox, Harvey, Daugh-
erty to ruin Woodrow Wilson for the time being and to crash the
hopes of mankind for world peace."[4]

Chancellor did first-hand research in Blooming Grove, the
community where the Hardings had grown up, and spent two
weeks interviewing the area's oldest inhabitants. He claimed
that Elizabeth Madison Harding, the future President's great
grandmother had been colored. The town had been a terminus
of the underground railway and perhaps half of its residents
were Negro or partly Negro. Dr. H. F. Alderfer, who spent five
years of research on Harding and his contemporaries, covered
the same territory in the 1920s. While he himself doubted that
Harding was an octoroon, he found that this was the general
belief of Marion and Blooming Grove people. Adams covered
the same ground in 1938 and reached the same conclusion.

Back in 1849, there was a sensational murder case in Central
Ohio. Two partners in a smithy, David Butler and Amos Smith,
had a quarrel in the course of which Smith told Butler he had
"a nigger wife." Butler hurled a wrench at his tormentor and
killed him. When the issue was raised by the defense, the jury
found that it was not slanderous to call Mrs. Butler a Negro,
since her family, the Hardings, had always been so classified.
Mrs. Butler was the sister of George Tryon Harding, the great-
grandfather of Warren G. Harding who, according to Chancellor, had married a Negro woman.[5]

Harding's father told a Syracuse newspaper that his son had
been named "Warren Gamaliel, after an uncle, a Methodist
preacher."[6] According to Chancellor, Warren Gamaliel Bancroft was a Negro minister.[7] Harding's attitude was one of un-
certainty. He once told James Miller Faulkner, a political re-
porter and an old friend: "How do I know, Jim? One of my
ancestors may have jumped the fence."

---

[4]*Ibid*, p. 278. Dr. Chancellor was a Democrat, a Presbyterian and a great
admirer of Woodrow Wilson. The people he lists as manipulating Harding were
leading Republican politicians of the day.
[5]*Ibid*, p. 282. Adams checked this against an affidavit in the Marion County
Court House.
[6]*Syracuse Post Standard*, November 1, 1926.
[7]Adams, *Incredible Era*, p. 282.

In Alderfer's judgment, the campaign of villification against him because of his alleged tincture of Negro blood had a profound effect on Harding's personality.[8] "When one reads some of his vituperative, insulting, coarse editorials of the early period of his editorship, it is impossible not to see that his anger, rage, and hatred for his tormentors was being transferred from the real issue."[9]

Harding's dignity and silence won him sympathy and support among large sections of the white electorate and also won him Negro votes. The campaign of calumny, one that was almost certainly engineered, in part at least, by the Ku Klux Klan, backfired. As for Chancellor, he was fired from his teaching post and his publications concerning Harding were suppressed, collected and physically destroyed with a thoroughness that would have done credit to a European totalitarian state.[10]

Campaign Promises, Presidential Policies

Immediately after World War I, the South was concerned with loss of its black labor supply. Accordingly William G. McAdoo, Wilson's Secretary of the Treasury and a Georgian by birth, issued an order "preventing anyone in the North from prepaying the transportation of a Southern Negro who wished to come North."[11] At the instigation of the NAACP, Senator Harding intervened and persuaded McAdoo to rescind the order.

In 1920 the NAACP requested Harding and two other aspirants for the Republican Presidential nomination to make public their stand on issues important to Negroes: government patronage, the right to vote, anti-lynching legislation, and the withdrawal of American armed forces from Haiti. Harding was the only one of the candidates who replied to the NAACP demands. Avoiding a specific commitment on any of the points raised, he stated that he believed the Republican Party should make "every becoming declaration on behalf of the Negro citizenship, which the conscience of the Party and the conditions

---

[8]Harding had no specifically Negro features. If his great-grandmother married a white man, it is probable that she herself was of mixed blood, which would reduce Harding's negritude to less than one-eighth his total ancestry.

[9]Quoted in Adams, *Incredible Era*, p. 250.

[10]For the full story of this suppression, v. *Ibid.*, p. 277–83.

[11]Kellogg, *NAACP*, I, 221, ftn. 49, citing *Crisis*, XIX (March 1920), p. 243.

of this country combine to suggest." This masterpiece of ambiguity and evasion satisfied large numbers of Negro voters and ensured their support. As the campaign progressed, candidate Harding committed himself in favor of anti-lynching legislation and government jobs for Negroes to such an extent that some Southern white politicians suspected that he "intended to strike at the heart of white supremacy."[12]

In his first message to Congress as President, Harding kept his promise to the Negroes and urged legislation "to rid the stain of barbaric lynching from the banner of a free and orderly representative democracy." In the *post bellum* South, lynching had developed into a customary method of summarily putting to death Negroes for real or alleged offenses and for keeping the colored population subdued and terrorized. Between 1882 and 1951, according to the records kept by Tuskegee Institute, 4,730 persons were lynched in the United States, of whom 1,293 were white and 3,437 Negro. While the majority of the victims were hanged, some were burned at the stake with shocking cruelty. Some 41 percent of the people who met death at the hands of lynch mobs were accused of homicide, another 25 percent of rape and attempted rape, and 1.8 percent of insulting white people.

By the time Harding was inaugurated, the plague of lynching was on the wane. Thus, between 1882 and 1901, from 96 to 230 people were murdered by lynch mobs annually; in the 1902–1935 period, the annual toll fell to between eight and 99. Harding's statement against lynching was applauded by James Weldon Johnson, the executive secretary of the NAACP, and even the liberal-to-radical *Nation* praised the Republican President for taking a position "in marked contrast to the attitude of the Wilson administration which sought, ostrich-like to evade the whole (race) question."[13]

Following through on his message to Congress, Harding endorsed the Dyer anti-lynching bill, which passed the House in January 1922 only to be bottled up in the Senate Judiciary Committee. When lynchings occurred in the South in May, Harding was urged to force the bill out of committee, but he moved

[12]Robert K. Murray, *The Harding Era* (Minneapolis, 1969), pp. 397–98.
[13]Murray, *Harding Era*, p. 398.

circumspectly because of the diehard opposition of Southern Senators. Finally the Dyer bill reached the floor of the Senate in a special session in the winter of 1922. Southern Senators retaliated with an effective filibuster. Faced with the alternative of having their entire legislative program stalemated while the upper house was regaled with endless oratory, Harding and the Republican leadership decided to drop the bill.

In the 1920 elections, Harding had carried the Border States of Maryland, Kentucky, Missouri and Oklahoma. The Republican Party had won in one Southern State, Tennessee, and had cut deeply into the traditional Democratic majorities elsewhere in the South. Harding saw this as an opportunity to transform the Republican Party into the majority political organization throughout the nation. To achieve this end, it was essential that the "black and tan" leadership of the Party below the Mason and Dixon Line be replaced. By 1921, the Republican Party in Virginia had been transformed from a Negro-led to a white-dominated political organization. Harding realized that to attain a two-party system in the South it was essential that the Republicans be under White leadership, but he was not prepared to yield to the pressure of advisors who insisted that the party be exclusively White and that faithful Negro supporters be ousted. He wrote a White supporter that the Republicans should not "inconsiderately wave aside all those who have heretofore carried the party banner through years of adversity. Some of them are deserving."[14]

He hoped for "a national attitude of mind calculated to bring about the most satisfactory possible adjustment of relations between the races." On the matter of government jobs, which was of such vital importance to Negro spokesmen, Harding wanted to go further than the traditional policy of giving the Negro token employment. In a memorandum to his Cabinet, Harding stated that he wished to place "a few representative colored Republicans into administrative activity" and directed all department chiefs to find "a couple of suitable places for colored appointees."[15] At the same time, he assured spokesmen of the White South that he would not "add to the irritation there

---

[14] *Ibid.*, p. 399.
[15] Andrew Sinclair, *The Available Man* (New York, 1965) p. 230.

by the appointment of Negroes to federal office." Nor did Harding reverse Wilson's policy of segregating Negro from White government employees in the nation's capital. By mid-1922, the result of Harding's policy of favoring government patronage for Blacks was the presence of 14 Negroes in governmental jobs paying $3,000 and more. Of these, the most important was Solomon P. Hood, Minister to Liberia.[16] Harding's Secretary of Commerce, Herbert Hoover, appointed no Negroes at the $3,000 level, explaining that he had been unable to find any that were qualified.

Equal Rights, Unequal Abilities

Harding enunciated his guiding policies toward the Negro and toward the South in a major address delivered in Birmingham on October 26, 1921, to an audience of 30,000, the Black third of which was seated in a separate section from the White majority. Referring to Lothrop Stoddard's popular work on race, *The Rising Tide of Color,* [17] Harding observed that the racial problem was not a peculiarly American affliction but was worldwide. His guiding principle would be political and economic equality of opportunity coupled with segregation in social matters. "Politically and economically there need be no occasion for great and permanent differentiation, for limitations of the individual's opportunity, provided that on both sides there shall be recognition of the absolute divergence in things social and racial." He believed that Negroes as well as Whites rejected "every suggestion of social equality" and that there must be a realistic recognition of "a fundamental, eternal, and inescapable difference."

Harding stressed that he believed in racial cooperation, but not in "racial amalgamation." Segregated education should be fostered for Negroes with a stress on vocational and trade schooling. Since immigration had been restricted, there was little prospect that the United States would ever again admit "such armies of laborers landing on these shores as have come in the past." This meant a great opportunity for Negroes to do

[16]Murray, *Harding Era,* p. 401.
[17]Lothrop Stoddard, *The Rising Tide of Color against White World-Supremacy* (New York, 1920).

"the simpler, harder, manual tasks." Negro education should not be oriented toward the professions, but toward developing competence in manual tasks. As the demand for Black workers in the North raised wages, the South would have to offer the Negroes better pay and better working conditions if it proposed to retain its labor force.

This perspective of the Negro displacing the White immigrant streams from southern and eastern Europe, which in the past had provided the North with its industrial labor force, seems remarkably prescient, especially from a President who has been labeled a drunkard, a lecher, an ignoramus and a political cipher. Where Harding's prediction went astray was in his assumption that the Negro would perform the tasks needed by industrial America efficiently enough for his services to be in hot demand. He was unable to foresee that the Black man, unlike his European White predecessor, would remain in the slums, suffer most from unemployment, and be concentrated in the most unskilled occupations except where governmental pressure was exerted to change that state of affairs.

Mussolini once announced that he wanted to make his Ethiopian subjects good Africans and not bad Europeans. Harding put the same idea less succinctly. He observed that "a black man cannot be a white man . . . He should seek to be, and he should be encouraged to be, the best possible black man, and not the best possible imitation of a white man."

The franchise should be based on a fair literacy test and educational qualifications. "Let the black man vote when he is fit to vote; prohibit the white man voting when he is unfit to vote."

Politically, he did not want "the colored people to be entirely of one party" (his own), nor did he want the White men of the South to vote solidly Democratic. He thought the Solid South was a political anachronism and that Americans of all sections and races should vote in accordance with the issues and not in accordance with parochial loyalties to region or ethnic group. "We cannot go on," Harding said, "as we have gone on for more than half a century, with one great section of our population, numbering as many people as the entire population of some significant countries of Europe, set off from real contribution to solving our national issues, because of a division on race lines."

The Birmingham speech was applauded by the nation's press. Southern newspapers heartily approved Harding's support of segregation. The *New York Globe* and the *Los Angeles Times* thought his approach the most candid and intelligent statement on the racial issue of his generation.[18]

His demand for equality of political opportunity, coupled with frank recognition of the "eternal difference" between the races and their mutual desire to live apart, was applauded by the moderates of both North and South. Extremists and rabble-rousers in the South, such as Senator Tom Heflin of Alabama, castigated the President for "seeking to improve" on the handiwork of "God Almighty" who had "fixt limits and boundary lines between the two races." The more intransigent Negro leaders also rejected the speech. W. E. Burghardt Du Bois demanded that Harding be repudiated at the polls for his "inconceivably dangerous and undemocratic" denial of social equality.[19]

As the Harding era moved relentlessly toward its inglorious end, the organized Negro pressure groups turned decisively against the President. He was blamed for having failed to end educational and political discrimination and given little credit for having made the attempt despite the intransigent opposition of the White South. He was assailed for not having withdrawn American armed forces from Haiti, a move which the State Department and its Secretary, Charles Evans Hughes, had successfully thwarted. He was attacked for his failure to get the Dyer anti-lynching bill enacted. Yet a bill of this sort would be introduced in every session of Congress and blocked by Southern filibuster or threat of filibuster until the Roosevelt Administration. "The fate of the Dyer Bill comes as the culmination of a series of disappointments to the colored people during the present administration," NAACP leader James Weldon Johnson proclaimed.[20]

[18]Sinclair, *Available Man*, p. 234.
[19]*Ibid.*, p. 235.
[20]Murray, *Harding Era*, p. 398.

Above all, Harding lost the support of the organized and vocal element in the Negro community because of his failure to deliver the goods on the issue most vital to it—the matter of loaves and fishes. The expected harvest of government jobs had not materialized. The fact that Northerners, such as Hoover, had refused to appoint colored candidates because they did not consider them competent was disregarded.

Harding gave his afterthoughts about patronage and the Birmingham speech in a letter to his friend, Malcolm Jennings:

> Now and then a petty little partisan squirt or some blackguard sheet cried out in opposition (to the Birmingham speech), but the leading papers of the South were more than hearty in their commendation. I doubt now myself if it was worth while to have made the effort. The impelling reason was the claim of the negro politicians for the performance of the things written into our platform and promised in the campaign. The negroes are very hard to please. If they could have half the Cabinet, seventy-five percent of the Bureau Chiefs, two-thirds of the Diplomatic appointments and all the officers to enforce prohibition perhaps there would be a measure of contentment temporarily, but I do not think it would long abide. Moreover, I am pretty well convinced that the public man who thinks he is going to break the solidarity of the South is dreaming.[21]

Coolidge and Hoover

Harding's efforts to shape a more moderate racial policy than that of his predecessor Woodrow Wilson were partially successful, but his effort to provide the Republican party with a solid base in the South bore little fruit. If there was any middle ground of compromise between Senator Tom Heflin and W. E. Burghardt Du Bois, President Harding failed to discover it. When the Harding Administration collapsed in a miasma of corruption and scandal, spiced with rumors of illicit Presidential booze and sex, succeeding Chief Executives were not tempted to build upon its foundations.

Calvin Coolidge had little contact with the Negro or his problems. When he was called upon to express his views on the Negro's constitutional rights, however, he did so with clarity and vigor. Thus, on August 9, 1924, he wrote a letter to a Charles

[21]Sinclair, *Available Man*, p. 240.

F. Gardner of Fort Hamilton, New York, which stated his position fully:

> My dear Sir:
> Your letter is received, accompanied by a newspaper clipping which discusses the possibility that a colored man may be the Republican nominee for Congress from one of the New York districts. Referring to the newspaper statement, you say:
> 'It is of some concern whether a Negro is allowed to run for Congress anywhere, at any time, in any party, in this, a white man's country. Repeated ignoring of the growing race problem does not excuse us for allowing encroachments. Temporizing with the Negro whether he will or will not vote either a Democratic or a Republican ticket, as evidenced by the recent turnover in Oklahoma is contemptible.'
> Leaving out of consideration the manifest impropriety of the President intruding himself in a local contest for nomination, I was amazed to receive such a letter. During the war 500,000 colored men and boys were called up under the draft, not one of whom sought to evade it.[22] They took their places wherever assigned in defense of the nation of which they are just as truly citizens as are any others. The suggestion of denying any measure of their full political rights to such a great group of our population as the colored people is one which, however it might be received in some other quarters, could not possibly be permitted by one who feels a responsibility for living up to the traditions and maintaining the principles of the Republican Party. Our Constitution guarantees equal rights to all our citizens without discrimination on account of race or color. I have taken my oath to support that Constitution. It is the source of your rights and my rights. I propose to regard it and administer it, as the source of the rights of all the people, whatever their belief or race. A colored man is precisely as much entitled to submit his candidacy in a party primary, as is any other citizen. The decision must be made by the constituents to whom he offers himself, and by nobody else. [23]

Herbert Hoover wrote a perceptive and detailed analysis of the character structure, temperament and capacities of the Chinese, among whom he had lived and worked as a young engineer, but made no similar analysis of the Negro. His ex-

---

[22]Coolidge's letter was weakened by this absurd assertion. Substantial minorities of all the races concerned attempted to escape induction.
[23]Calvin Coolidge, *Foundations of the Republic* (Freeport, 1968), pp. 71–72.

pressed opinions on the Negro's problems and prospects were few, brief and entirely in conformity with the emerging national liberal consensus of opinion.

"The Whig party," Hoover wrote, "temporized, compromised upon the issue of slavery for the black man. That party disappeared. It deserved to disappear. Shall the Republican Party deserve to receive any better fate if it compromises upon the issue of freedom for all men, white as well as black?"[24]

Hoover said that the Negro race, in the sixty years since emancipation, had made progress which "surpassed the most sanguine hopes of the most ardent advocates." He asserted that the Negro people had increased their wealth "more than one hundred and thirty times," an assertion that would have been more impressive if they had not been deprived, as slaves, of the privilege of owning any property at all. Hoover said that the Negro people had "reduced its illiteracy from 95 percent to 20 percent. . . . its death rate by one-half," and had "produced leadership in all walks of life that for faith, courage, devotion, and patriotic loyalty ranks with all the other groups in our country." The "greatest single factor in the progress of the Negro race has been the schools, private and public, established and conducted by high-minded self-sacrificing men and women of both races."[25]

These utterances were neither original nor intellectually stimulating. They had a sententiousness of phrasing and absence of spontaneity that suggested the presence of that indispensable Presidential crutch, the ghostwriter. No depreciation of Hoover's great mental powers is intended. He merely concentrated them on issues he considered important. He had only a marginal interest in the problems of the Negro and not a vast amount of sympathy for his leaders' aspirations.

The Hoovers faced a major social crisis when the President's wife decided to give a tea party for the wives of the members of the Congress. The problem was that a Negro, Oscar De Priest, had been elected to the House on the Republican ticket from Chicago, the first member of his race to sit in Congress

---

[24]Ray Lyman Wilbur and Arthur Mastick Hyde, *The Hoover Policies* (New York, 1937), p. 629.
[25]*Ibid.*, p. 78.

during the Twentieth Century. The White House social secretary declared that Mrs. De Priest must be invited; other members of the President's staff feared that to do so would alienate
Southern Senators and Representatives. Mrs. Hoover gave four
tea parties for wives of Congressmen, excluding Mrs. De Priest.

"Finally, Mrs. Hoover decided to ask Mrs. De Priest to a special tea," Arthur M. Schlesinger, Jr. has written, "at which
guests could be individually warned in advance about the ordeal
to which they were about to be subjected. When the day arrived,
Mrs. De Priest seemed to the White House usher the most composed person there. 'In a short while Mrs. Hoover retired from
the room, and Mrs. De Priest in perfect form made her exit, no
doubt to the relief of all, and yet leaving behind a feeling of
admiration at the way she conducted herself.' "[26]

Hoover, according to W. E. Burghardt Du Bois, made "fewer
first-class appointments of Negroes to office than any other
President since Andrew Johnson." Negroes were refused admission to governmental cafeterias and, when the Gold Star
Mothers were sent to France to visit their sons' graves, the
Negro contingent sailed on inferior ships and was given poorer
quarters. Hoover's Vice President, Charles Curtis, who had
been born on Indian land and whose mother was half-Indian,
refused to shake the hand of a Negro who formed part of a
racially mixed delegation that had come to see him.[27] This disinterest in, and marked aversion for, Negroes seemed strange
in an Administration whose Chief Executive was a Quaker and
therefore heir to a long Abolitionist tradition.

[26]Arthur M. Schlesinger, Jr., *The Age of Roosevelt: The Politics of Upheaval*
(Boston, 1960), pp. 427–28.
[27]*Ibid.*, p. 428.

CHAPTER TWENTY

Roosevelt, Truman and the Rise of Negro Political Power

> I did not choose the tools with which I must work. Southerners, by reason of seniority rule in Congress, are chairmen or occupy strategic places on most of the Senate and House committees. If I come out for the anti-lynching bills now, they will block every bill I ask Congress to pass to keep America from collapsing. I just can't take the risk.
>
> —Franklin Delano Roosevelt to Walter White, Executive Director of the NAACP[1]

When he was inaugurated for his first term in March 1933, Franklin Delano Roosevelt seemed to be an unknown quantity on race issues. As a Harvard student he had urged Southern colleges to follow the example of his *alma mater* and admit colored students; when Assistant Secretary of the Navy in the Wilson Administration, he had interceded to get a commission for a Negro doctor; and, as his political horizons widened, he grasped the importance of wrenching the Negro vote from the Republican Party.

On the other side of the medal, he used the word "nigger" as a young, aspiring politician and served amicably throughout World War I as Assistant Secretary of the Navy under that arch-segregationist, Josephus Daniels of North Carolina. There is no evidence that he ever protested Navy segregation policies, which were stricter even than those of the Army. Roosevelt and Daniels remained friends throughout the former's life and

[1]Tamara K. Hareven, *Eleanor Roosevelt* (Chicago, 1968), p. 120.

Roosevelt chose Georgia as his "second home."[2]

During the 1920 campaign, when he was candidate for Vice President, Roosevelt revealed what some Negroes thought was an arrogant attitude toward their race when he boasted, "I wrote Haiti's constitution myself and, if I do say it, I think it is a pretty good constitution." Republican Presidential candidate Harding promptly retorted that, if elected, he would not "empower an Assistant Secretary of the Navy to draft a constitution for a helpless neighbor in the West Indies and jam it down their throats at the point of bayonets borne by United States Marines." The Roosevelt reaction was to deny he had made the statement attributed to him, but reporters who had been present gave him the lie.[3]

As Governor of New York State, Roosevelt had done little for Negroes in terms of either jobs or legislation. In 1929, he was accused by Republicans of having entertained Negroes at a lunch; he denied the charge. In his 1932 Presidential campaign, he appealed for the Southern white vote and chose as his running mate John Nance Garner of Uvalde, Texas.[4]

Roosevelt never worked out a consistent philosophical attitude on the problems of the Negro or on racial issues in general. His political genius, his ability to resolve issues and to inspire the enthusiasm and devotion of tens of millions of people, both in America and overseas, were not the result of any marked analytical powers of mind, education or scholarship. At Groton he had been a mediocre student and at Harvard no better. While Roosevelt wore a Phi Beta Kappa key, he had not earned it, but acquired honorary membership from a small women's college when he was Governor of New York. He studied law at Columbia University, after his stint at Harvard, but failed to graduate. Serving briefly as a law clerk in the firm of Carter, Ledyard and Milburn, he was restricted in his activities by a memorandum from Ledyard to the office manager, ordering him "under no circumstances to put any serious piece of litigation" in Roosevelt's hands.[5]

Roosevelt reached manhood imbued with a disinterest in, or

[2]Schlesinger, *Upheaval*, pp. 430–31.
[3]Lela Stiles, *The Man Behind Roosevelt* (New York, 1954), p. 69.
[4]Schlesinger, *Upheaval*, p. 431.
[5]John T. Flynn, *The Roosevelt Myth* (New York, 1948), p. 260.

aversion to, reading books. Frances Perkins, his Secretary of Labor, who knew him well from his early days in New York politics to his death, recalled that he was not a student, knew nothing about economics, and admitted that he had never read a book on the subject. So profound was his ignorance of finance that, in the worst economic crisis of the century, he appointed a friend and fellow country-gentleman, Henry Morgenthau, Jr., to the key post of Secretary of the Treasury.[6] Edward J. Flynn, who was closely associated with FDR in the latter's gubernatorial years and who ran his 1940 campaign, said that he never saw the President read a book. Others denied this and said they recollected having seen him reading detective stories or books on the Navy.[7]

Roosevelt's vast knowledge was acquired more by conversation and by listening than by reading and study. Hence his views were plastic; his attitudes changed quickly with circumstance, and he was more than usually adroit at tacking to avoid political pitfalls and to reap ephemeral political advantages.

Anti-Lynching Legislation

During Roosevelt's first term, Negroes benefited from his public works program, expanded unemployment relief and Civilian Conservation Corps, but suffered from those aspects of the Agricultural Adjustment Act which operated to drive marginal and inefficient small farmers off the land.

At the instigation of an official of the Julius Rosenwald Fund, Roosevelt was persuaded in the summer of 1933 to see that somebody in government was concerned exclusively with the problems of Negroes. The President suggested that the matter be handled by Harold L. Ickes, the Secretary of the Interior, who had been head of the NAACP in Chicago. Dr. Clark Foreman, a white liberal from Georgia, was appointed to a position in Interior, his salary being paid by the Rosenwald Fund. Foreman was succeeded by Dr. Robert C. Weaver, a Negro with a Harvard Ph. D. in economics. In the National Youth Administra-

---

[6]When asked by newspapermen how he determined the dollar price with the United States off the gold standard, Morgenthau replied that a professor who worked in the Treasury wrote it down daily on a piece of paper and gave it to him.

[7]Flynn, *Myth*, p. 261.

tion, Mary McLeod Bethune, a colored educator, headed the Office of Minority Affairs and was partly responsible for a program which taught 300,000 illiterate Negroes how to read.[8]

Efforts to raise the wages of labor through the National Recovery Act increased the displacement of Negro by White workers. In October 1933, 18 percent of the Black population was unemployed; by January 1935, despite some economic recovery nationally, the figure had risen to almost 30 percent. The more radical and pro-Negro elements in the Roosevelt Administration reacted by pushing Blacks into middle-echelon jobs in Government and seeing to it that the new agencies hired or subsidized millions of Negroes who had been forced out of private employment by the NRA program.

At the instigation of Walter White, the national leader of the NAACP, Senator Edward P. Costigan of Colorado introduced an anti-lynching bill in early 1934 with Senator Robert F. Wagner of New York as co-sponsor. White worked through Eleanor Roosevelt, the President's wife, who was indefatigable in pressuring and even pestering her husband.

The bill made county officers financially liable for lynchings which occurred in their bailiwicks. Roosevelt had publicly condemned lynching as a "vile form of collective murder" and added that he condemned "those in high places or in low who condone lynch law." Although the Costigan measure had been approved quickly by the Senate Judiciary Committee, which at the time had only three Southerners among eighteen members, it had no chance of enactment unless the President agreed to put it in his package of "must" legislation.

Roosevelt was reluctant to do this. He believed that the bill would irrevocably antagonize Southerners in Congress and jeopardize legislation he considered more important. He told the press that he had doubts that the bill was either workable or constitutional. When Eleanor Roosevelt engineered an interview for Walter White with her husband, the President recognized at once that the Negro leader had been coached and remarked angrily: "Somebody's been priming you. Was it my wife?"

Despite White's failure to make headway, Mrs. Roosevelt

[8]Schlesinger, *Upheaval,* p. 436.

continued to apply pressure[9] and finally got FDR to permit her to tell Senator Robinson of Arkansas, the Majority Leader, "If in a lull, the anti-lynching bill can be brought up for a vote, the President authorizes the sponsors to say that the President will be glad to see the bill passed and wishes it passed."[10] This was not enough to sway Robinson and the bill failed to reach the Senate floor.

Even though lynchings had decreased from a peak annual figure of 230 to a total of 61 for the entire 1935-62 period, proponents of the Costigan measure continued to press for anti-lynching legislation. In 1937 the bill was brought to the Senate floor, where it received the urgent support of Senators Wagner of New York and Guffey of Pennsylvania. Southern Senators, such as Tom Connally of Texas, opposed the measure as an unconstitutional usurpation of State power by the Federal Government and revived the spectre of Reconstruction and military rule over the South. Less reputable Southern Senators relied on the tawdry assertion that passage of the measure would encourage the Negroes to "insolence" and crime.

The *coup de grace,* however, was administered by a distinguished Senator of impeccable liberal credentials, William E. Borah of Idaho, who "tore the Federal bill to pieces legally and traditionally. He cited numerous Supreme Court decisions to prove that one sovereignty may not interfere with the machinery of another. He showed how a State itself—Illinois—could legally hold its peace officers responsible for damages incurred by mob violence and ended by saying he would always resist the encroachment of arbitrary power. When sufficient political demonstration had been made, proponents let the bill be laid aside, and the President made no protest. But the material for a 'white supremacy' campaign had been gathered for use whenever the Administration moved wholly to annex the legislators of the South."[11]

Roosevelt "was often annoyed with his wife's techniques," according to the biographer of Eleanor Roosevelt, but "would not prohibit her from publicly advocating anti-lynching legisla-

[9]Hareven, *Eleanor,* p. 121.
[10]*Ibid.*
[11]Arthur Krock, *In the Nation: 1932-1966* (New York, 1966), "The White Supremacy Issue," August 24, 1938, p. 61.

tion. When she asked him, 'Do you mind if I say what I think?'
he said, 'No, certainly not. You can say anything you want. I can
always say, "Well, that is my wife; I can't do anything about
her." ' "[12]

The new executive director of the NAACP appraised the respective roles of husband and wife by characterizing FDR as a
friend of the Negro "only insofar as he refused to exclude the
Negro from his general policies that applied to the whole country." He believed that Eleanor Roosevelt had supplied "the personal touches and the personal fight against discrimination"
from which the President "reaped the political benefit."[13]

Roosevelt's perhaps calculated political defeat on the anti-
lynching bill was related to a winning strategy that had been
elaborated by Senator Joseph F. Guffey of Pennsylvania. Back
in 1932 Robert L. Vann, publisher of the *Pittsburgh Courier,* the
largest Negro newspaper in the State, had convinced Guffey
that the Democrats had a chance of capturing a substantial
portion of Pennsylvania's 280,000 black votes. Guffey persuaded
James A. Farley and Louis Howe to set up an effective Negro
division in campaign headquarters and to go out and tell colored voters to "turn Lincoln's picture to the wall" because their
debt to the Republican Party had been "paid in full."[14]

In 1934, Joe Guffey used this strategy to pick up about 170,000
votes and oust the incumbent Republican Senator in an upset
victory. Two years later, Roosevelt was running for re-election
against Governor Alfred M. Landon of Kansas. One of the
Republican campaign slogans read: "The Democratic Party of
the United States is the implacable foe of the Negro race."
George S. Schuyler, the distinguished conservative columnist
of the *Pittsburgh Courier,* called President Roosevelt "a man
who could speak sympathetically about the tortured Jews of
Europe, but was too callous or too cowardly to speak likewise
about the tortured Negroes of America."[15]

This rhetoric had little or no effect on Negro votes. The
Guffey strategy, as executed by that master of political

[12]Hareven, *Eleanor,* p. 123.
[13]*Ibid.,* p. 124.
[14]Schlesinger, *Upheaval,* p. 430.
[15]George Wolfskill and John A. Hudson, *All But the People: Franklin D.
Roosevelt and his Critics, 1933–39* (New York, 1969), pp. 89, 92.

manipulation Jim Farley, swung practically 100 percent of the Negro vote behind FDR in 1936 and this was enough to give him the needed majorities in the decisive, populous industrial States of the North and the Midwest. Agitation and propaganda in favor of Federal anti-lynching legislation, which was a natural emotional rallying-point for Negroes, was part of this grand political design. In reaction, Southern politicians secured their home territory by vigorous filibustering against the anti-lynching bills, whenever they raised their hydra heads, and by oratory in glorification of white supremacy.[16]

At the same time, diehard Southerners were distressed at what they regarded as increasing Negro power and social integration in Washington. A 1936 editorial in the *Rosslyn* (Virginia) *Chronicle* expressed outrage at a photograph of Mrs. Roosevelt seated beside a Negro woman "so near together that their bodies touched." Gerald L. K. Smith, the pro-fascist politician, charged that "modernist churchmen, academic sentimentalists, Communists, and New Dealers, all operating under the leadership of Eleanor Roosevelt" were trying to achieve wholesale miscegenation and "mongrelization."[18] Outright fascists, such as Silver Shirt *Fuehrer* William Dudley Pelley, called the New Deal the Jew Deal and charged that the Jews were behind the CIO campaign to unionize Negro workers in the South and that the hidden purpose was to overthrow white rule in Dixie.[19]

Southern political leaders such as Senator Josiah William Bailey of North Carolina were torn between their sympathy for New Deal policies designed to aid the impoverished States they represented and dislike and fear of Roosevelt's pro-Negro policies. Bailey dreaded capture of the Democratic Party in such great Northern centers as New York, Pennsylvania and Chicago by Negroes. He thought them "common fellows of the baser sort" because "they have no idea of political service. Their only thought is of political patronage."[20]

In 1944, the Administration threw another sop to Negro voters, as a means of enlisting their support behind Roosevelt's

[16]Krock, *Nation,* p. 61.
[18]Wolfskill and Hudson, *People,* p. 91.
[19]*Ibid.*
[20]John Robert Moore, *Senator Josiah William Bailey of North Carolina* (Durham, 1968), pp. 165–66.

fourth-term candidacy. Anti-poll tax legislation was introduced although it had little chance of passage. Responsible Southern Senators such as Bailey pointed out the hypocrisy of claiming that a $1.50 poll tax was depriving the poor voter of his livelihood, while, at the same time, compelling all workers to join trade unions and have union dues deducted from their pay envelopes, regardless of their inclinations or wishes.

By 1944, Negroes were sufficiently powerful in the Democratic Party so that an able Vice-Presidential candidate, James F. Byrnes of South Carolina, would be vetoed by Sidney Hillman and the Political Action Committee (PAC) as unacceptable to labor and northern Negroes. In a fury, Bailey wrote Senator Harry F. Byrd of Virginia, whom he supported as Democratic standard-bearer against Roosevelt:

"I make no threats, but I will say that when Sidney Hillman and the Communist crew in the name of the C.I.O.[21] come in the doors and windows of the party in which my father and I lived and served, I will go out."[22]

The politics of Roosevelt's alliance with the Negro are much more readily discerned than Roosevelt's convictions about the Negro. The nearest thing we have been able to find to a statement about racial equality is FDR's address to the White House Correspondents' Association in March 1941. "We believe that the rallying cry of the dictators," he said on that occasion, "their boasting about a master-race, will prove to be stuff and nonsense. There never has been, there isn't now, and there never will be, any race of people on the earth fit to serve as masters over their fellow men."[23]

These sentiments were, of course, directed specifically against Hitler and the Nazis at a time when Roosevelt's speeches were primarily directed at mobilizing American public opinion for the conflict that faced the nation. To assume that these were Franklin Delano Roosevelt's considered opinions about the comparative ability of different races to rule, outside

---

[21]Congress of Industrial Organizations, a labor federation rival to the American Federation of Labor, which had been started by John L. Lewis, leader of the coal miners' union.

[22]Moore, *Bailey*, pp. 218–19.

[23]Quoted in Thomas H. Greer, *What Roosevelt Thought* (East Lansing, 1958), pp. 164–65.

of the Nazi context, would be gratuitous. In fact, one cannot even assume that the quoted remarks were written by Roosevelt since, during the early part of 1941, he was in the habit of asking as many as half a dozen people to submit drafts of whatever speech he proposed to make.[24]

The Truman Years

The death of Franklin D. Roosevelt in the spring of 1945 brought Harry S. Truman into the Presidency. He had neither been informed of such vital matters as the atomic bomb project nor taken into Roosevelt's confidence on the structure which the latter envisaged for the postwar world. Faced with as momentous decisions as any American Chief Executive has ever had to face, Truman at first paid little attention to the problems of the Negro and the complaints of Negro pressure groups.

"Truman's private political views were not liberal," a journalistic source wrote in 1950. "He. . . . believed in legal rights for Negroes, but not in social equality."[25]

One of the new President's early steps in the race relations field was to see that Roosevelt's wartime Fair Employment Practices Committee was continued into peacetime America. Truman also appointed a Committee on Civil Rights to have "our Bill of Rights implemented in fact." He stated that progress in this direction had been achieved, but it was not fast enough. He suggested that the United States in 1947 faced a situation in which Ku Klux Klan terrorism might be revived.[26]

In late 1947 the Commission made a Report advocating sweeping legislation to protect American minority groups, and the President promptly asked Congress to implement its recommendations. Those that concerned Negroes established civil rights groups in Congress and the Department of Justice and a permanent Commission on Civil Rights; urged stronger civil rights statutes; Federal protection of the right to vote; Federal anti-lynching legislation; establishment of a perma-

[24]One of the authors submitted such a draft in April 1941.

[25]Robert S. Allen and William V. Shannon, *The Truman Merry-Go-Round* (New York, 1950), p. 10.

[26]Harry S. Truman, *Memoirs: Years of Trial and Hope* (Garden City, 1956), II, 181.

nent Fair Employment Practices Commission, and home rule in the District of Columbia.

Faced with this sweeping legislative program and threatened by a bolt of the Southern States, the 1948 Democratic National Convention platform committee made an astute political compromise. It endorsed Truman's civil rights program up to its "Constitutional limits," but avoided mentioning any specific plank. This was designed to win Black votes in the North and simultaneously assure the South that the threat was not to be taken seriously.[27]

Representatives of the anxious South, however, offered an amendment, reasserting States' rights. Since this was designed to nullify the plank, it was badly defeated. The radical Americans for Democratic Action (ADA) then offered a specific and sweeping civil rights program, which carried the key States despite the desire of Truman and his supporters for compromise. The Southern delegates bolted the Convention and the President was faced with a *fait accompli* by the radical wing.[28]

Truman expressed his personal convictions clearly and succinctly in his *Memoirs.* "The Constitutional guarantees of individual liberties and of equal protection under the law clearly place on the federal government the duty to act when state or local authorities abridge or fail to uphold these guarantees."[29]

While "the military establishment—particularly the Navy— had been strongly opposed to my policy of integration in the armed services, I [Truman] had forced it into practice. Then they discovered that no difficulty resulted from integration after all.[30] Integration is the best way to create an effective combat organization in which the men will stand together and fight."[31]

Truman also thought that Jim Crow practices "would be inconsistent with international commitments and obligations." Otherwise, we could not "expect to influence the immense

---

[27]Arthur Krock, *Nation,* "Even Grant Left Them Their Horses," July 14, 1948, p. 134.

[28]*Ibid.,* pp. 134–35.

[29]Truman, *Memoirs,* II, 180.

[30]More than twenty years after this naive and optimistic assertion, the armed forces would complain that discipline, troop security and combat morale were being menaced by racial strife between Blacks and Whites.

[31]Truman, *Memoirs,* II, 183.

masses that make up the Asian and African peoples."[32] Actually, the Japanese had their pariah caste, the Etas; the Indians based their entire society on an elaborate system of *varna,* or caste, the literal meaning of *varna* being *color:* and most of the newly-fledged African states were based on the subordination of one tribe, or group of tribes, by another; and, in such cases as the Malagasy Republic, these tribal differences were of a fundamentally racial nature. But while Truman was widely read on such subjects as the American Civil War, he was less thoroughly grounded in world history and the structure of foreign societies.

Truman was proud of the fact that, when Dixiecrat Presidential candidate H. Strom Thurmond was told that the President was "only following the platform that Roosevelt advocated," Thurmond replied: "I agree, but Truman really *means* it."[33]

His stand, Truman believed, had been "shamefully distorted and misrepresented by political demagogues and press propaganda" to make it appear that he wished to legislate social integration.

"My appeal for equal economic and political rights for every American citizen," Truman pointed out, "had nothing at all to do with the personal or social relationships of individuals or the right of every person to choose his own associates. The basic Constitutional privilege which I advocated was deliberately misconstrued to include or imply racial miscegenation and intermarriage. My only goal was equal opportunity and security under the law for all classes of Americans."[34]

[33]Truman, *Memoirs,* II, 183.
[34]*Ibid.*

CHAPTER TWENTY-ONE

The Turbulent Years of Eisenhower and Kennedy

> The old code of equity law under which we live commands for every wrong a remedy, but in too many communities, in too many parts of the country, wrongs are inflicted on Negro citizens for which there are no remedies at law. Unless the Congress acts, their only remedy is in the street.
> —John F. Kennedy, 1963 television address on the integration crisis at the University of Alabama.

As we move finally into the contemporary period, we are faced with a variety of problems, some of them new ones. The first of these is to disentangle the views of the major protagonists without getting lost in the labyrinthine maze of race riots, demonstrations, Federal court orders, administrative changes in the Federal Government affecting the Negro, legislation and Congressional debates. To cover this area with any degree of competence would have meant writing a very different book, essentially a political history of race relations in the United States during the past two decades. And this has been far from our intention.

A second difficulty is that Presidential utterances during this period become increasingly stereotyped: the enunciation of lofty sentiments and aspirations tends to displace calm analysis of national problems; logic takes a back seat to peroration. We have decided to refrain from reproducing this Presidential rhetoric wherever possible since it is more often eloquent than instructive.

A third difficulty is that race policies during this period were forged, to a very great extent, by the Supreme Court. Throughout this book, we have deliberately avoided including Chief Justices of the United States and Associate Justices of the Supreme Court in the roster of American statesmen whose views we have discussed. The reason for this is not any lack of regard on our part for the intellectual and political calibre of men such as John Marshall, Roger B. Taney, Salmon P. Chase, Charles Evans Hughes, Oliver Wendell Holmes, Louis B. Brandeis or Felix Frankfurter. Rather it is that their philosophy is embedded in their judicial opinions and these opinions cannot be presented coherently without a legal analysis. We have thought it wise to avoid this terrain.

A final difficulty is propinquity. We have omitted President Lyndon Baines Johnson from consideration, not from any desire to exclude him from the ranks of American statesmen, but because the evidence on the Johnson Administration is simply not available. The memoirs and analyses by participants in these events are almost wholly unwritten and, therefore, any consideration of Johnson's views as President would be superficial.[1] We have omitted discussion of President Nixon for similar reasons.

Eisenhower and School Desegregation

On May 17, 1954 the Supreme Court handed down an epochal unanimous decision which ended racial segregation in the public schools of the United States.[2] In his memoirs, President Eisenhower recalled:

> I refused to say whether I either approved or disapproved of it. The Court's judgment was law, I said, and I would abide by it. This determination was one of principle. I believed that if I should express, publicly, either approval or disapproval of a Supreme Court decision in one case, I would be obliged to do so in many, if not all, cases. Inevitably, I would eventually be drawn into a public statement of disagreement with some

---

[1]The available biographies of Johnson and accounts of his Administration as of mid-1970 included Eric F. Goldman's *The Tragedy of Lyndon Johnson* (New York, 1969) and Sam Houston Johnson's *My Brother Lyndon* (New York, 1969). Both books leave much to be desired.

[2]*Brown v. Board of Education*, 347 U.S. 483 (1954).

decision, creating the suspicion that my vigor of enforcement would, in such cases, be in doubt. Moreover, to indulge in a practice of approving or criticizing Court decisions could tend to lower the dignity of government, and would in the long run, be hurtful.

Immediately after this careful enunciation of a policy designed to buttress the constitutional division of governmental power between the executive, legislative and judicial branches, Eisenhower added this significant sentence:

"In this case I definitely agreed with the unanimous decision."[3]

The veracity of this assertion was directly challenged by Arthur Larson, one of Eisenhower's close advisers at the time, in a book published a year before the latter's death. This challenge is not directed at General Eisenhower's integrity, but at the accuracy of his recollection of events at a time when his memory may have been impaired by heart attacks and other illnesses. On the whole, we are inclined to accept Larson's version of the matter, both for the reason just given and because the views which Larson imputes to Eisenhower are consistent with the latter's general political philosophy of moderation.

Exactly a week after the Little Rock crisis—on the morning of October 1, 1957—Eisenhower said, according to Larson, that, while he was determined not to take sides on the merits of the Supreme Court's verdict, he personally thought that "the decision was wrong."[4]

Eisenhower expressed the opinion that the Court should have insisted that equal educational facilities be offered both races, but should not have required race integration. Shocked at this view, Larson reiterated the Supreme Court's contention that, "segregation has a tendency to retard the educational and mental development of Negro children because of the feeling of inferiority generated by the very fact of separation." Eisenhower listened patiently, then retorted:

[3]Dwight D. Eisenhower, *The White House Years: Waging Peace, 1956–1961* (Garden City, 1965), p. 150.
[4]Arthur Larson, *Eisenhower: The President Nobody Knew* (New York, 1968), p. 124.

"Yes, I am thoroughly familiar with that argument, but I do not find it compelling."[5]

A year earlier, Larson had submitted a draft of Eisenhower's acceptance speech on being renominated for President by the Republican Party. The President threw out the phrase, "that ugly complex of injustices called discrimination." He emphasized "his distaste for the word 'discrimination'," adding that he had lived in the South and understood the Southern viewpoint. The fact that the Negro was entitled to "political and economic opportunity did not mean necessarily that everyone has to mingle socially—'or that a Negro should court my daughter.' "[6]

Eisenhower realized that the Supreme Court school desegregation decision would compel the South to accept a social revolution, one which would overthrow the existing fabric of institutions and state laws. This would be doubly unpalatable to the White majority because it had been imposed, not by an elected body, but by judicial fiat. Moreover, it was an interpretation of the Constitution which diametrically contradicted the interpretation which the Supreme Court had upheld over the past fifty years.

Eisenhower and Integration

"Since my boyhood," Dwight D. Eisenhower wrote in his memoirs, "I had accepted without qualification the right to equality before the law of all citizens of this country, whatever their race or color or creed. In World War II, I had affirmed my belief in this principle through orders desegregating many Red Cross clubs, while, during some stages of the fighting, I had sent into previously all-white units Negro replacements who not only fought well but also encountered little or no resentment from their comrades."[7]

[5]*Ibid.*, p. 126.
[6]*Ibid.*, p. 127.
[7]Eisenhower, *Waging Peace*, p. 148. This view was more favorable than that of Secretary of War Stimson, who wrote: "The performance of the only Negro infantry division sent into combat (in World War II) as a whole was disappointing, but smaller units (including elements of the same division) did better." Henry L. Stimson and McGeorge Bundy, *On Active Service in Peace and War* (New York, 1947), p. 464. "Negro troops had not in the main won glory for themselves in combat during World War I," the same authors observed, p. 462.

In his first State of the Union Message (1953), Eisenhower urged that segregation be ended in Washington, D.C., so it could "become a showplace of peaceful civil rights progress."[8] Desegregation was accomplished, but the hope proved ill-founded. Seventeen years later, the nation's capital had become a jungle, in which violence and crime were rampant, which seethed with racial hate, and which was scarred by massive Negro riots in which White businesses and homes were looted, burned and gutted.

Informed by Maxwell M. Rabb, his Secretary of the Cabinet and an all-out opponent of segregation, that Negroes were being deprived of their right to vote in the South, Eisenhower called for new civil rights legislation in 1956 to authorize the Department of Justice to obtain preventive relief in civil rights cases.

This "sinister and iniquitous proposal," as 83 Southern Congressmen termed it, was blocked in the Senate. In 1957 Eisenhower resubmitted it, but Senator Richard B. Russell of Georgia tried to have it sent back to the Judiciary Committee, where it faced a slow but certain death. Although backed by Senators William Fulbright, John F. Kennedy and Lyndon B. Johnson, this maneuver was defeated. The reason these liberal palladins turned their backs on civil rights, in Eisenhower's opinion, was that they had made a deal with the South to get Dixie support for the "monster" Hell's Canyon Dam on the Snake River in Idaho, "one of the biggest, and in my opinion, most unjustified federal reclamation projects of the Twentieth Century. . . , a dream of those who championed complete federal domination in electric power production."[9]

At the instigation of Attorney General Herbert Brownell, a New York liberal Republican and no friend of the South, Eisenhower submitted a civil rights bill which gave the Federal courts power to punish violators through contempt actions. The reason for this punitive method was that Brownell and other Northern liberals feared Southern juries would not decide civil rights cases against the defendants. They termed an amend-

[8]Eisenhower, *Waging Peace,* p. 150.
[9]*Ibid.,* p. 155.

ment stipulating the right to jury trial "a shield for the offender."[10]

The Administration's circumvention of jury trials was denounced by Senator Russell of Georgia as a "cunning device to integrate the races." Lyndon Johnson vigorously, but unsuccessfully, opposed Brownell's plan, declaring: "The people will never accept a concept that a man can be publicly branded as a criminal without a jury trial."[11] Despite these protests, the bill was enacted substantially as the Administration wished it, adding further to the bitterness and sense of outrage of the White South.

The great integration crisis of the second Eisenhower term occurred at Little Rock, Arkansas in 1957. The conflict started when a White mother brought action in State Chancery Court to direct the school board not to proceed with integration. At the hearing, Arkansas Governor Orval Faubus testified that a drawerful of pistols had been taken from White and Negro students. Predicting that "violence, bloodshed and riots" would result from implementation of the integration plan, he urged that it be set aside.

The next day, U.S. District Judge Ronald N. Davies, a North Dakotan serving temporarily in Arkansas, heard an hour-and-five-minute argument by counsel, but no evidence, then set aside the Chancery Court order, reading an opinion which Faubus claimed "had already been drawn up and read before the meeting began." In a second hearing, lasting five minutes, the Judge ordered integration at once.[12]

Faubus decided to defy the court order. It was ironical that he should thus make himself the symbol of the intransigent South. He had attended Commonwealth College, a training school for left-wing organizers; had proclaimed "I'm not a segregationist"; had sent his only son to a racially integrated university, and had won a large majority of the Negro votes in his gubernatorial campaign. Nonetheless, Faubus believed that the Federal court order would cause race riots in Little Rock and that

[10]Sherman Adams, *Firsthand Report* (New York, 1961), p. 340.
[11]Eisenhower, *Waging Peace,* p. 158.
[12]Governor Orval E. Faubus, radio and television address, September 26, 1957.

he was bound by oath as Governor to maintain order in the
State.

President Eisenhower was committed against using the military to enforce court orders. "I can't imagine any set of circumstances," he told a news conference on July 17, 1957, "that would ever induce me to send Federal troops into. . . . any area to enforce the orders of a Federal court." He opposed the "extremists on the Negro side of the question" because they "did not seem to understand that, although federal troops could be sent into the South to enforce desegregation laws, soldiers cannot force the state authorities to keep the schools from closing their doors against white and Negro children alike."[13]

Yet, in the Little Rock crisis, Eisenhower acted firmly against what he regarded as defiance of the law of the land. He announced that he would "use the full power of the United States, including whatever force may be necessary, to prevent any obstruction of the law and to carry out the order of the Federal court." Troops were moved into Little Rock. The ensuing worldwide publicity was so slanted, in many instances, as to make the United States appear a racist state. By focusing international attention on the Negro's grievances, race leaders were given the stature and prestige they needed to intensify their demands and take increasingly militant steps to polarize conflict.

Did Eisenhower have any alternatives? When President Roosevelt devalued the dollar in 1933, some outstanding contracts required payment in gold or gold's dollar equivalent. Plaintiffs appealed to the Supreme Court that they were entitled to additional sums to offset the dollar devaluation. They lost their case. Had the Court decided in their favor, Roosevelt had prepared a statement that, because of overriding considerations of national interest, he had decided to ignore the Court decision. In the Little Rock affair, it could well have been argued that the duty of the State Governor to maintain law and order by whatever legal means seemed to him appropriate took priority over the Federal court order.

In any event, by acting as he did, Eisenhower committed the Chief Executive, it would seem, to act as the enforcement

[13]Adams, *Report,* p. 339.

agency of the Federal courts. Arthur Krock, the perceptive head of the Washington Bureau of the *New York Times,* immediately recognized the nature of this commitment "with consequences to race relations and respect for the National Government that one can only hope will not be as grave as their portent."[14]

In the field of race relations, Eisenhower's overriding objective was to see that all Americans received that equal treatment under law to which the Constitution entitled them. He considered protection of the Negro's right to vote paramount because, once he was secure in his franchise, the Negro could use political power to assert his other rights.

This approach did not imply special legislation or special favors for Negroes or any other minority group. Eisenhower did not consider that, as President, he was under any moral obligation to crusade against segregation where no governmental facilities were involved. Believing in individual liberty, he thought that Americans should be free to choose their own associates in the private sphere. He had doubts about social integration and misgivings concerning desegregation of the public schools by judicial fiat. Wherever he could do so without permitting flouting of Federal laws and Federal court orders, he would go to great lengths to damp down racial strife and advance national unity. He was skeptical about the efficacy of ideological panaceas as agents to revolutionize established *mores.* He believed that the Negro was entitled, not to favoritism, but to that equality of opportunity and equal protection of the laws which are American birthrights.

Kennedy! from Moderate to Militant

During his long quest for the Presidency, John F. Kennedy, like other Democratic aspirants of the post-FDR era, had to find a means of keeping Negro support without losing Southern white backing. He backed the jury-trial amendment to Eisenhower's Civil Rights Bill and, for doing so, was branded a "compromiser with evil" by Roy Wilkins, leader of the NAACP. When Governor John Patterson of Alabama announced his support of Kennedy as Democratic candidate for the Presidency,

[14]Arthur Krock, *Nation,* "A 'Condition' Refutes a Theory," p. 283.

Negro spokesmen sounded the alarm and Adam Clayton Powell demanded that the Convention repudiate JFK for accepting the backing of "Negro-hating" Southerners.[15] While Powell was a notorious racist agitator who had been attacked by the *New York Times* for his pro-Communist activities and would later be ousted from the House of Representatives for nepotism and other unsavory practices, he was a political power to be reckoned with in Harlem.

Kennedy made the reasonable reply that Negroes should judge him on the basis of his civil rights stand and not on the basis of who endorsed him in the South. While it was true that he had once breakfasted with Governor Patterson, he added, he had also lunched with Thurgood Marshall, the NAACP lawyer, and "no implication can be drawn from either of these meetings."

Jackie Robinson, a Negro baseball player turned politician, found this statement evidence that Kennedy's "opinion of the intelligence of Negro Americans must be very low indeed." Through logical processes known only to himself he concluded that "Senator Kennedy is not fit to be President of the United States." Subjected to this sort of emotional abuse, Kennedy tried to smooth the feelings of Negro politicians by telling them that Patterson's endorsement was "the greatest cross I have to bear." However, he did not repudiate it.[16]

The Democratic candidate lost little time in mending his fences, gaining the trust of the militant Negro leaders, and securing the Negro vote. He put Harris Wofford of Notre Dame Law School on his staff to handle Negro relations. He held conferences with Negro leaders at which he agreed "to obtain consideration of a civil rights bill by the Senate early next session that will implement the pledges of the Democratic platform."[17]

During the campaign, Kennedy went even further and prom-

---

[15]Victor Lasky, *J.F.K. The Man and the Myth* (New York, 1963), pp. 247–253. This book is devoted to proving that John F. Kennedy was an unprincipled opportunist, interested only in personal power. Dubious as the thesis may appear to be, the data assembled by its author is impressive and useful.

[16]*Ibid.*, p. 255.

[17]Arthur M. Schlesinger, Jr., *A Thousand Days* (Boston, 1965), p. 929.

ised "to use all the resources of [the] office" to "provide the leadership, the determination and the direction. . . . to eliminate racial and religious discrimination from American society."[18] This was a momentous step because there was no authority in the Constitution for Presidential crusading against discrimination where no public facilities were involved. Taken literally, the pledge would have committed Kennedy to use the leviathan powers of the White House to ensure that social clubs, professional associations, athletic teams and private gatherings were racially mixed.

During the election campaign, Dr. Martin Luther King, Jr. was jailed in Georgia for violation of probation in a traffic case. Richard M. Nixon refused to comment on the matter, but Kennedy seized his great opportunity and made a widely publicized telephone call to Mrs. King, expressing sympathy. Eisenhower observed after the votes had been counted that Kennedy had won the election with "a couple of telephone calls." Nixon observed sorrowfully: "I just didn't realize such a call could swing an election."[19]

Once elected, Kennedy decided against introducing still another civil rights measure. He believed that a few dramatic protests against segregation, which would stir the imagination of the Negro masses, plus the lavish bestowal of loaves and fishes on prominent members of the race, were better calculated to maintain their political support. The main dramatic step was to have the President's brother Bobby resign from the Metropolitan Club because it excluded Negroes and to have John F. Kennedy publicly endorse the action. Robert C. Weaver, the Negro economist who had served under FDR, was named Housing Administrator; two Negroes were given key positions in the State Department; another was named Assistant Secretary of Labor; still another was designated Ambassador to Norway; Thurgood Marshall was elevated to the Supreme Court; Black candidates for judgeships received preferment, and eager Kennedy aides searched for Negroes who might be considered qualified for top-echelon and middle-echelon government

[18] *Ibid.*
[19] Lasky, *J.F.K.*, p. 493.

jobs. Vice President Lyndon B. Johnson, who had once characterized the Truman Civil Rights program as "a farce and a
sham—an effort to set up a police state in the guise of liberty,"
played a prominent role in the fashionable quest for colored
talent.[20]

Toward Upheaval

If these moves were designed to ensure racial harmony in the
United States they did not succeed, and 1963 was scarred by
race clashes, particularly in Birmingham where the authorities overreacted with widely publicized violence. At the same
time, a new Negro leadership was emerging which advocated
terrorism, supported the Communist movement in several of
its various forms, and was increasingly committed to the destruction of the United States.

In May 1963, Attorney General Robert F. Kennedy called a
conference with prominent Negroes such as James Baldwin,
Lena Horne, Lorraine Hansberry, Harry Belafonte and Kenneth
Clark. Bobby Kennedy had hoped to build bridges toward a rational and responsible leadership; instead, he found appalling
ignorance, searing hatred and wild accusations.

"They didn't know anything," Kennedy told Arthur M. Schlesinger, Jr. "They don't know what the laws are—they don't know
what the facts are—they don't know what we've been doing or
what we're trying to do. You couldn't talk to them as you can
to Roy Wilkins or Martin Luther King. . . . It was all emotion,
hysteria. They stood up and orated. They cursed. Some of them
wept and walked out of the room." Others remained silent
while Robert Kennedy was attacked and vilified; then went to
him privately to express their appreciation of his efforts. When
he asked why they hadn't spoken up to defend him before the
others, their reply was: "If I were to defend you, they would
conclude I had gone over to the other side."[21]

This meeting did not serve as a warning tocsin, but rather
induced the Kennedy Administration to redouble its efforts to
appease the Negro militants and convince them of its good
intentions. In his campaign Kennedy had said that the Presi-

[20]Schlesinger, *A Thousand Days*, p. 933.
[21]*Ibid.*, p. 963.

dent "must exert the great moral and educational force of his office to bring about equal access to public facilities, from churches to lunch-counters, and support the right of every American to stand up for his rights, even if he must sit down for them."

This statement contains two harbingers of a new policy. The first was the assertion that churches and lunch-counters were public facilities. Here, President Kennedy was not trying to close the chasm between Church and State established by the First Amendment. Rather he was stretching the notion of public facilities to give some tincture of Constitutional authority to the proposition that it was a legitimate function of the President to crusade against racial exclusion in every aspect of American life.

The second significant innovation was the implication that illegal conduct was justified and entitled to Presidential approval provided a substantive grievance existed. Advocacy of illegal action was implied in the assertion that the President should support Negroes who "sit down" for their rights.

These people, needless to say, were not sitting on their own property, ruminating over their complaints. They were sitting at lunch-counters to prevent others from being served and to force the owners of these counters to serve them, even if local ordinances prohibited their doing so. They were sitting or lying in the offices of public officials who did not conduct their duties in a manner which pleased them. In doing so, they were often guilty of trespass and malicious interference with whatever the work of the office which they occupied happened to be. Others sat or lay in the halls of Congress, in churches which refused to pay them "reparations" for the past slavery of the Negro race, in restaurants which did not wish to serve them, and in many other places which had incurred their displeasure or which were legally barred to them.

This was merely the beginning of John F. Kennedy's flirtation with advocacy of illegal action by Negro demonstrators. Commenting on violence in Birmingham on May 22, 1963, the President said:

"I think there may be other things we can do which will provide a legal outlet for a desire for a remedy other than having to engage in demonstrations which bring them (the Negroes) into conflict with the forces of law and order. . . . As it is today, in many cases they do not have a remedy, and therefore they take to the streets, and have the kind of incidents that we had in Birmingham."[22]

This was merely an explanation of the reasons for Negro violence. As the race crisis intensified, the President inched closer to the role of apologist for lawless mobs. After stating, on June 9, 1963, that he was concerned about demonstrations that developed into riots, Kennedy added: "But you can't tell people 'don't protest.' " (If the protest was illegal, why not?)

And in a national television address concerning the integration crisis at the University of Alabama and his proposed civil rights legislation, Kennedy said late in 1963:

"The old code of equity under which we live commands for every wrong a remedy, but in too many communities, in too many parts of the country, wrongs are inflicted on Negro citizens for which there are no remedies at law. *Unless the Congress acts, their only remedy is in the street.*"[23]

This open advocacy of mob violence by the chief executive officer of the American Government seemed in conflict with his oath to uphold the Constitution and the laws of his country. Marking a high-water mark in the tide toward unconditional justification and support of Negro demands, it was promptly echoed by the more radical supporters of the Kennedy Administration. Thus, Adlai E. Stevenson, the American Ambassador to the United Nations, told an audience at Colby College that "Even a jail sentence is no longer a dishonor but a proud achievement." The audience presumably was to infer that the laws of the United States were so evil and unjust that it was an honor to break them. If Stevenson really believed this, listeners might have asked, why did he continue to serve as a public official?

Two years later Hubert Horatio Humphrey, by then Vice President of the United States, joined the chorus of high officials who condoned violence and disobedience of the laws. He

[22]Arthur Krock, *Nation,* "Shift in Civil Rights Policy," July 21, 1963, p. 335.
[23]Quoted by M. Stanton Evans, *The Liberal Establishment* (New York, 1965), p. 186. Italics supplied.

predicted "open violence" in all American cities unless Federal rent subsidy legislation was enacted. This prediction seemed to many to be an invitation. As matters turned out, the subsidy was legislated and violence swept the cities anyhow.

Humphrey continued his address with the statement that he would hate to "be stuck on a fourth floor tenement with rats nibbling on the kid's toes—and they do—and with garbage uncollected—and it is. . . ." If he found himself in such a predicament, he added: "I think you'd have more trouble than you have had already, because I've got enough spark left in me to lead a mighty good revolt under those conditions."[24]

Most of the nation's press was shocked at the spectacle of the Vice President glorifying rioting and speculating about his own abilities as a riot leader. It occurred to some commentators that Americans had been faced with the problem of rats in their houses or apartments in the past. They had not reacted with the blind violence which Humphrey advocated, but had plugged up the ratholes and used the energy and ingenuity for which Americans used to be famous to solve their own problem themselves.

Our narrative closes on November 22, 1963, the day of President Kennedy's assassination in Dallas. Looking backward over the almost two centuries of the nation's existence, a pessimistic observer might conclude that racial discontent, strife and hatred were as seething and widespread as at any previous time in the life of the United States as a Republic. This state of affairs existed despite the fact that Americans had spent billions of dollars to improve the education, housing and job opportunities of the Negro minority. A more concentrated and prodigious national effort had gone into this venture, during the two decades just past, than any other nation had ever expended on a submerged class, caste or ethnic group at any time.

[24]Allan H. Ryskind, *Hubert* (New York, 1968), pp. 323–24.

CHAPTER TWENTY-TWO

The Balance Sheet

It's always been my belief that the white folks and the colored folks simply don't like one another.
—William Faulkner, as quoted by the *New York Times*, March 8, 1958.

From the inauguration of George Washington in 1799 to the end of World War I, the pattern of American political thought concerning slavery and the Negro showed an extraordinary and somewhat astonishing consistency. There was a national consensus on both topics, one that was shared, in the main, both by the statesmen and political leaders of the nation and by public opinion.

Some have viewed American history during this period in terms of a struggle between those who wished freedom for the Negro and those who desired to keep him enslaved, between those who demanded equality for all races and those who accepted the dominant status of the White majority, between those who wished the assimilation of the Negro in American society and those who wished him excluded from that society. This view of the past is, in our opinion, erroneous.

If there is one single point that emerges with crystal clarity from the record as we have sought to decipher it, that point is the substantial agreement of the leaders of American government and public opinion on several fundamental propositions.

There was opposition to slavery and the slave trade both on moral grounds and because of objection to the Negro's presence on American soil. The extent to which anti-slavery sentiment was a complex combination of ethical condemnation and fear that an element had been introduced into American society which threatened the nation's security has been shown over and over again in our expositions of American political opinion.

The Negro was deemed an alien presence in American society who could not be assimilated without destroying or largely impairing the homogeneity and national cohesion of the Republic. As Jefferson so eloquently put it: "We have the wolf by the ears, and we can neither hold him, nor safely let him go. Justice is on one scale, and self-preservation in the other."[1]

A fundamental reason for believing the Negro to be unassimilable as a citizen was the conviction of most American statesmen that the Black man was mentally and morally inferior. This view was expressed with great clarity by Thomas Jefferson. In addition to being the predominant opinion of the South, it was shared by such political leaders as Henry Clay, Stephen A. Douglas and Abraham Lincoln. Among the Abolitionists, Charles Sumner could speak of Negroes as "moving masses of flesh, unendowed with anything of intelligence above the brutes;" Thaddeus Stevens would concede that those he knew were "not qualified to vote"; Ralph Waldo Emerson would find them degraded because of "sin"; Henry Wilson would deny "the mental or the intellectual equality of the African race" and William H. Seward would call them "a foreign and feeble element . . . incapable of assimilation . . . unwisely transplanted into our fields" and "unprofitable to cultivate." The dominant viewpoint of the next three decades was, if anything, considerably more unfavorable.

In the liberal and progressive camp, Theodore Roosevelt voiced the judgment that "as a race and in the main they are altogether inferior to the whites." President William Howard Taft told a Negro audience that they were adapted "to be a race of farmers first, and all the time." Woodrow Wilson wrote of the "easy faith, the simplicity, the idle hopes, the inexperience of children" of the newly emancipated Southern Negroes and thought that their "masterless homeless freedom" made them

[1]Thomas Jefferson to John Holmes, April 22, 1820.

"the more pitiable, the more dependent, because under slavery they had been shielded." The Socialist Party showed itself truly a disciple of Karl Marx, in respect at least to the latter's hatred of the Negro race, when it officially characterized them in 1903 as "lynchable human degenerates."

These strongly negative views were shared by most intellectuals though the latter did not, of course, express them with the vulgarity, intemperateness and hatred of some of the Socialists and Southern radical rabble-rousers. The labor historian John R. Commons thought the Negro to be "indolent and fickle." Josiah Royce, one of America's leading philosophers, believed the race would remain "primitive" because of "innate" causal factors. Charles Francis Adams, Jr. visited sub-Saharan Africa and returned to write of the "awful corollary" to the savagery of that continent posed by the Negro presence in the United States. Urging that free societies must consist of "homogeneous equals," he denied the Negro could be accepted as a citizen and even doubted his entitlement to equality under law.

Whether these views were sound or prejudiced, temperate or exaggerated, based upon science or based upon bias are issues beyond the scope of the present book. Our subject is what a certain class of Americans thought about slavery and the Negro. A related topic is how and why they arrived at these opinions and what formative forces shaped their social philosophies. To examine the verifiability of their beliefs would involve us either in the sort of petulant scolding of historical characters which has become a deplorable hallmark of even some of the more scholarly modern liberal and radical works on the American Negro, or else would involve a serious examination of the opinions advanced by American statesmen in the light of the entire complex of relevant scientific evidence. The first alternative we rejected as none of the business of the historian. The second alternative we declined because an evaluation of the evidence concerning innate differences in the psychology and mentality of the various races would require another book, at least as long as this one.

Given a consensus that the Negro was physically and psychically different from the White majority and that his inherent mental ability was much lower, the conclusion was drawn by most American political leaders that he could not be assimilated as a full-fledged citizen. From the earliest days of the Republic, the most insistent question asked about the Negro was not whether he should be slave or free on moral grounds, but what was to be done with him.

There was virtual unanimity that he should not be assimilated if that could be avoided. Therefore, the policy almost unanimously advocated by responsible Americans during the first sixty years of the Republic's existence was colonization. Jefferson's proposal was that the Negroes should be freed only on condition that they be deported to Africa or to some suitable place in the West Indies. There were differences of opinion on such matters as whether the colonization should be voluntary or enforced, whether it should apply exclusively to Negroes already free or to the entire Negro population, and whether the area to be colonized should be in Africa, the Antilles, Central America or some reserved "negro pen" within the boundaries of the United States. Allowing for these differences in implementation, the colonization solution was accepted and endorsed by Bushrod Washington, John Jay, Thomas Jefferson, James Madison, James Monroe, Chief Justice John Marshall, Henry Clay, Daniel Webster, Chief Justice Roger B. Taney, Stephen A. Douglas and Abraham Lincoln. It was endorsed by Southern slaveholders and Northern Abolitionists alike. The deportation dream faded only after President Lincoln's successive failures to establish viable Negro colonies in Panama and Haiti and only after the emancipation of the slaves destroyed the Government's ability to compel the Blacks to leave the country.

Colonization ventures continued to be attempted after 1865, but with scant success. The great majority of Negroes knew that they were much better off in the United States than in any other country which might be willing to accept them.

Under slavery, the alternatives had been bondage or deportation. The colonized Negro was separated from White society by distance; the slave was so separated by status. There was a dialectical interrelation between the two solutions. The progress of manumission of slaves was impeded by the fact that free Negroes were despised, detested and subjected to every possible sort of affront, discriminatory practice and indignity almost everywhere in the United States. Planters were willing to free slaves if they would go to Africa or the West Indies as permanent settlers; they were not willing to add to the desperate and degraded free Negro population.

Once slavery had been outlawed, the alternatives changed. It was no longer a choice between physical separation through deportation and status separation through slavery. The alternatives became separation through subordinate status and assimilation through some measure of equality. The latter was embraced by many of the Reconstruction Radicals during the first decade after Appomattox. Curiously enough, it was supported briefly by such former Confederate leaders as Alexander H. Stephens. An alliance between the Negro and White poor was the cornerstone of the thrust for Populist power as late as the 1890s.

Yet this alternative did not prove viable. The Abolitionists and Reconstruction radicals quickly became disillusioned with the Negro's progress in the *post-bellum* South. As we have shown, some of them became transformed into ardent advocates of white supremacy and Negro subordination below the Mason-Dixon Line. Nor did the Populist honeymoon with the Negro masses prove lasting.

The reasons customarily advanced for the fragility of these movements toward assimilation and some measure of political equality range from an evil conspiracy by Southern bourbons, to Populist disillusionment with the willingness of the Negroes to sell their votes to the White establishment, to the ignorance and benighted character of the poor Whites.

Without wholly repudiating any of these suggested causes, we should like to suggest that a more fundamental divisive force was the character of the modern nation.

Nation is defined in the *Oxford English Dictionary,* the ultimate literary and scholarly authority on English speech, as "an extensive aggregate of persons, so closely associated with each other by common descent, language, or history, as to form a distinct race or people, usually organized as a separate political state and occupying a definite territory." The root of *nation* is *nasci,* meaning to be born, thus indicating the role of lineage in the origins of nationality.

The Negroes could not, of course, claim common descent with the Anglo-Saxons. Their history had little in common with that of the descendants of European settlers. The institutions of the two races were disparate. Even the Negro language was as distinct from English as, say, Catalán is from Spanish. What was lacking in short was that common ground of tradition and heritage out of which most viable nations have arisen.

The common ground that remained for political cooperation was *convenience* and *self-interest.* Hence, Tom Watson, the most eloquent Populist spokesman in favor of a Negro-White political alliance, stressed *convenience* as its mainspring. Convenience, however, is temporary and changeable. When the apparent advantages of the Negro alliance were outweighed by its seeming liabilities, Thomas Watson and many of his colleagues became transformed overnight into intolerant and brutal advocates of racial repression.

With slavery a thing of the past, colonization a bygone dream and efforts at assimilation shipwrecked, not only the South, but the nation as a whole, turned toward an empirically devised system of separation and subordination. Its cornerstone in the South was denial to the Negro of almost all the basic rights of American citizenship, including particularly the right to vote. In the nation as a whole, strict segregation was imposed, both by law and by custom, in all areas of potential contact between the two races. This Jim Crow system was a substitute for slavery or colonization in that it had the same fundamental purpose of preventing contact on any terms suggesting equality.

Unlike slavery, however, the *de facto* system of segregation and subordination was administered, not by the patrician South, but by the masses. Where slavery had involved responsibility on the part of the master and paternalistic concern for the welfare of the slave, the new system entailed no responsibility and total unconcern. The old way was predicated on noblesse oblige, the new way on animosity.

The continuity of these attempted solutions and their underlying similarity of purpose was suggested by some musings of President Theodore Roosevelt in 1901. He could find "no solution to the terrible problem offered by the presence of the Negro on this continent." Yet "inasmuch as he is here and can neither be killed nor driven away," the only wise and Christian course was to treat "each black man and each white man strictly on his merits as a man, giving him no more and no less than he shows himself worthy to have." This was not a recipe for equality, since Roosevelt deemed the Negroes, as a whole, to be inferior; it was a recipe for eliminating the criterion of race and judging each individual on the basis of his own character, intelligence and worth.

We conceive the mainstream of American thought and purpose on slavery and the Negro to be one of consensus. Its two fundamental tenets were opposition to slavery and aversion to the Negro presence.

An alternative conception sees the central theme as one of struggle. The protagonists are the Abolitionists, some of whom wished full freedom, equality and even social and sexual mixing for the two races, and the pro-slavery Southerners, who regarded servitude as intrinsically desirable for the Negro, envisaged an Athenian democracy in which the Negro did all physical work, and even recommended reopening the African slave trade so the poor Whites could join the slave-owning class.

Both the Abolitionist and the Calhoun viewpoints seem to us unrepresentative of American thought and incompatible with the national temperament. The Abolitionists were a despised and persecuted minority. In the North as well as the South they were hounded, mobbed and sometimes murdered.

The Southern pro-slavery ideologists were men of more substance and power. They were neither despised nor persecuted in their own part of the country, but they were nonetheless a minority during the first half-century of this nation's existence. The Presidents of the Virginia dynasty agreed with Northern political leaders, such as Alexander Hamilton and John Adams, that slavery was immoral in itself and ruinous to the character of the White master class. With the rise of the Jacksonians to national power, the moral repudiation of slavery by American Presidents became the exception rather than the rule, but this was, in part at least, the reflection of a more pragmatic, empirical and materialistic attitude—a shift in interest from political philosophy to the practical politics of power. Even in this morally more insensitive age, the panegyrists of slavery were in a minority. Andrew Jackson, James K. Polk and other Southern leaders of the period regarded Calhoun as a fanatic whose obsessive need to raise the slavery issue on all occasions, and thus divide the nation, bordered on treason.

The Southerners of the Calhoun school became the predominant voice of the South only at a time when the conflict over slavery had become so polarized that civil war was imminent. The Abolitionists gained in respectability and power during substantially the same period and for the same reason. Once the nation was irrevocably divided into two hostile camps, the zealots and extremists of each side had their day. As the conflict escalated, Abolitionists and pro-slavery ideologists entrenched their power over their factions, drawing the more moderate masses toward their own fratricidal ideologies.

The Calhoun ideology did not reflect the viewpoint of the South, except under the stress of approaching and actual war, because its vision of an aristocratical society of White masters, lording it over African slave gangs which performed all physical work, was contrary to American conceptions of democracy. The Abolitionist ideology similarly failed to reflect the Northern viewpoint because it was predicated on conceptions of race equality and the desirability of a multiracial republic which had never been accepted by the people of either region. Both philosophies then were reflections, not of the continuing American view, but of the pathology of civil conflict.

As the Nineteenth Century came to a close, William Graham Sumner, professor of political and social science at Yale, worked on the final draft of his *magnum opus, Folkways.*[3] The underlying theme of this stimulating work was that the laws of militant reformers cannot change a society's *mores,* for the latter are the warp and woof of the social order. "Folkways" were the stable substratum of organized society: "Each individual is born into them as he is born into the atmosphere, and he does not reflect on them, or criticize them any more than a baby

[3]William Graham Sumner, *Folkways: A Study of the Sociological Importance of Usages, Manners, Customs, Mores, and Morals* (New York, 1906).

analyzes the atmosphere before he begins to breathe it."

Sumner believed that the Negro's future in America would be determined by the conduct of the White people among whom he lived and that every attempt to change this condition by outside interference was either useless or pernicious.

"In our Southern states, before the civil war," he wrote,

> Whites and blacks had formed habits of action and feeling toward each other. They lived in peace and concord, and each one grew up in the ways which were traditional and customary. The Civil War abolished legal rights and left the two races to learn how to live together under other relations than before. The whites have never been converted from the old mores. . . . The two races have not yet made new mores. Vain attempts have been made to control the new order by legislation. The only result is the proof that legislation cannot make mores. We see also that mores do not form under social convulsion and discord. It is only just now that the new society seems to be taking shape. There is a trend in the mores now as they begin to form under the new state of things. It is not at all what the humanitarians hoped and expected. *The two races are separating more than ever before. The strongest point in the new code seems to be that any white man is boycotted and despised if he 'associates with negroes.'* Some are anxious to interfere and try to control. They take their stand on ethical views of what is going on. It is evidently impossible for anyone to interfere. *We are like spectators at a great natural convulsion.* The results will be such as the facts and forces call for. We cannot foresee them. *They do not depend on ethical views any more than the volcanic eruption on Martinique contained an ethical element. . . . The mores which once were a memory. Those which any one thinks ought to be are a dream. The only things with which we can deal are those which are.*[4]

It was thus that the relationship between White men and Black men in the South appeared to a sagacious conservative observer as the Twentieth Century dawned. The new century was to carry in with it novel and unpredictable forces that Sumner could not have envisioned and that would magnify the power of what he called *stateways* (laws, categorical imperatives, directives) and would lessen that of his beloved *folkways*. Primary among these changes would be the unprecedented

[4] *Ibid.,* pp. 77–78. Emphasis supplied.

centralization of communications and the technological power to direct these communications instantaneously into almost every home in the nation. Stentor, the Greek warrior in the struggle with Troy "whose voice was as powerful as fifty voices of other men," was merely a whisper compared to the new media of the mass press, cinema, radio and television. Communism and Nazism were early demonstrations of the almost omnipotent power of these technological *stentors* to persuade multitudes and nations of absurdities, to change animosity into love and affection into hatred, to induce millions to die willingly for those fallacies and lies that the central authority chose to proclaim to the masses whose brains it dominated.

The use of these *stentors* was not a totalitarian monopoly, but being a matter of technological and scientific mastery, a technique that reached its greatest development in the United States. As the nation advanced toward the twilight years of the Twentieth Century, new and uneasy equilibria were created in the area of race relations.

The *stentors* proclaimed the equality of all races, not merely in respect to rights, but in respect to intelligence, ability and character as well. The Negro, who had previously complained that he was an "invisible man" in the eyes of White society, was given a prominence in television and the cinema disproportionate either to his numbers or to the affection in which he was held. He was portrayed as a paragon of nobility of soul, intelligence, fatherly wisdom and self-sacrifice. Any departures from high-mindedness in his conduct were attributed to White oppression. An immoral or stupid Negro became as uncommon on television as a corrupt FBI man or a drunken priest.

The American people spent a considerable part of their lives in this dream world of *stateways,* to use Sumner's term, of the boob tube, to use the vernacular, or of the *stentor,* as we prefer to put it. During the rest of the day and night, they were faced with more practical problems. Some of these involved the Negro. Neighborhoods were deteriorating into slums; public schools became jungles; Negroes demanded admission to universities without passing qualifying examinations and sometimes resorted to arson when their demands were refused; a rising crime wave made streets, neighborhoods and whole cities unsafe.

Some of these problems created a contradiction between the world of the *stentor* and the world of observed reality, causing ambivalence and tension in the minds of the White majority. The apparent consensus of public opinion in favor of racial integration, registered by public opinion polls but seemingly belied by recurrent racial strife, may have represented nothing more than a highly unstable equilibrium, the chief force for instability being the contradiction between propaganda and reality.

From the end of World War II to the inauguration of Richard M. Nixon, American governmental policy moved steadily from advocacy of desegregation to support of race blending in schools and neighborhoods. It moved from the principle of equality of rights to that of preferential treatment for Negroes.

The original school desegregation decision said nothing more than that children should not be deprived of the right to attend any given public school by reason of their race.[5] By 1970, this had been expanded to authorize compelling local authorities to transport children to schools outside their residential neighborhoods in order to achieve a racial mix corresponding to that of the population. Similarly, the original court decisions upholding equal access to governmental jobs, regardless of race, were transformed into their direct opposite, preferential hiring of Negroes in public jobs and consequently deliberate violation of the Fourteenth Amendment to the Constitution.[6]

The reasoning behind some of these strange developments was foreshadowed by an *amicus curiae* brief submitted to the Supreme Court in the school desegregation case by President Truman's Attorney General. "Racial discrimination," that official declared, "furnishes grist for the Communist propaganda mills, and it raises doubts even among friendly nations as to the intensity of our devotion to the democratic faith." Attorney General McGranery then incorporated what he called an "au-

---

[5] *Brown v. Board of Education,* 347 U.S. 483 (1954).

[6] "No State shall make or enforce any law which shall abridge the privileges or immunities of citizens of the United States; nor shall any State deprive any person of life, liberty, or property, without due process of law; nor deny to any person within its jurisdiction the equal protection of the laws."

thoritative statement" from Secretary of State Dean Acheson, which stated in part: "The hostile reaction among normally friendly peoples, many of whom are particularly sensitive in regard to the status of non-European races, is growing in alarming proportions. In such countries, the view is expressed more and more vocally that the United States is hypocritical in claiming to be the champion of democracy while permitting the practice of racial discrimination here in this country.[7]

One of the present authors commented on this essay by Mr. Acheson ten years ago in the following terms:

> If the Court of 1952 was prepared to weigh political factors in making a Constitutional interpretation, Acheson's memorandum was subject to criticism because of its oversimplification and calculated omissions. It was true that Southern treatment of the Negro was resented abroad. The Supreme Court knew this. What it did not know and was in no position to judge was the total effect of a desegregation decision in terms of the world position and prestige of the United States.
>
> Would it split or unite the country? Would it convince the world that the United States was the champion of racial equality? Or would it focus international attention for years to come on race struggle and race hatred in the United States, placing these ugly aspects of American life under a global spotlight? These were questions which an American Secretary of State should have attempted to answer provided he thought it was proper for him to inject himself into the case at all.[8]

These misgivings have, it would seem, been amply justified by the course of events. The United States has undertaken an historically unparalleled effort to raise the Negro by governmental action to the political, cultural, social and economic level attained by the White man. In the pursuit of this objective, it has spent billions of dollars. It has promoted men to positions for which they are not qualified solely because they are Black. It has persuaded universities to admit students who do not qualify educationally or mentally exclusively because of their

---

[7] *Brief for the United States as Amicus Curiae, In the Supreme Court of the United States, October Term 1952, Brown v. Board of Education of Topeka,* pp. 1, 7.

[8] Nathaniel Weyl, *The Negro in American Civilization* (Washington, 1960), pp. 255–56.

color. It has filled some of the highest positions in the executive
and judicial branches of government on the basis of race and
without regard to merit.

The reward the United States has reaped is to be denounced
across the world as a racist state and as a recrudescence of
Hitlerism. By contrast, the Japanese, who continue to oppress
one and a half million Etas, have been silent about their mis-
conduct and it has passed unnoticed. The Indians, who have
abolished caste more in name than in fact, remain immune
from world criticism even though their untouchables are still
largely pariahs. The masochistic traditions of liberal Protes-
tantism, reformed Judaism and modern Catholicism to the contrary, those who publicly display their sores are tagged with the
leper's bell.

Having completed this long excursion into the history of our
country, we ask ourselves what does it all mean and what useful purpose, if any, does it serve? Somebody once said that those
who refuse to learn from history must re-experience it. That is
true. It is also true that one cannot copy the solutions of history
because the past is not the present, nor is the present the future.
Particularly, in the present era of accelerated change in all
aspects and parameters of human existence, a slavish imitation of past solutions is inappropriate.

Nevertheless, we should like to hazard an answer to two
pressing questions.

Is it the lesson of American history that different races cannot peacefully coexist in the same society?

We think not. Fortunately, we have the example of Hawaii,
in which Japanese, Chinese, Polynesian and White populations
and the various mixtures resulting from their heterogeneity
coexist harmoniously on the basis of cooperation and with
minimal racial strife. The fundamental difference between the
condition of the non-Whites of Hawaii and the Negroes of
mainland United States is that the former have advanced to a
status of approximate cultural, intellectual, economic and political parity by their own efforts. Hawaiians of Oriental ancestry are accepted because they have proved themselves equal to
the American challenge. Their educational progress, their self-
reliance, courage and capacity for hard work, their creative

contributions in the arts, sciences, business, government and the professions have made them generally admired. In short, negative attitudes toward the Negro are due less to his racial difference than to his failure to meet the challenges of American life as effectively as other peoples.

Nowhere is the pace of change and innovation faster than in the United States. No people is more receptive to new ideas, new ways of doing things, new challenges. In recent decades, the American people have shown themselves more ready to accept newcomers of other races and from other lands than most Europeans. The requirement for such acceptance, however, is the ability to adapt to an advanced, free society and to meet its multiple challenges successfully.

The second question is: What policies toward the Negro are practical and constructive?

Obviously, slavery, colonization and the *de facto* racial subordination and oppression which prevailed roughly between Appomattox and the New Deal are unacceptable.

Two possible general avenues of approach remain.

The first is that represented by the ultra-liberal ideology on race. It presupposes that race differences are superficial and that no significant psychic differences between races exist. "Race prejudice" is said to be caused exclusively by the pathological condition of the prejudiced. To combat prejudice, governmental action is applied to compel interracial association regardless of the wishes of either ethnic group. White and Black children are forced to mix in the same schools and live in the same neighborhoods. On the theory that any superior position enjoyed by the Whites is due to prejudice and unfair advantage, governmental action of a compensatory sort is taken to bring the Negro up to the White level. This means denying scholarships, appointments, jobs and promotions to the best qualified applicants if they happen to belong to the majority race. To the extent that race quotas rather than ability determine promotion, American science, technology, medicine, the professions, and governmental and business leadership will inevitably suffer.

In education, the dominant egalitarian philosophy has stressed concern for the disadvantaged. Consequently, the best educational resources of the nation have been deployed on the mentally below-average pupils of both races, on children who are incapable of making any contribution of significance to their society. The intelligent students, forced into the strait-jacket of this slow-motion system, find that the schools shackle their minds instead of challenging them. Many acquire a profound antipathy to formal education; many become dropouts. The gifted have become the orphans of American education. The nation is engaged in squandering and stultefying its most promising human resources.

The second profoundly adverse consequence is alienation. The more the policies of racial favoritism and enforced inter-racial association are applied, the more apparent and militant is Negro rejection of American society. When masses of mentally and academically unqualified Negroes are pushed into the universities, they are humiliated by failure and angered by rejection. This creates a racist, revolutionary element which demands the destruction of all academic standards and, when frustrated, retaliates with mob violence, arson and terror.

Negro alienation from American society has reached greater proportions than at any period in our history. This alienation is correlated with the increased association and competition between the two races which has been forced upon both ethnic groups by doctrinaire bureaucrats.

The suggested alternative policy is simple and consonant with the traditions and principles of American society.

Government should continue to act to ensure that no citizen is denied his civil rights or access to public schools, public office or any other governmental facility because of race.

In the private sector, individuals should have the right to associate or refuse to associate with anybody they please without interference by governmental authority.

Racial mixing of schools, neighborhoods and residential complexes according to bureaucratically prescribed formulas is an abuse of governmental power. It is the business of the state to see that people are not deprived of their rights because of their race; it is not the business of the state to decide how they should be mixed in relation to race.

Favoritism in governmental appointment, promotion, scholarship or entry into any educational institution on the basis of race is a violation of the Fourteenth Amendment and should be outlawed. Any compensatory advantages given to Americans because of an unfavorable economic, social or educational environment should apply to all persons so handicapped, not merely to those racially so handicapped.

Government, we believe, should endeavor to enforce equality of rights and equality of opportunity. It should not impose equality of rewards. In our society, rewards are supposed to be proportionate to contributions. Those who achieve more receive more.

These suggestions presuppose a return to those traditional values of an open and free society which are such a vital element in the American dream. The alternative of racial quotas and official ethnic discrimination is more reminiscent of Czarist Russia, the Soviet Union and Nazi Germany than of the Free World.

APPENDIX

Old World Influences on American Slavery

> The lower sort are by nature slaves, and it is better for them as for all inferiors that they should be under the rule of a master. For he who participates in rational principles enough to apprehend, but not to have, such a principle is a slave by nature. Whereas the lower animals cannot even apprehend a principle; they obey their instincts. And indeed the use made of slaves and of tame animals is not very different; for both with their bodies minister to the needs of life. . . . It is clear, then, that some men are by nature free, and others slaves, and that for these latter slavery is both expedient and right.
>
> —Aristotle, *Politics,* Book I, Chapter 5, *1254ᵇ-1255ᵃ* (Benjamin Jowett translation.)[1]

The architects of the American Republic derived their ethical and legal views concerning slavery from the Scriptures, from the classical writers of the Graeco-Roman world and from the British and French writers of the Enlightenment. Thinkers such as Montesquieu, Rousseau, Voltaire, Locke and Hume were engaged in undermining the authority of revealed religion as the fountainhead of law, politics, and government and substituting a rationalist critique, resting on *a priori* philosophizing concerning natural rights, man in a state of nature and the social contract. This revolutionary movement from religion to rationalism was well under way at the time of the

[1]The numbers and letters refer to the pages and columns of the Berlin Greek edition.

Constitution, but by no means completed. Hence the statesmen who created the American Republic had intellectual roots deeply imbedded in the Bible and the classics. When they sought for historic examples, analogies or guidelines to action, they were as likely to focus their attention on Greece, Judea or Rome as on that Eighteenth-Century England from which their ancestors had come.

All the Mediterranean civilizations had tolerated slavery and most positively accepted it as a desirable social institution. None of the Greek schools of philosophy advocated the emancipation of slaves as a moral imperative. Perhaps the closest approach to an Abolitionist position was that of such neo-Stoics as Dio Chrysostom and Seneca, who urged humane treatment of bondmen. Stoicism regarded slavery as a mere accident of human existence and observed that any man could free himself from slavery by committing suicide. The aim of life was not external, but internal, freedom. The latter required an attitude of indifference toward fortune and circumstance. Any man who was a philosopher and who had the necessary strength of character could attain that freedom.

The Old Testament regulates the relationship between master and slave in some detail. Thus in LEVITICUS (xxv: 39–55), God instructs the Children of Israel to enslave the heathen and their progeny forever, but to employ poor Jews as servants only, and to free them with their children on the year of jubilee.[2] As for impoverished Jews, "They are My slaves whom I brought out of Egypt, they shall not be sold as slaves are sold." But, "The children of those who have settled and lodged with you and such of their family as are born in the land. . . . may become your property, and you may leave them to your sons after you; you may use them as slaves permanently."

The laws of Moses provided that Israelites could be enslaved, but at the end of six years were to be set free. If they were married when enslaved, their wives were to be set free with them. If their masters gave them wives during their terms of bondage and children resulted from the union, then the men were to be freed to go away alone, leaving their wives and

[2] *The New English Bible* (Oxford University Press, Cambridge University Press, 1970), both here and elsewhere.

children behind as slaves. "But if the slave should say, 'I love
my master, my wife, and my children; I will not go free,' then
his master shall bring him to God: he shall bring him to the door
of the door-post, and his master shall pierce his ear with an awl,
and the man shall be his slave for life."[3]

The treatment of slaves was humane by classical standards.
No bondman could be made to work on the Sabbath
(DEUTERONOMY V: 14.) Slaves could be beaten, but if the slave
died on the spot, the master must be punished. "But he shall not
be punished if the slave survives for one day or two, because he
is worth money to his master." That is to say, it was assumed
that the death was accidental, because no prudent man would
deliberately destroy his own property (EXODUS XXI: 20–21). The
same Mosaic laws provided that, if a master blinded his slave
or knocked out one of his teeth, the slave was to go free (EXODUS
XXI: 26–27). An interesting provision covered the case of a man
who had intercourse with a slave girl who had been assigned to
another man and had not been ransomed. "They shall not be put
to death, because she has not been freed." Instead, the girl's
seducer was required to offer a sacrificial ram to God, after
which he was to be forgiven (LEVITICUS XIX: 20–22).

The injunction that Israelites were never to be enslaved is
repeated throughout the Old Testament. Thus, the prophet
Oded prevents the Children of Israel from enslaving 200,000
defeated Judeans (II CHRONICLES XXVIII: 8–15). The prophet Jeremiah complained that Zedekiah, King of Judah, having made
a covenant with God to free all his Hebrew slaves after the
sixth year, had done so, but had promptly re-enslaved them. For
this offense, the Lord would deliver them "to the sword, to
pestilence, and to famine" and would make the besieging
Babylonian army sack and burn the cities of Judah and make
them "desolate and unpeopled" (JEREMIAH 34: 17, 22).

The putative heinousness of the crime of enslaving impoverished Jews can be measured by the fact that Jeremiah attributes the destruction of Judean power and the Diaspora that
followed it to this transgression.

By the time of Christ, Palestine was perhaps the only corner
of the Roman Empire in which slavery was not rife. Particu-

[3]EXODUS, XXI: 5–7.

larly after the return from the Babylonian Captivity, Jewish slaves began to enjoy the protection of an intricate, evolving rabbinical code which safeguarded them against mistreatment and exploitation. The Pharisees interpreted the law as requiring that Jewish masters treat those of their slaves who were co-religionists as they treated themselves, providing them with equally good food, wine and lodging. Since the rabbinical courts tended to enforce such regulations, the holding of Jewish slaves by Jews soon became unprofitable. As for the Jewish slaves of Gentiles, there were very few of them prior to the capture of Jerusalem by Titus in A.D. 70, since Jews considered it a cardinal religious duty to ransom co-religionists held in bondage. The paucity of Jewish slaves of non-Jews is confirmed by a scrutiny of the record of manumissions at the great commercial center of Delphi from the Third to the First Century B.C.[4]

The Pharisees effectively opposed the slavery of non-Jews to Jewish masters, particularly during the centuries immediately preceding the birth of Christ. "He who multiplies female slaves, increases licentiousness," they exhorted, "While he who multiplies male slaves, increases robbery." They objected to them as an alien and unassimilable element which threatened the integrity of the Jewish people and the power of the Jewish religious leaders over their flock. On these grounds, they also strongly opposed manumission, for the emancipated slave acquired the same status under Jewish law as the proselyte. The abundance and low wages of labor combined to make slavery unnecessary and at times unprofitable. These factors made Palestine virtually unique in the Roman Empire at the time of Christ, for it lacked both a large population of slaves and that large and powerful element of freedmen which played such a major role in the administration of the Empire under the Claudian and Julian houses.[5]

---

[4]Another reason for the meager supply of Jewish slaves was the more humane attitude of the Hebrews than that of their contemporaries. At a time when exposure of unwanted children was common in Egypt and Rome, the practice was illegalized among Jewry. While Jewish thieves could be sold into slavery, debtors could not.

[5]Salo Wittmayer Baron, *A Social and Religious History of the Jews, Volume I: Ancient Times, Part I* (New York, 1952), pp. 267-71.

If the New Testament devotes considerably less attention to slavery than the Old, the reasons include the fact that the institution was already on the wane in Palestine by that time and that the early converts to Christianity were people too poor, for the most part, to own slaves. In numerous places, St. Paul urges slaves to obey their masters with full hearts and without equivocation. "Slaves, give entire obedience to your earthly masters," he wrote from prison, "not merely with an outward show of service, to curry favour with men, but with singlemindedness, out of reverence for the Lord. Whatever you are doing, put your whole heart into it, as if you were doing it for the Lord and not for men, knowing that there is a Master who will give you your heritage as a reward for your service." Then Paul adds: "Masters, be just and fair to your slaves, knowing that you too have a Master in heaven."[6]

Peter goes beyond this and orders slaves to obey even unjust orders of their masters, pointing out that there is greater merit in submitting to punishment when one is innocent than when one is guilty of an offense. "Servants, accept the authority of your masters with all due submission, not only when they are kind and considerate, but even when they are perverse. For it is a fine thing if a man endure the pain of undeserved suffering because God is in his thoughts. What credit is there in fortitude when you have done wrong and are beaten for it? But when you have behaved well and suffer for it, your fortitude is a fine thing in the sight of God."[7]

In his epistles to the Ephesians and Colossians, Paul also urged masters to "give up using threats; remember you both have the same Master in heaven, and he has no favourites," but the stress was on the obligation of the slave to obey and this duty was absolute, in no way conditioned by the conduct of the slave's master. In St. Paul's first epistle, to Timothy, Christian slaves are ordered to obey their Christian masters even more faithfully than if they were heathen: "If the masters are believers, the slaves must not respect them any less for being their Christian brothers. Quite the contrary; they must be all the better servants because those who receive the benefit of

[6]COLOSSIANS III: 22–25.
[7]I PETER 2: 19–21.

their service are one with them in faith and love."[8]

In his letter to Philemon, a Christian, St. Paul appeals to him to take back his runaway slave, Onesimus, "whose father I have become in this prison," not as a bondsman, but "as a dear brother, very dear indeed to me and how much dearer to you, both as a man and a Christian."[9] Like the other early Christians, Paul believed that the Second Coming was imminent and hence the status of slaves in this world was of little importance. The converted slaves were to be accepted on an equal basis by free Christians as "the Lord's freedmen" (I CORINTHIANS 7:22.)

Paul made it abundantly clear that the Christian Church was not to be a community of equals, but comparable to the human body, in which each organ serves a special purpose. As for women in church, "They have no license to speak, but should keep their place as the law directs. If there is something they want to know, they can ask their own husbands at home. It is a shocking thing that a woman should address the congregation."[10] The Church was also hierarchically ordered:

"Now you are Christ's body, and each of you a limb or organ of it. Within our community God has· appointed, in the first place apostles, in the second place prophets, thirdly teachers; then miracle-workers, then those who have gifts of healing, or ability to help others or power to guide them, or the gift of ecstatic utterance of various kinds. Are all apostles? Do all speak in tongues of ecstasy? Can all interpret them? The higher gifts are those you should aim at." This conception of the Christian community as an organic, articulated religious body with its various gradations of rank would be used by later generations as a justification for slavery.

The Bible has many references to slavery and its rights, duties and obligations, but it does not refer anywhere to Negro slavery. This is not at all remarkable since the institution of human bondage was one with which the Jews were familiar during the first millennia of their history, but the Negro race was a branch of mankind with which they had only occasional contact.

[8]I TIMOTHY 6: 1–2.
[9]PHILEMON 10: 16.
[10]I CORINTHIANS XIV: 34–35.

Justification for the enslavement of Negroes specifically and
the belief that they had been set apart by God uniquely for this
role would be derived by later generations of Biblical interpret-
ers from the story of Noah and his sons and the Table of Nations. After the Waters of the Flood had subsided.

"Noah, a man of the soil, began the planting of vineyards. He
drank some of the wine, became drunk and lay naked inside his
tent. When Ham, father of Canaan, saw his father naked, he
told his two brothers outside. So Shem and Japheth took a cloak,
put it on their shoulders and walked backwards, and so covered
their father's naked body; their faces were turned the other
way, so that they did not see their father naked. When Noah
woke from his drunken sleep, he learnt what his youngest son
had done to him, and said:

> 'Cursed be Canaan,
> slave of slaves
> shall he be to his brothers.'

And he continued:

> 'Bless, O LORD,
> the tents of Shem;
> May God extend Japheth's bounds,
> Let him dwell in the tents of Shem,
> may Canaan be their slave.' "[11]

There are obscurities and ambiguities in this story which
have not escaped the attention of Biblical scholars. Elsewhere
in *Genesis* Ham is identified as the second son, not the youngest. The offense was committed by Ham, yet it was Canaan, one
of Ham's four sons, who was singled out for divine punishment.
The transgression of Ham seems trifling to modern readers and
the retribution disproportionate.

Freud offered an Oedipal interpretation of the Curse of Canaan and speculated that the real offense had been the castration of Noah. There is some textual support for this hypothesis
in the Midrashic literature of the Third to Seventh Centuries
A.D., where Noah accuses Ham in these words: "You have pre-

[11]GENESIS IX: 20–27.

vented me from doing something in the dark."[12] Other Jewish exegetic literature of the period accuses Ham of having had intercourse in the Ark or of copulation with a dog.

Such Patristic Fathers as St. Jerome and St. Augustine saw the Curse of Canaan as the Biblical justification for slavery, but failed to associate bondage with the Negro race specifically. Jewish theologians, writing in the Talmudic and Midrashic literature of the first six centuries of the Christian era, were naturally aware of the fact that Ham meant "dark" and "hot". They associated his punishment with his color accordingly and suggested that "Ham was smitten in his skin," that Noah told him that his "seed will be ugly and dark-skinned," and that he was the father of Canaan "who brought curses into the world, of Canaan who was cursed, of Canaan who darkened the faces of mankind," of Canaan "the notorious world-darkener."[13] The *Koran* followed closely in this tradition of imputing black skin to divine punishment for some unforgivable sexual offense by claiming that the Negro's swarthiness was caused by exposure to the fires of hell.

Upon these foundations, an ideological justification for the natural slavery of Negroes was erected. The similarity between Ham and *Khem,* the Egyptian word for black, reinforced the inference that Noah's youngest son was the ancestor of the Negro race. The sons of Ham are listed as Cush (Ethiopia), Mizraim (Egypt), Phut (Put) and Canaan (GENESIS X:6 and I CHRONICLES I:8.) The first three were exempted from the divine curse and, in fact, Cush "was the father of Nimrod, who began to show himself a man of might on earth."[14]

From this, scholars might have concluded that the peoples of Africa were not set aside for perpetual slavery, but merely the descendants of Canaan, that is to say, the Canaanites, who lived in Palestine and whose lands the Children of Israel coveted. Yet, by the beginning of the Seventeenth Century, the identification of Negroes with the people cursed by God and condemned to eternal slavery was widespread. George Sandys'

[12]Jordan, *Black,* p. 36.
[13]*Ibid.,* p. 18.
[14]GENESIS X:8.

account of his trip to Cairo in 1610 refers to Negroes from the
upper Nile offered for sale there as "descended of *Chus,* the
sonne of cursed *Cham;* as are all of that complexion."[15] A commentary on St. Paul, published in London in 1641 or 1643, declares: "This curse to be a servant was laid first upon a disobedi-
ent sonne *Cham,* and wee see to this day, that the *Moores
Chams* posteritie, are sold like slaves yet."[16]

Thus, the Bible accepted the institution of slavery, but contributed little toward its rational analysis. The fundamental
message of the Old Testament on the subject was that Jews
might enslave alien tribes at will, but not their fellow Jews, for
God had made a covenant with all the children of Israel. Regulations, which were humane in relation to the harsh customs of
the age, were prescribed for the management of Jewish servants, and non-Jewish slaves and both classes were protected
against certain types of punishment. When we turn to the New
Testament, the focus narrows and the stress is almost exclusively on the unconditional obedience which slaves owe their
masters. The primary interest here is not the rational organization of a social institution, but the prescription of righteous
conduct by the slaves, many of whom were Christians, so that
they might enter the Kingdom of Heaven.

Plato and Aristotle

For a more penetrating analysis of the relationship of slavery
to the good society, one must turn to the Greeks and, in particular, to Aristotle. When one does so, the field of vision becomes
immediately enlarged. The Greeks are concerned with the
moral justification for slavery in general and they are able to
present this issue in terms of a relationship between man and
man, quite irrespective of any special favors promised to a
particular tribe or people by the Deity. They seek to distinguish
between those who are slaves by nature and those who are
slaves by accident. They define the limits of slavery, considered
as an institution of mutual dependence within the moral

---

[15] *Relation of a Journey Begun An: Dom: 1610. . . .* London: 2nd edition, 1621.
Quoted in Jordan, *Black,* p. 60.
[16] Paul Bayne(s), *An Entire Commentary upon the Whole Epistle of the
Apostle Paul to the Ephesians. . . . ,* London 16(41). Quoted by Jordan, *Black,*
p. 62.

confines of a just society. In terms of these and similar considerations, they deal with the relationship between master and slave and the system of rewards and punishments that should define that relationship.

The institution of slavery was a vital element in the economy of Greece and the ratio of slaves to freemen increased from the age of Pericles to that of Alexander. The distinguished British historian of classical slavery, Moses I. Finley, observed that "the cities in which individual freedom reached its highest expression—most obviously Athens—were cities in which chattel slavery flourished."[17] At the time of its cultural peak, Athens may have had 115,000 slaves to 43,000 citizens.[18] In Sparta, the ratio of helots to citizens was higher, perhaps seven to one, but the helots were more comparable to serfs than to chattel slaves. Chios in the Fifth Century was believed to have had 100,000 slaves, primarily to cultivate the overrated and excessively sweet wine of that island. Of the great Italian colonies of the Greeks, Sybaris earned its reputation for luxury and idleness from the fact that all manual labor was performed by slaves and all work which was excessively noisy and might disturb the repose of the free citizens was performed by them beyond the city's confines.[19]

Plato's attitudes toward slavery form part of his fundamental philosophical system, one which is both dualistic and hierarchic with its opposition between mind *(logos)* and matter, form and formlessness, spirit and body, being and non-being. The dualism involved, however, is not comparable to that of Medieval Christianity, in which Satan was conceived of as a supreme force for evil in perpetual struggle with God, or the similar Zoroastrian conflict between Ormuzd and Ahriman. To Plato, evil is essentially non-being, formlessness, the absence of beauty, truth, order or the breath of the spirit.

Applying this hierarchical view to the social world, the slave is inferior, not as an active, energetic organized entity, striving

[17]Moses I. Finley (Ed.), *Slavery in Classical Antiquity: Views and Controversies* (Cambridge, 1960), p. 72.
[18]A.W. Gomme, *The Population of Athens in the Fifth and Fourth Centuries B.C.* (Oxford, 1933), pp. 21, 26, 47. Cited in Will Durant, *The Story of Civilization, Part II: The Life of Greece* (New York, 1939), p. 255.
[19]Davis, *Slavery,* pp. 66–67.

for evil, but as incompleteness of being. Plato opposed the enslavement of Greek citizens as a punitive measure, but accepted slavery as a matter of course for "barbarian" peoples accustomed to despotism and unfit for freedom. His practical proposals were directed toward strengthening the discipline masters exerted over their bondmen and raising the barriers between citizens and the servile population. He opposed allowing the manumitted slave to become a citizen and provided that he must leave the city after a stipulated period of time, must continue to serve his former master, and could be reduced to servitude again at will. In the ideal society, slavery should be hereditary.

In the *Laws*, Plato's *alter ego*, the Athenian Stranger, notes the apparent contradiction that "many a man has found his slaves better in many ways than brethren or sons, and many times have they saved the lives and property of their master," yet it is also true "that the soul of the slave is utterly corrupt, and that no man of sense ought to trust them."[20]

As for the management of slaves, the Athenian Stranger recommends that no master should have slaves who come from the same country and speak the same language, because, if they speak different tongues, "They will be more easily held in subjection." Slaves should be treated with more consideration than equals, for the test of a man's love of justice is how he deals with his inferiors. Slaves, however, ought not to be "admonished as if they were freemen, which will only make them conceited. The language used to a servant ought always to be that of a command, and we ought not to jest with them."[21]

If a slave strikes a freeman, the latter shall "put him in chains, and inflict on him as many stripes as he pleases."[22] When a female slave conceives by a male slave, the child shall belong to the master of the woman. If a free woman has intercourse with a male slave, the progeny belong to the owner of the male. If a child is born to a slave by her master, master

---

[20]Plato, *Laws*, Book VI, 776 (Jowett Translation). Great Books of the Western World, *7*, 709b–c. (The Britannica Great Books edition will be cited, unless specifically otherwise stated, for Herodotus, Aristotle, Epictetus, St.Augustine, St. Thomas Aquinas, Spinoza, Montaigne, Hobbes, Locke, Hume, Montesquieu, Rousseau, Adam Smith, J. S. Mill and Hegel.)

[21]*Ibid.*, Book VI, pp. 777–78.

[22]*Ibid.*, Book X, p. 882.

and child shall be exiled. If it is born to a woman and her slave, then the woman and the child shall be sent away.[23]

Aristotle considers slavery one of the most basic institutions of society. "He who thus considers things in their first growth and origin," he writes,

> whether a state or anything else, will obtain the clearest view of them. In the first place, there must be a union of those who cannot exist without each other; namely, of male and female, that the race may continue. . . . and of natural ruler and subject, that both may be preserved. For that which can foresee by the exercise of mind is by nature intended to be lord and master, and that which can with its body give effect to such foresight is a subject, and by nature a slave; hence master and slave have the same interest.[24]

Among the barbarians, "No distinction is made between women and slaves, because there is no natural ruler among them: they are a community of slaves, male and female."[25]

Aristotle realized that slavery in the classical world arose because of defeat in war. The prisoners taken by the victor in an unjust war and sold into slavery, particularly those of noble birth, could not be considered natural slaves.

> And again, no one would ever say that he is a slave who is unworthy to be a slave. Were this the case, men of the highest rank would be slaves and the children of slaves if they or their parents chance to have been taken captive and sold. Wherefore Hellenes do not like to call Hellenes slaves, but confine the term to barbarians. Yet, in using this language, they really mean the natural slave of whom we spoke first; for it must be admitted that some are slaves everywhere, others nowhere. The same principle applies to nobility. Hellenes regard themselves as noble everywhere, and not only in their own country, but they deem the barbarians noble only when at home, thereby implying that there are two sorts of nobility and freedom, the one absolute, the other relative.[26]

The slave existed in a dual capacity. As a slave, he was a mere living instrument; but, as a man, he was also a human being.

[23] *Ibid.*, Book X, p. 930.
[24] Aristotle, *Politics,* Book I, *1252*[a].
[25] *Ibid.*, Book I, *1252* [b].
[26] *Ibid.*, Book I, *1255*[a].

This is a contrast that the Constitution of the United States recognized implicitly when it counted each slave for purposes of taxation and representation as three-fifths of a citizen. It was also recognized in the codes of the Southern states, which denied the slave such basic human rights as that of testifying in his own behalf, but which also provided the same punishment for his murder as for that of a free man.

Nobody can feel friendship "toward lifeless things," Aristotle observed. "But neither is there friendship toward a horse, or an ox, nor to a slave *qua* slave. For there is nothing common to the two parties; the slave is a living tool and the tool a lifeless slave. *Qua* slave then one cannot be friends with him. But *qua* man one can; for there seems to be some justice between any man and any other who can share in a system of law or be party to an agreement."[27]

The slave is a possession: "He who is by nature not his own but another's man, is by nature a slave; and he may be said to be another's man who, being a human being is also a possession. And a possession may be defined as an instrument of action, separable from the possessor."[28]

The relationship between master and slave was analogous to that between mind and body. In a man, the mind should control the body. In a society, those who were mentally and morally equipped to rule should, in Aristotle's view, be masters over the natural slaves. The virtues of slaves *as* slaves were limited to those qualities which enabled them to serve effectively as instruments, such as bravery and self-control.

When he compared the status of household slaves with that of artisans and laborers, Aristotle found the former preferable. "For the slave shares in his master's life; the artisan is less closely connected with him, and only attains excellence in proportion as he becomes a slave. The meaner sort of mechanic has a special and separate slavery; and whereas the slave exists by nature, not so the shoemaker or other artisan."[29] Needless to say, Aristotle considered that neither slaves nor free artisans and mechanics should be citizens. They were "necessary people" to the community, but not entitled to share in its govern-

---

[27] Aristotle, *Nichomachean Ethics*, Book VIII, *1161ᵇ* (W. D. Ross translation.)
[28] Aristotle, *Politics*, Book I, *1254ᵃ*.
[29] *Ibid.*, Book I, *1260ᵃ–1260ᵇ*. This foreshadows Calhoun's view that chattel slavery and free labor were essentially identical relationships.

ment. This effort to prevent free men from taking up manual or menial occupations which resembled the work of slaves was designed to raise the barrier of separation between the servile population and the free.

Aristotle's views concerning the treatment of slaves are more liberal than those of Plato. He dissents sharply from the latter's maxim that they should be spoken to only in tones of command, pointing out that, precisely because the natural slave is mentally inferior, he must be taught and admonished.

"Of possessions," Aristotle writes, "That which is the best and worthiest subject of economics comes first and is most essential. I mean man . . . Three things make up the life of a slave, work, punishment and food. To give them food but no punishment and no work makes them insolent; and that they should have work and punishment but no food is tyrannical and destroys their efficiency. It remains therefore to give them work and sufficient food; for it is impossible to rule over slaves without offering rewards, and a slave's reward is his food."[30]

There were a few dissenting voices in the Graeco-Roman world from the Aristotelian doctrine of natural slavery. The dissent took the form of asserting with the Stoics the fundamental equality and identity of mankind; of conceding differences in ability, but denying inequality of rights; or of denying that those who wielded power and freedom corresponded to Aristotle's natural masters. Thus, the Sophists held that there was no differentiation in nature between free men and slaves. Diogenes, the Cynic, when offered for sale as a slave, described his trade as a master of men. His belief that power in the world did not accrue to those who were naturally masters was part of his generally revolutionary stance as a "citizen of the world" and a champion of cannibalism and incest. Lions were not the natural slaves of their keepers, Diogenes asserted, "for fear is the mark of the slave, whereas wild beasts make men afraid of them."[31]

Among the more eloquent repudiators of the doctrine of natural slavery was Epictetus, the Stoic philosopher, who had been brought to Rome as the slave of a courtier of Nero, named Epaphroditus, who had lamed him by breaking his leg. While

[30]Aristotle, *Oeconomica,* Book I, 1344ᵃ–1344ᵇ (E.S. Forster translation.)
[31]Quoted in Davis, *Slavery,* p. 74.

still a slave, Epictetus attended the lectures of Musonius Rufus, the Stoic philosopher. After buying his freedom, Epictetus was expelled from Rome around A.D. 90 for suspected republicanism and returned to Nicopolis in northern Greece, where he expounded Stoic doctrines for the rest of his life, owning, as he put it, only earth, sky and a cloak.

When you call for warm water and the slave brings you tepid instead, or is nowhere to be found in the house, Epictetus said, "Then not to be vexed or not to burst with passion, is not this acceptable to the gods? . . . Will you not remember who you are, and whom you rule? that they are kinsmen, that they are brethren by nature, that they are the offspring of Zeus? 'But I have purchased them, and they have not purchased me.' Do you see in what direction you are looking, that it is toward the earth, toward the pit, that it is toward those wretched laws of dead men? but toward the laws of the gods you are not looking."[32]

Most American statesmen who had had a classical education had some familiarity with Plutarch's *Lives* and had been, to a greater or lesser degree, influenced by that writer's praise and strictures. The biography of Marcus Cato was particularly pertinent to the issue of slavery and the abuse of power. After pointing out that Cato never paid more than 1,500 drachmas for a slave, purchased only "able sturdy workmen, horse-keepers and cow-herds; and these he thought ought to be sold again when they grew old," Plutarch commented:

"Yet certainly, in my judgment, it marks an over-rigid temper for a man to take the work out of his servants as out of brute beasts, turning them off and selling them in their old age, and thinking there ought to be no further commerce between man and man than whilst there arises some profit by it . . . It is doubtless the part of a kind-hearted man to keep even worn-out horses and dogs, and not only take care of them when they are foals and whelps, but also when they are grown old."[33]

Plutarch added that, after "feasts for his friends and colleagues in office, as soon as supper was over, Cato used to go with a leathern thong and scourge those who had waited or dressed the meat carelessly." He put slaves to death when they

[32]Epictetus, *Discourses* (George Long translation), Book I, Chapter 13.
[33]Plutarch, *The Lives of the Noble Grecians and Romans, Marcus Cato* (Dryden translation).

were condemned by their fellow servants and engaged in "odious" usury, lending money to his own slaves rapaciously and at unconscionable interest rates.

The Christian Revolution

From the reign of Nero on, the trend of Roman law was to alleviate the condition of slaves. Masters were denied the right to kill their slaves or sell them to serve as gladiators. Officials were appointed in all provinces to hear the complaints of slaves. Instead of the older provision that, when a master was murdered, all slaves not in chains or totally disabled must be put to death, the law was modified to require only that those slaves who were within hearing at the time of the murder be put to the torture. The later Antonines adopted the Stoic conception of the essential equality of man and, as a consequence, "The slave code of Imperial Rome" compared, in Lecky's opinion, "not unfavourably with those of some Christian nations."[34]

Christianity further alleviated the condition of slaves and restricted the untrammeled power of their masters. The first Christian emperors reinforced the rule of the Antonines denying the right of masters to kill their slaves. They went further and called it murder, providing intent could be proved. On the theory of the Mosaic Law that no rational man would willingly destroy his property,[35] the first Christian Caesars ruled that homicidal intent might only be presumed if certain atrocious tortures had been employed. If the slave died under ordinary tortures, his death was assumed to be accidental. The Church outlawed the formerly common way of executing slaves, that of crucifixion, since it seemingly vulgarized the manner of Christ's death. Other drastic penalties remained in force. If a woman had intercourse with her slave, the mistress was put to death and the slave burned alive. Any slave who accused his master of any offense, other than high treason, was burned alive without investigation of the charges and regardless of their truth or falsity.

Justinian's *Institutes* reshaped and codified the laws of Rome two centuries after the conversion of Constantine to

---

[34]William Edward Hartpole Lecky, *History of European Morals from Augustus to Charlemagne* (New York, 1869), I, 327.

[35]Hence the Mosaic rule that, if the slave lived two days after torture, his master was exonerated of his murder.

Christianity and one century after Alaric's sack of the Eternal City. Despite the fact that they were the intellectual creation of an age which enshrined tradition and distrusted innovation in any form, the *Institutes* embodied three major reforms in the sphere of slavery. The encumbrances of emancipation which had arisen during the era of the pre-Christian Caesars were swept aside. The disabilities and invidious conditions which had degraded the class of freedmen were abolished and the latter were virtually merged into the population of free-born Roman citizens. Finally, the *Institutes* permitted free women to marry slaves if the slaves's masters consented and permitted masters to marry their slaves if they emancipated them, all children of such unions to be free.

Despite the fact that by the Fourth Century the Church had become a great slave-owning institution and had acquired some of the intellectual attitudes of the master class,[36] manumission was deemed an act of exemplary Christian virtue. St. Melanie was credited with freeing 8,000 slaves; St. Ovidius of Gaul with 5,000; Chromatus, an official of Trajan, with 1,250. By the Thirteenth Century, when Christians found it hard to find slaves to emancipate, they bought pigeons and let them fly away on high church festivals.[37]

This Christian enthusiasm for the liberation of slaves stemmed in part from the teachings of Gregory the Great, who asserted that Christ's mission on earth had been to liberate man from the bondage of sin and to restore him to his natural condition of freedom which had existed before the Fall. Consequently, the manumission of slaves, who were free by the law of nature and chattel only by the laws of nations, was an act of Christian virtue.[38]

The improvement of the condition of Roman slaves was not entirely the result of a moral advance in society. As the status of slaves was bettered, that of free men deteriorated. Under the later Emperors in the West, and under Diocletian in partic-

---

[36]Sumner, *Folkways*, p. 290.

[37]Lecky, *European Morals*, II, 73–74.

[38]Davis, *Slavery*, p. 92. The Ulpian and Justinian Codes had both held that slavery was not justified by natural law, but merely by the laws of nations, that is, the existing complex of social relationships enforced by statute. This meant that slavery did not rest on any moral imperative. Western Europe adopted this approach to slavery and it formed the rationale for Common Law decisions concerning the status of slaves until about A.D. 1800.

ular, the empire became a static, tradition-bound socialistic bureaucracy, in which all innovation and initiative were stifled; trade and industry were chained by guilds; Romans were bound by birth to their labor or trade; the burden of taxes was so intolerable that those who sought to escape this crushing punishment by volunteering for military service in the legions were branded as criminals.[39]

With the economic disintegration of the Roman Empire, the great latifundia of Sicily and northern Africa, whose slave gangs had provided grain for the empire, fell into desuetude. The general economic retrogression entailed a retreat from the metropolis with tributary sources of supply toward the small self-sufficient units that would characterize the European economy of the Dark Ages. The more sophisticated enterprises of slave-operated plantation and mine were supplanted by the subsistence agriculture of serfdom and the local self-sufficiency of the manor.

While the Patristic Fathers accepted the institution of slavery and never repudiated it, the moral revolution imposed by Christianity made characteristics which had formerly been regarded as slavish, such as meekness, docility and turning the other cheek, appear commendable. Pride, which Aristotle and the Greeks had deemed a virtue, was now considered a deadly sin.[40] The Graeco-Roman attitude of contempt for the slave class and the servile character, so marked in Plautus, Cicero and other classical writers, was transformed into its opposite.

The most influential of the Church fathers in Roman times, St. Augustine, held that slavery was not part of natural law. God "did not intend that His rational creature, who was made in His image, should have dominion over anything but the irrational creation—not man over man, but man over the beasts. And hence the righteous men in primitive times were made

<hr/>

[39]"For a man to join the army when he has no right to do so," Arrius Menander said, "is a serious crime." Vilfredo Pareto, *The Mind and Society* (New York, 1935), 2550. (The reference is to Pareto's paragraphs, not his pages.)

[40]"Now the man is thought to be proud who thinks himself worthy of great things, being worthy of them; for he who does so beyond his deserts is a fool, but no virtuous man is foolish or silly. . . . For he who is worthy of little and thinks himself worthy of little is temperate, but not proud; for pride implies greatness, as beauty implies a good-sized body, and little people may be neat and well-proportioned but cannot be beautiful." Aristotle, *Nichomachean Ethics,* Book IV, Chapter 3, *1123 ᵇ*.

shepherds of cattle rather than kings of men." Slavery arose, St. Augustine argued, because of man's sin and, "This is why we do not find the word 'slave' in any part of Scripture until the righteous Noah branded the sin of his son with this name. It is a name, therefore, introduced by sin and not by nature. The origin of the Latin word for slave is supposed to be found in the circumstance that those who by the law of war were liable to be killed were sometimes preserved by their victors, and were hence called servants. And these circumstances could never have arisen save though sin. For even when we wage a just war, our adversaries must be sinning."

St. Augustine conceded that, "There are many wicked masters who have religious men as their slaves, and who are yet themselves in bondage . . . And beyond question it is a happier thing to be the slave of a man than of a lust; for even this very lust of ruling, to mention no others, lays waste men's hearts with the most ruthless dominion. Moreover, when men are subjected to one another in a peaceful order, the lowly position does as much good to the servant as the proud position does harm to the master." St. Augustine then repeated the admonition of the Apostle Paul that slaves obey their masters "heartily and with good will . . . not in crafty fear, but in faithful love."[41]

From the standpoint of the Medieval Christian theologian, the slave was more to be envied than the master. The former was merely the slave of a man; the latter was the slave of his lusts. By accepting slavery and practicing humility and obedience, the slave would improve his chances of entering the Kingdom of Heaven. The master, by contrast, if he displayed the arrogant and imperious conduct toward his servants typical of his class, would jeopardize his immortal soul.

Early Slavery and the Negro

In Merovingian times, the markets of Western Europe were flooded with impoverished people from Russia and the Balko-Danubian area who had been brought from the East as slaves, because they were prisoners of war, because they had sold themselves for debt, because they had been born into bondage,

---

[41]St. Augustine, *The City of God*, Book XIX, Chapter 15 (Marcus Dods translation.)

or because they were once free men who had married slave women. The word *slave* has the same derivation as *Slav* and by the Seventh Century A.D. bondmen were so preponderantly of East European origin that *slave* displaced the Latin word *servus*. These slaves were mere chattel and the penalty for killing another man's slave was the same as for killing his horse. Yet slaves could be enfranchised formally before king or Church and the marriages of slaves were legitimate and sanctified unions.[42]

In England, villeinage, an institution in many respects analogous to slavery, had virtually disappeared by the Fourteenth Century and William Harrison was correct when he declared in 1577: "As for slaves and bondmen we have none, naie such is the privilege of our countries by the especiall grace of God, and bountie of our princes, that if anie come hither from other realms, so soone as they set foot on land they become so free of condition as their masters, whereby all note of servile bondage is utterlie remooved from them."[43] In France in the Thirteenth Century, Philip the Fair had asserted that man is naturally free and had therefore liberated the serfs of Valois.[44] Since the free cities had charters which released them from the more onerous bonds of the feudal system, they became asylums of freedom for slaves. By the late Middle Ages, a common German saying was *"Stadtluft ist frei Luft."*[45]

Yet to imagine that there was a steady and unilinear progression from slavery toward either serfdom or freedom between the fall of the Roman Empire in the West and the discovery of America would be to do violence to the evidence of history. Much light has been shed on this period in David Brion Davis's brilliant and scholarly *The Problem of Slavery in Western Culture*, which we have already cited in several instances.

In England, 10 percent of the persons enumerated in the *Domesday Book* (A.D. 1086) were slaves, and these could be put to death by their owners with impunity. On the Iberian Penin-

[42]C. W. Previte-Orton (Ed.), *The Cambridge Shorter Medieval History* (Cambridge, 1952), I, 165.

[43]William Harrison, *Historicall Description of Britaine.* Quoted by Jordan, *Black*, p. 49.

[44]Davis, *Slavery*, pp. 7–8.

[45]"City air is free air."

sula, slavery was kept alive by the religious wars between Christians and Moors, in which both sides enslaved and sold their prisoners. As a result, chattel slavery had an unbroken existence in Spain and Portugal from the fall of the Roman Empire in the West to the revival of the Mediterranean slave trade.[46]

During the Viking age, Norse merchant sailors sold Russian slaves in Constantinople, receiving spices and silks as return cargo. The slave trade was important to the economy of the merchants and princes of Kievan Russia. Venice grew to prosperity and power partly as a slave-trading republic, which took its human cargo from the Byzantine Empire and sold some of the more promising females for the harems of Islam.[47]

"The Italians," Davis writes, "not only created joint stock companies, commercial bases or *fondachi,* and a highly organized slave trade, but in the colony of Cyprus they established plantations where imported bondsmen were employed in the cultivation of sugar cane. By 1300, indeed, there were Negro slaves on Cyprus, which had become virtually a prototype for the West Indian colonies."[48]

Thus Venetian and Genoese slave traders devised several of the institutions which would characterize the African slave trade and the plantation economies of the Southern States and of tropical America. The fall of Constantinople to the Turks in A.D. 1453 delivered a fatal blow to this prosperous institution of Mediterranean slavery. The great trade routes from Russia southward to Egypt and the Levant were cut, while Turkish sea power soon dominated the Mediterranean. The prices of slaves to Christian buyers became prohibitively high. Mediterranean slavery soon changed its form and direction. Turkish and other Muslim raiders harried the coastal towns and settlements of the European Mediterranean and overhauled Christian vessels in that sea, taking slaves for ransom, labor or the harems of the cities of Islam.

During these long centuries, Negro slavery had not been unknown. That the Greeks had some Negro slaves is suggested by

[46]Davis, *Slavery,* p. 41.
[47]*Ibid.,* p. 42.
[48]*Ibid.*

the fact that Herodotus, writing in the Fifth Century B.C., proclaimed that the semen of Negroes was black, and that Aristotle flatly contradicted him.[49] Perhaps because they were encountered chiefly in the role of slaves, possibly for other reasons, Negroes were regarded as inferior in many of the societies which had early contact with them. In the early centuries of Islam, slaves were protected and given specific rights but, as slave traders penetrated interior Africa and returned with Negroes, the predominant view changed. Negroes were considered "as a docile race who were born to be slaves"; the word *abid,* meaning slaves, was increasingly confined to Negroes; the latter occupied a degraded position, as the evidence of the *Thousand and One Nights* shows, and were despised and reduced to pariah status in medieval Egypt. Although the *Mamelukes* who ruled Egypt were themselves theoretically slaves, being generally children of such Christian minorities in Islam as the Circassians, they revolted in A.D. 1498 when the Sultan married off the chief of his Negro arquebusiers to a white slave girl, They exterminated the black troops, and forced the authorities to give in to their demands.[50]

The Chinese imported some Negro slaves as early as the Eighth Century of the Christian era. They identified natural slaves as those who were black; considered them inferior; and, to preserve purity of their blood, forbade slaves to copulate with free men or free women on pain of death. These darker slaves, who were not necessarily Negroes but included some Persians, were tattooed or mutilated to set them apart from Chinese society.[51]

The Mongol Kalmucks of the Volga developed an aristocracy of Whites ("white bones, white flesh") as against the common people ("black bones, black flesh").[52] The *rigsmal* describes the

---

[49]Aristotle said: "Herodotus does not report the truth when he says that the semen of the Aethiopians is black, as if everything must needs be black in those who have a black skin, and that too when he saw their teeth were white." *On the Generation of Animals,* Book II, *736ª.*

[50]Davis, *Slavery,* 50. Earlier, the Sultan had aroused the fury of the Mameluke knights by arming the Negro slaves with arquebuses; previously, they had been unarmed personal servants.

[51]Davis, *Slavery,* p. 51.

[52]Michael Prawdin, *The Mongol Empire* (London, 1952), p. 25. "Bones" was used to designate men; "flesh" to designate women.

thrall infant, destined for slavery, as "swarthy" with "a curving back and sharp, protruding heels."[53] Portugal imported large numbers of Negro slaves to work her estates in the southern provinces and to do menial labor in the cities from A.D. 1444 on. The province of Algarves became preponderantly Negro, according to Du Bois, and by the middle of the Sixteenth Century Lisbon itself had more Negroes than Whites.[54] These Negroes, together with the Moorish slaves, constituted the "lowest rank of slaves" from the outset in both Spain and Portugal. In 1515, the Portuguese king ordered that they be denied Christian burial and thrown into "a common ditch" called the *Poço dos Negroes.*[55]

Utopians and Lawyers

Despite the fact that he exalted property rights to such an extent that he believed fathers should have the traditional Roman power of life and death over their children, Jean Bodin (1530–1596) was an uncompromising enemy of slavery. He asserted that the institution had died out in France as early as the Twelfth Century and that a slave became free merely by touching French soil. Bodin believed that the state was an organic unit like the human body and that, therefore, all its members and elements must be recognized as such.[56] The history of slavery convinced him that the institution corrupted whatever it touched. He recommended the gradual emancipation of slaves and the granting of citizenship to those who were not aliens.

Sir Thomas More's *Utopia* (1516) provides for bondmen to do "all vile service, all slavery and drudgery, with all laboursome

---

[53]Roland B. Dixon of Harvard, who wrote *The Racial History of Man* in 1923, believed that these *thralls* were proto-Negroid. A more modern view is that they may have been aboriginal Beaker Folk from the Mediterranean or perhaps Laplanders. v. Bertil J. Lundman, *The Racial History of Scandinavia,* I.A.A.-E.E. Reprint No. 7.

[54]W. E. Burghardt Du Bois, *Black Folk Then and Now* (New York, 1939), pp. 132–133.

[55]Davis, *Slavery,* p. 53. However, *poço* means "well" or "hole", not "ditch".

[56]Davis, *Slavery,* p. 112. Bodin's analogy with the human body was: "There be in mans body some members, I may not call them filthie (for that nothing can so be which is naturall) but yet so shamefull, as that no man except he be past all shame, can without blushing reveale or discover the same: and doe they for that cease to be members of the same bodie?" *The Six Bookes of a Commonweale,* 1574–76(?), A3–A9, A35, A64.

toil and base business."⁵⁷ The citizens of Utopia do not indiscriminately enslave prisoners of war nor do they buy slaves on
the market, unless the latter were previously convicted of
crimes so serious that they are punished by enslavement or
death. Such slaves they bring home, paying little for them "yea,
getting them for gramercy." They keep them in "continual
work and labour" and in fetters.⁵⁸ There are also slaves who
violated the laws of Utopia and these "they handle hardest,
whom they judge more desperate, and to have deserved greater
punishment . . ." Finally, there is a third class of slaves, "When
a vile drudge, being a poor labourer in another country doth
choose of his own free will to become a bondman among
them."⁵⁹ These they treat almost "as gently as their own free
citizens" and permit to leave the community whenever they
wish to do so.

Lord Edward Coke, the great liberal historian of English
jurisprudence, followed the authority of the Thirteenth Century jurist, Bracton, instead of using his own eyes, and thus
made the egregious error of assuming that villeinage existed in
his own time. He erroneously derived Negro slavery from this
extinct institution. The chief justification for slavery, Coke
held, was Scriptural: "This is assured, That Bondage or Servitude was first inflicted for dishonouring of Parents: For Cham
the Father of Canaan . . . seeing the Nakedness of his Father
Noah, and shewing it in Derision to his Brethren, was therefore
punished in his Son Canaan with Bondage."⁶⁰

Coke adduced an alternate origin of slavery. The primitive
communist society which prevailed before the Flood was supplanted by one based on private property. Wars then broke out,
men were taken prisoner and it was ordained that "he that was
taken in Battle should remain Bond to his taker forever, and he
to do with him, all that should come to him, his Will and Pleasure, as with his Beast, or any other Cattle, to give, or to sell, or

⁵⁷Sir Thomas More, *Utopia* (translated by Ralph Robinson), (New York,
1951), p. 73.
⁵⁸*Ibid.*, p. 97.
⁵⁹*Ibid.*, p. 98.
⁶⁰Sir Edward Coke, *The First Part of the Institutes of the Laws of England*
(1628), Lib. II, Cap. XI.

to kill."[61] The last power was abused and was, therefore, taken away from ordinary captors and vested only in the king. Coke added that men could also be slaves because they were sentenced to bondage for crime, because they sold themselves, or because they were born slaves. In *Calvin's Case* (1608) Coke, who was then Chief Justice of England, declared that there is perpetual warfare between Christians and heathen, that the latter are subjects of the Devil and may therefore justly be killed and, if it be just to kill them, it is also just to impose the lesser punishment of enslaving them.

As the Western world moved from the Age of Faith toward the Enlightenment, other conflicting crosscurrents of thought affected opinion on slavery and the status of the Negro. The Curse of Canaan and abundant textual evidence suggested that the Bible approved the institution of slavery, regarded nations and peoples as unequal in quality and in rights, and conceived of a hierarchic organization of the religious community. Yet the main thrust of religious teaching was anti-slavery on the grounds that all men were equal in respect to Original Sin and as children of God.

Therefore anti-religious and anti-Christian thinkers tended to emphasize racial differences and even, in a few daring instances, to suggest separate acts of creation. Paracelsus (Theophrastus Bombastus von Hohenheim), the physician and alchemist whose neo-Platonist and iconoclastic views made him suspect to devout Christians, believed that Negroes were descended from apes or, at the very least constituted a separate species. Giordano Bruno, the anti-Christian mystic who was burned at the stake in 1600 by the Inquisition, entertained similar opinions.[62]

At the close of the Seventeenth Century, Edward Tyson dissected an orang-utan and published his findings that it anatomically resembled man. Earlier in the same century, Marcello Malpighi (1628–1694) had discovered the layer of the skin which bears his name and had also found that the pigment which differentiates the Negro from other races was located in

[61]Coke, *Institutes,* Lib. II, Cap. XI.
[62]Davis, *Slavery,* p. 452.

this stratum.[63] At about the same time Anton Leeuwenhoek, inventor of the microscope, had said that Negro blood differs chemically from that of other races.[64]

Hugo Grotius, whose great intellectual achievement was to liberate international law from Scriptural authority, justified slavery as part of the chain of authority and status which defines society and preserves social order. He followed Aristotle in believing that some men are destined by nature to be masters, and others to be slaves. His successor, Baron Samuel von Pufendorf (1632–1694), also defended slavery on the grounds that there are men who are incapable of governing themselves and who need a master.

Thus, as Western man moved toward the Age of the Enlightenment, there was no clear evidence that a moral repudiation of slavery by the intellectual leaders of the era was impending. In fact, the weakening authority of revealed religion seemed to forebode a revival of the Aristotelian doctrine of natural slavery, based on observations derived from the natural sciences. That this did not occur is partially due to the fact that the Enlightenment created its own *a priori* deductive system of natural rights and social contract, which was almost as antihistorical and as hostile to deriving conclusions solely from observed, empirical scientific evidence, as theology had been in previous centuries.

From Scholasticism to Social Contract

With the end of the Middle Ages and the emergence of new Christian faiths to challenge Catholicism, the foundations of political science began to shift from Biblical authority and natural law to the concept of social contract. A primitive society was envisaged in which men banded together and formed governments by agreement for their own interest and protection. One of the radical differences between this approach and those that had immediately preceded it was that it presumed that at least the original sanction for government had been

---

[63]The melanocytes, which form melanin, are in the deepest layer of the dermis, the *stratum germanittivum*, or Malpighian layer.
[64]Davis, *Slavery*, p. 454.

popular consent. This consent was putatively based on individual concepts of self-interest and the entire notion of social contract presupposed an original state of affairs in which men had been juridically and politically equal. Perhaps the most revolutionary aspect of this new protohistorical hypothesis was that it justified human institutions, not in terms of Divine purpose or conformity with the laws of nature, but in terms of human convenience. To some of the political theorists of social contract, this original compact may have seemed an historical fact. To more realistic exponents of the doctrine, and notably to Thomas Hobbes and David Hume, the social contract was merely a convenient hypothesis without concrete existence in time or place.

Thomas Hobbes did not invent the theory of social contract. It had been propounded earlier by George Buchanan (1506–1582), by Juan de Mariana (1537–1624) and by John Milton in his 1649 tract *On the Tenure of Kings and Magistrates.* But Hobbes gave the doctrine structure and articulation and created an intellectual climate in which Western political theorists would think in terms of this imaginary compact for the next century and a half.

Born in 1588, Hobbes lived to the age of 92, much of the time in exile, surviving the reigns of the first Stuarts and the Commonwealth and living well into the Restoration. Hobbes is generally considered to be one of the pillars of conservatism in political theory, but his credentials are dubious. A thoroughgoing materialist, he was forced to flee France because of Catholic clerical persecution and, as an old man in England, was charged with atheism and denied permission to publish anything on ethics. In politics, he was a supporter of unlimited royal autocracy, of a single established church dominated by the Crown, and of persecution of dissenters and heretics. One might say that Hobbes' Chinese counterpart was the authoritarian school of the Legalists. Like most upholders of absolutism, he was unsympathetic to the aristocratic conception of a complex society, based on numerous gradations of power and status. He believed in a government of men, not laws, observing:

"And therefore this is another error of Aristotle's politics, that in a well-ordered Commonwealth, not men should govern, but the laws. What man that hath his natural senses, though he can neither write nor read, does not find himself governed by them he fears, and believes can kill or hurt him when he obeyeth not? Or that believes the law can hurt him; that is, words and paper, without the hands and swords of men?"[65]

Hobbes also rebuked Aristotle for believing that some men were significantly abler, more intelligent and better than others:

"Nature hath made men so equal in the faculties of body and mind, as that, though there be found one man sometimes manifestly stronger in body or of quicker mind than another, yet when all is reckoned together the difference between man and man is not so considerable that one man therefore claim to himself any benefit to which another man may not pretend as well as he."[66] In terms of mental abilities, "I find yet a greater equality amongst men than in that of strength."[67]

Men lived in a state of nature before they made a social compact to provide government and order for them. Being equal, they were constantly in conflict or on the brink of conflict. "Hereby it is manifest that during the time men live without a common power to keep them all in awe," Hobbes wrote, "they are in that condition which is called *war;* and such a war is of every man against every man. For war consisteth not in battle only, or the act of fighting, but in a tract of time, wherein the will to contend by battle is sufficiently known." During this era prior to government, "Every man is enemy to every man." Hence, there is no security, no industry, no agriculture, no navigation, no foreign trade, no comforts, no science, no history, no arts and no letters. That which prevails is that "which is worst of all, continual fear, and the danger of violent death; and the life of man, solitary, poor, nasty, brutish, and short."[68]

To end this state of affairs, men transfer by agreement their right to make war upon each other and to kill one another to a government. In return, the government establishes and main-

---

[65]Thomas Hobbes, *Leviathan, Or, Matter, Form, and Power of a Commonwealth Ecclesiastical and Civil* (1651), Part IV, Chapter 46.
[66]*Ibid.,* Part I, Chapter 13.
[67]*Ibid.*
[68]*Ibid.*

tains order. Absolute monarchy is the best form of government because the centralization of power and the unambiguous dynastic rules of descent minimize the danger of lapses into anarchy. Morality derives from the quest for order. Order is maintained by concentration of power. Hence, when a sovereign or a nation is no longer able to protect its subjects, the latter are entitled to desert it and seek another protector. This view justified both submission to a foreign conqueror and transfer of allegiance from a king to a band of regicides who had effectively seized power. This denial of any morality, other than that derived from power, made Hobbes suspect to the Royalists whom he supported.

Given his authoritarian conception of society, Hobbes' beliefs concerning human equality could have been anticipated. Virtually all theories of absolute political power rest on the assumption that the subjects form a homogeneous mass or can be shaped into that form by propaganda, rewards and coercion. His egalitarianism made Hobbes sharply reject Aristotle's views on natural slavery:

"The question who is the better man has no place in the condition of mere nature, where (as has been shown before) all men are equal. The inequality that now is has been introduced by the laws civil. I know that Aristotle in the first book of his *Politics*, for a foundation of his doctrine, maketh men by nature, some more worthy to command, meaning the wiser sort, such as he thought himself to be for his philosophy; others to serve, meaning those that had strong bodies, but were not philosophers as he; as if master and servant were not introduced by consent of men, but by difference of wit: which is not only against reason, but also against experience."[69]

Aristotle had called the relationship of master and slave between superior and inferior people natural because he believed it necessary to their preservation. Hobbes retorted that, however stupid the potential slave, he would not consent willingly to slavery, because he would prefer to be his own master. Nor could the relationship arise from conflict because, in such a struggle, the wise men would seldom get the upper hand over the stupid ones.

[69] *Ibid.*, Part I, Chapter 15.

Hobbes also denied that slavery had originated as an automatic consequence of victory in war. For captives, "commonly called *slaves,* have no obligation at all; but may break their bonds, or the prison; and kill, or carry away captive their master." However, if the prisoner agrees to become a slave, as he may do in return for the conqueror's sparing his life, then he becomes the absolute possession of his master:

"The master of the servant is also master of all he hath, and may exact the use thereof; that is to say, of his goods, of his labour, of his servants, and of his children, as often as he think fit. For he holdeth his life of his master by the covenant of obedience; that is, of owning and authorizing whatever the master shall do. And in case the master, if he refuse, kill him, or cast him into bonds, or otherwise punish him for his disobedience, he is himself the author of the same, and cannot accuse him of injury."[70]

From the sombre authoritarianism of Hobbes, one turns with relief to Michel Eyquem de Montaigne (1533–1592), whom Gibbon considered one of the only two men "of liberality" who lived in "those bigotted times" and whom Sainte Beuve characterized as "the wisest Frenchman who ever lived." The son of a Gascon officer, who won his peerage in war, and a mother who was of Spanish Jewish descent though converted to Christianity, Montaigne remained a Catholic probably long after he had ceased to believe in God and expressed a quiet, humanistic skepticism which had a more corrosive effect on the minds of his contemporaries than the more strident voices of iconoclasts. He elaborated no theory of chattel slavery and certainly did not seek to justify the institution but, in the labyrinthine maze of his *Essays,* suggested that man undervalues liberty and that the lowly should be treated with justice.

And the majority of free persons surrender, for very trivial advantages, their life and being into the power of another; the wives and concubines of the Thracians contended who should be chosen to be slain upon their husband's tomb. . . . The form of the oath, in that rude school of fencers, who were to fight it out to the last, was in these words: "We swear to suffer ourselves to be chained, burned, beaten, killed with the sword, and to endure all that true gladiators suffer from their master, religiously engag-

[70] *Ibid.,* Part II, Chapter 20.

ing both bodies and souls in his service";... this was an obligation
indeed, and yet there were, in some years, ten thousand who
entered into it and lost themselves in it. When the Scythians
interred their king, they strangled upon his body the most
beloved of his concubines, his cup-bearer, the master of his horse,
his chamberlain, the usher of his bed-chamber and his cook; and
upon his anniversary they killed fifty horses, mounted by fifty
pages, whom they impaled up the spine to the back of the throat,
and there left them planted in parade about his tomb. The men
that serve us do it more cheaply, and for a less careful and favourable usage than that we entertain our hawks, horses, and dogs
with.[71]

Concerning the punishment of inferiors, Montaigne recommended never to "lay a hand upon our servants, whilst our
anger lasts... Faults seen through passion appear much greater
to us than they really are, as bodies do when seen through a
mist. He who is hungry uses meat; but he who will make use of
chastisement should have neither hunger nor thirst to it."[72]

A thinker who wielded far more influence than either Montaigne or Hobbes was John Locke (1632–1704). "Even before his
death," the Durants wrote, "he had reached in philosophy a
reputation surpassed only by Newton's in science; men already
spoke of him as '*the* philosopher.' "[73] According to Spengler,
"The rationalism of the Continent comes wholly from Locke."[74]
Locke influenced Samuel Adams and his philosophy shaped
much of the Federal Convention of 1787. Thomas Jefferson was
one of his most uncritical admirers. Toward the close of his
diplomatic mission in France, Jefferson instructed the American painter John Trumbull to find him life-size busts of Newton, Bacon and Locke and to put all three of them on a single
canvas, since he considered them to be "the three greatest men
that have ever lived, without any exception, and as having laid
the foundation of those superstructures which have been
raised in the physical and moral sciences".[75] Trumbull con-

---

[71]Charles Eyquem de Montaigne, *The Essays*, II, 12. (Charles Cotton translation.)
[72]*Ibid.*, II, 31.
[73]Will and Ariel Durant, *The Story of Civilization: Part VIII, The Age of
Louis XIV* (New York, 1963), p. 590.
[74]Spengler, *Decline*, II, 308.
[75]Thomas Jefferson to John Trumbull, February 15, 1789.

vinced Jefferson that this conception was esthetically defective and the latter settled for three separate portraits to be hung together. More than a year later, when the Cabinet was meeting in Jefferson's house, Alexander Hamilton noticed the Trumbull paintings of Sir Isaac Newton, Sir Francis Bacon and John Locke and asked who these men were. They were the "trinity of the three greatest men the world had ever produced," Jefferson replied. "The greatest man that ever lived," Colonel Hamilton retorted, "was Julius Caesar."[76]

Locke's *Concerning Civil Government, Second Essay,* was published in 1690, almost forty years after Hobbes' *Leviathan* and on the heels of the "glorious revolution" which ended Stuart rule and which it was partially designed to justify. The state of nature was not one of war by each against all, but a condition of primitive communism. Men graduated from this to private property, which in turn derived from labor. Finding that government was necessary, each person surrendered his individual right to judge and punish to a sovereign. The conclusion which Locke drew was that ultimate sovereignty resided in the people from whom it had sprung. Whenever government ceased to live up to its obligation under the social contract of maintaining order and justice, it lost its legitimacy; sovereignty reverted to the people, and the people had the right and duty to overthrow it. These ideas were to be recapitulated in resounding prose with no consequential alteration of substance by Thomas Jefferson in the Declaration of Independence. Property, in Locke's view, was sacred. "Government has no other end but the preservation of property." he wrote, and added: "The supreme power cannot take from any man part of his property without his consent."[77]

Slavery, in Locke's opinion, was a violation of the law of nature. "The natural liberty of man is to be free from any superior power on earth, and not be under the will or legislative authority of man, but to have only the law of Nature for his rule. The liberty of man in society is to be under no other legislative power but that established by consent in the commonwealth, nor under the dominion of any will, or restraint of any

[76]Dumas Malone, *Jefferson,* p. 287.
[77]John Locke, *Concerning Civil Government, Second Essay,* No's. 94 and 138.

law, but what that legislative shall enact according to the trust put in it."

If so, how did men become slaves? By selling themselves to others, some writers had claimed. Locke repudiated this view: "This freedom from absolute, arbitrary power is so necessary to, and closely joined with, a man's preservation, that he cannot part with it but by what forfeits his preservation and life together. For a man, not having the power of his own life, cannot by compact or his own consent enslave himself to any one, nor put himself under the absolute, arbitrary power of another to take away his life when he pleases. Nobody can give more power than he has himself, and he that cannot take away his own life cannot give another power over it."

If a man could not sell himself, how could slavery be justified? Only, Locke replied, if a person forfeits his life by committing some crime and the person having the lawful power to punish that crime with death refrains from doing so. The most common specific case was that of soldiers who fought in an unjust war and then became captives. As Locke expressed it:

> Indeed having by his fault forfeited his own life by some act that deserves death, he to whom he has forfeited may, when he has him in his power, delay to take it, and make use of him to his own service; and he does him no injury by it. For, whenever he finds the hardship of his slavery outweighs the value of his life, it is in his power, by resisting the will of his master, to draw on himself the death he deserves.
>
> 23. This is the perfect condition of slavery, which is nothing else but the state of war continued between a lawful conqueror and a captive, for if once compact enter between them, and make an agreement for a limited power on the one side, and obedience on the other, the state of war and slavery ceases as long as the compact endures; for, as has been said, no man can by agreement pass over to another that which he hath not in himself—a power over his own life.[78]

The fact that people were said to have sold themselves into slavery in the time of the ancient Jews did not seem to Locke to invalidate his analysis. He noted that these bondmen could not have been, strictly speaking, slaves because "the master of

[78] *Ibid.,* Chapter IV. Of Slavery.

such a servant was so far from having an arbitrary power over his life that he could not at pleasure so much as maim him, but the loss of an eye or tooth set him free."

The most enduring contribution of Locke to the slavery doctrines of the Enlightenment was the thesis that no man could sell himself into slavery because he did not have power to dispose of his own life. In one form or another, this doctrine was taken up by such thinkers as Montesquieu and Blackstone and hence became embedded in the Anglo-Saxon philosophy of law. The Lockean view that slavery was just only when its victims were the prisoners of war of a side which had waged an unjust conflict undermined any moral support to which the African slave trade might have laid claim. The slaves were generally seized in raids on comparatively peaceful hinterland villages by warlike coastal tribes. The purpose of these raids was simply to get slaves to sell or barter to the Europeans in the coastal factories and they could not by any stretch of the imagination be described as just.

Montesquieu, Rousseau and Hume

The influence of Montesquieu on American statesmen before the Civil War derived mainly from his emphasis on the need for checks and balances within a constitutional system. Montesquieu was one of the authorities cited in the debates over the Federal Constitution. His *magnum opus, The Spirit of the Laws,* influenced Samuel Adams. As a young man, Jefferson not only read Montesquieu carefully, but copied numerous quotations from the French political scientist in his notebooks, adding critical comments of his own.[79] In later decades, Montesquieu's political philosophy exerted a considerable influence on John Calhoun and helped shape Daniel Webster's thinking.[80]

Where Locke reasoned deductively from general moral principles and *a priori* hypotheses concerning the rights of man, the state of nature and the social contract, Montesquieu devoted a great deal of attention to the effect of such physical and material factors as climate on human character and institutions. His *Spirit of the Laws* is a systematic treatise on govern-

[79]Malone, *Virginian,* pp. 176–77.
[80]Parrington, *Main Currents,* II, 73, 75–76, 306.

ment, but one illustrated by an immense amount of historical and anthropological material on the comparative customs and institutions of different peoples. Montesquieu considered slavery in terms of natural rights philosophy; he was influenced by the English theorists of social contract and by John Locke in particular; but he also broke new ground by advancing the hypothesis that climatic and other physical factors predisposed certain races and peoples to a docile acceptance of chattel slavery. His consideration of the peculiar institution is entitled, "Book XV. In What Manner the Laws of Civil Slavery Relate to the Nature of the Climate."

"Slavery, properly so called," Montesquieu begins, "is the establishment of a right which gives to one man such a power over another as renders him absolute master of his life and fortune. The state of slavery is in its own nature bad. It is neither useful to the master nor to the slave; not to the slave, because he can do nothing through a motive of virtue; *nor to the master, because by having an unlimited authority over his slaves he insensibly accustoms himself to the want of all moral virtues, and thence becomes fierce, hasty, severe, choleric, voluptuous, and cruel".* [81] The italicized clause was taken to heart by Thomas Jefferson. In a much quoted passage from his *Notes on the State of Virginia,* Jefferson arraigned slavery in a manner that was almost a paraphrase of Montesquieu as "a perpetual exercise of the most boisterous passions, the most unremitting despotism on the one part, and degrading submissions on the other." He added that the masters and their children gave "loose" to "the worst of passions" and were "thus nursed, educated, and daily exercised in tyranny." [82]

Montesquieu, like Jefferson, was more concerned with the corrupting influence of slavery on the citizens of a free society than with the wrongs, injuries and insults suffered by the slave class.

"In despotic countries, where they are already in a state of political servitude," Montesquieu wrote, "slavery is more tolerable than in other governments . . . Hence the condition of a

[81]Charles de Secondat, Baron de Montesquieu, *The Spirit of Laws* (translated by Thomas Nugent, revised by J. V. Pritchard), Geneva, 1748. Book XV, I. (Emphasis supplied.)
[82]Jefferson, *Notes,* (Peden, ed.), pp. 162–63.

slave is hardly more burdensome than that of a subject . . . In democracies, where they are all upon equality; and in aristocracies, where the laws ought to use their utmost endeavours to procure as great an equality as the nature of the government will permit, slavery is contrary to the spirit of the constitution: *it only contributes to give a power and luxury to the citizens which they ought not to have.*"[83]

Montesquieu next proceeded to reject the customary view that slavery was justified as it arose from pity and a decision to spare the lives of prisoners of war. "It is false that killing in war is lawful, unless in a case of absolute necessity; but when a man has made another his slave, he cannot be said to have been under a necessity of taking away his life, since he actually did not take it away. War gives no other right over prisoners than to disable them from doing any further harm by securing their persons. All nations, excepting a few cannibals, concur in detesting the murdering of prisoners in cold blood."

Still less could slavery be justified as the sale of themselves by debtors to their creditors. "Neither is it true that a freeman can sell himself. Sale implies a price; now when a person sells himself, his whole substance immediately devolves to his master; the master, therefore, in that case, gives nothing, and the slave receives nothing . . . If it is not lawful to a man to kill himself because he robs his country of his person, for the same reason he is not allowed to barter his freedom. The freedom of every citizen constitutes a part of the public liberty, and in a democratic state is even part of the sovereignty."[84]

Having rejected these views and also Locke's assertion that slavery is justifiable as a substitution for lawful sentence of death, Montesquieu examines the belief that "the right of slavery proceeds from the contempt of one nation for another, founded on a difference in customs," and answers that "knowledge humanises mankind, and reason inclines to mildness; but prejudices eradicate every tender disposition." He examines the assertion that Christians are entitled to enslave heathen. "This was the notion that encouraged the ravishers of America in their iniquity. Under the influence of this idea they founded

[83]Montesquieu, *Spirit.* (Emphasis supplied.)
[84]*Ibid.*, Book XV, 2.

their right of enslaving so many nations; for these robbers, who would absolutely be both robbers and Christians, were superlatively devout."

This is followed by the not entirely ironic Chapter Five, *Of the Slavery of the Negroes,* which is worth quoting extensively:

> Were I to indicate our right to make slaves of the negroes, these should be my arguments . . .
>
> Sugar would be too dear if the plants which produce it were cultivated by any other than slaves.
>
> These creatures are all over black, and with such a flat nose that they can scarcely be pitied.
>
> It is hardly to be believed that God, who is a wise Being, should place a soul, especially a good soul, in such a black ugly body.
>
> It is so natural to look upon colour as the criterion of human nature, that the Asiatics, among whom eunuchs are employed, always deprive their blacks of their resemblance to us by a more opprobrious distinction . . .
>
> The negroes prefer a glass necklace to that gold which polite nations so highly value. Can there be a greater proof of their wanting common sense?
>
> It is impossible for us to suppose these creatures to be men, because, allowing them to be men, a suspicion would follow that we ourselves are not Christians.

Montesquieu then discusses slavery in tyrannies. "In all despotic governments people make no difficulty in selling themselves; the political slavery in some measure annihilates the civil liberty." And in Russia, "the Muscovites sell themselves very readily: their reason for it is evident; their liberty is not worth keeping."

The rational origin of slavery, Montesquieu believed, was a torrid climate.

> There are countries where the excess of heat enervates the body, and renders men so slothful and dispirited that nothing but the fear of chastisement can oblige them to perform any laborious duty: slavery is there more reconcilable to reason; and the master being as lazy with respect to his sovereign as his slave is with regard to him, this adds a political to a civil slavery.
>
> Aristotle endeavours to prove that there are natural slaves;

but, what he says is far from proving it. *If there be any such, I believe they are those of whom I have been speaking . . .*
Natural slavery, then, is to be limited to some particular parts of the world. In all other countries, even the most servile drudgeries may be performed by freemen. Experience verifies my assertion. Before Christianity had abolished civil slavery in Europe, working in the mines was judged too toilsome for any but slaves or malefactors: at present there are men employed in them who are known to live comfortably . . .
No labour is so heavy but it may be brought to a level with the workman's strength, when regulated by equity, and not by avarice. The violent fatigues which slaves are made to undergo in other parts may be supplied by a skilful use of ingenious machines . . .
I know not whether this article be dictated by my understanding or by my heart. Possibly there is not that climate upon earth where the most laborious services might not with proper encouragement be performed by freemen. Bad laws having made lazy men, they have been reduced to slavery because of their laziness.[85]

Cold climates, Montesquieu asserted, made men vigorous in body and mind, "patient and intrepid" and qualified for "arduous enterprises." Warm climates, on the contrary, drained "energy and courage," made men effeminate and "almost always rendered them slaves."

In Europe, with its extensive temperate zone and climate gradually changing with latitude from warm to cold, there is "no very extraordinary difference" between the northern and southern people. The fact that the plains are intersected to form many valleys and protected areas serves to create "many nations of a moderate extent" and this "has formed a genius for liberty that renders every part extremely difficult to be subdued and subjected to a foreign power."

But in Asia, sparsely inhabited deserts and icy mountain ranges and plateaus massively restrict the temperate area. There is an abrupt gradation and a sharp contrast between the cold and the torrid zones. The enormous, uninterrupted plains are propitious to the establishment and maintenance of autocratic empires. Consequently, There reigns in Asia a servile

[85] *Ibid.*, Book XV, 5–7. (Emphasis supplied.)

spirit, which they have never been able to shake off, and it is impossible to find in all the histories of that country a single passage which discovers a freedom of spirit; we shall never see anything there but the excess of slavery.[86]

As for Africa, it "is in the same climate like that of the south of Asia, and is in the same servitude."[87]

This brilliant, pioneering application of geography to politics had surprisingly little influence either on the American mind or on the dialectics of the long American controversy over Negro slavery. It is interesting to note that the seeming refutations of Montesquieu's prophecy that the Asian land mass would always remain servile—Japan, Formosa, and the Philippines—are islands or archipelagos in which the geographic conditions favorable to slavery which Montesquieu posited are partially or entirely absent.

Of the other British thinkers who exercised some influence on the American mind during the formative years of the United States, Oliver Goldsmith considered the Negroes the "gloomy race of mankind" and held that the torrid climate of their habitat made made them "stupid, indolent and mischievous."[88] Adam Smith in *The Wealth of Nations* (1776) opposed slavery as an inefficient form of production. Samuel Johnson approached the problems of slavery and the Negro with, in Boswell's opinion, "zeal without knowledge." His Abolitionist enthusiasm was sufficiently intense for him to have been accused of toasting the next servile insurrection in the West Indies.[89]

Edmund Burke devoted little attention to the problem of slavery, but he considered that the institution was natural and that Negroes must be ruled with great firmness. Emancipation would do them injustice. Slaves were often fond of their masters and would refuse "a general wild offer of liberty." While gradual reforms in the institution were desirable, "The cause of humanity would be far more benefited by the

---

[86] *Ibid.*, Book XVII. How the Laws of Political Servitude Bear a Relation to the Nature of the Climate, 5–6.

[87] *Ibid.*, Book XVII, 7.

[88] Oliver Goldsmith, *An History of the Earth, and Animated Nature* (London, 1774), pp. 228, 239–240. Quoted in Davis, *Slavery*, p. 456.

[89] *Ibid.*, p. 413.

continuance of the [African slave] trade and servitude, regulated and reformed, than by the total destruction of both or either."[90]

The great naturalists were concerned, not with slavery, but with the place of the different races in the scheme of things. Linnaeus refused to apply the hierarchic concept of the Great Chain of Being to man. He recognized four major racial groups. Of these, the Europeans were "sanguine, brawny, acute, inventive" and *"governed* by customs." Asiatics were "melancholy, rigid, *Severe,* haughty, covetous" and governed by "opinions." The American Indians were "choleric, erect, *Obstinate,* content, free" and *"Regulated* by habit." The Negro, or African man, was "phlegmatic, relaxed, *Crafty,* indolent, negligent" and *"Governed* by caprice."[91] Buffon, Linnaeus' illustrious successor, thought Negroes had degenerated from a higher type of man.[92]

The French Encyclopedists were, with few exceptions, champions of the equality of mankind and the abolition of slavery. Diderot specifically attacked slavery. However, they did not make a major impact on the minds of American statesmen. Even the influence exerted by Jean Jacques Rousseau (1712–1778) was slight. He appealed to radicals and to such popularizers as Thomas Paine. Jefferson was familiar with his work, but then, Jefferson read almost everything. As for John Adams, he greeted the French Revolution with the observation that he didn't know "what to make of a republic of thirty million atheists" and blamed the French predicament on the "encyclopedists and economists, Diderot and D'Alembert, Voltaire and Rousseau."[93]

The Social Contract (1762) begins with a denial of any possible moral justification for slavery, one which in essence recapitulates the reasoning of Locke and Montesquieu. "Since no man has a natural authority over his fellow, and force creates no right," Rousseau argues, "we must conclude that conventions form the basis of all legitimate authority among

[90]Edmund Burke, *Works* (Boston 1866), VI, 257–98. Quoted in Davis, *Slavery,* p. 398.
[91]Reprinted in Jordan *Black,* pp. 220–21.
[92]Buffon also believed that the orang-utan lusted for Negro women.
[93]Quoted in Parrington, *Main Currents, I,* 323–324.

men."[94] He concludes: "The right of slavery is null and void, not only as being illegitimate, but also because it is absurd and meaningless."[95]

Rousseau was fairly well read in international law and he took pains to attempt to refute those pro-slavery observations he found or thought he detected in such authorities as Grotius and Pufendorf. "Grotius denies that all human power is established in favour of the governed, and quotes slavery as an example. His usual method of reasoning is constantly to establish right by fact. It would be possible to employ a more logical method, but none could be more favourable to tyrants."[96]

Rousseau emphasized his belief that men were essentially equal, not only in rights, but in abilities, in a state of nature. After telling his readers that the Emperor Caligula had reasoned that either kings must be gods or men must be beasts, Rousseau observed:

> Aristotle, before any of them, had said that men are by no means equal naturally, but that some are born for slavery, and others for dominion.
> Aristotle was right; but he took the effect for the cause. Nothing can be more certain than that every man born in slavery is born for slavery. Slaves lose everything in their chains, even the desire of escaping from them: they love their servitude, as the comrades of Ulysses loved their brutish condition. If then there are slaves by nature, it is because there have been slaves against nature. Force made the first slaves, and their cowardice perpetuated the condition.[97]

This classical and eloquent statement of the environmental analysis of slave inferiority and in favor of the equality of races in innate gifts was to be quoted only very occasionally in the great American slavery debates, largely because of a parochial American prejudice in favor of English, and against French philosophers.

David Hume (1711–1776), the Scottish epistemologist, political scientist and historian, wielded a large influence on the American political mind during the formative years of the

---

[94]Jean Jacques Rousseau, *The Social Contract or Principles of Political Right* (translated by G. D. H. Cole), 1762, Book I, 4.
[95]*Ibid.*
[96]*Ibid.*, Book I, 2.
[97]*Ibid.*, Book I, 2.

Republic. Samuel Adams read him; he was one of the few political philosophers who had a major impact on Alexander Hamilton; he was frequently cited as an authority during the debates on the Federal Constitution. John Adams was familiar with Hume's writings. In 1863, the crucial year of the American Civil War, Abraham Lincoln withdrew the five volumes of Hume's *History of England from the Invasion of Julius Caesar to the Revolution of 1688* from the Library of Congress one at a time: the manner of withdrawal indicates that the President found time to read them.[98]

Thomas Jefferson regarded Hume as an arch reactionary, whose works "infect" American youth with "the poison of his own principles of government." He noted that an Englishman named John Baxter had "performed a good operation" on Hume: "Wherever he has found him endeavoring to mislead, by either the suppression of a truth or by giving it a false coloring, he has changed the text to what it should be, so that we may properly call it Hume's history republicanized."[99] Jefferson wholeheartedly recommended that this forgery be foisted on American readers as the authentic Hume so that their minds should not be poisoned by opinions with which he, Jefferson, found himself in disagreement.

In his essay, "On National Characters," Hume delivered himself of some ethnic generalizations of a sweeping sort. He believed that European Jews were "as much noted for fraud" as Armenians were for "probity." Modern Romans were distinguished by "subtlety, cowardice, and a slavish disposition." In the Near East, "the integrity, gravity, and bravery of the Turks, form an exact contrast to the deceit, levity, and cowardice of the modern Greeks." While he was skeptical of Montesquieu's attribution of national character to climate, Hume had a scarcely more flattering view of the Negro:

> I am apt to suspect the Negroes to be naturally inferior to the Whites. There scarcely ever was a civilized nation of that complexion, nor even any individual, eminent either in action or speculation. No ingenious manufactures amongst them, no arts, no sciences. On the other hand, the most rude and barbarous of

[98]Sandburg, *War Years*, II, 310.
[99]Leonard W. Levy, *Jefferson and Civil Liberties* (Cambridge, Mass., 1963), pp. 144–45.

the Whites, such as the ancient Germans, the present Tartars, have still something eminent about them, in their valour, form of government, or some other particular. Such a uniform and constant difference could not happen, in so many countries and ages, if nature had not made an original distinction between these breeds of men. Not to mention our colonies, there are Negro slaves dispersed all over Europe, of whom none ever discovered any symptoms of ingenuity, though low people, without education, will start up amongst us, and distinguish themselves in every profession. In Jamaica, indeed, they talk of one Negro as a man of parts and learning; but it is likely that he is admired for slender accomplishments, like a parrot who speaks a few words plainly.[100]

Blackstone and the Common Law

Despite the authority of Lord Coke and despite the enormous British economic stake in the slave trade,[101] British courts handed down decisions which were almost consistently anti-slavery in character. Toward the close of the Seventeenth Century Lord Chief Justice Holt handed down a landmark decision which included the rule, "As soon as a Negro comes into England, he becomes free." Abolitionists seized on this decision, persuaded Negro slaves in England to abscond, baptised them, and then took legal action to validate their freedom.

In 1772 Baron Mansfield, Lord Chief Justice of the King's Bench, issued an epochal decision which he feared might cost slaveowners £700,000. The question at issue was whether Somerset, a Negro slave, could be returned by force to Virginia or should be granted habeas corpus. Mansfield observed that the only form of slavery recognized by English law, villeinage, had been extinct for centuries. Since slavery was contrary to natural law, the issue then boiled down to one of whether England should recognize the laws of Virginia and extend comity to them. He replied that the institution of slavery was "so odious

[100]David Hume, *Essays, Literary, Moral, and Political,* 1741. Essay XX, Of National Characters, footnote.
[101]At the time (1790), England was shipping 38,000 Blacks to the Americas annually, as against the 36,000 shipped by all other countries combined, according to the eighteenth century pro-slavery historian of the West Indies, Bryan Edwards.

that nothing could be suffered to support it but positive law."[102] The result was to free all slaves in Great Britain automatically. This had the incidental effect of transforming a class of house servants into homeless and destitute wanderers on the streets of London, thus compelling the Abolitionists to experiment with free Negro colonization in Sierra Leone.

Three generations of American statesmen and politicians were to learn their law from Blackstone's *Commentaries*. Regarded as an oracle in the United States, Sir William Blackstone was somewhat less esteemed in his native England. Thomas Jefferson, with habitual exaggeration, denounced Blackstone and Hume as demons of reaction who had made "tories of all England" and were corrupting "young Americans" with their "wily sophistries." Blackstone had "done more towards the suppression of the liberties of man, than all the million of men in arms of Bonaparte."[103] This denunciation of him as an enemy of human liberty notwithstanding, Blackstone never wavered in his inflexible opposition to chattel slavery as morally iniquitous and contrary to natural law. He adopted Montesquieu's ideas on the subject, giving their author full credit, "undefiled by any idea or originality of his own."[104]

Blackstone followed Montesquieu and Locke in rejecting the justification of slavery as arising from war, from the sale of one's self to another and from hereditary status. Slavery is abhorrent to natural law. "Liberty by the English law depends not upon the complexion; and what was said even in the time of Queen Elisabeth is now substantially true,—that the air of England is too pure for a slave to breathe in." There was no inconsistency, Blackstone argued, between this fact and the circumstance that English slavers manned by British crews transported thousands of Negroes from African to American slavery. The captives on these ships were free men, but were unable to actualize their freedom because there were no magistrates aboard to whom they could apply for the writ of habeas

---

[102]Weyl, *American Civilization,* 15–22.
[103]Thomas Jefferson, *Writings* edited by H. A. Washington, (Washington, 1853–54), VI, 335.
[104]F. T. H. Fletcher, *Montesquieu and English Politics, 1750–1800,* (London, 1939), p. 232.

corpus. Should any of the slave ships touch on British ports, their cargoes would become free as soon as they made application to the courts.

As for the view of Lord Coke that Christians could rightfully enslave heathen, Blackstone thundered:

"Hence too it follows, that the infamous and unchristian practice of withholding baptism from negro servants, lest they should thereby gain their liberty, is totally without foundation, as well as without excuse. The law of England acts on general and extensive principles: it gives liberty, rightly understood, that is, protection, to a Jew, a Turk, or a heathen, as well as to those who profess the true religion of Christ.[105]

The law of England, Blackstone asserted,

abhors, and will not endure the existence of slavery within this nation; so that when an attempt was made to introduce it, by statute of 1 Edw. VI. x. 3, which ordained, that all idle vagabonds should be made slaves, and fed upon bread and water, or small drink, and refuse meat, should wear a ring of iron round their necks, arms, or legs; and should be compelled, by beating, chaining, or otherwise, to perform the work assigned them, were it never so vile; the spirit of the nation could not brook this condition, even in the most abandoned rogues; and therefore this statute was repealed in two years afterwards. And now it is laid down, that a slave or negro, the instant he lands in England, becomes a freeman; that is, the law will protect him in the enjoyment of his person, and his property.[106]

Thus, the Graeco-Roman world, the Old Testament, the teachings of the Apostle Paul and the Theology of the Patristic Fathers agreed in upholding chattel slavery as a just institution. The weight of Christian authority, from earliest times to the Reformation, was applied to persuade slaves that they must obey their masters regardless of the justice or injustice of the conduct of the latter.

With the emergence of moral and political philosophy from under the influence of the Catholic Church, the ethical basis of slavery was challenged and denied. The thinkers of social con-

[105]Sir William Blackstone, *Commentaries on the Laws of England* (1765), Book I, Chapter XIV.
[106]*Ibid.*

tract and of the Enlightenment agreed in finding slavery contrary to the law of nature. The three European thinkers of the Seventeenth and Eighteenth Centuries who wielded most influence on the statesmen who shaped the emerging American Republic—Locke, Blackstone and Montesquieu—asserted, not unanimously but each in articulate and luminous fashion, that slavery was not merely contrary to the law of nature, but a moral enormity as well.

Index of Personal Names

Subject Index

Abolition of Slavery: Franklin on, 23–4; Madison on, 105–9; Garrison on, 159–64; Lee on, 180; 211.

Abolitionists: Jackson on, 121; Benton on, 122; Webster and, 140–1; 158–71; Tilden on, 261; Croly on, 289–90; 380; 382.

Africa, T. Roosevelt on need for White rule, 303–4.

Africans, T. Roosevelt on accomplishments of, 304–5.

Alienation, 390.

American Colonization Society: Clay and, 132–3; Garrison on, 161–3.

American Philosophical Society, 72–3.

American Socialist Party, 293–6.

Amistad, 113.

Anti-Semitism: J. Q. Adams and, 113–4; Watson and, 284; Bryan and, 286.

Aryan Race, T. Roosevelt on, 300.

Aryan Superiority, Watson on, 283.

Athens, Slavery in, 152, 400–7.

Bible, 393–400.

Biddle University, speech at by Taft, 322–4.

Birth of a Nation, 336–7.

Black Domination, Watson on, 283.

Canaan, Curse of, 398–400.

Caucasians: M. Lease on, 279–80; Berger on, 295.

Cayenne (French Guiana), 41–2.

Chinese, Compared to Japanese by T. Roosevelt, 300–1.

Chinese Exclusion, Blaine on, 256–7.

Chiriqui Concession, 215–7.

Civil Rights, Truman on, 359–60.

Civil War and Reconstruction, Discussion of by T. Roosevelt and Rhodes, 306–11.

Civilized Races, T. Roosevelt on, 302–3.

Colonization, of Negroes: Jefferson on, 83–5; Madison on, 106–7; Monroe on, 110; J. Q. Adams on, 111; Clay on, 132–5; Lincoln on, 214–29; Stevens on, 240; Pike on, 249; Douglass on, 271; 379.

Colored Race, Taft on, 323–4.

Committee on Civil Rights, 359.

Compromise of 1850: Clay on, 135–6; Webster on, 139–40.

Creole, 137–8.

Cyprus, Slavery in, 206.

DeBow's Review, 189, 206.

Democracy, Corruption of by Slavery, J. Adams on, 80–1.

Democracy, and Race, T. Roosevelt on, 299–300.

Deportation, Distortion of Taft's views on, 322–4.

Discrimination, J. Kennedy on, 371–4.